END OF IMMUNITY

Holding World Leaders Accountable for Aggression, Genocide, War Crimes, and Crimes against Humanity

CHILE EBOE-OSUJI

Prometheus Books

Essex, Connecticut

PB Prometheus Books

An imprint of The Globe Pequot Publishing Group, Inc.
64 South Main Street
Essex, CT 06426
www.globepequot.com

Distributed by NATIONAL BOOK NETWORK

British Library Cataloguing in Publication Information Available

Library of Congress Cataloging-in-Publication Data

Names: Eboe-Osuji, Chile author.
Title: End of immunity : holding world leaders accountable for
  aggression, genocide, war crimes, and crimes against humanity / by Chile
  Eboe-Osuji, PhD.
Description: Lanham, Maryland : Prometheus, [2024] | Includes
  bibliographical references and index. | Summary: "In End of
  Immunity, former president of the International Criminal Court Chile
  Eboe-Osuji probes the history and theory of the concept of immunity for
  heads of state, underscoring tribunal achievements, pointing out gaps in
  the existing framework of accountability and the hypocrisies that
  produced them, and offering workable solutions to the loopholes that
  government leaders still use to escape consequences today"—Provided by
  publisher.
Identifiers: LCCN 2024009661 (print) | LCCN 2024009662 (ebook) | ISBN
  9781633889903 (cloth) | ISBN 9781633889910 (epub)
Subjects: LCSH: Government liability (International law) | Criminal
  liability (International law) | Responsibility to protect (International
  law) | Criminal justice, Administration of—International cooperation. |
  Treaty of Versailles (1919 June 28)
Classification: LCC KZ4080 .E23 2024 (print) | LCC KZ4080 (ebook) | DDC
  345/.04—dc23/eng/20240617
LC record available at https://lccn.loc.gov/2024009661
LC ebook record available at https://lccn.loc.gov/2024009662

∞™ The paper used in this publication meets the minimum requirements of
American National Standard for Information Sciences—Permanence of Paper for
Printed Library Materials, ANSI/NISO Z39.48-1992.

To a world that rejects the power of any human being to unleash organized violence and hope for impunity.

We do not accept the paradox that legal responsibility should be the least where power is the greatest. We stand on the principle of responsible government declared some three centuries ago to King James by Lord Chief Justice Coke, who proclaimed that even a King is still "under God and the law."—U.S. Supreme Court justice Robert H Jackson[1] *(June 1945)*

With regard to the question of international law, well, we are making international law, and all we can claim is that international law should be based on justice.—David Lloyd George[2] *(November 1918)*

CONTENTS

Preface   vii

Prologue   xiii

CHAPTER 1   A Gap in the Framework   1

CHAPTER 2   Aggression: A "Supreme Crime"   25

CHAPTER 3   Three Peace Conferences for Law Reform   57

CHAPTER 4   Article 227 of the Versailles Treaty   67

CHAPTER 5   The Preparatory Background to Article 227   75

CHAPTER 6   The Legislative Scope of Article 227   149

CHAPTER 7   Dutch Refusal to Surrender the Kaiser   167

CHAPTER 8   The Leipzig Letdown   185

CHAPTER 9   London Conference of 1945   191

CHAPTER 10   Norms of Nuremberg   205

CHAPTER 11   Affirmation of the Nuremberg Norms   213

CHAPTER 12   Post-Nuremberg Administration of International
             Criminal Justice   233

CHAPTER 13   Divine Right of Kings   241

CHAPTER 14   Times, They Are A-Changin'   257

CHAPTER 15   The Right to Peace: A New Order of Accountability   269

Conclusion   277

Epilogue: The Fallacies of the "Delegation Theory"
of Jurisdiction of International Courts   283

Acknowledgments   289

Notes   291

Index   357

About the Author   375

PREFACE

Late in the production of this book, the U.S. Supreme Court rendered its decision in *Trump v. United States*, in which the majority held that the president of the United States enjoys "absolute immunity" from judicial inquiry in all exercise of official presidential power. Leading off the dissent against that ruling, Justice Sotomayor protested that the new ruling amounted to the president being a king above the law in the use of official power. Although this book is not about the immunity of a head of state and government in domestic law, the fascinating story of the doctrine of *legibus solutus* that placed kings and emperors above the law is told fully in chapter 13 of this book. Those most interested in that particular history will not lose the plot of this book if they begin reading it from that chapter.

This book's purpose is to provide usable information to readers interested in the evolution of international law as regards the accountability of heads of state and government for international crimes—specifically the crime of aggression, genocide, crimes against humanity, and war crimes. The general reader—whether or not a lawyer—curious about the possibilities and the limitations of holding supreme power accountable for those crimes may skim the book for that information. There are ample historical vignettes beyond the familiar that the average reader will find interesting, even entertaining. Legal professionals, and those who make (or assist in making) policy decisions at the national or international level about accountability for international crimes, will also find much new information and insights to help them in their important work.

Beyond the prologue, the book begins with a discussion in chapter 1 about a gap that exists in the current framework of international law constructed for purposes of accountability for the crime of aggression. The discussion is usefully provoked by questions of accountability for Russia's war of aggression in Ukraine. The discussion recalls the story of what many consider "big power hypocrisy," which created a regrettable gap in that regard. To conclude the chapter, I offer suggestions on how to close that gap.

Continuing with the theme of aggression, chapter 2 traces the development of international law from the pre–World War I era (during which wars of aggression were accepted as the prerogative of sovereigns able to wage them) to the post–World War I era (during which wars of aggression began to be viewed as international crimes deserving of prosecution).

Chapter 3 loops back to the beginnings of international law's momentum to regulate the manner of fighting wars. The momentum began with two purely diplomatic peacetime conferences, the First Hague Peace Conference of 1899 and the Second Hague Peace Conference of 1907. Upon the adjournment of the 1907 conference, the convening plenipotentiaries calendared a third peace conference eight years thence. But World War I intervened in 1914 to disrupt the planned meeting. Upon conclusion of the war in November 1918, the third peace conference, so to speak, did take place—but in the more postbellum conditions of a devastating war. That gave the 1919 conference a decided focus of a determination to adjust international law, by giving it teeth to punish those who would violate its prohibitions during armed conflict, notwithstanding that the culprits might be heads of state.

Chapter 4 focuses on the treaty provision that introduced into international law, for the first time, the idea that a head of state can be held criminally responsible for committing an international crime—with no immunity accorded to him. This is article 227 of the Versailles Treaty of 1919, a monumental outcome of the Paris Peace Conference, which reshaped international law in a revolutionary way. It communicated the resolve of the Allies and Associated Powers to prosecute Kaiser Wilhelm II, the German emperor and king of Prussia, before an international tribunal.

Chapter 5 gives close-up views of precisely how that adjustment of international law came about during the Paris Conference. The reader is taken into the conference rooms, to relive the intense dogfights and battles of wits that were fought for that law reform. We also get a detailed view of the preparatory work that was done ahead of the Paris Peace Conference by the British government under Prime Minister David Lloyd George and the French government under Premier Georges Clemenceau, underscoring their united determination to change international law to ensure the trial of the kaiser, and future heads of state who commit international crimes.

Chapter 6 engages a sustained consideration of the enduring scope of article 227 of the Versailles Peace Treaty by clearing up some of the misunderstandings that have been left in academic discussions about it over the years. The chief misunderstanding is the casual impression that the U.S. government was opposed to article 227, thus limiting the importance to be attached to it as an enduring precedent for the development of international law along the lines of rejection of immunity for heads of state. The discussion in chapter 6 corrects that impression. Indeed, the U.S. secretary of state at the time, Mr. Robert Lansing, had relentlessly opposed the idea that was codified in that provision and tried hard to enlist President Wilson's support to the same cause. In the end, however, it was Wilson himself who scripted (in his own words) the initial text of article 227, having caved in to the intense pressure brought upon him by UK prime minister David Lloyd George and French premier Georges Clemenceau. The significance of Wilson's drafting of article 227 himself and his support for its effectuation (discussed in chapter 7) have largely gone underappreciated in the scholarship on the subject.

With new historical insights, chapter 7 discusses the Dutch government's refusal to surrender the former emperor of Germany, Kaiser Wilhelm II, to the Allies for his trial before an international tribunal, as contemplated in article 227. The discussion in the chapter notes that the Dutch (perhaps not entirely aware that Wilson supported the idea of surrendering the kaiser for trial) were emboldened by their intelligence of Lansing's opposition to prosecuting the kaiser, who by then had been granted asylum in the Netherlands. Indeed, because of Lansing's famous opposition to surrendering the kaiser, many scholars on the subject wrongly assume that the U.S. government presided over by Wilson was opposed to the idea of surrendering the kaiser to the Allies for trial. There is great underappreciation of the historical fact that the first draft of the Allies' diplomatic note to the Dutch government demanding the surrender of the kaiser was, in fact, prepared by Lansing at the specific instructions of Wilson, who supported the demand for the surrender of the kaiser so that he would be tried before an international court. The chapter also examines the significance of certain diplomatic instructions that Lansing later gave to his subordinates at the U.S. embassies in The Hague and Paris, which had the effect of undermining Wilson's unrevised inclination to have the kaiser surrendered for trial before the international criminal tribunal that the Allies proposed to create. We also see that the timing of those diplomatic instructions from Lansing came when Wilson was incapacitated with a stroke. Upon his recovery, Wilson demanded Lansing's resignation as secretary of state, citing Lansing's general disloyalty to him in relation to the Paris Peace Conference.

Chapter 8 deals with the Leipzig trials that were conducted by Germany, in an effort to stave off the Allies' demand to hand over the German war crimes suspects for trial by the Allies. On the Allied list of suspects were very high-profile Germans—their top military brass and statesmen—who were considered German heroes from previous wars. The Leipzig trials were widely viewed as a sham. But it set the stage for how the Allies would handle matters in the aftermath of World War II.

Chapter 9 recalls the Allies' resolve to prosecute Adolf Hitler and the leadership of Germany at the end of World War II. Having learned the lessons of World War I and the failure of accountability, the Allies were determined to ensure that justice was done this time. Unlike the unsuccessful efforts to create an international tribunal for World War I, an endeavor that Robert Lansing had stridently opposed despite Wilson's ultimate support for the prosecution, the post–World War II efforts were spearheaded by the Americans, represented by former attorney general and incumbent Supreme Court justice Robert H. Jackson, and supported by two successive U.S. presidents, Franklin D. Roosevelt and his successor Harry S. Truman.

Chapter 10 elaborates on how the seeds of the legal norm of accountability that were first planted at the Paris Peace Conference in 1919 now germinated more decisively, in the context of another law reform that resulted from the efforts to prosecute the leaders of the German and the Japanese governments in both Nuremberg and in Tokyo. This time, the efforts were much more successful. Although the Allies always had Hitler in their sights for prosecution after the war, he eluded their hopes of doing so when he committed suicide shortly before the end of the war. But all his surviving colleagues at the apex of the Third Reich leadership were prosecuted, and many of them received the death penalty. Similar fate befell the Japanese wartime cabinet of Prime Minister Hideki Tojo who was tried, convicted, and hanged. So, too, were many of his cabinet colleagues. The emperor of Japan was spared prosecution. The chapter concludes with the deduction that sparing the emperor was consistent with the law, since the emperor is understood to be largely a ceremonial head of state, as are most modern monarchs such as the British monarch.

Chapter 11 tracks the story of how the legal norms that were applied in the Nuremberg legal process were transformed into norms of modern international law, beginning with their affirmation by the United Nations General Assembly as general principles of international law. Those principles of international law are what are now referred to as the "Nuremberg Principles." They include the principles that wars of aggression are crimes in international law; and that heads of state do not enjoy immunity when prosecuted for international crimes.

Continuing with the theme of the previous chapter, chapter 12 tracks how the Nuremberg Principles, especially the rejection of immunity for heads of state accused of international crimes, received consolidation in international law during the period following the Nuremberg and the Tokyo trials, particularly in the work of the international criminal tribunals created in the 1990s and later.

In light of contemporary scholarship, a minority of which effectively insists on preserving in our own times the age-old idea of head-of-state immunity, chapter 13 examines the origins of the notion of immunity of heads of state, tracing it back to the Middle Ages and the ancient doctrine of divine right of kings. According to that doctrine, the king was seen as God's vicar on earth, and was accountable only to God and to no earthly powers.

Continuing with that theme, chapter 14 examines how the doctrine of divine right of kings has since been abandoned as part of the law in many countries. Rulers are now generally held accountable under the very national laws that once gave them immunity. At any rate, the doctrine of the divine right of kings, to the extent that it held sway, operated only in the relationship between the king and his subjects. It did not extend to relations between warring kings.

In a new proposal, chapter 15 explores ways in which international law can be shored up to accentuate the risks of accountability for those who wage wars of aggression in particular. The shoring up needs to be done not only by closing some of the gaps in the framework of criminal prosecution but also requires recognizing peace as an actionable human right, according to which victims are given the right to bring civil proceedings against authors of wars of aggression and their accomplices. Such civil proceedings would diminish the appetite of war mongers and those who enable them.

The epilogue dispels the "delegation theory," which some academics have sought to rely upon to give syllogistic respectability to their objection to accountability of heads of state and government for international crimes.

In the conclusion, the double-edged nature of immunity is under-scored in the sense that, while immunity may exempt its subject from the judicial process, it also means denying political leaders the protection of an impartial judicial process, when they fall from power under the clouds of suspicions or accusations of atrocities. Devoid of such judicial protec-tion (which operates on the core basis of presumption of innocence unless proven guilty in a fair trial where they may be acquitted of the charges brought against them), their alternative fate becomes exposure to "politi-cal" or "mob" action—which may entail summary exile from home and loved ones, extrajudicial execution, or public lynching, following condem-nation in the court of public opinion.

PROLOGUE

In the spring of 2021, U.S. president Joe Biden sounded strident warnings to the world that Russian president Vladimir Putin was mobilizing his troops for a massive invasion of Ukraine.[1] It seemed a surreal prospect. Such things no longer happened in Europe. In the recollection of many, the last time someone did that sort of thing was eighty-two years earlier, when Adolf Hitler, history's prime exemplar (and reminder) of how evil can manifest in human form, invaded Poland.

"What nonsense!" intoned the Russian government, as Biden continued to sound the alarm bell with increasing amplitude throughout 2021 and into 2022. Biden was engaging in nothing but a "hollow and unfounded attempt to incite tensions," countered the Russians.[2]

A hopeful world seemed keen to believe the denials. Never mind that Russia annexed the Ukrainian territory of Crimea in March 2014. Optimism encouraged a certain sense of distinction between a full-scale invasion of Ukraine and the earlier annexation of Crimea. After all, the Russians always had military presence in the Crimea, at least since 1783. During the Cold War, Sevastopol, the largest city in Crimea, was the principal naval base of the Soviet Black Sea Fleet. After the collapse of the Soviet Union and Ukraine's independence as a separate country, Ukraine agreed to lease Sevastopol to Russia, in view of Russia's insistence that the seaport was always crucial to its national security.[3] It was, therefore, one thing for the Russians to convert their tenancy agreement in Crimea into absolute domain in 2014: it was quite a different story to imagine them going beyond that to invade the entirety of Ukraine.

Even Ukrainian president Volodymyr Zelensky seemed inclined to hope that Biden's warning of an imminent Russian invasion was unnecessary hyperbole. At the end of January 2022, he urged Biden to stop creating "panic," which, in his assessment, was damaging Ukraine's economy.[4]

"There are signals even from respected leaders of states," said Zelensky in an obvious reference to Biden, "they just say that tomorrow there will be war. This is panic—how much does it cost for our state?"[5]

Less than one month later, on 24 February 2022, Russian forces invaded Ukraine full on, on the orders of President Putin.[6]

According to figures published on 21 November 2023, less than two years into the war that continues to rage as I write, the United Nations (UN) monitoring service estimated that more than 10,000 Ukrainian civilians have been killed and more than 18,500 injured. By the UN's account, even those were conservative estimates.[7]

Many of the victims of the war have been Ukrainian children. As of 1 June 2022, the Ukrainian government marked the death of 243 children, 446 wounded, and 139 missing.[8] And according to UNICEF, up to 5.2 million children have needed humanitarian assistance as a result of the war.[9]

⌒

The tale of heart-rending misery that aggressive wars, genocides, and crimes against humanity—let alone war crimes—have inflicted on humanity even in the modern era that we like to call "civilized" always induces feelings of déjà vu to those whose only plight is to observe from afar. But it is a tale that should be captured and framed and mounted at every bedside and on every doorway, so that we can see it as we go to bed at night, as we rise in the morning, and as we leave our homes and when we return. It is a moving picture that we must keep at the forefront of our minds—every day; lest we forget, as we always do when the universal umbrage against the latest manmade horror has subsided.

I begin this book by recalling, once more, that the Nazi leadership of the Third Reich plunged the world into a calamitous Second World War that devasted life in Europe and beyond, including Germany itself, when it launched a full-scale invasion of Poland on 1 September 1939. It is surely a hackneyed tale. But it still demands reprising—much like that prized piece of somber painting that hangs above the hearth. It hangs there to remind us.

A perpetual emblem of that war's turpitude remains the Nazi regime's cold-blooded extermination of up to 11 million innocent lives. About 6 million of the number were Jewish. The remaining 5 million were Roma, Jehovah's Witnesses, gay men, suspected communists, and others.

When the horror of the Holocaust was no longer fresh, a quarter of a century or so having passed, the Khmer Rouge in Cambodia launched another extermination project against our shared humanity. The regime, it is conventionally estimated, murdered as many as 3 million people: because it was possible, and the world would not care.

Again, about a quarter of a century later, during the 1990s, when the Cambodian horror was no longer fresh, and the Holocaust tale was even more stale, there came the deep cut of another genocide on the body and soul of humankind. As the world looked on, more than eight hundred thousand people were murdered in Rwanda: because they were Tutsi.

Seven decades after World War II ended in 1945—and it was the war that finally galvanized the world into seeing aggressive war for the crime that it always was—Russia invaded Ukraine in February 2022, in another devastating war of aggression, in full view of the whole world. As indicated earlier, the war in Ukraine has destroyed whole neighborhoods and livelihoods and human lives and minds and dreams.

Those are only some, not all, of the stories of the worst brand of deliberate atrocities that have been our collective experience as the human race.

But why are these depravities remarkable? They are remarkable because the apparatus of government leadership directly committed them or enabled or condoned their commission. In each case, the head of the government in question was suspected of or proved to be implicated.

Russian president Vladimir Putin, notably, informed the TV-viewing world that he was the man who ordered his troops to unleash the distressing mayhem in evident display in Ukraine. The worry cannot be casually dismissed that this may escalate into nuclear warfare.

In Germany, Adolf Hitler, the führer, or leader, of the Nazi regime, unleashed a similar crime of aggression in 1939 under the cover of which he also committed genocide. In Cambodia, Pol Pot was the head of a similarly genocidal Khmer Rouge regime. In Rwanda, Theonéste Bagosora was the effective head of the Rwandan government during the anti-Tutsi genocide that was unleashed promptly upon the death of the actual president, Juvénal Habyarimana, whose airplane was shot down in the incident that became the immediate trigger for the genocide.

In a combined stroke of aggressive war and crimes against humanity, Liberian president Charles Taylor aided an armed conflict in neighboring Sierra Leone in the 1990s, so that he could gain access to its natural resources, especially diamonds. The modus operandi of the rebel groups he backed included rampant sexual violence against women and the amputation of hands and arms of helpless civilians. In the fact pattern of evildoing, it would have made no difference if these amputations were done under anesthesia. But they weren't.

∾

Putin's accountability before the bar of justice and the logistics of bringing it about remain burning questions as I write this—a matter we will explore in this book. Hitler and Pol Pot died before justice could get its hands at them. But Karl Dönitz, Hermann Göring, and Rudolf Hess, all of them deputy leaders of the Third Reich, were all tried by the International Military Tribunal in Nuremberg (IMTN). Dönitz was the last head of state of Germany when Hitler chose suicide rather than face justice. Dönitz thus became Germany's head of state for one week, before Germany surrendered to the Allies on 7 May 1945. Chief among the charges against Dönitz and his codefendants were the crime of aggression and crimes against humanity. The latter was the best that could be done at the time to account for the atrocities committed against innocent civilians, the worst of which was the Holocaust. The term "genocide" had not yet been coined.

Fifty years later, Rwanda's Théoneste Bagosora was also tried by an international court—the International Criminal Tribunal for Rwanda (ICTR)—including for the crime of genocide and crimes against humanity. I led the trial team that prosecuted him. Charles Taylor was similarly prosecuted at the Special Court for Sierra Leone (SCSL) for crimes against humanity. I served on the appeal team that prosecuted him.

In each of those cases, the instrument establishing the tribunal precluded the defendants from pleading that their official position—including as head of state—entitled them to immunity from prosecution.[*] Bagosora and his defense counsel wisely left the matter well alone. But not Charles

---

[*] Notably, just as article 7 of the Charter of the International Military Tribunal at Nuremberg had barred the plea of official position immunity including for heads of state, so too did article 6(2) common to the Statute of the International Criminal Tribunal for Rwanda and the Statute of the Special Court for Sierra Leone, as well as article 7(2) of the Statute of the International Criminal Tribunal for the former Yugoslavia.

Taylor. He made a frontal run at his indictment with the plea but was unsurprisingly smacked down by the judges of the SCSL.

Beyond the texts of those international documents and judgments that forbade the plea of immunity, any correct appraisal or understanding of the substance or spirit of customary international law—meaning legal standards to which the international community has become accustomed—must reveal unambiguous rejection of immunity for persons including heads of state accused of international crimes. The anti-immunity feature of international law was not fortuitous. It was a deliberate policy in international lawmaking, as we shall see in this book.

Indeed, any insistence that customary international law had *ever* recognized immunity for heads of state before an international court is an insistence enabled either by a systematic misunderstanding of the actual operation of customary international law's rules of recognition or a stubborn rejection of the progress of international law since Woodrow Wilson's idea of an organized international community caught on at the end of World War I.

That progress was precisely designed to wean our civilization from the gory habit of warfare that was feared as brooking eventual perdition for that civilization, in light of its own ever-unfolding capabilities and malignities.

As the stories in this book will make clear, Wilson and his fellow heads of government of the most powerful nations on earth, which the Allied and Associated Powers represented, were determined to spur on "the intelligent development of international law" in the aftermath of the "Great War."[10]

Enthusing to that project, French premier Georges Clemenceau, the host of the Paris Peace Conference of 1919, said this: "Today we have a perfect opportunity to carry into international law the principle of responsibility which is at the basis of national law."[11]

British colleague David Lloyd George put the point of their project more directly. "With regard to the question of international law," he said, "well, we are making international law, and all we can claim is that international law should be based on justice."[12]

"In one sense," waxed Wilson, unsurprisingly philosophical, "this great, unprecedented war was fought to give validity to international law, to prove that it has a reality which no nation could afford to disregard; that, while it did not have the ordinary sanctions, while there was no international authority as yet to enforce it, it nevertheless had something behind it which was greater than that, the moral rectitude of mankind."[13]

"If we can now give to international law the kind of vitality which it can have only if it is a real expression of our moral judgment," he continued, "we shall have completed in some sense the work which this war was intended to emphasize."[14]

Wilson ultimately saw the matter in these rhapsodic terms: "In a sense the old enterprise of national law is played out. I mean that the future of mankind depends more upon the relations of nations to one another, more upon the realization of the common brotherhood of mankind, than upon the separate and selfish development of national systems of law; so that the men who can, if I may express it so, think without language, think the common thoughts of humanity, are the men who will be most serviceable in the immediate future."[15] In the language of the times, then and now, he would have meant men and women.

⌒

The primary purpose of this book is to recall and retrace with clarity the journey of international law's rejection of immunity for anyone—including heads of state in particular—when they are suspected or accused of atrocities that international law has proscribed as crimes and are especially facing prosecution before international courts. International law's rejection of such immunity was a striking feature of the determination of Wilson and his fellow heads of government to adjust international law and emphasize its critical role in the affairs of humanity coordinated more systematically (also a novel idea) within a multilateral international order.

The deliberate approach or methodology that I employ in this writing is what I call the narrative synthesis of the historical evolution of international law. By that, I mean piecing together, in a composite story, the ways in which major historical events and personalities played a role in shaping our evolving civilization in ways that have concrete, identifiable form today as regards the accountability of those who sit at the summit of power and abuse it by committing crimes of aggression, genocides, crimes against humanity and war crimes. It is a manner of forensic historiography, involving the distillation and analysis of historical information for purposes of drawing serviceable legal inferences or conclusions.

The major figures who played that role include French premier Georges Clemenceau; British prime ministers David Lloyd George and Winston Churchill; U.S. presidents Woodrow Wilson, Franklin D. Roosevelt, and Harry S. Truman; and, yes, Putin's strongman predecessor Joseph Stalin, the Soviet premier.

These statesmen were advised and represented by eminent lawyers. From Great Britain were Lord Birkenhead, the Lord Chancellor (formerly Sir Frederick E. Smith, KC, Attorney General); Viscount Hanworth, Master of the Rolls (formerly Sir Ernest Pollock, KC, Solicitor General); and Sir Hartley Shawcross, KC, Attorney General. From France, there were Professor Ferdinand Larnaude (dean of law of the University of Paris) and his colleague Professor Albert de La Pradelle. There was Edouard Rolin-Jaequemyns from Belgium and Nikolaos Politis from Greece. From the United States, there were Robert H. Jackson, Francis Biddle, and Henry L. Stimson.

These were in their eras the giant jurists of the leading nations. Their thinking and work between the ends of the two world wars played enduring roles in reforming international law to include within it the norm of accountability of those who commit international crimes, even when they are heads of state.

In a manner of speaking, the intellectual battle that questions the existence of the resulting rules of international law is really an insurgency. Nevertheless, it is an insurgency that must be taken seriously. For, complacency has been known to allow many an insurgency to destabilize or overthrow a sensible order of things, unleashing chaos.

Hence, the present battle of ideas engages the need to cast in compelling light what international law actually *says*—not what it *ought to say* according to anyone's opinion—about the accountability of high political power for wars of aggression and other international crimes.

It bears keeping in mind, specifically, that the insurgency battle of ideas comprises the efforts of people whose interests—or even sheer predisposition to intellectual mooting exercise that the publish-or-perish culture of academe can press some scholars into—encourage the view (1) that international law may not have developed to the extent of recognizing aggression as a *crime* (a view that might have been implicated in Russia's invasion of Ukraine in 2022, the U.S. invasion of Iraq in 2003, and the Iraq invasion of Kuwait in 1991); or (2) that international law may not have developed to the extent of creating a universal expectation of accountability for every head of state accused of committing the crime of aggression, genocide, war crimes, or crimes against humanity.

Hence, any project such as this book, which aims to demonstrate the *actuality* of the law (as opposed to the *desirability* of it being so), must, to those extents, show how the law came to be, and the road traveled to get there.

Then again, for those who are (or desire to be) familiar with the basic notions of international law, that exercise is only a function of demonstrating the reality of the source of international law known as customary international law, which is at once the most preponderant source of international law as it is the source most prone to debate.

Unlike treaties, which are agreements that states have reduced to writing usually after extensive negotiations of the words and phrases and their meanings, the rule of recognition for customary international law comprises two elements. One is consistent practice of states in their international relations, and the other is what international lawyers call *opinio juris*. The Latin phrase simply refers to the *mindfulness of law* or *law regarding*. This is in the sense that what was done or the practice adhered to in a particular instance was motivated by a sense that the law was being followed or being laid down to be followed. In other words, it was a matter of law and not a matter of comity of nations or mere grace or courtesy (like laying down the red carpet for a visiting head of state) that a certain thing was done, a practice followed.

It is that dual requirement of consistent state practice and *opinio juris* that makes customary international law vulnerable to debate. But the best antidote to such debates is the evidence of existence of the practice and the *opinio juris*. And that evidence is primarily in documents that demonstrate the establishment of the rule.

By hewing closely to historical documents, I shall engage in an excavation project, so to speak, digging up very old documents that have been long and deeply buried and tamped down by the dross of time and unending traffic and bustle of activities. Some of these documents have for long been buried so deep, out of sight and out of mind, that their incidence or significance lies beyond the consciousness of many who now claim expertise in the subject matter that those documents engage. Because the documents demonstrate the consciousness of what was done, in the deliberate reform and reorientation of international law, I shall disinter and resurrect them. This requires deliberate and extensive references—even lengthy quotations—from them. The strategy of including lengthy quotations resurrects and re-presents those historical documents. More importantly, it minimizes conjecture, interpretation, and debates as to what the documents were intended to communicate.

Writing about natural right in 1953, Leo Strauss remarked that the "issue of natural right presents itself today as a matter of party allegiance. Looking around us, we see two hostile camps, heavily fortified and guarded."[16] The same is true of the fraught debates about immunity of heads of state from accountability for international crimes. It is indeed a battle of ideas.

The most striking evidence of that battle of ideas is seen in the aggressive harassment and bullying that a minority of scholars and their followers have in recent times directed at anyone who recalls the norm that says state officials, particularly heads of state, enjoy no immunity in international law when they are accused of committing crimes of aggression, genocide, war crimes, and crimes against humanity. Indeed, largely due to the vulnerability of customary international law to debate, many who follow the current work of the UN's official law reform think tank, known as the International Law Commission (ILC), may be forgiven to think it taboo to refer to that anti-immunity norm. The taboo impression results from the fast and furious storm that gets unleashed against any authoritative restatement of that norm of international law, notwithstanding that it has consistently rejected such immunity since 1919.

The immunity-tolerant scholars—their methods have also earned them the sobriquet of "pro-immunity advocates"—who unleash that storm appear to adopt the strategy of branding any restatement of the rule against immunity as a novel proposition that is "controversial" at best, counting on diplomacy's low tolerance for controversies. The value or effect of such branding is to throw the smoke-bomb of doubt at the very existence of the anti-immunity norm in the first place, thereby claiming or gaining a beachhead for possible renegotiation of that rule in our own times. At least that was the scenario between 2006—when ILC member Roman Kolodkin (the legal adviser at the Russian Ministry of Foreign Affairs) introduced the topic of immunity of state officials from foreign criminal jurisdiction for examination at the ILC,[17] acting as the first rapporteur for the study[18]— and Russia's invasion of Ukraine in 2022.

It may be noted, as a matter of public interest, that in 2022 Judge Kirill Gevorgian (a former departmental colleague of Kolodkin at the Russian Ministry of Foreign Affairs) was one of only two judges[19] of the International Court of Justice who dissented[20] from the overwhelming majority who reproached Russia for the invasion of Ukraine.[21] This surely does not mean that there is any connection—direct or indirect—between Kolodkin's introduction of the immunity question in the work program of the ILC in 2006 and the Russian invasion of Ukraine sixteen years later.

What is clear, however, is that those implicated in the crime of aggression against Ukraine stand to benefit from any strategy or outcome that erroneously controverts either the legal norm that makes aggressive war a crime or the legal norm that denies immunity to heads of state or other government officials suspected or accused of international crime.

As will be seen, the erroneous controversion of the anti-immunity norm was aggressively attempted in 2017 in the context of the draft article 7 of the ILC's Draft Articles on Immunity of State Officials from Foreign Criminal Jurisdiction, which a different rapporteur, Concepción Escobar Hernández of Spain, had produced reprising the anti-immunity norm. On that occasion, Kolodkin and ILC members from other powerful nations—specifically, the United States, the United Kingdom, China, and Germany, appeared to raise doubt about the norm.

What gave the development a particularly alarming dimension was that the ILC study was initially presented in 2006—and accepted by the UN General Assembly in 2007—as having an *exclusive* bearing at the level of relationship between states. The Americans had flushed out General Manuel Noriega from his position as president of Panama and prosecuted him in the United States on drug trafficking charges. Should the courts of Belgium claim to exercise criminal jurisdiction, as they attempted to do, over American or Congolese officials for war crimes and crimes against humanity? Should a judge in Spain seek the extradition of the former Chilean president to stand trial in Spain for torture?

The International Court of Justice adjudicated that question in the *Arrest Warrant* case in 2002 as regards Yerodia Ndombasi, a Congolese foreign minister that Belgium wanted to prosecute in Belgium. So, too, had the British House of Lords dealt with the question as concerned Augusto Pinochet of Chile. Both highly respected courts came to different conclusions.

So, Kolodkin could claim that there was an objective need for the ILC to clear up the matter once and for all, by conducting a comprehensive and focused study of the question and possibly formulate a treaty to guide the matter at the level of relationship between states, given the many ways that the matter arises at that level.

"The question of the immunity of State officials from foreign criminal jurisdiction," offered Koldokin in 2006, "has begun to attract greater attention in recent years."

According to him, "This is connected to a large extent with the growth of the concept of protection of human rights, a decline in willingness to tolerate gross violations of human rights, and efforts to combat terrorism, transnational crime, corruption and money laundering."

"Society," he wrote, "no longer wishes to condone impunity on the part of those who commit these crimes, whatever their official position in the State." But, in Kolodkin's view, society's rejection of impunity is not all there is to life in international relations. As he put it, "At the same time it can hardly be doubted that immunity of State officials is indispensable to keep *stable* inter-State relations."[22]

Yet, in proposing the study, Kolodkin did not intend the question to perturb the jurisdiction of international criminal courts and tribunals. This is because it had been settled since the Nuremberg proceedings—in which the Soviet Union, together with France, the United States, and the United Kingdom, played a major role—and followed by consistent provisions in the founding instruments of every international tribunal since Nuremberg that there is no immunity before international criminal tribunals.

It was for those reasons that Kolodkin specified as follows as his opening recommendation: "The discussion should cover *only* immunity from domestic jurisdiction. The *legal regime of this* institution, as noted above, *is distinct* from the legal regime of immunity from international jurisdiction."[23]

But, eventually, something quite different began to happen. The ILC study that the UN General Assembly authorized following its initial presentation as having *exclusive* bearing on the ability of *states* to prosecute each other's officials (for sundry transnational crimes, including corruption, money-laundering, terrorism, drug trafficking, etc.) afforded an opportunity for some scholars to reorientate that inquiry—through the back door—into the purview of the jurisdiction of international courts to try genocides, crimes against humanity, war crimes, and the crime of aggression. This reorientation occurred notwithstanding that it was originally promised that the inquiry would not go there.

That pivot—the object of which was to blur the distinction between the jurisdiction of international courts and the jurisdiction of national courts—was an intellectual sleight of hand executed through a potpourri of fallacies.

Perhaps the most meretricious of those fallacies is the argument that any limitation in one state's ability to exercise prosecutorial jurisdiction over heads of state or officials of another state must similarly limit the jurisdiction of an international criminal court. As the argument goes, this is because states cannot do "through" an international mechanism anything they cannot do alone. To some very busy lawyers in a hurry—let alone the average diplomat at the UN who is not a lawyer—the sound bite and "common sense" of that argument have a compelling ring. It is, however, a rather unfortunate argument from an international lawyer. I explain why in a technical essay in the epilogue to this book, for the benefit of those especially interested in that debate.

◠

As should be clear by now, the need to write this book resulted from rumblings of agitation that seek to revive immunity for heads of state.

In 2019, the Appeals Chamber of the International Criminal Court (ICC) delivered its judgment in *Jordan Referral re Al-Bashir*, an appeal concerning the claim of immunity for Omar Al-Bashir who was president of Sudan at the material time of the events. He was under an ICC arrest warrant that required all member states of the ICC Statute (the "Rome Statute") to arrest and surrender him to the ICC. The Hashemite Kingdom of Jordan (a member state of the Rome Statute) declined to do so during his trip to Amman in 2017—he was attending the conference of the League of Arab States. The Jordanian authorities claimed that they refrained from arresting him because he enjoyed immunity under customary international law. In the judgment (in which I was involved), the ICC Appeals Chamber held that customary international law never recognized immunity for heads of state accused of international crimes in proceedings before international courts.

◠

What made this newfound tabooing of the anti-immunity norm especially concerning is its coincidence with the reign of Donald Trump as U.S. president, a mercurial powerful leader who seemed to have made it a defining creed to erase much that the international community had achieved in its age of enlightenment that followed the end of World War II—even threatening to destroy Iran's cultural heritage, a threat that many correctly identified as an international crime.[24] Two years after Trump's departure from office, Vladimir Putin decided to invade Ukraine in a blatant war of aggression.

◠

Two years before the Appeals Chamber's judgment in *Al-Bashir*, the same agitation that seeks to revive immunity for heads of state was on evident display at the ILC. Escobar Hernández, the ILC special rapporteur on immunity of state officials from foreign criminal jurisdiction, proposed draft article 7 and commentary, also saying that there is no immunity in international law for those accused of international crimes.* The proposal led to extended fractious debates at the ILC. The noise and the emotion alone left the impression of rupture right down the middle. In the end, a recorded vote was called—a highly unusual event in ILC procedures. The result revealed that it was only a small vocal minority of eight members that had been kicking up the storm. An overwhelming majority—twenty-one members—favored it. One member abstained.[25] But not even that humbling defeat of the opposing standpoint was able to calm down the noise. A subsequent *AJIL* Unbound symposium,[26] an online companion to the *American Journal of International Law*, took up the subject and attracted five contributors. None of them was warm toward the ILC draft article 7. Three percent of the voices who opposed the draft at the ILC—and even so was in a small minority—now represented 20 percent of the voices that argued robustly against the draft at the *AJIL* Unbound symposium, with an article asking "Immunity *Ratione Materiae* of State Officials from Foreign Criminal Jurisdiction: Where Is the State Practice in Support of Exceptions?" All of which would lend to the impression that the greater part of the world—than was actually the case—was against the proposition that there is no customary international law immunity for those accused of perpetrating international crimes.[27]

Documentary evidence of the prevailing mood at the ILC may be found in the vote explanation offered by the ILC member from China. He complained that the draft article had been adopted despite strong opposition expressed by several members—actually the strong opposition came from the ILC members from Germany, Russia, the United Kingdom, and the United States. Such a hasty decision, continued the ILC member from China, went against the fine tradition of the commission. He fully agreed with the three ILC members, from Russia, the United States, and the United Kingdom, respectively, and wished in turn to express his strong opposition to the Drafting Committee's decision regarding draft article 7.[28] He acknowledged, ultimately, that only a minority were against the draft. Nevertheless, the numbers for or against a proposition should not be the

---

* In the relevant respect, article 7 to Draft Articles provides as follows: "Immunity *ratione materiae* from the exercise of foreign criminal jurisdiction shall not apply in respect of the following crimes under international law: (a) crime of genocide; (b) crimes against humanity; (c) war crimes; (d) crime of apartheid; (e) torture; (f) enforced disappearance."

only basis for decision-making. In the circumstances, it would be "*reckless to proceed on the basis of majority rule.*"[29]

The brooding cloud against the draft floated from the Palais de Nation in Geneva (where the ILC usually conducts its business) to the UN Headquarters in New York (where its work is debated at the Sixth Committee of the UN General Assembly). The sense of the atmosphere is sufficiently conveyed in a three-and-a-half-page statement that Germany's representative* delivered during the seventy-second session of the UN General Assembly toward the end of 2017.[30] Clearly calculated to encourage widespread and sustained opposition to the draft article,† the statement noted that the subject had been "one of the most controversial" in the history of the ILC[31]—even unusually resulting in a recorded vote.[32] And in one stride, the statement excoriated both the draft article and its accompanying commentary, along with an unmistakable back-handed swipe at the competence of the special rapporteur who produced them.[33]

In an interesting twist, in 2020, the federal prosecutor general of Germany specifically repudiated, in effect, the position espoused by the German delegate at the Sixth Committee in 2017. In a case he was prosecuting in Germany, involving an Afghan soldier accused of committing war crimes in Afghanistan, the federal prosecutor general firmly expressed the view that customary international law does not recognize immunity for officials charged with international crimes before foreign courts.[34] The federal prosecutor correctly observed that the controversy at the ILC or the UN General Assembly Sixth Committee (no doubt mindful of Germany's support of that controversy in 2017 in both forums) does "not demonstrate" that customary international law recognized immunity in relation to international crimes.[35] According to him, the contrary views "were mainly based on an incomplete and partly incorrect analysis"[36] of customary international law.

---

* Notably, the German member of the ILC presided over the debates that resulted in the recorded vote and had taken sides against the proposal. Having voted against the draft, he explained his vote by observing, among other things, that "the exceptions to immunity *ratione materiae* formulated in the draft article were not based on customary international law, nor had it been established that there was any trend to that effect." See UN International Law Commission, Provisional Summary Record, 12.

† Notable in that regard are the following passages: "Germany welcomes the fact that the commentary to the article as adopted by the Drafting Committee reflects the vast differences of opinion within the Commission. This is underlined by the unusual event of a recorded vote for the adoption of draft article 7 by the ILC. However, we believe this point could be made even clearer. It also urgently needs to extensively address the equally controversial reception of the article by States in their statements in the Sixth Committee as well as on other occasions." And: "Germany continues to observe this project closely and strongly encourages others to do so as well." UN International Law Commission, Provisional Summary Record, 5.

The research reported in this book bears out the position of the federal prosecutor of Germany, and why the storms that have followed the proposition were always misguided and must be firmly confined to their teapot.

A GAP IN
THE FRAMEWORK

On 19 November 2021, I received an unexpected e-mail from Mark Agrast, who was then the executive director of the American Society of International Law (ASIL), the world's premier society of international lawyers. Agrast wrote to inform me that the ASIL would be awarding me the society's Goler T. Butcher Medal for 2021. According to the citation, the "medal is awarded to a distinguished person of American or other nationality for outstanding contributions to the development or effective realization of international human rights law."[1] The medal would be formally conferred at the April 2022 annual conference of the ASIL.

It is a coveted prize. I was naturally delighted at the unexpected gesture. I decided to deliver a public lecture on a topic of current interest to human rights law. In light of the debate that the work of the International Law Commission had generated at the United Nations (UN), concerning the immunity of state officials and agents from the criminal jurisdiction of foreign national courts (which I described in the prologue), I decided to deliver a lecture titled "Accountability of Sovereign Power for International Crimes." Through an ensuing round of e-mails between Agrast and me, we agreed on 4 February 2022 that I would deliver that lecture.

I should mention that the date was 4 February 2022—not yet 24 February, when Russian forces would invade Ukraine. As of that date, I had no particular plan to discuss the conduct of any particular serving head of state. To the extent necessary, my aim was to limit discussions of exemplary villainy to the conducts of the historical figures whose behaviors had compelled international law to develop the norm of individual criminal responsibility for everyone accused of international crimes, including heads of state. Notable examples include Kaiser Wilhelm II (the German emperor who unleashed the unprecedented carnage that was World War I), Adolf Hitler (the German Nazi führer who not only was determined to succeed where the kaiser had failed but also whose holocaust against Jews and others introduced the term *genocide* into the global lexicon of law and society), Pol Pot (the Khmer Rouge leader of Cambodia responsible for one of the world's more notorious extermination projects in more recent history), and Théoneste Bagosora (the strongman of Rwanda who was the effective leader of his country during a genocide against Tutsis for which he was convicted).

Then, in a stunning live show of the perennial relevance of the topic of accountability of supreme power for immoderate misanthropy, Russian president Vladimir Putin ordered his troops to invade Ukraine on 24 February 2022, in a blatant war of aggression—one of the most serious forms of criminal conduct in international law.

President Biden, much to the discomfort of aides at the White House and allies like French president Emmanuel Macron, did not hold back in repeatedly calling Putin a "criminal" in the eyes of international law, even a genocidal one, who must be brought to justice. Other leaders like Canadian prime minister Justin Trudeau and UK prime minister Boris Johnson have, at least, shaded that view of President Putin.

Unsurprisingly, Putin's invasion of Ukraine was the major media news of the era—possibly since World War II. As the former president of the International Criminal Court (ICC) and an expert in that aspect of international law, I found myself a frequent guest of major media houses—from Al Jazeera, BBC, CNN, and MSNBC, to *Newsweek, Christian Science Monitor,* and so on—to express a view and to help their audiences make sense of it all from the point of view of international law.

One of the questions fielded was what to make of Biden's labeling of Putin as an international "criminal." From the perspective of international law, the answer was fairly straightforward.

It all depended on what Biden had in mind in the name-calling. It was not interesting to me, I said, if Biden's *only* purpose was to engage in scurrilous denigration of a fellow political wielder of the biggest military power. But if Biden was signaling the strong resolve of his government and their allies to align themselves behind accountability for international crimes, notwithstanding that the suspect is the head of state of any nation (strong or weak), then Biden's attitude toward Putin would be entirely consistent with international law as I understood it.

The purpose of this book is to illuminate that understanding.

As we will see along the way, President Biden broke no new ground in calling for the prosecution of another head of state or head of government for international crimes.

At the end of World War I, French premier Georges Clemenceau and UK prime minister David Lloyd George—eventually joined by U.S. president Woodrow Wilson—called for the prosecution of Kaiser Wilhelm II (emperor of Germany and king of Prussia) after they defeated him in battle. And they took concrete steps to try to realize that objective, a revolutionary idea at the time.

In the middle of World War II, U.S. president Franklin D. Roosevelt, UK prime minister Winston Churchill, and Soviet premier Joseph Stalin communicated their shared resolve to prosecute Adolf Hitler and other leaders of Germany's Third Reich.

Those were early developments that charted the course of international law in ways that have endured today. I shall return to that discussion in due course. But, first, a necessary digression.

"Oh, No! There's a Gap in the Accountability Framework!"

International law reserves especial censure for the crime of genocide, crimes against humanity, war crimes, and the crime of aggression.

Genocide connotes any of a number of acts committed against an ethnic, national, religious, or racial group calculated to annihilate them in whole or in part as such. The most classical of such genocidal acts is homicide committed against the group. Crimes against humanity consist of widespread or systematic attacks against a civilian population: in the manner of conducts such as murder, extermination, enslavement, torture, persecution, forcible transfer of populations, enforced disappearances, apartheid, sexual violence, and other inhumane acts. Genocide and crimes against humanity can be committed in peacetime and during war. But war crimes are crimes that soldiers commit, or their commanders condone or order them to commit, during war. Such crimes include the targeting or the mistreatment of civilians—or doing the same to soldiers who are no longer able to fight because of injuries, sickness, or captivity. In addition to crimes against persons, war crimes can also come in the manner of attacks against civilian property, by either pillaging them or by directing attacks against public buildings, hospitals, places of worship, or heritage property and cultural monuments.

Generally speaking, the crime of aggression means to commence a war against another state that had not attacked (or was not about to attack) the aggressor state.

International lawyers familiar with the negotiation of the crime of aggression provisions of the Rome Statute—that is, the treaty that established the ICC to try individuals and not states accused of international crimes—are used to hearing the crime of aggression described as "special" among all the other international crimes. As it was suggested by those who take that view, the reason for it is that aggressive war is a crime that people in effective political or military leadership of countries are uniquely situated to commit. I'm not sure that the crime of aggression deserves a "special" status for that reason. I'm rather satisfied that the reason itself is ill conceived. I'm of the firm view that prosecuting ordinary soldiers for fighting wars of aggression will exert the pressure of law against that crime. Aggression will then be put on par with other international crimes, which soldiers are not free to commit on the orders of their superiors.

A Reason Not to Treat the Crime of Aggression as "Special"

Not long ago, CNN published a story titled "Russian Officer Reveals Why He Risked It All to Quit Putin's War."[2] The piece tells the story of how the pangs of conscience and fear combined eventually to drive one Russian military officer to go straight to his field commander and do something brave: resign his own commission on the spot. He did this, it seems, from inside Ukraine after he had taken part—apparently reluctantly—in the early phase of the invasion. Of course, the idiom "risked it all," as the phrase was used in the story's caption, means in context that, in resigning his commission, the soldier risked court-marshal and worse.

The CNN story also shows that the officer in question was neither unique in his action, nor the first to do so. Other soldiers, it seems, had resigned from the Russian army at the very outset, rather than take any part at all in the invasion.

The resignation of these soldiers may well throw a more sensible light upon a certain assumption that is implied as an important fact when establishing the legal norm—lawyers call this a "legislative fact"—regarding accountability for the crime of aggression. Here, that assumption shines through in the view that the crime of aggression is so "special" that the fault element of it rests exclusively with the political or military leadership of a country. According to that assumption, no field officer or ordinary soldier has a moral choice except to fight a war of aggression once so commanded by the political or military leader of his or her country. Consequently, field officers and soldiers bear no criminal responsibility under the Rome Statute for the crime of aggression. In effect, they are innocent agents incapable of formulating and retaining what lawyers call the *mens rea* of a crime—that is, the mindfulness of wrongdoing that the law requires before attributing criminal guilt to the apparent culprit—beyond the physical act (i.e., the *actus reus*) of the crime. A typical example of an innocent agent would be an innocent child that a corrupt adult sent to commit a crime; or a third party that was, say, the hand that actually gave a poison pill to a friend having been tricked into thinking he was giving his beloved friend a vitamin pill.

But, the ineptitude of the reasoning, which limits the culpability for the crime of aggression to those in a position to order it, becomes apparent if you consider that the same reasoning must exclude from culpability anyone else who was merely obeying an order to commit a crime, any crime at all (say rape) though he knew he was committing a crime. According to the known general rules of recognition in criminal law, it makes no difference that the one type of crime (specifically aggression) uniquely needs a superior order to unleash it, while another crime (say rape) is one that typically requires no such order yet can be committed pursuant to a superior order. All that matters is that anyone concerned in the crime knew they were involved in actualizing a crime in playing the role they played.

In the course of an open lecture that I delivered at Stanford Law School on 10 May 2022, I questioned the correctness of the arrangement that excludes foot soldiers from punishment for the crime of aggression. More than that, there is a serious question about the continuing usefulness of that arrangement in a post-Nuremberg world order that desires to suppress wars of aggression, using international criminal law. I argued, amongst other things, that the needed fortification of the international order against future wars of aggression requires an adjustment to international law as expressed in the Rome Statute. The needed adjustment is that criminal jeopardy for the crime of aggression should be extended to foot soldiers, too; but without diluting the existing regime that focuses that criminal responsibility on persons who occupy positions that allow them to exercise control over or to direct the political or military actions of their states.

It was always an odd arrangement, in my view, to exclude from punishment those upon whose participation the crime entirely depends for effective execution. This is regardless of the criminal responsibility of the political and military leadership who actually ordered the crime of aggression to begin with. The oddness of the arrangement is demonstrable indeed. Consider this hypothetical scenario: Gigantia and Minoria are neighboring states with strained relations due to the orientation of the leadership of Minoria away from Gigantia toward the Group of Prosperous and Progressive Nations (GPPN)—an alliance of wealthy states ideologically opposed to Gigantia—to whom Minoria has applied for membership. In its own circumstances, Minoria is a multiethnic country, comprising the Minori (as the predominant ethnic group) and Gigans (a minority ethnic group that has ethnocultural ties to Gigantia). The two ethnic groups are embroiled in an internal armed conflict in Minoria, because the Gigan minority wants to steer the direction of Minoria's national policies away from GPPN and toward Gigantia. In a final act of frustration, the emperor of Gigantia decides to resolve the "Minorian problem" once and for all. To that end, he issues a proclamation involving three orders to his forces: (1) invade Minoria to pacify it by annexation, and quell the foolish clamor about joining GPPN; (2) kill every Minorian troop they encounter and take no prisoners, to prevent later insurgency under the new postinvasion arrangement; and (3) kill as many Minori civilians as possible and reduce their numbers below a level that would make it practically impossible for the "Minorian problem" to rear its ugly head again in future.

In international law, the first order involves the crime of aggression, the second involves war crimes, and the third genocide. The order to commit all three international crimes comes from the same leader; and they all depend on field officers and soldiers to execute them. That is to say, the emperor's orders will be completely frustrated if the rank and file mutinied and refused to obey them.

But, for some peculiar reason, under the Rome Statute, the field officers and soldiers *can* be held criminally responsible for executing the second and the third orders (war crimes and genocide, respectively) but *not* the first (aggression).

The distinction is entirely short-sighted. For one thing, it leaves unperturbed the peremptory capability of political and military leaders of states to wage wars of aggression, a crime in international law. By *peremptory capability*, I mean the ability of a leader to produce results merely by communicating her will for that action.

But one way to throw a wrench into the works of that capability is by using the law to interfere in the relationship between the leader (who gives the order) and the subordinates (expected to obey). This will be done by extending to the military rank and file the criminal jeopardy for the crime of aggression.

Doing that would realign the crime of aggression with the rest of international criminal law whose development was set in motion at Nuremberg. According to that law, the duress of truly coercive orders—such that leaves the subordinate no moral choice but to obey—is no total defense to a charge of international crime. But judges can consider such a plea, to lighten the punishment to be imposed after criminal conviction. A sentence so mitigated may entail a minimal prison term, other nominal punishment, or even a suspended sentence. But there may be those who willingly—even enthusiastically—executed criminal "orders" that may have left them a moral choice to do something different, because they shared the vision of the order. They should get their just deserts. But, in excluding foot soldiers from punishment for the crime of aggression, the current framework of international law precludes that outcome.

Only fastidious academic self-indulgence—especially luxuriated in from the safety of an ivory tower or other environment that accentuates one's detachment from what the famous American jurist Oliver Wendell Holmes Jr. once described as "the incommunicable experience of war"[3]— will embolden anyone to debate the justice of holding accountable the actual perpetrators of the crime of aggression, on the quibble that only their ultimate commanders ought to be held responsible for it.

But, to also hold the rank and file criminally responsible for the crime of aggression will have the following added advantages. It will give more soldiers in the position of the Russian officer in the CNN story an objective reason—beyond their own qualms and fears—to refuse to fight wars of aggression. And those who refuse to fight will have a legal defense—furnished by international law—for refusing to fight. That is to say, international law will punish the soldier for taking part in the war of aggression. Regrettably, the current arrangement does not afford that excuse to soldiers who may need it to justify their refusal to fight in a war of aggression. In effect, international law has left them completely to the whims of their leaders. "What is your problem, Captain Boris?" a commander may ask. "Since international law imposes no criminal jeopardy on you for fighting a war of aggression," he may reason, "international law does not forbid *you* from participating in a war of aggression. So, by refusing to fight, you will be court-martialed, and you have no legal defense whatsoever."

Now, rendering that reasoning unavailable to political leaders will make their orders of wars of aggression more vulnerable to legitimate and practical objection from the soldiers who would be the almost literal cannon fodders for such wars, and the families left to mourn their permanent loss or disability, even as the leader who ordered them to war may have continued to enjoy power, privilege, and possibly glory for any gains perceived to come from the war, as those "gains" will be attributed to his leadership and his peremptory capability to wage the war.

I must, of course, anticipate the query whether this proposed adjustment may not end up translating into prosecution of only field officers and foot soldiers for the crime of aggression. I may, of course, begin by noting that wars of aggression waged by a powerful state do in fact translate, as it were, into the risk of casualties for field officers and foot soldiers and their arrest for war crimes. Those outcomes are typically not the fate of the political leadership who ordered the war to begin, only to stay back in their capitals or safer locations, protected by heavy security bunkers and phalanxes.

Still, extending criminal responsibility to the rank and file for the crime of aggression doesn't have to translate into their prosecution for that crime—to the practical exclusion of the political leaders who ordered the war of aggression.

Understandably, that concern results from the strange view that, at the ICC, no one may be tried in their physical absence from the courtroom. The view is strange because it arises more from an incomplete universal view of the administration of criminal justice than a compelling interpretation of the Rome Statute. During my time as a judge at the ICC, I had occasion to question the correctness of that view in a lengthy judicial opinion in which I set out all the national and international judicial precedents that support the idea of prosecuting people who knowingly choose to stay away from their own trials as a stratagem to frustrate them.[4]

There is no necessary injustice in prosecuting accused persons *in absentia* at the ICC if they have adequate notice of the proceedings against them. This should include prosecuting political leaders accused of the crime of aggression. Notably, Martin Bormann was so prosecuted and convicted at Nuremberg. More recently, as amply discussed in the judicial opinion referred to earlier, the United Nations Human Rights Committee, the European Court of Human Rights, and the UK House of Lords have all ruled that there is no necessary injustice in prosecuting accused persons *in absentia*.

But, even if the proposed adjustment to the regime of the crime of aggression were to translate into prosecuting only the rank and file, since they are as a practical matter the ones most likely to be arrested in the process of committing the crime of aggression, then so be it. Neither justice nor humanity—as represented by victims of the crime of aggression or by courtroom practitioners whose work has brought them in close proximity to the pain of victims of war—will be troubled by the reality that soldiers who did the actual shooting, shelling, killing, and destruction are held accountable for the crime of aggression they executed, notwithstanding whether those who ordered them into the war were also prosecuted for the same crime.

In the end, even if that is what the adjustment entails, perhaps that's the whole practical point of the adjustment. It is up to field officers and foot soldiers to mutiny against orders to commit the crime. It is up to them to tell their political leaders, "No, I'll not fight your aggressive war, because I'm more likely than you to die or be prosecuted for your crime. You go fight your war yourself, if it is that important to you."

To conclude the point, the rank and file who do the actual killing and destruction that wars of aggression portend are the *principal* perpetrators of that crime. Their preclusion from criminal responsibility for the crime of aggression is not only incongruent to the idea of criminal law in general but also to international criminal law in particular. The commission of international crimes often implicates the culpability of superiors: yet individual criminal responsibility is contemplated for both the superior and the subordinate in proportion to their moral guilt. Generally, in criminal law, obedience to a superior's order is not an absolute defense against a criminal charge. But in mitigation, judges can take into account the incidence of any superior order that left the subordinate no moral choice but to commit the crime as commanded. So it is for genocide, crimes against humanity, and war crimes. In that sense, the crime of aggression is not truly unique, merely because it is leaders who order them to be committed. Leaders can also order their subordinates to commit war crimes, crimes against humanity, and genocide: yet both the perpetrating subordinate and the ordering superior are held punishable. There is no reason that the crime of aggression should be treated differently.

Perhaps just as important is the reality that the preclusion of the rank and file from criminal responsibility for the crime of aggression potentially is akin to killing soldiers with kindness—literally speaking—by denying them the one legal excuse they may have to refuse to fight a war of aggression in which they may be killed (as became the fate of the many Russian soldiers who died fighting a war of aggression in Ukraine). The excuse they need (but which they are denied) is that they will not fight a war of aggression because international law will hold them individually criminally responsible for the war.

So, extending criminal responsibility to the rank and file will put pressure on the political or military leadership of countries against embarking on wars of aggression, as many officers and soldiers will have legally afforded reason to refuse to fight.

A Reason to Treat the Crime of Aggression as Special

For the foregoing reasons, at least, I'm not convinced that the crime of aggression warrants the treatment it has thus far received as a "special" crime for which *only* political or military leaders of states may be punished.

There is, however, a different reason that gives the crime of aggression status as a truly *special* crime. That reason was supplied in 1946, in the judgment of the International Military Tribunal at Nuremberg. "To initiate a war of aggression . . . is not only an international crime;" wrote the judges, "it is the supreme international crime differing only from other war crimes in that it contains within itself the accumulated evil of the whole."[5]

It was an apposite observation that invites no elaborate explanation. It is enough to say that most of history's genocides, notably, let alone crimes against humanity and war crimes, have been committed under the cover of armed conflict. Wars are accepted Saturnalia of sundry homicide. How much more morally complicated can it be, then, if the occasion of war is also used as a cover to exterminate a racial, ethnic, religious, or national group that was always loathed? Perhaps no one would notice the genocide.

It is against that background of "accumulated evil of the whole" of international crimes that the execration of Russia's war of aggression against Ukraine—in our own era—must be appreciated.

The Gap in the Framework

It is, of course, a matter of much interest that leaders of Western nations and much of their citizens now want Putin personally prosecuted for the crime of aggression he brought upon Ukraine, among other international crimes. Former prime minister of the United Kingdom Gordon Brown became the leader of that outcry for accountability.[6]

There's a problem, though. There's a gap in the available international framework of accountability—in relation to the crime of aggression. And now, those who want Putin prosecuted are ruing that gap.

Notably, the Rome Statute's provisions on the crime of aggression are drafted in the diffident manner of ensuring that the ICC does not exercise jurisdiction over a citizen or the territory of a state that is not party to the Rome Statute, unless the UN Security Council refers the situation in question to the ICC. For present purposes, let us call this "the first limitation."

There is yet a second limitation that underscores that different approach to accountability for aggression. This engages the question whether the ICC can even exercise jurisdiction over the crime of aggression in relation to the nationals of a member state of the Rome Statute that had not specifically "opted in" to be bound by the Rome Statute's provisions on the crime of aggression. But we can leave that second limitation to one side for now, because it does not concern Russia, which is not a state party. Russia is only concerned with the first limitation.

We see that limitation in the combined operation of two provisions of the Rome Statute—article 15*bis*(5) and article 15*ter*(1)—that delineate the ICC's jurisdiction in relation to the crime of aggression.

Article 15*bis*(5) provides that as regards "a State that is not a party to this Statute, the Court shall not exercise its jurisdiction over the crime of aggression when committed by that State's nationals or on its territory."

It is important to note that it is only in relation to the crime of aggression—not genocide, crimes against humanity, or war crimes—that we have a specific provision that says that the ICC cannot exercise jurisdiction over nationals or the territory of a state that is not a party to the Rome Statute. Because the ICC has jurisdiction over Ukraine, the ICC can prosecute the nationals of Russia, including Putin, for genocide, war crimes, or crimes against humanity they committed in Ukraine. But the ICC cannot similarly prosecute a Russian national—notably Putin—for the crime of aggression committed in Ukraine.

As noted earlier, the only exception to that limitation is when the UN Security Council refers the situation to the ICC prosecutor for investigation and prosecution. And we see that in article 15*ter*(1), which provides that the "Court may exercise jurisdiction over the crime of aggression in accordance with article 13, paragraph (b), subject to the provisions of this article." Article 13(b) says that the Court may exercise its jurisdiction with respect to a crime outlawed in the Rome Statute if: "A situation in which one or more of such crimes appears to have been committed is referred to the Prosecutor by the Security Council acting under Chapter VII of the Charter of the United Nations." Article 13(b) is rather limiting, in the following ways: the Security Council is the only organ of the UN that the Rome Statute recognizes as entitled to refer a situation to the ICC for investigation and prosecution; and, the Security Council may only make that referral when acting under Chapter VII of the UN Charter, where the utmost power of the UN—the power to even use military force—is laid down.

The result of the first limitation is that the ICC cannot now be the proper forum to try Putin (and his colleagues in the Russian leadership) for the crime of aggression. This is because Russia is not a state party to the Rome Statute. Consequently, only the UN Security Council can trigger the investigation and prosecution of Russian nationals for the crime of aggression they committed, by referring the matter to the ICC. But that will not happen as regards Russia's invasion of Ukraine, because Russia will veto any such referral from the Security Council.

What to do now? Immediately following Russia's invasion of Ukraine in February 2022, desperate efforts got under way to cover that gap by seeking to create an ad hoc special international tribunal to prosecute the crime of aggression in Ukraine. The United Kingdom's Gordon Brown emerged as the champion of the cause.

A Deliberate Gap

As a matter of principle, any effort to ensure accountability—including the effort to hold Putin accountable—must be applauded. But the line must be drawn at the point where the intended "special tribunal" for the crime of aggression in Ukraine would be so "special" that the effective outcome of the effort is to manipulate international law to snare only some people who receive negative branding in the chorus of the more dominant sections of the world's mass media renowned for bias. Following this, the world would return to business as usual, in the sense of shutting the gate of accountability once more, in ways that leave untroubled the other leaders from the most favored nations who may do the same thing in future that Putin did in 2022. Experience makes it foolish to see the Russian invasion of Ukraine as the first time a powerful nation invaded a weaker one in recent times. The reason that the invasion of Ukraine did not excite the same level of indignation everywhere in the world as President Biden wanted was because many around the world saw no real difference between Russia's invasion of Ukraine in 2022 under false pretenses and America's invasion of Iraq in 2003 under false pretenses, supported by the British government in which Gordon Brown served as deputy prime minister.

Hence, a sensible approach to international law draws a line against an *ad hominem* approach to the framework of accountability for the crime of aggression.

It may be recalled that the American delegation drew precisely that line against selective accountability during the London Conference of 1945, when the Allies were negotiating the modalities of the Nuremberg trials. It is an irony of history that the Russian delegation was determined then to press "a definition [of crimes] which . . . had the effect of declaring certain acts crimes only when committed by the Nazis."[7] The American delegation firmly opposed that approach to international lawmaking, "even if it meant the failure of the Conference."[8] The Americans insisted that "the criminal character of . . . acts could not depend on who committed them and that international crimes could only be defined in broad terms applicable to statesmen of any nation guilty of the proscribed conduct."[9] The American argument ultimately prevailed. "At the final meeting the Soviet qualifications were dropped and agreement was reached on a generic definition acceptable to all."[10]

Precisely the same concern would trouble the creation of a "special" tribunal for the crime of aggression in Ukraine, without ensuring that there is a generic jurisdiction in a permanent international court to be exercised under similar conditions in future. In other words, it is surely sensible to work to create a special tribunal to prosecute Putin for the crime of aggression in Ukraine. But it will be entirely wrong to create such a special tribunal without closing the gap in relation to the crime of aggression in the Rome Statute, so that anyone who commits the crime of aggression in future may be held accountable regardless of who the person may be.

∾

This gap was not an oversight. It resulted precisely and directly from pressure that was brought to bear during the negotiation and drafting of the aggression provisions of the Rome Statute. That pressure came mostly from the U.S. government of the day,[11] joined by others among the five permanent members of the UN Security Council.[12]

At the time, *all* the permanent members of the Security Council (including the Right Honorable Mr. Brown's own country even when he was the prime minister) insistently pushed to give the Security Council the *sole* authority—famously called the "trigger"—to decide whether the crime of aggression may be prosecuted at all at the ICC in any given case. Translated into realpolitik, that insistence meant that *all* the permanent members of the Security Council were pushing to give themselves—including Russia—the power to veto the prosecution of the crime of aggression at the ICC. And that is exactly what is happening now, even in the compromise version of the arrangement that was eventually accepted. That compromise version is the limitation reflected in the combined operation of article 15*bis*(5) of the Rome Statute (which denies the ICC jurisdiction over the crime of aggression committed by nationals of a state like Russia that is not a member state of the Rome Statute) and article 15*ter*(1) (which allows the court to exercise jurisdiction in those circumstances only when the UN Security Council refers the matter to the ICC).

᧖

Perhaps a 2015 piece in the *American Journal of International Law* by two renowned American scholars says much about the gap that now exists in the Rome Statute in relation to the crime of aggression. As they put it, "the crime of aggression issue has prominently figured" in the "rocky" relationship between the United States and the ICC.[13] "The treatment of aggression," they wrote, "contributed significantly to the sense of disappointment with which the United States reacted to the ICC treaty adopted at Rome (the Rome Statute)."[14]

Shortly before the Kampala Conference of June 2010, where the aggression provisions of the Rome Statute were to be adopted for the first time, the Council on Foreign Relations, an influential American think tank, published a report notably asserting that the ICC's exercise of jurisdiction over the crime of aggression "would jeopardize U.S. cooperation with the Court."[15] In that regard, the author of the report wrote as follows:

> Prosecuting aggression risks miring the court in political disputes regarding the causes of international controversies, thereby diminishing its effectiveness and perceived legitimacy in dispensing justice for atrocity crimes. ICC jurisdiction over aggression also poses unique risks to the United States as a global superpower. It places U.S. and allied leaders at risk of prosecution for what they view as necessary and legitimate security actions. Adding aggression to the ICC's mandate would also erode the primacy of the UN Security Council in managing threats to international peace.[16]

The message of that quote accurately sums up the position of the United States as then understood in relation to giving the ICC jurisdiction over the crime of aggression, independent from the control of the UN Security Council.

It is thus clear enough from that perspective that the sentiments that resulted in limiting the ICC's jurisdiction in relation to the crime of aggression were as follows:

Rationalization: The crime of aggression is not a justiciable political matter. But that argument raises this question: Does aggression become justiciable only when a "special tribunal" is created to prosecute it on a case-by-case basis? Or when the Security Council manages to authorize the prosecution?

Rationalization: ICC jurisdiction over the crime of aggression poses a unique risk to the United States as "a global" superpower. But that argument raises this question: Does that concern preclude any other state that may qualify as "a global superpower" or sees itself as such? Should accountability for the crime of aggression serve its purpose only when it entails no risk to a global superpower, but lose that purpose when it entails that risk?

Rationalization: "An ICC jurisdiction over the crime of aggression will place the U.S. and allied leaders at risk of prosecution for what *they* view as necessary and legitimate security actions." But that argument raises this question: If the leaders of the United States and its allies must be spared the risk of prosecution for what "*they* view as necessary and legitimate security actions," on what credible basis should the nationals of any other state be excluded from a class of persons who must also be spared the risk of prosecution for what *they*, too, view as necessary and legitimate security actions? Should the leaders of Russia be excluded from that class of protection for what they have now declared as *necessary and legitimate security action*—in Crimea and in mainland Ukraine—to the horror of the whole world?

Rationalization: "Adding aggression to the ICC's mandate would also erode the primacy of the UN Security Council in managing threats to international peace." But that argument invites the following considerations. The Security Council ended up having that primacy to trigger prosecution for the crime of aggression in relation to Russia. And that has directly led to the inability to prosecute Russian leaders for their invasion of Ukraine. What is more, must accountability fail when cops go rogue? The purpose of the UN Security Council is to manage in good faith threats to international peace and security. But what happens when, as in the invasions of Ukraine and Iraq, the culprits of the threat to or disturbance of international peace and security are powerful members of the Security Council itself?

The foregoing considerations must show that it is not plausible to create a "special tribunal" uniquely to prosecute Putin, and then draw the line of accountability at the crime of aggression when committed by the leaders of other nations.

Other Questions Attending the Creation of a Special Tribunal

Anyone familiar with international relations would know how difficult it is to create international criminal tribunals—permanent or ad hoc—in the context of a cold war. And the world is now effectively in the middle of a second cold war. In the event, the following questions arise. Some leaders of the G7 may now want to create such a tribunal. But would the 135 countries of the G77 go along with any effort to create such a tribunal in the context of the UN—which is the most authoritative context in which to create it? Can this be done without the cooperation of the G77 in the context of the UN—merely by avoiding the UN in the first place or altogether and reaching back to the Nuremberg Tribunal model that was used in 1945, when much of the world was under colonial rule and the UN had not been created to be the clearinghouse for efforts to manage and maintain international peace and security? Perhaps such a tribunal could be created by the Council of Europe in an effort to prosecute Putin, in the same way that the African Union created a special chamber in Senegal to prosecute Hissène Habré, the former president of Chad. But will European leaders have the political stomach or unity to do so? Vladimir Putin is no Hissène Habré, nor is Russia Chad, and it was not easy for the AU to set up the special chamber in Senegal.

These are some of the difficult questions arising. And I haven't got the answers. I merely raise the questions.

The Hard Lessons of Political Expediency

What the world cannot afford is to ignore the hard lessons that the invasion of Ukraine has taught about short-sighted political expediency. It was politically expedient to limit the reach of the Rome Statute in relation to the crime of aggression, to save the leaders of powerful nations from accountability. And then the chickens came home to roost, with Russia's invasion of Ukraine under the orders of President Putin.

It would be foolish to brush that hard lesson aside and carry on as if nothing happened; as if the gap in the Rome Statute was an oversight, when it really resulted from the deliberate policy of self-interest that ignored the central message of Robert H. Jackson, delivered more than seventy years earlier in a lecture titled "The Rule of Law among Nations." In the middle of Russia's brutal invasion of Ukraine in 2022, America's political leaders who never wanted international law to reign over them and their nationals now want that law to reign over the leadership of

Russia and its citizens. But, at the end of World War II, Jackson presciently warned Americans against that attitude. As he put it in what may be termed the "Jackson Doctrine":

> It is futile to think . . . that we can have an international law that is always working on our side. . . . We cannot successfully cooperate with the rest of the world in establishing a reign of law, unless we are prepared to have that law sometimes operate against what would be our national advantage.[17]

It is important to stress that message. The point is not to rub the faces of the architects of the gap (that exists in the aggression provisions of the Rome Statute) in their own costly folly. It is only necessary to stress the mistake of ignoring Jackson's counsel, to avoid normalizing its routine repetition. It is not too much to imagine that had the United States demonstrated a willingness to be bound by the Rome Statute and its aggression provisions, there would, first, have been no gap in the Rome Statute in the first place, and second, it might have added a layer of deterrence against Russia's invasion of Ukraine in 2022. Unless, of course, it is accepted implicitly that Russia's invasion of Ukraine—or any other future invasion of Ukraine or of any other country—is a good bargain for sparing America's leadership the risk of prosecution for the crime of aggression should they face that prospect. But that trade-off is not America's alone to make. In a world in which a war of aggression is a threat to international peace and security in more ways than are readily appreciated at any given time, it is a question for the international community.

The Need to Amend the Rome Statute

It is against the foregoing background that I stress the need for corrective amendment of the Rome Statute; whether or not a special tribunal for the crime of aggression in Ukraine is established, but more so if it is. One minimum way to do that is to delete article 15*bis*(5) of the Rome Statute, which provides that as regards "a State that is not a party to this Statute, the Court shall not exercise its jurisdiction over the crime of aggression when committed by that State's nationals or on its territory." That deletion will bring the crime of aggression to a level of parity with genocide, crimes against humanity, and war crimes, which currently do not have the kind of limitation to ICC's jurisdiction that article 15*bis*(5) entails.

And, to a greater effect, it will be helpful to amend article 13(b) of the Statute: in a way that allows the ICC to exercise jurisdiction when the

UN General Assembly either refers a situation to the ICC prosecutor or when UN member states make such a referral upon the specific recommendation of the General Assembly pursuant to the specific resolution of the General Assembly, when the Security Council fails to make a needed referral because of the use of the veto power. One way that the UN General Assembly can make that referral directly as it now does with requests for advisory opinions from the ICJ—or by inviting member states to do so jointly or severally—is through the "Uniting for Peace" procedure, a rarely used procedure specifically designed to work around the occasions when the veto power is used in obvious bad faith to block the Security Council from performing its functions. Notably, the Uniting for Peace procedure originated in the UN General Assembly resolution 377A (V) of 3 November 1950, to contain the Soviet Union's exercise of veto power that blocked the Security Council from taking measures to protect the Republic of Korea from North Korea's war of aggression.[18]

It must be pointed out in this connection that the cleanest solution would obviously be an arrangement in which a clear construction of the UN Charter would have enabled the General Assembly to make a direct referral to the ICC, possibly using the Uniting for Peace procedure. Such a clean solution, however, may be difficult in light of the text of articles 10 to 12 of the UN Charter, which tends to limit the powers of the General Assembly to only *discussions* and *recommendations*. Life in its nonlinear reality must then make do, if need be, with the solution that involves only recommendations from the General Assembly to UN member states to make the needed referral to the ICC. It will then be for the ICC judges to determine whether such a referral—derived from the recommendation of the General Assembly—would be sufficient to anchor the jurisdiction of the ICC in situations of article 13(b) of the Rome Statute, which currently entitles the Security Council to refer situations to the ICC prosecutor, under Chapter VII of the Charter. In any circumstance in which the veto power was used to prevent a needed Security Council referral, it would be difficult to envision the ICC judges declining to accept jurisdiction pursuant to an alternative referral from the UN General Assembly, made under an amended provision of the Rome Statute that entitles the UN General Assembly to make that referral when the Security Council has been prevented from making the referral itself.

Here, I must recall an Igbo parable. It holds that the dog would have you serve him his food, as you may, and leave him to worry about wresting it from the spirits of your ancestors (who also have an interest in the same food as served).

From the perspective of that parable, it may be that ICC judges would consider the Chapter VII power of the Security Council in the context of the power's overarching need. That need is the maintenance of international peace and security through the United Nations as the global clearinghouse of action. But when the Security Council as the UN organ with the primary function in that regard is disabled from acting, due to the selfish or improper motives of one or more of the permanent members, then the General Assembly must—as a function of incidental power—perform that function itself on behalf of humanity. Such a construction, if made, would not be the first time that an international court would have construed an incidental power to exercise the crucial function of an organization, where no such power had been spelled out in the constating instrument.[19]

Sovereign Immunity before the Special Tribunal for Aggression in Ukraine

We must, of course, contend with a further matter regarding Putin's accountability for the crime of aggression in Ukraine. That is to say, even if it is possible to set up the special tribunal for that crime of aggression, there is one big question that must be addressed. It is the question of immunity.

That question asks whether it is even possible to prosecute Putin for the crime of aggression, or indeed any other international crime for that matter, given that he is a head of state. And that question is subsumed in the main frame of this book.

For now, I'm naturally expected to recall that when I served as the president of the ICC and presided over the *Jordan Referral re Al-Bashir* appeal in 2019, the Appeals Chamber comprehensively addressed the question of immunity in relation to the work of the ICC.[20] The Chamber held that customary international law never recognized head-of-state immunity in the processes of an international criminal court; and that article 27 of the Rome Statute, which precludes the plea of immunity at the ICC, is fully consistent with a proper understanding of customary international law.

The Turn of the Wind Vane

The main arguments of the immunity apologists are fully discussed in the epilogue of this book, pointing out the many fallacies that have fueled that scholarship. There is no need to repeat the discussion here.

Suffice it to observe here that the warts of providence have their way of catching out voluble scholarship. It was, of course, more than surprising to see the leading apologist of head-of-state immunity now turn around and argue that President Putin can be prosecuted before the special international tribunal that Gordon Brown now wants to set up.[21]

Efforts were actually made to explain this turn of the wind vane by the argument that any immunity that a head of state enjoys in international law before the courts of equal sovereigns can be overcome by resorting to the *jurisdiction of Ukraine* to prosecute President Putin of Russia, notwithstanding the original premise of immunity of sovereigns from the criminal jurisdiction of foreign *national* courts. That original premise is expressed in the doctrine of equality of sovereigns. And in recent years, the immunity-tolerant scholars have attempted to use syllogism to import that premise into the sphere of jurisdictions of *international* criminal courts.

But, now, in an effort to ensure the prosecution of Putin for the crime of aggression, the thought leaders of the immunity-tolerant scholarship appear to have registered an about-face. In the process, the following argument was made: Ukraine is fighting a war of self-defense in Ukraine; that right of self-defense on the territory of Ukraine even entitles it to effect regime change in the Kremlin. The special international tribunal would "derive" its jurisdiction from Ukraine; hence, it would be "far-fetched" to say that the special tribunal would not have jurisdiction to try President Putin of Russia, since the tribunal would have "derived" its jurisdiction from Ukraine's right of self-defense.[22]

By that argument, it must then be accepted that the Special Court for Sierra Leone was correct in deciding that it had jurisdiction to try Liberia's president, Charles Taylor, because the Special Court derived its jurisdiction from Sierra Leone, which had the right of self-defense against Liberia, including the right to remove Charles Taylor from power in Monrovia. Notably, the law professor at the early vanguard of efforts to prosecute Putin on the basis of the argument reported above had earlier repeatedly rebuked the Special Court for Sierra Leone for rejecting the plea of immunity for Charles Taylor.[23] Perhaps the hue and cry raised against Putin has ushered in salutary epiphany.

There is surely much to the argument that belligerency customarily encompassed the right to defeat an adversary and assert dominion over its leadership, to the fullest extent possible. And this is not limited to a state fighting a war of self-defense. It is a right of belligerency in general—even if no longer imported by the old Latin slogan *Vae victis!* It is what explained, for instance, the extrajudicial banishment of Napoleon Bonaparte into exile, by the concert of European powers then at war with France. This is because the draconian right to punish a belligerent adversary without resorting to the due process of law must include within it the right to punish him by resorting to the due process of the law—as was the case in Nuremberg and Tokyo. Indeed, Robert H. Jackson made that point in the first few words of his opening statement at the trial of the major war criminals at Nuremberg. "That four great nations, flushed with victory and stung with injury stay the hand of vengeance and voluntarily submit their captive enemies to the judgment of the law," he said, "is one of the most significant tributes that Power has ever paid to Reason."[24]

That is a theme to which Jackson was to return a little later. "At the very outset," he said, "let us dispose of the contention that to put these men to trial is to do them an injustice entitling them to some special consideration."[25]

"These defendants," he continued, "may be hard pressed but they are not ill used. Let us see what alternative they would have to being tried."[26]

In explaining how it was that the legal process was not unjust to the defendants, though it subjected them to the usual hardship (or jeopardy, as lawyers would say) of a criminal trial, an experience to which the more lowly placed German soldiers being tried in the Allied zones of occupation were also facing, Jackson continued, "For these defendants, however, we have set up an International Tribunal and have undertaken the burden of participating in a complicated effort to give them fair and dispassionate hearings. That is the best-known protection to any man with a defense worthy of being heard."[27]

But, how so? Jackson answered:

> If these men are the first war leaders of a defeated nation to be prosecuted in the name of the law, they are also the first to be given a chance to plead for their lives in the name of the law. Realistically, the Charter of this Tribunal, which gives them a hearing, is also the source of their only hope. It may be that these men of troubled conscience, whose only wish is that the world forget them, do not regard a trial as a favor. But they do have a fair opportunity to defend themselves—a favor which these men, when in power, rarely extended to their fellow countrymen. Despite the fact that public opinion already condemns their acts, we agree that here they must be given a presumption of innocence, and we accept the burden of proving criminal acts and the responsibility of these defendants for their commission.[28]

But the failure of the immunity-tolerant scholarship to sufficiently account for this factor before Putin exploded in Ukraine as late as 2022 is but one among numerous reasons that the immunity-tolerant scholarship is such a whited sepulcher.

Some questions arise: Does the theory of "derivative" jurisdiction of an international tribunal (now used to justify the view that Putin may be tried by the special international tribunal that Gordon Brown champions) apply exclusively to the right of self-defense or the right to defeat and assert radical dominion over a belligerent adversary? Should that theory of "derivative" jurisdiction not also follow in every case in which the jurisdiction of an international criminal court is said to "derive" by some reasoning from the national jurisdiction? Should that derivative jurisdiction of an international criminal court not also flow from the situation in a national jurisdiction where a tyrant sovereign has put himself "in a state of war"[29] against the population or a segment of it, thus entitling them to resistance, rebellion, and revolution, such as were implicated in the many historical instances in which rulers lost their heads or necks in the hands of their own subjects? And if a population or segment of it is entitled to execute their tyrant ruler with or without a judicial process, why should the same entitlement be denied expression on the international plane, where it may be more convenient to establish an international tribunal that will "derive" its own jurisdiction from that domestic source, for purposes of bringing the due process of law to bear in the trial of a sociopathic sovereign who will be precluded from pleading his own immunity?

Ultimately, all the Swiss cheese exceptions and gerrymandering in legal reasoning on immunity does is betray the deep fallacy propagated in the immunity-tolerant scholarship, in the erroneous insistence that customary international law recognized head-of-state immunity before an international court trying an international crime.

Instructively writing in the eighteenth century, Emer de Vattel observed that the truth of limited inviolability of despotic sovereignty "is acknowledged by every sensible writer, whose pen is not enslaved by fear, or sold for hire."[30] That reproach of transactional scholarship has not lost its resonance in the twenty-first century. There are modern academics whose scholarship is *always* consistent in its alignment with the preferences of the axis of geopolitical power or with countries and organizations that had retained them as consultants and counsel in topical legal questions of the day.

Against that background, it was always difficult to see where one would demarcate the acceptable limits of a theory of sovereign immunity that would sit well with some twenty-first-century constituencies, but which theory would have legally served impunity on a platter to Adolf Hitler and Pol Pot for the crime of genocide, merely because they were heads of state.

The crime of genocide—that is the legacy of Adolf Hitler and Pol Pot—is often described as "the crime of all crimes." One would think it astonishingly immoral of any legal theory to permit any human being—even a head of state—to escape from accountability for that odious crime.

It is encouraging to see that people now also recognize the immorality of allowing President Putin to escape accountability for the invasion of Ukraine—another crime also seen as a supreme international crime. We may recall here the characterization that the Nuremberg Tribunal gave to wars of aggression, as "the supreme international crime differing only from other war crimes in that it contains within itself the accumulated evil of the whole." Notably, Russian prosecutors and judges were full participants in the judicial process that resulted in that jurisprudence—and that pronouncement—in 1946.

❧

In the final analysis, Putin and all other heads of state and heads of government are accountable in international law for international crimes. They do not enjoy immunity before an international criminal court for international crimes. But the reason that heads of state do not enjoy immunity in customary international law for international crimes, when prosecuted before international courts, flows not merely from a principle of natural law discoverable through the path of morality alone.

The rejection of immunity resulted rather from a deliberate principle of positive law formulated as such by the powerful nations that hewed the path of international law at the material time. That is the story of this book.

AGGRESSION: A "SUPREME CRIME"

2

From the perspective of modern international law, four types of conduct are now generally accepted as classical international crimes. They are war crimes, crimes against humanity, genocide, and the crime of aggression.

Strictly speaking, jurisprudence of international law has been reluctant to recognize any hierarchy among these crimes.[1] They are all odious. But "at the level of general appreciation," some of them are readily perceived instinctually as worse than the others. Not even international judges and lawyers can entirely escape the pull of that sentiment.[2] It is in that sense that genocide and the crime of aggression provoke heightened fear and revulsion in comparison to the other international crimes. This could be because of the essential feature of these crimes as conduct that inflicts hurt and destruction to a mass of humanity as such.

The emotive status of genocide as a crime of crimes requires no extensive discussion. All that is needed to settle that status at any given time is to point to the Holocaust as the prime example of the crime. And that, quite rightly, puts an end to any debate about the status of the crime as supreme evil. The execrable status of genocide is such that no government can boldly claim that its own conduct can fit the factual elements of that crime, leaving only the legal characterization of the conduct to reasonable debate.

ᐤ

The international crime that tends to provoke debate is the crime of aggression. There is, of course, no shortage of ostensible scholarly arguments offered to justify opposition to its proscription. Ultimately, however, it says so much that tiny nations like Lichtenstein and weak ones like Belgium will be at the vanguard of that proscription. Could this be because the leaders of the more powerful nations would prefer to reserve for themselves the ability to engage in the very conducts that international law characterizes as the crime of aggression? After all, that is how many of the past leaders of the powerful states settled on territories, expanded their spaces, or acquired new colonies. Even Belgium did the same in the past. And Russia's invasion of Ukraine suggests that there are still leaders of modern states who would like to keep using those tactics to acquire or expand their current territories.

Regrettably, this attitude has had the unfortunate tendency to dull the edge of the moral stench of the crime of aggression.

⌒᎒⌐

An early indication of the moral miasma of aggressive war is evident in how the classical Dutch jurist Hugo Grotius treated it in his 1625 legal classic on the law of war and peace titled as such in the Latin of the day, *De Jure Belli ac Pacis*. That book settled the reputation of Grotius as the "father of international law" as he is generally regarded. As part of his treatment of aggressive wars, Grotius quoted with approval St. Augustine's view to the effect that wars of aggression are nothing short of "wholesale robbery."[3] Grotius also cited other eminent authorities to the same effect.

Philo of Alexandria notably elaborated even further that theme of aggressive war as armed robbery: "Now men who have acquired the strength of robbers lay waste whole cities, taking no thought of punishments, because they appear to be stronger than the laws. These are men whose nature is unsuited to civil life, who seek after tyrannies and despotisms, who carry out plundering on a large scale, concealing under the respected names of government and authority what is more correctly called robbery." Grotius found "these views" to be "in excellent accord" with those of Curtius, Justin, Seneca, and Augustine.[4]

But this newfound tendency to dull the stench of aggressive wars in our own more enlightened times is primarily attributed to the conduct of the leading Western nations. The actions and words of these leaders at various times have clearly signaled ambivalence toward wars of aggression, once they had managed to secure the prosecution and conviction of Axis leaders following criminal proceedings under the charters of the Nuremberg and Tokyo tribunals that the same Western nations had drawn up following World War II describing wars of aggression as international crimes.

One infamous action that signaled that ambivalence was the invasion of Iraq in 2003 by a coalition of countries, led by the United States with the United Kingdom as the prominent second mate, employing the debunked claim that Saddam Hussein had built and kept weapons of mass destruction.[5] Although the world opinion was even then sufficiently clear that the invasion of Iraq was an aggressive war,[6] notwithstanding the thuggish disposition of Saddam Hussein, the Iraqi leader who had invaded Kuwait earlier, it is not difficult to imagine how much more the global outrage would have been if the architects and culprits of the kind of invasion inflicted on Iraq were leaders who come from the global axes that do not enjoy the warm embrace and cheer-leading of the Western media.

Indeed, that dissipation of the moral stench of aggressive war remains paradoxically palpable even in the context of Ukraine's invasion by a leader who comes from such a global axis of low respect in the Western media. This time, the aggression norm skepticism is felt from the non–Western axis. That phenomenon is evident in the fact that thirty-five United Nations (UN) member states abstained from a UN General Assembly resolution (of 3 March 2022) that condemned Russia for the invasion.[7] The mainstream of Western mind-set has struggled to understand that the invasion of Iraq is implicated in those abstentions. The abstainers see no material difference between the U.S.-led invasion of Iraq and Russia's invasion of Ukraine, the condemnation of which is now championed by the same United States that led the invasion of Iraq. That is one way that the conduct of the leading Western nations has continued to confuse global sentiments against aggressive wars.

Another way that the leading Western nations operated to dull the moral stench of aggressive war has been through their opposition to giving the International Criminal Court (ICC) independent jurisdiction over the crime of aggression. That problem is sufficiently discussed elsewhere in this book.

The attitude implicated in the foregoing discussion, however, should not detract from the story of how the crime of aggression came into its sobriquet as a "supreme crime" in international law. That story began long before World War I.

The Story before World War I

"And at this day, in this part of the world," wrote Thomas Hobbes in 1651, "private duels are, and always will be honourable, though unlawful, till such time as there shall be honour ordained for them that refuse, and ignominy for them that make the challenge.'"⁸ As of 2022, private duels have surely acquired the ignominy for those who make the challenge, in addition to being unlawful. The same goes for wars of aggression between nations.*

It was during the nineteenth century that international law started experiencing the end of a frontiers-style laissez-faire attitude to wars in general. The old attitude had been generally hands off to those who would make war. The *Vae victis!* understanding seemed to be the only guiding rule. The vanquished were at the mercy of the victors, for a fate that included but was not limited to war crimes prosecutions, enslavement, banishment, and summary execution of even the ruler. And, of course, the conquered lands were up for annexation or colonization.†

---

* Indeed, there is a storied connection between war and duels. In an address to the Council on Foreign Relations (8 August 1932) underscoring shifting attitudes toward wars after World War I, U.S. secretary of state Henry L. Stimson observed that war "is no longer to be the source and subject of rights. It is no longer to be the principle around which the duties, the conduct, and the rights of nations revolve. It is an illegal thing. Hereafter when two nations engage in armed conflict either one or both of them must be wrongdoers. . . . We no longer draw a circle about them and treat them with the punctilios of the *duelist's* code. Instead we denounce them as lawbreakers": Henry L. Stimson, "The Pact of Paris: Three Years of Development," special supplement, *Foreign Affairs* 11, no. 1 (1932): iv (emphasis added). Hugo Grotius was an early authority for the duel-war connection. As he put it in 1625: "For the Latin word, *Bellum*, war, comes from the old word, *Duellum*, a duel, as *Bonus* from *Duonus*, and *Bis* from *Duis*. Now *Duellum* was derived from *Duo*; and thereby implied a difference between two persons, in the same sense as we term peace, unity, from *Unitas*, for a contrary reason." Hugo Grotius, *De Jure Belli ac Pacis*, bk. 1, chap. 1 (1625). In his typical fashion, Carl von Clausewitz, the famous German classical publicist on warfare, got directly to the point: "I shall not begin by expounding a pedantic, literary definition of war, but go straight to the heart of the matter, to *the duel. War is nothing but a duel on a larger scale. Countless duels go to make up war*": Carl von Clausewitz, *On War* (1832), ed. and trans. Michael Howard and Peter Paret (Princeton, NJ: Princeton University Press, 1976), 13, emphasis added. Unsurprisingly, leading voices of the post–World War I peace movement did their best to recall the duel-war connection in hopes of outlawing war in international law in the same way that duels were eventually outlawed in national laws. Salmon Levinson notably drew that analogy, as he argued that dueling lasted as long as an "'affair of honor' could be made the occasion of a duel. But, after many failures to regulate and moderate dueling, it was called by its right name, 'murder,' and then it met its proper legal fate. 'Vital interests' and 'national honor' in the affairs of nations are like the 'affairs of honor' in the relations of individual men. War, not sanctioned by an international court, must, like dueling, be called murder." See John Stoner, *S. O. Levinson and the Pact of Paris* (Chicago: University of Chicago Press, 1943), 24. See also S. O. Levinson, "The Legal Status of War," *New Republic*, 9 March 1918, 171–73.

† As St. Augustine put it in his *De Civitate Dei*, "SET justice aside then, and what are kingdoms but fair thievish purchases? For what are thieves' purchases but little kingdoms, for in thefts the hands of the underlings are directed by the commander, the confederacy of them is sworn together, and the pillage is shared by the law amongst them? And if those ragamuffins grow up to be able enough to keep forts, build habitations, possess cities, and conquer adjoining nations, then their government is no more called thievish, but graced with the eminent name of a kingdom, given and gotten, not because they have left their practices, but because now they may use them without danger of law. Elegant and excellent was that pirate's answer to the great Macedonian Alexander, who had taken him: the king asking him how he durst molest the seas so, he replied with a free spirit: 'How darest thou molest the whole world? But because I do it with a little ship only, I am called a thief: thou, doing it with a great navy, art called an emperor'": St. Augustine, *De Civitate Dei*, trans. John Healey (London: Eld, 1610), bk. 4, chap. 4.

But the gradual process of regulation of warfare started with the Paris Declaration of 1856, following the Crimean War of 1853–1856. It sought to regulate certain aspects of maritime warfare. Specifically, it aimed to abolish privateering, enshrined the duty to respect neutrality, and indicated the circumstances under which naval blockades would be recognized in international law.[9]

The next regulatory landmark came in the form of the Lieber Code, adopted by President Lincoln's administration in 1863, to regulate the conduct of Union soldiers during the American Civil War. Although a domestic instrument of the United States—as its formal title "Instructions for the Government of Armies of the United States in the Field" reveals—it was a distillation of understood principles of international law from academic research and writing.[10] The document itself paid forward the knowledge, as subsequent efforts to regulate international law at the global level also ended up borrowing generously from the Code.*

In a further development, the first Geneva Convention was adopted in 1864. It owed much to the humanitarian campaigns of a Swiss businessman, Henry Dunant, who witnessed the harrowing battle of Solferino during the Second Italian War of Independence in 1859, in which scores of thousands of wounded soldiers needlessly died because they were not properly cared for.[11]

The focus of the instrument was that wounded and sick soldiers shall be given relief and succor, without distinction on the basis of nationality; and that the neutrality of medical establishments, medical units, and medical personnel giving that care was to be guaranteed.

By 1868, martial science and technology had started developing harrowing weapons. The Russian military science had come up with bullets that exploded on contact with human flesh. Thus, in 1868, the Russian government organized an international military commission, which came up with the St. Petersburg Declaration of 1868. By that instrument, the contracting parties engaged mutually to renounce the use of any bullet that is either explosive or charged with fulminating or inflammable substances. In the premises of that undertaking, the drafters took care to express what remains the essential anxieties and overarching aims of humanitarian law. These include the desire that the progress of civilization should have the effect of alleviating as much as possible the calamities of war; that the only legitimate object that states should endeavor to accomplish during war is to

---

* The international instruments inspired by the Lieber Code include, notably, the Brussels Declaration of 1874 and the regulations annexed to the Hague Conventions of 1899 and 1907 on laws and customs of war on land.

weaken the military forces of the enemy; that, for that purpose, it is sufficient to disable the greatest possible number of men; that this object would
be exceeded by the employment of arms that uselessly aggravate the sufferings of disabled men or render their death inevitable; and that the employment of such arms would, therefore, be contrary to the laws of humanity.
In essence, the Declaration of St. Petersburg set off the development of
customary rule of international law prohibiting the use of arms, projectiles,
methods, and materials of a nature to cause unnecessary suffering.[12]

Although an international conference that Czar Alexander II had
sponsored in Brussels in 1874 did not achieve its aim of an international
agreement on a more elaborate convention, another attempt in The Hague
in 1899 was more successful. The outcome document of the 1874 conference was left only at the level of declarations,[13] the Brussels Declaration of
1874 was only a hortatory statement of recommended practices that were
binding on no one.

Czar Alexander II's grandson, Czar Nicholas II, had called the First
Hague Peace Conference in 1899, for purposes of an agreement to bring
the prevailing order of arms race to an end.[14] It was indeed the first truly
momentous milestone in the international effort to regulate the laws of
war.[15]

The conference did not achieve its intended purpose of arms limitation. But it produced three conventions and three declarations. It was, at
the time, the most extensive attempt made in international law to regulate
warfare. These instruments sought to address a range of needs, including
peaceful settlement of international disputes;[16] regulation of wars on land;[17]
adapting the Geneva Convention of 1864 into the sphere of maritime
warfare;[18] the launching of projectiles and explosives from balloons;[19] the
use of asphyxiating or deleterious gases during war;[20] and the use of bullets
that expand or flatten easily in the human body.[21]

Eight years later, in 1907, the second Peace Conference was convened in The Hague, during which instruments of the First Hague Peace
Conference were revised, expanded, modified, and supplemented. All in
all, fourteen instruments were adopted—thirteen conventions and one
declaration. Besides reissuing revised versions of the documents adopted
in 1899 on peaceful settlement of international disputes,[22] regulation of
wars on land,[23] adapting the Geneva Convention of 1864 into the sphere
of maritime warfare,[24] and the launching of projectiles and explosives
from balloons,[25] the 1907 Conference saw the adoption of new treaties
in relation to the limitation of the use of force for the recovery of contract debts;[26] the opening of hostilities;[27] the rights and duties of neutral

powers and persons during war on land[28] and at sea;[29] the status of enemy merchant ships at the outbreak of hostilities;[30] the conversion of merchant ships into war ships;[31] the laying of automatic submarine contact mines;[32] bombardment by naval forces in time of war;[33] certain restrictions on the exercise of the right of capture in maritime war;[34] and the establishment of an international prize court to adjudicate whether property (mostly vessels) captured or seized during war could lawfully be retained as war prizes by their captors.[35]

At the end of the Second Hague Peace Conference, the participants agreed to convene another peace conference in eight years—the same interval between the first and the second peace conferences. That third peace conference would have taken place in 1915; however, World War I intervened in 1914. So it was that the peace conference that would have taken place to develop international law of war further, in the more serene circumstances as the first two conferences, had then to repair to Paris in 1919, at the conclusion of the war. It took on the traditional aspects of peace conferences at the end of a war, where the conquerors would impose terms of settlement upon the losers. And the Paris Peace Conference of 1919 was remarkable for producing some quite precipitous developments in international law and international relations.

World War I and the Paris Peace Conference of 1919

World War I decidedly changed the old view of war, when battles such as that at Waterloo (June 1815) represented the worst of epic battles beyond the age when wars were fought with spears and swords and other rudimentary weapons. Fought in open plains and farm fields in June 1815, the Battle of Waterloo registered a combined casualty figure of about fifty thousand men for the armies of Napoleon and his opposing alliance of the Duke of Wellington and Gebhard von Blücher (the Prussian field marshal).[36]

In contrast, World War I saw claims of 1.4 million dead[37] and 3.74 million wounded[38] soldiers on the side of France alone—not counting those on the side of the British Empire and Italy.

"The burdens of this war," Woodrow Wilson lamented later, "have fallen in an unusual degree upon the whole population of the countries involved. I do not need to draw for you the picture of how the burden has been thrown back from the front upon the older men, upon the women, upon the children, upon the homes of the civilized world, and how the real strain of the war has come where the eye of government could not reach, but where the heart of humanity beats."[39]

⌒

International law had to be adjusted to meet the new threat. The British and the French governments stepped up to lead the project of that adjustment. In the remarks he made on 18 November 1918 to the Committee of Enquiry into Breaches of the Laws of War (the Macdonell Committee), Sir Frederick E. Smith, the attorney general of England and Wales, the future Lord Birkenhead, framed the need for law reform in these terms: "Our own view is that *an aggressive War* was forced upon the world by an ambitious and unscrupulous power, and that the challenge so developed involved *the whole future of the Public Law of States*."[40] Painting a picture of the weakness of international law thus far in restraining wars of aggression and punishing how they were fought in fact, Smith spelled out what his government perceived of the attitude of Germany's leadership.

"In other words," he said, "the challenge which proceeded from Germany meant this, and it meant nothing else: We think that we are strong enough to conquer the world; believing ourselves strong enough to conquer the world we care nothing for all the doctrines of International Law; if we win, and we are convinced that we are strong enough to win, the inherent weakness of International Law immediately makes itself manifest, in other words, inasmuch as we shall be the conqueror, inasmuch as International Law has no sanctions which it can apply to the conqueror, it is a matter of the most complete indifference to us whether in the judgment of those, whom by our hypothesis we shall have vanquished, we have broken International Law or not."[41]

Smith acknowledged that had Germany prevailed in that war—and they came close to doing so[42]—"public law and the sanctity of treaties would have disappeared in our day and our generation from the world."[43]

Against that background, the British government took it upon itself to do its utmost to "re-establish the authority of International Law."[44] To that end, Smith vowed that "we are determined to take any steps that are necessary to reassert, and to reassert under circumstances of the utmost possible notoriety, the authority of those doctrines."[45]

To the British government, the project of reestablishing the authority of international law, in the light of World War I that was unleashed aggressively, was a forward-looking project. As Smith put it, "with cool and passionless eyes into the future of the World, we are determined that our children and our grandchildren, and those even who come after them, shall be spared what this generation has gone through."[46]

He continued: "To us it seems that the most effective deterrent of all is that for all ages men who are tempted to follow the wicked and the bloody path which the Governors of the Central Empires have trodden during the last four years, shall have present before their eyes, not a picture merely of the brilliant and meretricious glamour of military success, but also the recollection that in this great conflict punishment attended upon crime."[47]

∽

At the end of the Macdonell Committee's inquiry, "Waging an Aggressive and Unjust War" and "Invasion of Belgium and Luxemburg in Breach of Treaties" were the first and second charges appearing atop their recommended list of crimes for which the German kaiser should be prosecuted before an international tribunal.[48]

The priority given to those charges was not accidental. As it was explained in the committee's report, "One of the main objects of bringing him to trial would be defeated if foremost among the charges to be made against him was not that of having long planned and deliberately instigated an aggressive and unjust war."[49]

Similarly ranking aggressive war in priority, professors Ferdinand Larnaude and Albert Geouffre de La Pradelle, the University of Paris jurists commissioned by the French government to study the matter of the German kaiser's criminal responsibility, considered that *"Guillaume II peut être accusé d'avoir commis des crimes, et les crimes qu'il a commis—guerre préméditée dans l'injustice, violation de la neutralité de la Belgique et du Luxembourg."* ("William II may be prosecuted for having committed crimes, and the crimes which he has committed—an unjust premeditated war, the violation the neutrality of Belgium and Luxemburg.")[50]

∽

Eventually in the report of the Paris Peace Conference Commission of Responsibility of the Authors of the War and the Enforcement of Penalties, while acknowledging aggression a crime, the commission recommended abandoning—on that occasion—the project of prosecuting the kaiser for starting a war of aggression, for the reasons we will review later. They recommended instead that the kaiser be prosecuted for violation of laws and customs of war or war crimes.

David Lloyd George did not receive warmly the recommendation to abandon prosecuting the kaiser for the crime of aggression. "Our commission declared itself against bringing to trial those who are in different degrees responsible for the declaration of war," he complained. "Personally, I regret this decision, but I accept it." Underscoring the need to deter wars of aggression of the future by prosecuting the sovereigns who start them, Lloyd George continued, "In my opinion, if we could hold the high and mighty men who unleashed such a scourge—the greatest of all—responsible for this greatest of all crimes, there would be less danger of war in future."[51]

In a certain detail, it is an important lesson on how delegates at diplomatic conferences do not always follow the marching orders of their political principals. Apparently before this meeting, Lloyd George and his private secretary, Philip Kerr, had attempted in vain to persuade Sir Ernest Pollock (Lloyd George's solicitor general) to secure a recommendation for prosecuting the kaiser for starting the war. In Kerr's words, Pollock's failure to do so was a "great pity."[52]

Although the technical commission of the Paris Peace Conference did not recommend prosecution on the charge of aggressive war, those inclined to see the glass as half full will perceive the possibility that the scope of the provision eventually drafted by President Wilson (in his own hand) on behalf of the Council of Four was broad enough to accommodate the crime of aggression within the terms of article 227 of the Treaty of Versailles. According to that provision, "Allied and Associated Powers publicly arraign William II of Hohenzollern, formerly German Emperor, for a *supreme offence against international morality and the sanctity of treaties*" (emphasis added).

Antebellum "international morality" might not have held the mere idea of wars of aggression in great disdain, yet the destructive force of this particular war changed things. There was no question that "international morality" had roundly condemned the unleashing of an aggressive war that took the lives of 1.4 million French men alone, not counting the casualty figures of the British Empire and Italy—and, of course, Belgium and Germany itself. With that consideration in mind, it is clear enough that the formulation of article 227 was broad enough to also cover the primary charge of starting an aggressive war, as contemplated in the recommendations of the Macdonell Committee and professors Larnaude and La Pradelle.

Notably, even as they opposed the prosecution of the kaiser for reasons discussed elsewhere in this book, Robert Lansing and James Brown Scott (respectively, the U.S. secretary of state and the renowned international law academic who accompanied him to the Paris Peace Conference) were clear in saying that "a nation engaging in a war of aggression commits a crime."[53] Indeed, Lansing and Scott did not disagree with the common desire at the Paris Peace conference, to the effect that wars of aggression and violations of laws and customs of war should be punished as crimes. As they expressed their differences, "War and those responsible for violations of the laws and customs of war should be punished for their crimes, moral and legal." The differences between Lansing and Scott on one side versus "their colleagues lie in the means of accomplishing this *common desire*."[54]

Accepting that wars of aggression and other crimes committed within them were undoubtedly "moral offences"[55] or "moral . . . crimes,"[56] Lansing and Scott still insisted that it was not appropriate to prosecute them before judicial tribunals, since international law had not, as of 1919, recognized wars of aggression as punishable crimes. Such moral offenses, they argued, might only be prosecuted before *other* forums. But they were not clear about what such other forums might be, nor the procedure to be followed in such forums.

In the end, however, the Council of Four were more concrete in their answer. They decided that the kaiser was to be arraigned "for a supreme offence against international morality and the sanctity of treaties"; the forum for his trial would be a "special tribunal . . . composed of five judges"; the "decision of the tribunal [would] be guided by the highest motives of international policy, with a view to vindicating the solemn obligations of international undertakings and the validity of international morality"; and it would be that tribunal's "duty to fix the punishment which it considers should be imposed."[57]

In other words, the kaiser was to be tried by an international judicial tribunal, using procedures and processes of a criminal trial.

The Paris Peace Conference of 1919 thus marked a turning point in the attitude of international law, in the direction of making wars of aggression not only illegal but also criminal.

Although the initial series of international law instruments focused less on proscribing war—given the interest and wont of the more powerful states in fighting them—than on making eventual wars more humane and respecting the rights and duties of neutral nations, there was no doubt that the beginning of regulating wars at all that started in 1856 (at the end of the Crimean War)[58] had the inevitable trajectory of making wars of aggression not only unlawful but also eventually criminal.

In terms of time lines, that trajectory bears an appreciable correlation to the pre-1919 era of martial laissez-faire, when there was no organized effort or mechanism at the multilateral level to manage matters of war and peace, with concomitant modulation of extremist views of national sovereignty. As there was no League of Nations that existed on a permanent basis to do so, it would have been unrealistic, if not counterproductively idle, to require nations to renounce wars of aggression. That organized approach was foreshadowed in the first and second Hague Peace Conferences and, eventually, consolidated and concretized in the establishment of the League of Nations in 1919 and its successor, the United Nations, in 1945. As the man who conceived of the League of Nations, Woodrow Wilson, described its nature:

> [I]t seems to me that we must concert our best judgment in order to make this league of nations a vital thing—not merely a formal thing, not an occasional thing, not a thing sometimes called into life to meet an exigency, but always functioning in watchful attendance upon the interests of the nations—and that its continuity should be a vital continuity; that it should have functions that are continuing functions and that do not permit an intermission of its watchfulness and of its labor; that it should be the eye of the nations to keep watch upon the common interest, an eye that does not slumber, an eye that is everywhere watchful and attentive.[59]

In 1919, the primary mission of the League of Nations was stated in the preamble to its Covenant: "In order to promote international co-operation and to achieve international peace and security . . . by the acceptance of obligations not to resort to war." But, by 1945, after two world wars, there was a more urgent and insistent mission for the United Nations, expressed at once in the very opening message of the charter: "WE THE PEOPLES OF THE UNITED NATIONS DETERMINED to save succeeding generations from the scourge of war."[60]

It must follow that the starting point in that *determination* is to make it illegal to wage wars of aggression.

Developments after World War I

The Stimson Perspective

It would be terribly romantic to suppose that the only reason that the U.S. government abandoned the name "Department of War" for its military bureaucracy, embracing "Department of Defense" instead, was because of the role that the United States played as the champion of the idea of renunciation of *war* as an instrument of national policy, as *required* by a general treaty of that name (known for short as the Briand–Kellogg Pact), which did not proscribe wars of *self-defense*.

But Henry Lewis Stimson deserves credit for elucidating more than seventy-five years ago why and how wars of aggression became criminal conducts in international law.

Stimson was a man whose views we cannot ignore in these matters. He took his first degree at Yale before studying law at Harvard.[61] He later practiced law and became a partner at the prestigious Wall Street firm that Elihu Root founded.[62] Stimson joined the U.S. Army during World War I and commanded an artillery battalion in France, achieving the rank of colonel.[63] He served in the administrations of five presidents between 1911 and 1945.[64] At the young age of forty-four, he had served President Taft as secretary of war in 1911. In 1929, President Hoover appointed the sixty-two-year-old Stimson to serve as secretary of state. Ten years later, following the outbreak of World War II, President Franklin D. Roosevelt appointed him the secretary of war, and President Truman retained him in that position upon Roosevelt's death in office in April 1945. Stimson served in that post until September 1945, upon the end of the war in the Far East following the U.S. atomic bombing of Hiroshima and Nagasaki that he recommended.

One biography of Stimson begins with the two-week Cuban Missile Crisis in the second half of October 1962 that tested the international order. The administration of the young and inexperienced President Kennedy secretly sought all the wise counsel it could get from those who had served their country during trying times of the past—including during the Second World War that ended only less than two decades earlier. One of those that Kennedy's lieutenants had consulted was a man who had served as an aide to Stimson during World War II. A notable piece of advice he gave was that "[T]he best service we can perform for the President is to try to approach this as Colonel Stimson would."[65]

In Godfrey Hodgson's book *The Colonel*, Stimson's stature in the history of U.S. foreign affairs—and, by extension, in international relations in general—is summed up as follows:

> Many articles and several books have been written about what is called American foreign-policy establishment, and one short answer to the question, Why did President Kennedy's advisers ask themselves, "What would Colonel Stimson have done?" might be: Because he was the founding father and patron saint of that establishment. . . .

Few Americans in the twentieth century served so long in high public life or over so long a period; none spanned in a single career so drastic a transformation of the United States' position in the world. Emperor Augustus boasted that he found Rome a city of brick and left it a city of marble. Henry Stimson first came to Washington when it was a quaint little southern town, and he left it as the unchallenged capital of the greatest power the world had ever seen.[66]

And zooming in on the correlation that America's emergence as a pioneering nuclear power bears to Stimson's own stature as a historical figure, Hodgson points out the "growth in American power conferred by the bomb, which was built under Stimson's authority and dropped on Hiroshima and Nagasaki on his orders."[67]

Stimson's closeness to America's pioneering science in the development of weapons of mass destruction—keenly alive to the unrivalled danger of that science—is particularly important to the question of criminalization of wars of aggression.

～

Thus, Stimson is an extremely important source of insight concerning the progressive development of international law from a period of resigned toleration of wars of aggression to the point of its resolute denunciation as criminal. As Stimson explained it, the change of attitude was triggered by World War I.

In an address he delivered before the Council on Foreign Relations in New York on 8 August 1932 titled "The Pact of Paris: The Three Years of Development," Stimson, the secretary of state at the time, tried to explain the significance of the Briand–Kellogg Pact, which his predecessor Frank B. Kellogg negotiated three years earlier in France with French foreign minister Aristide Briand. The treaty's adherents at the time comprised "virtually all of the nations of the world."[68]

Stimson rightly pointed out that "a large part" of international law, from its early beginnings, "had been a development of principles based upon the existence of war."[69] Although much of the developments in international law that occurred before World War I had focused on principles of neutrality and those of humanitarian law, international law had not sought "to abolish war but to narrow and confine its destructive effects."[70] The chief purpose of the resulting rules "was to produce oases of safety for life and property in a world which still recognized and legalized the destruction of human life and property as one of the regular methods for the settlement of international controversies and the maintenance of international policy."[71] But, then, along came the Industrial Revolution and great advancements in science, coupled with changes in social organizations, which "produced inevitable effects upon the concept of war."[72] In a sense, the world got smaller, so to speak, with the increased interdependence of the populations of nations even as they grew. "The civilized world thus became very much more vulnerable to war."[73] Notably, mechanization of warfare came with greater ease in the movement of armies, air forces, and navies across great distances with their ever more destructive ordnance.[74]

"By these changes on either side," Stimson explained, "the inconsistency of war with normal life became sharper and more acute; the destructiveness of war to civilization became more emphatic; the abnormality of war became more apparent. The laws of neutrality became increasingly ineffective to prevent even strangers to the original quarrel from being drawn into the general conflict."[75] And the Great War was the great epiphany, "and it became evident to the most casual observer that if this evolution were permitted to continue, war, perhaps the next war, would drag down and utterly destroy our civilization."[76]

Thus was awakened at the global level "a community spirit which can be evoked to prevent war."[77]

That sentiment helps explain why World War I was called "a war to end all wars," even before its own ending.[78] And at the end of that war, an unprecedented global mechanism, the League of Nations, was founded, pursuant to a covenant "which sought to reduce the possibility of war to its lowest terms."[79] Although it did not seek to abolish war entirely, it nevertheless marked "the beginning of a group sentiment which is wholly at variance with some of the old doctrines in respect to war."[80]

That ambition of abolishing war altogether followed nine years later with the adoption of the Briand–Kellogg Pact at Quai d'Orsay in Paris on 28 August 1928, known in the long form as a general "Treaty for the Renunciation of War as an Instrument of National Policy." Not only did the signatories and adherents "*condemn* recourse to war for the solution of international controversies, and *renounce* it, as an instrument of national policy in their relations with one another,"[81] they also agreed "that the settlement or solution of *all* disputes or conflicts *of whatever nature* or *of whatever origin* they may be, which may arise among them, shall *never* be sought *except* by pacific means."[82] The pact's wide adherence by most of the nations then independent signaled that war had "become illegal throughout practically the entire world." Being "an illegal thing," it could no longer be the source and subject of rights.[83]

In the course of a protracted armed conflict between Japan and China that began in September 1931, during which Japan occupied all of Manchuria, the United States informed both parties that it would not recognize any situation, treaty, or agreement that might result from that armed conflict. The American position was of the essence of the Briand–Kellogg Pact to which Japan and China were parties. Notwithstanding that the United States was not a member of the League of Nations, the Assembly of the League of Nations endorsed the American position[84]—which became known in international relations as the "Stimson Doctrine."

According to Stimson, the progression of international law from the negotiation and adoption of the covenant of the League of Nations to those of the Briand–Kellogg Pact signaled "a revolution in human thought" that was "not the result of impulse or thoughtless sentiment." Fundamentally, the two treaties were "the growth of necessity, the product of a consciousness that unless some such steps were taken modern civilization might be doomed."[85]

The London Agreement and Charter of the International Military Tribunal

As noted earlier, Stimson was secretary of war to the administrations of President Roosevelt and his successor, President Truman, during World War II. In that capacity, Stimson cosigned (with Secretary of State Edward Stettinius and Attorney General Francis Biddle) the Yalta Memorandum, which contained the official U.S. position that guided President Roosevelt's discussions[86] during the Yalta Conference—also known as the Crimean Conference—of February 1945. It was during this conference that Roosevelt, Churchill, and Stalin discussed the reorganization of postwar Germany and Europe.

Notably, the Yalta Memorandum maintained that the Axis leaders must face international criminal prosecution upon the conclusion of the war, rather than be put to summary execution without a trial. And, quite significantly for present purposes, one of the charges to be brought against them must be for "the waging of an illegal war of aggression with ruthless disregard for international law and the rules of war."[87] Stimson's War Department, again together with the State and the Justice departments, had contributed in the formulation of an American draft protocol of agreement for the international prosecutions canvassed at the margins of the San Francisco Conference for the United Nations Organization.[88] According to that draft protocol, "Launching a war of aggression" was one of the crimes to be prosecuted.[89] An accompanying memorandum from the American delegation in San Francisco also made clear that the crime of aggression had to be prosecuted as one of the charges.[90]

The Yalta Memorandum inspired subsequent negotiations en route to the London Conference of 1945 and at the conference itself, all of which made it perfectly clear that a primary objective of post–World War II settlement entailed the prosecution of the Axis war of aggression as criminal conduct.[91]

Those negotiations ultimately resulted in the London Agreement of 8 August 1945 to which was annexed the Charter of the International Military Tribunal (IMT). The charter indicates the crime of aggression as the first crime over which the tribunal was given jurisdiction, after which appeared war crimes and crimes against humanity. To that end, the second paragraph of article 6 provides as follows:

> The following acts, or any of them, are crimes coming within the juris-diction of the Tribunal for which there shall be individual responsibility:
>
> (a) CRIMES AGAINST PEACE: namely, planning, preparation, initia-tion or waging of a war of aggression, or a war in violation of international treaties, agreements or assurances, or participation in a common plan or conspiracy for the accomplishment of any of the foregoing.[92]

For France, the United Kingdom, the United States, and the Union of Soviet Socialist Republics, the London Agreement, together with the charter annexed to it, came into force on 8 August 1945, in accordance with article 7 of the London Agreement. It further came into force between September and December 1945 for fifteen other countries that subscribed to it as adherents. Those were Australia, Belgium, Czechoslovakia, Denmark, Ethiopia, Greece, Haiti, Honduras, India, Luxembourg, Netherlands, New Zealand, Norway, Panama, Paraguay, Poland, Uruguay, Venezuela, and Yugoslavia.[93]

The Jackson Perspective

On 2 May 1945, President Truman appointed Justice Robert H. Jackson to represent the United States at the London Conference of 1945 and as a chief of counsel for the United States at the resulting trial for the prosecu-tion of Nazi leaders before an international tribunal.[94]

In his capacity as the *representative* of the United States, Jackson spoke and acted on behalf of his country during the negotiations not only of the London Agreement but also the Charter of the IMT.

In a mission report that he submitted to President Truman during the summer of 1945, Jackson insisted that international law had already "thoroughly" denounced wars of aggression as a crime before the commencement of World War II. As he put it, "By the time the Nazis came to power it was thoroughly established that launching an aggressive war or the institution of war by treachery was illegal and that the defense of legitimate warfare was no longer available to those who engaged in such an enterprise. It is high time that we act on the juridical principle that aggressive war-making is *illegal and criminal.*"[95]

To demonstrate that proposition, Justice Jackson began with the Briand–Kellogg Pact and Stimson's 1932 address to the Council of Foreign Relations. Jackson further recalled that, in the Geneva Protocol for the Pacific Settlement of International Disputes (1924), the representatives of forty-eight states asserted through it that "a war of aggression constitutes . . . an international crime";[96] that by a unanimous resolution adopted in 1927, the Eighth Assembly of the League of Nations, consisting of forty-eight countries (including Germany), similarly declared that a war of aggression constitutes an international crime;[97] and that twenty-one nations at the Sixth Pan-American Conference that met in Havana in 1928 had adopted a resolution saying that "war of aggression constitutes an international crime against the human species."[98]

In article 6 of the eventual Charter of the International Military Tribunal annexed to the London Agreement of 1945 for the prosecution of the major suspects of the Nazi atrocities, the first set of crimes over which the tribunal was given jurisdiction were "crimes against peace" explained as "planning, preparation, initiation or waging of a war of aggression, or a war in violation of international treaties, agreements or assurances, or participation in a common plan or conspiracy for the accomplishment of any of the foregoing."

Not only did it fall to Jackson, as the chief prosecutor of the United States, to make the opening statement for the prosecution before the International Military Tribunal at Nuremberg, but it also fell to him to address the first charge in the indictment. It concerned common plan or conspiracy to commit or involved committing the crimes against peace, war crimes and crimes against humanity as described in the Charter.[99]

In the very first sentence of his opening statement, Jackson made it immediately clear that the undertaking was "the first trial in history for crimes against the peace of the world."[100]

"That attack on the peace of the world is the crime against international society which brings into international cognizance crimes in its aid and preparation which otherwise might be only internal concerns."[101]

The trial, Jackson insisted, was not an interesting exercise in scholarship, but "the practical effort of four of the most mighty of nations, with the support of 17 more, to utilize international law to meet the greatest menace of our times—aggressive war."[102]

"The common sense of mankind demands that law shall not stop with the punishment of petty crimes by little people," Jackson continued, inviting focus on the essence of the criminal responsibility for the crime of aggression as resting on political leadership. The law "must also reach men who possess themselves of great power and make deliberate and concerted use of it to set in motion evils which leave no home in the world untouched."[103]

To drive the essence of the crime home to his audience, Jackson pointed to the defendants as the "living symbols" of the crime of aggression that had made Europe miserable for so long: "We will show them to be living symbols of racial hatreds, of terrorism and violence, and of the arrogance and cruelty of power," he said.

"They are symbols of fierce nationalisms and of militarism, of intrigue and war-making which have embroiled Europe generation after generation, crushing its manhood, destroying its homes, and impoverishing its life."[104]

Jackson devoted a part of his opening speech to outlining the factual elements of the case for the charge of aggressive war.[105]

In the ensuing exposé, Jackson addressed the fallacy of the doctrine that had preserved until World War I the right of nations to wage wars of aggression. In the process, he took care to allude to the economic motives that powerful states had in preserving that doctrine.

In introductory classes to international law, law students are taught that general principles of law recognized by "civilized states" are sources of international law. That is to say, there need be no treaty or customary international law on a particular point for it to be accepted as constituting a principle of international law: as long as it can be shown that the principle in question is identifiable in the national laws of "civilized" nations.

That, in effect, was Jackson's starting point. "Of course, it was, under the law of all civilized peoples, a crime for one man with his bare knuckles to assault another," he began. And he asked, "How did it come that multiplying this crime by a million, and adding fire arms to bare knuckles, made it a legally innocent act?"

"The doctrine," he continued, "was that one could not be regarded as criminal for committing the usual violent acts in the conduct of legitimate warfare."

And, alluding to the sin of imperialism that Woodrow Wilson hoped in 1919 to see "swept away" as one of the "very foundations of this war,"* Jackson continued, "The age of imperialistic expansion during the eighteenth and nineteenth centuries added [to] the foul doctrine, contrary to the teachings of early Christian and international law scholars such as Grotius, that all wars are to be regarded as legitimate wars. The sum of these two doctrines was to give war-making a complete immunity from accountability to law."[106]

From that perspective, Jackson sensibly updated the progressive development of international law up to the Briand–Kellogg Pact of 1928. As he put it:

> This was intolerable for an age that called itself civilized. Plain people with their earthy common sense, revolted at such fictions and legalisms so contrary to ethical principles and demanded checks on war immunities. Statesmen and international lawyers at first cautiously responded by adopting rules of warfare designed to make the conduct of war more civilized. The effort was to set legal limits to the violence that could be done to civilian populations and to combatants as well.
>
> The common sense of men after the first World War demanded, however, that the law's condemnation of war reach deeper, and that the law condemn not merely uncivilized ways of waging war, but also the waging in any way of uncivilized wars—wars of aggression. The world's statesmen again went only as far as they were forced to go. Their efforts were timid and cautious and often less explicit than we might have hoped. But the 1920's did outlaw aggressive war.

---

* In the words of Wilson: "We are here to see, in short, that the very foundations of this war are swept away. Those foundations were the private choice of small coteries of civil rulers and military staffs. Those foundations were the aggression of great powers upon the small. Those foundations were the holding together of empires of unwilling subjects by the duress of arms. Those foundations were the power of small bodies of men to work their will upon mankind and use them as pawns in a game. And nothing less than the emancipation of the world from these things will accomplish peace." See Wilson, "Address to the Peace Conference in Paris," 3:178.

The re-establishment of the principle that there are unjust wars and that unjust wars are illegal is traceable in many steps. One of the most significant is the Briand–Kellogg Pact of 1928.[107]

In a point of emphasis, he insisted that "[a]ny resort to war—to any kind of a war—is a resort to means that are inherently criminal. War inevitably is a course of killings, assaults, deprivations of liberty, and destruction of property. An honestly defensive war is, of course, legal and saves those lawfully conducting it from criminality. But inherently criminal acts cannot be defended by showing that those who committed them were engaged in a war, when war itself is illegal."[108]

But, even if it was possible to make a credible case that the Nazi hierarchy then at trial for the crime of aggression were being tried under a law that was not clearly established as law before the Nuremberg Charter created that law in terms so clear, Jackson was prepared to make no apologies in creating that precedent in international law that must be followed in future. Insisting that it was the right thing to do, he said, "But if it be thought that the Charter, whose declarations concededly bind us all, does contain new law I still do not shrink from demanding its strict application by this Tribunal. The rule of law in the world, flouted by the lawlessness incited by these defendants, had to be restored at the cost to my country of over a million casualties, not to mention those of other nations. I cannot subscribe to the perverted reasoning that society may advance and strengthen the rule of law by the expenditure of morally innocent lives but that progress in the law may never be made at the price of morally guilty lives."[109]

Recall that Jackson's starting point was that the crime of aggression in international law had a confident source in the legal principle that proscribed violent aggression in the laws of every civilized nation. But here, he was even prepared to go further, in saying that since the construction of international law had been an ongoing project to which past generations had added according to the needs of their own times, the generation of Jackson's own era had every right and duty to contribute their own block to that ongoing building project by virtue of the Charter of the Nuremberg Tribunal. As he put it:

> It is true of course, that we have no judicial precedent for the Charter. But international law is more than a scholarly collection of abstract and immutable principles. It is an outgrowth of treaties and agreements between nations and of accepted customs. Yet every custom has its origin in some single act, and every agreement has to be initiated by the action of

some state. Unless we are prepared to abandon every principle of growth for international law, we cannot deny that our own day has the right to institute customs and to conclude agreements that will themselves become sources of a newer and strengthened international law. International law is not capable of development by the normal processes of legislation, for there is no continuing international legislative authority. Innovations and revisions in international law are brought about by the action of governments such as those I have cited, designed to meet a change in circumstances. It grows, as did the common law, through decisions reached from time to time in adapting settled principles to new situations. The fact is that when the law evolves by the case method, as did the common law and as international law must do if it is to advance at all, it advances at the expense of those who wrongly guessed the law and learned too late their error. The law, so far as international law can be decreed, had been clearly pronounced when these acts took place. Hence, I am not disturbed by the lack of judicial precedent for the inquiry it is proposed to conduct.[110]

Any debate about the validity of Jackson's argument of legal precedent can only matter in relation to the trial of the Nazi leaders in 1945, relative to the preceding period. That debate is entirely irrelevant in the subsequent march of international law, for the essence of the creation of the crime of aggression in the Charter of the Nuremberg Tribunal—which was adopted by four of the most powerful nations at the time and adhered to by nineteen other independent nations[111] and later affirmed by the United Nations[112]—is that the crime has since been recognized as such in international law.

In concluding on the point, Jackson left the judges with the parting thought flown on the poetry of Rudyard Kipling: "Civilisation . . . does not expect that you can make war impossible. It does expect that your juridical action will put the forces of international law, its precepts, its prohibitions and, most of all, its sanctions, on the side of peace, so that men and women of good will, in all countries, may have 'leave to live by no man's leave, underneath the law.'"[113]

The judges, however, would not respond until they had heard from another eminent jurist, Sir Hartley Shawcross, KC, who was the attorney general of England and Wales, and lead counsel for the British prosecutorial team.

The Shawcross Perspective

On the twelfth day of the proceedings, Shawcross addressed the tribunal as part of his mandate to outline the prosecution case on the second count of the indictment against the Nazi leaders on trial. The charge was that the defendants "participated in the planning, preparation, initiation, and waging of wars of aggression, which were also wars in violation of international treaties, agreements and assurances."[114]

As the attorney general of Great Britain, Shawcross was the chief law officer of the British Crown. In that capacity, he represented the views of Great Britain in the proceedings.

In his own turn addressing the tribunal, Shawcross observed that, in the period since the Paris Peace Conference of 1919, "[t]he statesmen of the world deliberately set out to make wars of aggression an international crime."[115] Thus, words to that effect in the Charter of the International Military Tribunal for Nuremberg were "no new terms invented by the victors to embody in this Charter."[116]

"They have figured," he said, "and they have figured prominently, in numerous treaties, in governmental pronouncements, and in the declarations of statesmen in the period preceding the second World War."[117] And he traced that reconfiguration of international law in the terms of a number of international multilateral and bilateral treaties and declarations, including but not limited to the Briand–Kellogg Pact of 1928.[118]

For Shawcross, the essential point in the development of international law boiled down to this: "Whatever the position may have been at the time of the Hague Convention, whatever the position may have been in 1914, whatever it may have been in 1918—and it is not necessary to discuss it—no international lawyer of repute, no responsible statesman, no soldier concerned with the legal use of armed forces, no economist or industrialist concerned in his country's war economy could doubt that with the Pact of Paris on the statute book a war of aggression was contrary to international law."[119]

Not shrinking from the distinction between mere illegality and sheer criminality, Shawcross argued that the horrors of war of aggression made it absurd for the law to dwell on that distinction, thereby avoiding criminal prosecution of those whose conduct violated the rule against waging a war of aggression.[120]

In any event, "[i]f this be an innovation," he insisted, "it is an innovation long overdue—a desirable and beneficent innovation fully consistent with justice, fully consistent with common sense and with the abiding purposes of the law of nations."[121] It was right that the charter of the tribunal should make the waging of a war of aggression a crime in international law. For "[i]t is a salutary legal rule that persons who, in violation of the law, plunge their own and other countries into an aggressive war should do so with a halter around their necks."[122]

The Tribunals' Perspectives

In their eventual judgment, at the end of the trial, the judges of the International Military Tribunal for Nuremberg (IMTN) wasted no time in their judgment in signaling their acceptance of the submissions of Jackson and Shawcross, to the effect that a war of aggression is a crime in international law. Not only that; it is also "the supreme international crime," said the tribunal. They put the point across so clearly in the opening segment of their judgment: "The charges in the Indictment that the defendants planned and waged aggressive wars are charges of the utmost gravity. War is essentially an evil thing. Its consequences are not confined to the belligerent States alone, but affect the whole world."[123]

In an observation that has enjoyed sustained resonance since then,[124] the tribunal reasoned, "To initiate a war of aggression, therefore, is not only an international crime; it is the supreme international crime differing only from other war crimes in that it contains within itself the accumulated evil of the whole."[125]

Following a discussion of the facts and circumstances revealed in the evidence presented to the tribunal, the judges found many of the alleged defendants guilty of waging a war of aggression or a war in violation of international treaties. As the tribunal put it, "The Charter defines as a crime the planning or waging of war that is a war of aggression or a war in violation of international treaties. The Tribunal has decided that certain of the defendants planned and waged aggressive wars against 12 nations, and were therefore guilty of this series of crimes."[126]

The tribunal then reviewed the international treaties that fostered peace, which the Nazi regime had violated. Key among these treaties was the Briand–Kellogg Pact of 1928, which the tribunal considered in the light of the preceding history.

Similarly, the tribunal considered it "important to remember that Article 227 of the Treaty of Versailles," which "provided for a special court . . . to try the former German Emperor 'for supreme offence against international morality and sanctity of treaties.' The purpose of this trial was expressed to be 'to vindicate the solemn obligations of international undertakings and the validity of international morality.'"[127]

In their judgment, the tribunal made certain important pronouncements about the provisions of the Charter of the Nuremberg

Tribunal—pronouncements that were to have profound implications to the future development of international law.

In that respect, the tribunal observed that the law of the Charter gave the tribunal jurisdiction—including over the crime of aggression as set out in article 6 of the Charter. In that regard, the "law of the Charter [was] decisive, and binding upon the Tribunal."[128]

There was, however, a larger legal implication to the making of the Charter. This was in the sense, first, that it was "the exercise of the sovereign legislative power by the countries to which the German Reich unconditionally surrendered; and the undoubted right of these countries to legislate for the occupied territories has been recognized by the civilized world."[129] No doubt, this allusion had to do with the fact that most independent nations had also subscribed to the Nuremberg Charter by the end of 1946.

The second large implication that the tribunal ascribed to the making of the Charter was that "[t]he Charter is not an arbitrary exercise of power on the part of the victorious Nations, but in the view of the Tribunal, as will be shown, it is the expression of international law existing at the time of its creation; and to that extent is itself a contribution to international law."[130] It was in that regard that the tribunal reviewed, as noted earlier, the progressive development of international law in a manner that repeatedly denounced the waging of aggressive war as unlawful—even making it a crime—in international law. These included not only the incidence of the Briand–Kellogg Pact but also of article 227 of the Versailles Treaty, as noted earlier.[131]

Still on how the law of the Charter bore larger implications to the development of international law, the tribunal engaged the submissions on behalf of the defendants to the effect that wars of aggression were acts of sovereign states by their very nature and, as such, entailed sovereign immunity for the accused state officials and agents. The tribunal rejected the submissions. As part of their reasoning, the tribunal declared that "[t]he principle of international law, which under certain circumstances, protects the representatives of a state, cannot be applied to acts which are condemned as criminal by international law. The authors of these acts cannot shelter themselves behind their official position in order to be freed from punishment in appropriate proceedings."[132]

In that regard, the tribunal invoked article 7 of the Charter, which provided the following: "The official position of Defendants, whether as heads of State, or responsible officials in Government departments, shall not be considered as freeing them from responsibility, or mitigating punishment."[133]

As the tribunal further observed, "the very essence of the Charter is that individuals have international duties which transcend the national obligations of obedience imposed by the individual state. He who violates the laws of war cannot obtain immunity while acting in pursuance of the authority of the state if the state in authorizing action moves outside its competence under international law."[134]

⌒

It is important to keep in view the reason that these pronouncements should have profound implications to the future development of international law. Those implications are immediately clear to the extent that the Nuremberg Tribunal expressed itself as recognizing existing principles of international law. In this regard, it is necessary to consider in turn the significance of UN General Assembly resolution 95(I) of 11 December 1946, through which the then fifty-five-member United Nations affirmed "the principles of international law recognized by the Charter of the Nürnberg Tribunal and the judgment of the Tribunal."[135]

This means that by virtue of resolution 95(I), the UN General Assembly not only recognized that wars of aggression are criminal conducts in international law—as both the Nuremberg Charter and judgment had declared—but also that there was no immunity for anyone in respect of the conducts that the charter recognized as crimes.

⌒

Notably in resolution 95(I), the UN General Assembly observed in the preamble "that similar principles have been adopted in the Charter of the International Military Tribunal for the trial of the major war criminals in the Far East, proclaimed at Tokyo on 19 January 1946."[136] The "Tokyo Tribunal," formally called the International Military Tribunal for the Far East, was the tribunal created by the U.S. occupation government under General Douglas MacArthur. The tribunal, composed of judges from ten nations, tried the surviving political leaders of Japan, except Emperor Hirohito (who was spared prosecution primarily for political reasons).

Indeed, as was the case in article 6 of the Charter of the Nuremberg Tribunal, article 5(a) of the Charter of the Tokyo Tribunal (promulgated on 19 January 1946) also gave that tribunal the jurisdiction over "Crimes against Peace: Namely, the planning, preparation, initiation or waging of a declared or undeclared war of aggression, or a war in violation of international law, treaties, agreements or assurances, or participation in a common plan or conspiracy for the accomplishment of any of the foregoing."

It is also important to note that article 6 of the Charter of the Tokyo Tribunal repudiated immunity on grounds of "official position, at any time" as well as on grounds that "an accused acted pursuant to order of his government or of a superior"; although that a subordinate was obeying orders might "be considered in mitigation of punishment if the Tribunal determine[d] that justice so require[s]."

That the official position did not afford immunity from accountability for the crimes indicated in the Charter of the Tokyo Tribunal was a norm of general application to all those crimes—including aggression as an international crime.

___

It is important to consider how the crime of aggression was treated at the Tokyo Tribunal in a trial that lasted from May 1946 to September 1947, thus consolidating the repudiation of wars of aggression as a general principle of international law that took hold after World War II.

Notably, the first thirty-eight counts of the indictment at the Tokyo Tribunal were concentrated on charges concerning the waging of a war of aggression (counts 1–36) or initiating hostilities (counts 37 and 38) against named countries.[137]

It is significant that those charges were anchored in the jurisdiction conferred upon the tribunal under article 5(a) of its charter. In substance, that provision was formulated in the same essential terms as article 6(a) of the Charter of the Nuremberg Tribunal.[138]

As was the case at the Nuremberg Tribunal, the Tokyo Tribunal in its own turn also had to deal with jurisdictional objections against the aggression charges. The tribunals' disposals of those objections also increased the consolidation of the general principle of international law in relation to the crime of aggression. For our purposes, the four main ones were these: (1) that the Allied powers acting through the supreme commander [had] no authority to include in the Charter of the Tribunal and to designate as justiciable "Crimes against Peace" described in article 5(a) as comprising the crime of aggression; (2) that aggressive war was not illegal as such, and merely by renouncing war as an instrument of national policy, the Briand–Kellogg Pact of 1928 did not enlarge the scope of international criminal law; (3) that war is an act of state for which there was no individual responsibility under international law; and (4) that the provisions of the Charter were, to the foregoing extent, illegal, as they violated the principle that forbade "ex post facto" legislation.[139]

As their starting point in resolving those jurisdictional objections, the judges observed that the Charter that created the Tokyo Tribunal was "decisive and binding on the Tribunal" in relation to the law therein stipulated.[140]

Nevertheless, the judges observed that to say that the tribunal was bound by the charter did not mean that the Allied powers or any victor nations had the right under international law to vest in a tribunal they established or enact or promulgate laws that are in conflict with recognized rules or principles of international law. Any such tribunal may be created, and powers conferred on it, "only within the limits of international law."[141]

Beyond those general propositions, the Tokyo Tribunal used the same reasoning template laid down by the Nuremberg Tribunal in resolving the more specific points of law engaged by the objections. This was unsurprising given the similarity of the objections, as seen earlier. Notable in that regard was the Nuremberg Tribunal's pronouncement that "[t]he Charter [was] not an arbitrary exercise of Power on the part of the victorious nations but [was] the expression of international law existing at the time" of the tribunal's creation.[142]

In those regards, the Tokyo Tribunal ultimately considered that the "opinions of the Nuremberg Tribunal and the reasoning by which they are reached this Tribunal is in complete accord. They embody complete answers to the . . . four . . . grounds urged by the defence as set forth above."[143]

In the circumstances, the judges of the Tokyo Tribunal considered that "in all material respects" the charters of both their tribunal and the Nuremberg Tribunal were identical. Hence, they preferred to express their "unqualified adherence" to the relevant opinions of the Nuremberg Tribunal rather than reason the matters anew in somewhat different language that may invite controversy and conflicting interpretations of the two sets of opinions.[144]

The import of those pronouncements is clear enough in the chronicles of the development of international law. Both the Nuremberg and the

Tokyo tribunals were at one in their views about the essential elements
of international law that they applied in the trials of German and Japanese
Axis leaders. Two striking aspects of that development in international law
were that a war of aggression is a crime in international law,[145] and that
official position—no matter how high—did not confer immunity from
accountability for international crimes.[146] Consequently, almost the entire
executive political leadership of both the wartime governments of Germany[147] and Japan[148] (with the singular exception of Emperor Hirohito*)
were prosecuted and convicted for the crime of aggression. And those
elements were sufficiently captured in what the United Nations General
Assembly affirmed in December 1946 as "the principles of international
law recognised by the Charter of the Nürnberg Tribunal and the judgment
of the Tribunal."[149]

The Stimson Perspective Updated

Stimson's views as U.S. secretary of state, as reviewed earlier, is an important commentary on the evolution of international law to the point of
proscription of wars of aggression.

Fifteen years later, following his service as the U.S. secretary of war
during World War II, and having played an instrumental role in the decision to prosecute the leadership of the Third Reich at Nuremberg, Stimson returned to reiterate why aggressive war *had* become an "illegal thing"
in international law. But, above all, his 1947 essay in *Foreign Affairs*, titled
"The Nuremberg Trial: Landmark in Law," is a magisterial primer on why
international law had to make war not only illegal but *criminal*—and how
the Nuremberg trial crystallized that progression.

He observed in that regard that the "surviving leaders" of the Nazi
regime had been indicted, tried, and judged in a proceeding whose magnitude and quality made it "a landmark in the history of international law."[150]
A point of significance of the reference to "surviving" Nazi leaders was
the allusion that Hitler did not survive the war. From all indications, as
discussed elsewhere in this book, the Allied leadership always had Hitler in
their sight as the primary target of any postwar accountability project under
contemplation during the war.

But speaking to those who observe or follow the progressive development of international law, Stimson noted that "great undertaking
at Nuremberg can live and grow in meaning . . . only if its principles

---

* Many would not find the emperor's exclusion from prosecution as a surprising outcome, given
that many constitutional monarchies had become largely ceremonial even by the 1940s.

are rightly understood and accepted."[151] It is not always clear how well modern pundits of international law understood the significance of that development.

Insisting that the Nuremberg "trial deserves to be known and valued as a long step ahead on the only upward road," Stimson pointed out that the prosecution of the Nazi leaders was the only reasonable course to be pursued following the conclusion of the war. As he outlined the options, there were "three different courses" that might have been followed when the Nazi leaders were captured. They were "release, summary punishment, or trial."[152]

Criminal trial following the due process of law—the course eventually followed—was the only reasonable approach in the circumstances. Release was out of the question, as it would have been an admission that the Nazi atrocities (including the Holocaust) engaged no question of accountability.

Summary execution—euphemistically referred to as "summary punishment" or "executive action"—was equally out of the question in Stimson's view, although it had been "widely recommended."[153] Stimson considered it the kind of barbarous method that defined the Nazi regime.[154]

It must, of course, be observed here as an aside that the protests of modern-day scholars who insist that heads of state must enjoy immunity in international law appear surprisingly oblivious to how their arguments retain the pressure on victorious nations to subject conquered enemies to summary execution, pursuant to the dictates of the ancient maxim *Vae victis!* and the accepted practice (particularly in the past) of execution or banishment without a trial.[155]

Adverting to the gradual process by which customary international law grows, Stimson recalled that "[i]nternational law is not a body of authoritative codes or statutes; it is the gradual expression, case by case, of the moral judgments of the civilized world. As such, it corresponds precisely to the common law of Anglo-American tradition."[156] And such is how the Nuremberg trial has enlarged international law. "We can understand the law of Nuremberg only if we see it for what it is—a great new case in the book of international law."[157]

The proscription of the crime of aggression and the subjection of rulers to accountability are two remarkable ways that the Nuremberg process enlarged international law.

In tracing the progressive development of international law along the path of proscribing aggressive wars, Stimson correctly identified World War I as the point of departure for law reform in the new direction. "Throughout the centuries, until after World War I," he observed, "the choice between war and peace remained entirely in the hands of each sovereign state, and neither the law nor the ordinary conscience of humanity ventured to deny that right. The concept of just and unjust wars is of course as old at least as Plato. But in the anarchy of individual sovereignties, the right to fight was denied to no people and the right to start a fight was denied to no ruler. For the loser in a war, punishment was certain. But this was not a matter of law; it was simply a matter of course. At the best it was like the early law of the blood feud, in which the punishment of a murderer was the responsibility of the victim's family alone and not of the whole community."[158]

Not only was accountability for aggressive war considered beyond the authority of international law, so too was the accountability of rulers. As Stimson observed, "So far indeed was this sovereign right of war-making accepted that it was frequently extended to include the barbarous notion that a sovereign ruler is not subject to the law."[159]

In those circumstances, all that international law could manage was to do its best to temper the brutalities of warfare once commenced, "[i]n obedience to the age-old instincts of chivalry and magnanimity."[160]

But the project of moderating "the excesses of war without controlling war itself"[161] became unsustainable in light of the advancements of human abilities enabled by "the extraordinary scientific and industrial developments of the nineteenth and twentieth centuries,"[162] which both increasingly shrinks the world as a battleground as it increasingly magnifies the spatial dimensions of war's destructive power. By the beginning of World War I in 1914, Stimson observed, "the world had been intertwined into a single unit and weapons had been so far developed that a major war could shake the whole structure of civilization. No rules of warfare were sufficient to limit the vast new destructive powers of belligerents."[163]

The devastations of the First World War—which for France's soldiers alone accounted for more than 1 million deaths and close to 4 million wounded[164]—thus "made it clear that old notions" of a laissez-faire attitude to wars of aggression "must be abandoned; the world must attack the problem at its root."[165] And that attack at the root of the problem began in 1918, at the conclusion of World War I and the resulting Paris Peace Conference of 1919. The repeated efforts made since then "to eliminate aggressive war as a legal national undertaking" culminated in the Briand–Kellogg Pact of 1928 in which the sixty-three nations that then comprised almost the entirety of independent nations agreed to renounce aggressive warfare.[166]

According to Stimson, the Briand–Kellogg Pact was "not an isolated incident of the postwar era."[167] Quite the contrary, "the whole world was at one in its opinion of aggressive war" during that period.[168] "In repeated resolutions in the League of Nations and elsewhere, *aggression was roundly denounced as criminal. In the judgment of the peoples of the world the once proud title of 'conqueror' was replaced by the criminal epithet 'aggressor.'"*[169]

Although that direction was halting between the first and the second world wars, it was also sufficiently palpable. According to Stimson, "the mandate for peace was overwhelming,"[170] though the mechanism to enforce it was less certain. But World War II forced the question.

"In early 1945," Stimson observed, "as it became apparent that the long delayed victory was at hand, the question posed itself directly: Has there been a war of aggression and are its leaders punishable?"[171] The Nuremberg Charter resolved those questions. According to it, "the responsible leaders of aggressive war were subjected to trial and conviction on the charge of crimes against peace."[172]

"Thus," concluded Stimson, "the Second World War brought it home to us that our repugnance to aggressive war was incomplete without a judgment of its leaders. What we had called a crime demanded punishment; we must bring our law in balance with the universal moral judgment of mankind. The wickedness of aggression must be punished by a trial and judgment. This is what has been done at Nuremberg."[173]

In other words, the Nuremberg process set in place the anchoring plate for international *jus puniendi*—the community's right to punish those who violate its criminal laws—in relation to the crime of aggression and other international crimes.

But, to appreciate fully the progressive development that Stimson outlined above, we must go back in time to capture in greater detail some of the major milestones of that development.

THREE PEACE CONFERENCES FOR LAW REFORM

3

> *War's effects have been so profound that to leave it out is to ignore one of the great forces, along with geography, resources, economics, ideas, and social and political changes, which have shaped human development and changed history. —Margaret MacMillan,* War

A French diplomat once expressed in beatific tones how some architects of international law see their work and the discipline. "We have endeavoured," he said, "to preserve intact the fundamental principles of that august law of nations which spreads like the vault of heaven over all nations and borrows the laws of nature herself, to protect the peoples of the world one from the other by inculcating upon them the essentials of mutual good-will."[1]

It should be possible, of course, to say the same thing in more earthbound ways. One way is to say that international law in all its aspects regulates modern life within the international community, in ways it is hoped will improve that life. Among those (but by no means limited to them) are the spheres of trade and commerce between nations, international air travel, haulage of goods, telecommunications, posts and telegraphs, common use of the high seas and of outer space, arctic exploration, and intellectual property.

Above all, it has been the need to blunt the violent bent of humankind, bared through wars, that has afforded the keenest spur for the advancement of international law. The 1648 peace treaties known as the *Peace of Westphalia*—which ended both the more immediate thirty-year war and longer eighty-year wars of Europe—are largely credited with setting international law upon its still-recognizable course. The challenge for statesmen and women (the era had regnant queens) was how to use law to modulate the predatory or the belligerent instinct in the relationships of nations. Russian czar Nicholas II was thus motivated to propose a world peace conference "to seek the most effective means of ensuring to the peoples a lasting peace, and of limiting the progressive development of military armaments"[2] and "to prevent war, if possible, or at least to mitigate its effects."[3]

Queen Wilhelmina of the Netherlands agreed to host the conference in one of her royal palaces—Huis ten Bosch (the Palace in the Woods)—in The Hague.[4] The result was the First Hague Peace Conference of 1899.

The convening plenipotentiaries did not agree to limit military expenditure.* But they adopted a set of outcome documents: three binding treaties and three nonbinding declarations, to try and make war more humane in the next wars should wars become inevitable.[†] In international law, *humanitarian law* or the *law of war* are (roughly speaking) the shorthand terms for the law covered in those kinds of documents.

As they were concluding the 1899 Peace Conference, the delegates agreed to meet again in a few years' time.[5] And they did, in 1907. And again it was in The Hague. Notably, at the time, there was no standing multilateral international organization, such as the United Nations that now convenes general meetings annually and many more meetings in between. The best that the world could manage before the twentieth century was to call occasional conferences once between many years.

As was the case at the First Hague Peace Conference in 1899, talks of limitation of armament at the Second Hague Peace Conference in 1907 was equally a nonstarter.[6] Nevertheless, the results in 1907 were much more thoroughgoing. There were fourteen outcome documents: thirteen

---

* In his closing remarks, the conference president, Baron Egor Egorovich Staal of Russia, delicately expressed the failure as follows: "If the First Commission, which had taken charge of military questions, the limitation of armaments and of budgets, did not arrive at important material results, it is because the Commission met with technical difficulties and a series of allied considerations which it did not deem itself competent to examine. But the Conference has requested the various Governments to resume the study of these questions. The Conference unanimously supported the resolution proposed by the first delegate of France, to wit: 'That the limitation of military charges, which at present weigh down the world, is greatly to be desired for the increase of the material and moral welfare of humanity'" (Carnegie Endowment for International Peace, *Proceedings of the Hague Conferences*, 224).

† As the sentiment was put in the very opening message of the preamble to the Hague Convention (II) relative to the Laws and Customs of War on Land (1899): "Considering that, while seeking means to preserve peace and prevent armed conflicts among nations, it is likewise necessary to have regard to cases where an appeal to arms may be caused by events which their solicitude could not avert."

binding treaties intended as binding and one hortatory declaration. They mostly consolidated and expanded the project of codifying the laws of war.

The 1907 Hague Conference was until then the most ambitious gathering of states for the purpose of developing international law. Forty-four nations had sent ambassadors.

The two conferences were truly epochal in the history of international relations. They "were the first truly international assemblies meeting in time of peace for the purpose of preserving peace, not of concluding a war then in progress."[7]

Once more, as the delegates were concluding the Second Hague Peace Conference, they recommended a third peace conference, "which might be held within a period corresponding to that which has elapsed since the preceding Conference, at a date to be fixed by common agreement between the Powers."[8] The lag time between 1899 and 1907 was eight years. Hence, the next peace conference would have taken place in 1915.

On 1 August 1914, Germany invaded Belgium and World War I broke out, lasting a grueling four years. So, the third peace conference for the further development of international law had to be postponed. However, in a manner of speaking, that third "peace conference" was effectively held—but under markedly different circumstances and not in The Hague. It was held in 1919, with its ceremonies taking place at the Versailles Palace in Paris—in the postbellum atmosphere of World War I.

The Paris Peace Conference developed international law in very significant ways, including by the international regulation of labor, and by way of coordination of international efforts for the common good, through the creation of a standing international organization—the League of Nations, which was the predecessor to the United Nations (UN).

A conscious and determined effort was made in Paris to develop international law along the following new lines: (1) individual criminal responsibility must be visited upon those who commit international crimes; (2) it is proper to create an international tribunal for that purpose; and (3) anyone arraigned before such an international tribunal will not enjoy immunity—regardless of status even as a head of state. It was a highly significant point of international law reform. Those were specific outcome norms of the Paris Peace Conference of 1919—the "third peace conference" of the world, as it were.

As we saw earlier in Henry L. Stimson's observations, those outcome norms were built upon at the conclusion of World War II. And they have since crystallized in subsequent general international practice accepted as law—what international lawyers call customary international law.

The Significance of the Paris Peace Conference of 1919

It should not be rude to observe that there are many in the modern era of international law and international relations who do not readily appreciate the enormity of the Paris Peace Conference of 1919, certainly in its physical dimension. As a background to our further discussion, it is necessary to recall here the grandiose undertaking that the conference was. Margaret MacMillan, the renowned Canadian historian who specializes in the World War I era, paints an adequate picture of the conference's grandeur.

For the first six months in 1919, she wrote, "Paris was the capital of the world."[9] The fabled city was sad, though beautiful as always. Its people were subdued, though its women remained "still extraordinarily elegant."[10] The restaurants were "still marvellous" when they could get supplies. The nightclubs still buzzed for couples seeking a good time.[11] The grass was "still green and a few flowers still bloomed."[12] Heavy rains had flooded the Seine, its waters rising, as Parisians reveled in the climes of an ended war that their side had won.[13]

It was into those circumstances that men and women assembled from all over the world. "To struggle with the great issues of the day and try to resolve them, statesmen, diplomats, bankers, soldiers, professors, economists and lawyers came to Paris from all corners of the world."[14]

"That winter and spring," wrote MacMillan, "Paris hummed with schemes, for: Jewish homeland, a restored Poland, an independent Ukraine, a Kurdistan, an Armenia. The petitions poured in, from the Conference of Suffrage Societies, the Carpatho-Russian Committee in Paris, the Serbs of the Banat, the anti-Bolshevik Russian Political Conference. The petitioners came from countries that existed and ones that were just dreams. Some, such as the Zionists, spoke for millions; others, such as the representatives of the Aland islands in the Baltic, for a few thousand. A few arrived too late; the Koreans from Siberia set out on foot in February 1919 and by the time the main part of the Peace Conference ended in June had reached only the Arctic port of Archangel."[15]

Among the most prominent of Paris's guests that winter and spring was U.S. president Woodrow Wilson. The significance of his presence, in relation to the conference's importance, is implicit in the following observation of MacMillan's: "No other American President had ever gone to Europe while in Office."[16]

The scale of the undertaking that was the Paris Peace Conference is usually cast in sharp relief when compared to the Congress of Vienna of 1815, convened to settle the geopolitical order of Europe following the Napoleonic Wars. "The problems faced by the peacemakers in Vienna, large though they were, were straightforward by comparison with those in Paris."[17]

The sizes of the delegations say it all. Lord Castlereagh, the British foreign secretary, "took just fourteen staff with him to the Congress of Vienna. But in 1919 the British delegation numbered nearly four hundred."[18] That was nearly thirty times more attendees. The comparative sizes of the delegations to the two conferences become exponentially clear enough if one considered that the Vienna conference was limited to Europe: with Austria, France, Portugal, Prussia, Russia, Spain, Sweden, and the United Kingdom as the participants.[19] By comparison, "more than thirty countries sent delegates to Paris, including Italy, Belgium, Rumania and Serbia, none of which had existed in 1815. The Latin American nations had still been part of the Spanish and Portuguese empires. Thailand, China, and Japan had been remote, mysterious lands. Now their diplomats appeared in Paris in pinstriped trousers and frock coats. Apart from a declaration condemning the slave trade, the Congress of Vienna paid no attention to the non-European world. In Paris, the subjects covered by the Peace Conference ranged from the Arctic to the Antipodes, from small islands in the Pacific to whole continents."[20]

David Lloyd George summed up the comparison. "The task with which the Peace Delegates have been confronted has indeed been a gigantic one," he wrote. "No Conference that has ever assembled in the history of the world has been faced with problems of such variety, of such complexity, of such magnitude, and of such gravity. The Congress of Vienna was the nearest approach to it. You had then to settle the affairs of Europe alone. It took eleven months. But the problems at the Congress of Vienna, great as they were, sink into insignificance compared with those which we have had to attempt to settle at the Paris Conference. It is not one continent that is engaged—every continent is affected. With very few exceptions, every country in Europe has been in this War. Every country in Asia is affected by the War, except Tibet and Afghanistan. There is not a square mile of Africa that has not been engaged in the War in one way or another. Almost the whole of the nations of America are in the War, and in the far islands of the Southern Seas there are islands that have been captured, and there are hundreds of thousands of men from those remote regions who have come to fight in this great world struggle."

"There has never been in the whole history of this globe anything to compare to it," Lloyd George wrote.[21]

Yes, MacMillan concurred, "The world has never seen anything quite like it and never will again."[22]

᠊᠑᠊

And as will become evident in the words and actions of Lloyd George, in addition to those important geopolitical settlements undertaken at the conference, he and his fellow leading statesmen of 1919 also came to Paris to *change* international law in an *intentional* way—in the specific and defining manner covered in this book. That is an important detail that does not always register sufficiently among many in the circles of modern international law and international relations.

An International *Jus Puniendi*

On a proper view, the three peace conferences (1899, 1907, and 1919) are amenable to composite appreciation as falling within the standards of classic penal regulation.

According to those standards, the legislator, first, prescribes the behavior that the citizen must abstain from (the subjective factor of penal regulation) and, second, lays down the consequences of failure to do so. The former is the subjective factor of penal regulation (in the sense of what falls within the control of the citizen); the latter is the objective factor (in the sense of what falls outside the control of the citizen).

The latter factor is what is otherwise known in Latin as *jus puniendi*, society's right to punish those who violate its cherished rules. It is the hallmark of penal regulation.

The first and second peace conferences of 1899 and 1907 supplied only the first factor, without the second, effectively making them hortatory appeals to "the better angels of our nature" as Abraham Lincoln once put the point. Indeed, the preambles to the outcome instruments ooze such sentiments.* But along came World War I to show the insouciant frequency with which the worst demons of human nature can terrorize

---

* The classic examples may be found in the preamble to the Hague Convention Respecting Laws and Customs of War on Land (1907). Among other things, it shows a readiness to accommodate "the appeal to arms" when it could not be averted by the care "to preserve peace and prevent armed conflicts between nations." The reader is informed that the treaty was "[a]nimated by the desire to serve, even in this extreme case, the interests of humanity and the ever progressive needs of civilization." It meekly informs that "these provisions, the wording of which has been inspired by the desire to diminish the evils of war, as far as military requirements permit, are intended to serve as a general rule of conduct for the belligerents in their mutual relations and in their relations with the inhabitants." And it concludes with the famous clause that Russian jurist Fyodor Fyodorovich Martens gave to international law: "Until a more complete code of the laws of war has been issued, the High Contracting Parties deem it expedient to declare that, in cases not included in the Regulations adopted by them, the inhabitants and the belligerents remain under the protection and the rule of the principles of the law of nations, as they result from the usages established among civilized peoples, from the laws of humanity, and the dictates of the public conscience."

the better angels, even flinging the world into a "welter of savagery"[23] in selfish ways, as the invasion of Ukraine has brought home even to all who are only experiencing it through the mass media in 2022 and later. By 1919, it had become clear that the invasion of Belgium in 1914 was a true moment of reckoning that fully exposed the serious inadequacies of the honors-based international humanitarian law system.

Professor Coleman Phillipson, who during the Paris Peace Conference reportedly worked much behind the scenes for the Crown Law Officers of England and Wales, and was held in high regard at the highest levels,[24] would have expressed the general wish of what needed to happen in international law after the war. "The main problem," he wrote, "to which men and nations should devote themselves is how to fortify it by such potent sanctions as will make its violation not merely dishonourable, but unprofitable to an offending member of the community of States."[25]

Senior members of the British government committed themselves to that theme. Notably, in his remarks to the Macdonell Committee of Enquiry into the Breaches of the Laws of War, Sir Frederick E. Smith, KC, the attorney general of England and Wales, the future Lord Chancellor Birkenhead, observed the following familiar discrepancy between international law and municipal law, the need for correction of which World War I brought to the fore: "The point of essential difference between Municipal Law and International Law has long been a commonplace with those who have written or thought upon such subjects. In our Municipal Laws punishment waits upon the wrong doer, and the presence of punishment—immediate, inevitable—is one of the primary and essential marks of a civilised community."[26] The allusion to developing international law along similar lines as municipal law in the imposition of criminal sanctions was not fortuitous. That ambition was a predominant feature of the speech he delivered to the New York State Bar Association a year earlier, instructively titled "Law, War and the Future."[27]

British prime minister David Lloyd George similarly declared himself in that regard in a speech he delivered in August 1918 to the National Council of Evangelical Free Churches, of which he was a member.[28] He was speaking about the need to form a real League of Nations after the war, including for purposes of enforcing international law. "As society is banded together for the punishment and repression of murder, theft, fraud, and all kinds of wrong and injustice inflicted by one individual upon another," he said, "so nations shall be banded together for the protection of each other and the world as a whole against the force, fraud, and greed of the mighty."[29]

"We have had treaties before," he returned to the theme a little later; "we must now know that we can give them reality. *Millions of young men from the British Empire, from France and Italy—and in due time there will be millions from America—are engaged in demonstrating at the risk of their lives to the Prussian war lords that the world has reached that stage of civilization where justice can be enforced against the most powerful nations that trample upon its decrees.*"[30]

As we will see later, this need to align international law with national law in the manner of imposing criminal responsibility upon those who violate international law through wars was also uppermost in the mind of French prime minister Georges Clemenceau, when he spoke about the opportunity they had to reflect into international law the same principles of "responsibility" that are "recognized by civilized nations." To Clemenceau it was necessary to translate "the essential principles of national law [regarding responsibility] into international law" in the new order of international law ushered in by the formation of the League of Nations.[31]

☙

The need to reform international law, by giving it punitive impetus beyond the hortatory aspirations of the first and second peace conferences at The Hague in 1899 and 1907, respectively, was to be actuated at the eventual third peace conference in Paris in 1919, upon the conclusion of World War I.

As we will see, historical records are replete with that *corrective, punitive intent* on the part of the leading members of the Allied and Associated states.

Ultimately, that intent is captured in both the text of article 227 of the Treaty of Versailles and in its legislative history. These include the proceedings of the Macdonell Committee (who advised the British government); the recommendations of legal experts who advised the French government; the proceedings of Sub-Commission III of the Paris Peace Conference Commission on the Responsibility of the Authors of the War and on Enforcement of Penalties; and the deliberations of the Council of Four leaders of the Allied powers.

☙

The urgency about adjusting international law along the lines outlined above was consistent in the governmental policy positions of the Allied and Associated Powers, as articulated by Georges Clemenceau and David

Lloyd George, the respective prime ministers of France and Great Britain. Notably, in an Inter-Allied meeting of 1 December 1918, attended by Clemenceau, Lloyd George, and Vittorio Orlando (the Italian prime minister), Clemenceau communicated his single-minded resolve "to bring the ex-Kaiser to justice," adding that "people everywhere would be satisfied if this could be done. They will feel that justice *will in future be done in the case of Kaisers and Kings just as much as in the case of common men.* If this could be achieved, it would be a magnificent advance and a moral revolution."[32]

At the conclusion of the Inter-Allied meeting of 1 December 1918, it fell to Lloyd George to send a telegram to President Woodrow Wilson (who had been unable to attend the meeting), notifying him of the decision arrived at during the meeting. The telegram informed of the resolve of the Allies to prosecute the ex-kaiser before an international tribunal. One of the rationales indicated for the measure was that "the certainty of inevitable personal punishment for crimes against humanity and international right will be a very important security against future attempts to make war wrongfully or to violate international law, and is a necessary stage in the development of the authority of a League of Nations."[33] As Lloyd George detailed years later in his memoirs of the Peace Conference, "President Wilson subsequently intimated that he was in agreement with the decision arrived at by the Allies on this subject."[34] It is not clear whether that particular indication of Wilson's agreement was to the telegram of 1 December 1918 or to their eventual agreement at the Paris Peace Conference to prosecute the kaiser. For present purposes, however, it is enough that Wilson agreed to the text of article 227 of the Versailles Treaty, which demanded the prosecution of the kaiser. Indeed, Wilson himself personally drafted the first version of that provision.

Notably, the German government's reaction to the Versailles Treaty that included article 227 afforded the Allied and Associated Powers another opportunity to convey their determination to adjust international law in a manner that incorporated the notion of *jus puniendi.* The occasion was the reply communicated to the German government by Clemenceau in his capacity as the president of the Paris Peace Conference. In the reply, he made sure to explain that the individual criminal responsibility provisions of the treaty—the height point of this was article 227—was "intended to mark a departure from the traditions and practices of earlier settlements, which have been singularly inadequate in preventing the renewal of war."[35]

In other words, this new approach of individual criminal responsibility was also "necessary as a deterrent to others who, at some later date, may be tempted to follow [the] example" of engaging in similar atrocities.[36] To drive home the intended adjustment to international law, he observed, "The Allied and Associated Powers indeed consider that the trial and punishment of those proved most responsible for the crimes and inhuman acts committed in connection with a war of aggression, is inseparable from the establishment of that reign of law among nations which it was the agreed object of the peace to set up."[37]

It is thus clear that, after World War I, the urgent task for the world and global policy makers of the day was how to protect future generations of humanity against the consequences of unconstrained warmongering so rampant in Europe as elsewhere.

It was a war in which "[t]wenty million men had died, twice as many again were wounded"[38]; in addition to other catastrophic economic costs, it had fully brought home how unsustainable the norm of aggressive war as an attribute, nay prerogative, of national sovereignty had become to the future of human civilization.

The backdrop of unprecedented carnage must have made that danger more immediate in 1919 than the danger of climate change was to the most passionate environmentalists in 2019. That statesmen and stateswomen and the best thinkers of the twenty-first century have struggled to find how to arrest and reverse the degradation of our climate and natural environment must enable an appreciation of the urgency the world faced in 1919 in establishing norms that would save the world from the danger of wars of the future and how they are fought.

The Paris Peace Conference of 1919 afforded the leadership of the Allied and Associated Powers the much-needed opportunity to build the required solutions into international law. Those solutions included enshrining the *jus puniendi* element into that gentle and dignified body of law, as Lloyd George indicated in his address of August 1918 to the National Council of Evangelical Free Churches. This would prove to be a foundational piece of international law for the ensuing decades and up to our present day.

ARTICLE 227 OF THE VERSAILLES TREATY

4

In the annals of international law, article 227 of the Versailles Treaty, adopted at the conclusion of the Paris Peace Conference in 1919, is an iconic piece of international lawmaking. It was the first occasion that the international community communicated the norm that those who act even in the position of heads of state enjoy no immunity from accountability for international crimes. It provided as follows:

> The Allied and Associated Powers publicly arraign William II of Hohenzollern, formerly German Emperor, for a supreme offence against international morality and the sanctity of treaties.
>
> A special tribunal will be constituted to try the accused, thereby assuring him the guarantees essential to the right of defence. It will be composed of five judges, one appointed by each of the following Powers: namely, the United States of America, Great Britain, France, Italy and Japan.
>
> In its decision the tribunal will be guided by the highest motives of international policy, with a view to vindicating the solemn obligations of international undertakings and the validity of international morality. It will be its duty to fix the punishment which it considers should be imposed.
>
> The Allied and Associated Powers will address a request to the Government of the Netherlands for the surrender to them of the ex-Emperor in order that he may be put on trial.

Some scholars have a tendency to miss the point of that provision. As will soon become clear, article 227 of the Versailles Treaty was not a flotsam casually tossed up in the aimless waves of the proceedings of the 1919 Paris Peace Conference. It was a centerpiece of the proceedings: a crowning achievement in a determined process of international social engineering that had that result in its sight. It marked the inception of an international law norm that has endured into our own times.

It is up to the international community to choose to reverse engineer that norm if they wish, in the same way that they introduced it in the first place. Until that is done, article 227 must be recognized for the norm that its architects intended to usher in.

Let's explore the full story of the norm's provenance.

"[W]e Are Making International Law"

Norms of international law, in any of the familiar sources, do not spring forth on their own. They result from human agency. Legal fictions, such as those that insist on the notion of equality of all states, serve important value. But even among equals, some will be leaders, as it is among all social animals. It is the leader-states that lead the world as it goes. And so it is in the making of international law. Professor Malcolm Shaw described that reality when, in relation to the making of customary international law, he observed thus: "Law cannot be divorced from politics or power and this is one instance of that proposition."[1] Indeed, the adjustment of *jus puniendi* (the right of society to use punishment to enforce respect for its laws) made to international law at the Paris Peace Conference was "one instance of that proposition" of which Shaw writes.

At the end of World War I, France and the United Kingdom were leader-states with clear-eyed determination to steer international law in the direction of using criminal punishment to enforce the rules of international law that value peace and abhor war. Keenly aware that there was no precedent for the adjustment they wanted to make, they were determined to correct that lack of precedent by creating the needed precedent to guide the future of international law. As noted earlier, David Lloyd George, the wartime British prime minister, announced his intent to see to that international *jus puniendi* when he declared, in his August 1918 speech to the National Council of Evangelical Free Churches, "We have had treaties before; we must now know that we can give them reality."[2] He continued, "[T]he world has reached that stage of civilization where justice can be enforced against the most powerful nations that trample upon its decrees."[3]

Lloyd George tells the story of how the statecraft of that reorientation of international law began. He starts the story at the Imperial Cabinet meeting of 20 November 1918. At Lloyd George's invitation, Lord Curzon briefed the Cabinet on his (Curzon's) recent discussion with French premier Georges Clemenceau in Paris about the need to prosecute Kaiser

Wilhelm II, the German emperor and king of Prussia. Clemenceau was apparently insistent on the prosecution and had commissioned two of France's leading legal experts to study the matter. But Clemenceau did not know what his legal experts would report back regarding the position of international law on the matter. Such was Curzon's report.

At the end of Curzon's briefing, Lloyd George added his own strong support to the idea of prosecuting the kaiser. "With regard to the question of international law," Lloyd George added, "well, we are making international law, and all we can claim is that international law should be based on justice."[4] Indeed, that was what the United Kingdom and France were doing as regards enshrining the *jus puniendi* element into international law—they were "making international law."

A case study in international lawmaking, as of 1919, will be found in the deliberations of the Council of Four leaders of the Allied and Associated nations—U.S. president Woodrow Wilson, Clemenceau, Lloyd George, and Italian prime minister Vittorio Orlando—also known in the history books as the "Big Four."[5] With Orlando as the weakest member, the "Big Four" were the personalities who truly made the decisions that the other delegates were required—or had no choice but—to follow at the Paris Peace Conference.[6]

"It seems to me that we have sorted out this question in its main outline," said Wilson.[7] With those words, Wilson signaled his eventual capitulation to the intense pressure that Clemenceau and Lloyd George exerted upon him to agree to the prosecution of the kaiser. The capitulation followed extended contretemps among the Big Four in their meetings of 2 and 8 April 1919, during which Lloyd George and Clemenceau had worked hard to dissolve Wilson's initial hesitant resistance to prosecuting the kaiser—resistance stoked by the strenuous objections of U.S. secretary of state Robert Lansing against trying the kaiser on grounds that the idea of individual criminal responsibility, before an international tribunal, for violation of international law was without precedent in international law—especially regarding a head of state.

But before concluding the discussion, Wilson fairly sought to hear from Orlando, who had been silent all the while.[8] Orlando made it abundantly clear that, notwithstanding his own personal views on the matter, the Italian position was the position of the two experts whom he had sent to represent Italy on the Commission on the Responsibility of the Authors of the War and on Enforcement of Penalties, which the Paris Peace Conference had tasked with studying the question of prosecuting the crimes committed during the war—including the crime of aggression. As the Italian experts on the commission had supported the majority in recommending the trial of the kaiser for war crimes and crimes against humanity, that would remain the position of Italy, said Orlando, which his own views were not intended to alter.[9]

Having said that, Orlando registered his own private reservations, which hinged on the absence of precedent for holding the kaiser individually responsible in international law for purposes of criminal punishment.[10] There was indeed an absence of precedent for prosecuting anyone, let alone a head of state, before an international criminal tribunal. That lack of precedent did not deter Clemenceau and Lloyd George. They rather saw it as a weakness in international law, which they were well placed to rectify. And they were determined to rectify that weakness.

Linked to Orlando's reservations about the absence of precedent was another concern: the doctrine of sovereignty. In Orlando's appreciation of prevailing international law, the kaiser and the German people were united in one sovereignty, such that the resulting responsibility is collective, not individual. "But we would be establishing a completely new principle," he worried, "if we wanted to punish as an individual a man who was acting as an instrument of the collectivity."[11]

Unimpressed, Clemenceau recalled the fates of Louis XVI of France and Charles I of England, both of whom were beheaded following criminal trials.[12]

"In both cases," countered Orlando, "the issue was a domestic one. In the international field, the law you are trying to establish can't be based on any precedent."[13]

But rather than dissuade him, the riposte had the opposite effect on Clemenceau. It propelled him into a resolute discourse on the significance of precedent and on sources of international law. Although Clemenceau was not a lawyer (he had trained as a physician and practiced medicine for a while[14]), he showed an impressive grasp of the essence of the process of lawmaking in international law; perhaps more so than Orlando the jurist.

"Was there a precedent when liberty was given to men for the first time?" Clemenceau began. "Everyone must assume his own responsibility, and I assume mine."[15]

And speaking of legal responsibility, he continued, "For me, one law dominates all others: that of responsibility. Civilisation is the organisation of human responsibilities."[16] He was evidently speaking about "responsibility" in the same sense that Lloyd George[17] and British attorney general F. E. Smith, QC,[18] had spoken about criminal responsibility following those who violated the tenets of criminal law in municipal settings.

In an apparent demonstration of understanding that "general principles of law recognised by civilised nations" can be a source of international law, although he did not articulate his arguments in those terms, Clemenceau continued his mini-tutorial on international law and legal responsibilities.

Whereas Orlando might have been content to leave the imposition of such criminal responsibility within only the domestic forums, where it had been all along, Clemenceau was intent on using the opportunity now presented to them—in the dawn of a new era of international law—to translate the idea onto the international realm.

"M. Orlando says: 'Yes, within each nation.' I say: 'In the international field.' I say this along with President Wilson who, by establishing the foundations of the League of Nations, has had the honour of transferring the essential principles of national law into international law."[19]

"What we want to do today," Clemenceau continued, "is essential if we want to see international law established. None of us doubts that William II bears responsibility for the war. I agree with M. Orlando on the solidarity of the German people with their sovereign. However, there is one man who gave the order, whilst the others followed it. We are told: 'It is better to exile him and to expose him to the scorn of the world, without convicting him.' It is a sanction which can be defended; it is not the one I prefer. Today we have a perfect opportunity to carry into international law the principle of responsibility which is at the basis of national law."[20]

With that, he circled back to the complaint about the absence of precedent. "There is no precedent? There never is a precedent. What is a precedent?" he asked, "I'll tell you. A man comes; he acts—for good or evil. Out of the good he does, we create a precedent. Out of the evil he does, criminals—individuals or heads of state—create the precedent for their crimes. We have no precedent? But that is our best argument. Was there a precedent in recent generations for the atrocities committed by the Germans during the present war—for the systematic destruction of wealth in order to end competition, for the torture of prisoners, for submarine piracy, for abominable treatment of women in occupied countries? To those precedents, we will oppose [i.e., confront with] a precedent of justice."[21]

At this point in his discourse, Clemenceau interjected a thought on how judges of the various nations and various legal traditions who would compose the international tribunal (that he and Lloyd George were pushing to create) would be charged to unite their consciences to distill the principles upon which they must rely to judge "the greatest crime in history."[22]

And then, just as he had opened his discourse with the theme of precedent, he returned to it for his conclusion. This was not as a source of weakness but as a source of strength for their project of steering international law in a new direction that contemplates accountability for violation of international law.

"If necessary, I will resign myself to a solution which is not mine," he said. "But I beg the heads of state to reflect that, if they follow my advice, they will do for their own glory an unprecedented thing—I admit it—in establishing international justice, which up to now has existed only in books, and which we will at last make a reality."[23]

Without a doubt, Clemenceau's performance was the coup de grâce to any resistance that lingered within the Big Four against the idea of trying the kaiser.

Wilson, who earlier had signaled his agreement to the general outline of the idea, now had to ask the one remaining "practical question" still troubling him: "We don't have the legal means to compel Holland to deliver the Kaiser to us."[24] Wilson's lingering concern now was how to compel the Dutch government to surrender the kaiser (then on asylum in the Netherlands) so that the Allies could prosecute him before the international criminal tribunal they would eventually designate in article 227 of the Versailles Treaty.

Orlando was now fully on board with the idea of prosecuting the kaiser. When next he spoke, he opined that "the only principle which justifies our action is M. Clemenceau's. I accept M. Clemenceau's views, because they raise us above legal technicalities; it is history that is taking place here, it is no longer law. If we consult the code, we will have great difficulty in finding what we seek there. If we speak only about international morality, it is different."[25]

That, of course, was largely an academic observation. Everyone had agreed that there was no precedent. They were only divided about what to do in the absence of precedent. The difference was that some people—notably Lansing and now Orlando before his eventual agreement with Clemenceau—were prepared to do nothing in the absence of precedent. Clemenceau and Lloyd George, for their part, insisted quite correctly that the circumstances required the immediate establishment of that precedent, which had been lacking all along in international law. In that insistence, they displayed a better appreciation of how laws are made throughout history—both in legislation and in jurisprudence—in the domestic legal order and on the international plain.

In legal and lay usage, the term *precedent* means the initial instance of a practice that marked a departure from an earlier order. Once that precedent is set, it forms a frame of reference for subsequent practice. It appeared to have escaped both Orlando and Lansing, but not Clemenceau, that precedents—notably in the legal sphere—result from human agency. Clemenceau and Lloyd George were fully prepared to set the new precedent for trying a head of state before an international tribunal for criminal violation of international law. They unequivocally declared their resolve to do just that.

THE PREPARATORY BACKGROUND TO ARTICLE 227

5

A proper understanding of the object and circumstances of article 227 of the Treaty of Versailles, to appreciate its value as a legal precedent for the future,[1] requires a close review of its groundwork as laid by the British and the French governments—the two nations that suffered the most casualties at the hands of the Germans during World War I.[2]

Once more, a golden thread that ran through those preparatory efforts comprised both (i) the realization that the idea of prosecuting Kaiser Wilhelm II before an international tribunal had no precedent to support it; and, (ii) a determination to correct that deficiency in international law.

A World War I *Volksgeist*

The impetus of lawmaking that was manifested in article 227 of the Versailles Treaty resulted from a phenomenon akin to what German jurists would call *volksgeist*, meaning "the spirit of the people"—in this sense, something of an international *volksgeist*.

The highly respected nineteenth-century German jurist Friedrich Karl von Savigny popularized the term *volksgeist*. He meant that law is an expression of the common will or spirit of the people and validated by their acceptance, rather than "the arbitrary will of a law-giver."[3]

The horrors of World War I had provoked a great outcry around the world, demanding punishment for the kaiser. Up until World War I, punishments of defeated enemies, including their political leaders, were usually exacted by political action—meaning summary banishment or execution involving no judicial process. *Vae victis!*

An early advocate of war crimes prosecutions—a more civilized approach—was the British attorney general, Sir Frederick E. Smith. In a speech he made to the New York Bar Association in January 1918, he preferred prosecution of war crimes suspects more than he saw viability in Woodrow Wilson's proposals for the League of Nations, thus provoking Wilson's displeasure.[4]

As of early August 1918, when Allied victory started looking realistic, the governments of the British Empire and of France started eyeing war crimes trials as part of any eventual peace treaty. "At the same time," according to James Willis, "the climate of public opinion among the Allied peoples virtually compelled adoption of this policy."[5]

Speaking at a meeting of the National Council of Evangelical Free Churches in August 1918, David Lloyd George indicated that his government's terms of settlement included *"above all,* making sure that war shall henceforth be treated as a crime, punishable by the law of nations."[6] Without a doubt, the trial of the kaiser was the most immediate way to signal that reorientation of international law.

The public opinion for war crimes prosecution was reinvigorated in France due to the widespread destruction of northern France, which German soldiers left in their wake as they retreated. The French newspaper *Le Temps* insisted on 25 August that *les coupables* (the guilty), including the kaiser, must stand trial.[7] On 17 September, Georges Clemenceau declared in the French Senate that nothing "could justify an amnesty for so many crimes."[8]

On 4 October, the same day that Germany admitted defeat by requesting an armistice, the French government issued a declaration, including the following:

> Conduct which is equally contrary to international law and the funda-
> mental principles of all human civilization will not go unpunished. . . .
> The authors and directors of these crimes will be held responsible morally,
> judicially, and financially. They will seek in vain to escape the inexorable
> expiation which awaits them.[9]

On 15 October, Stephen Pichon, the foreign minister, reiterated that message before the French Senate, who voted their unanimous approval without hesitation.[10] There was a chorus of support in the press.[11]

A similar mood prevailed in England. The *Times* and the *Daily Mail* unequivocally urged war crimes prosecutions.[12] The call for prosecution included, in the words of the *Daily Mail*, the trial of "Wilhelm II, the author of the war and of the order to murder prisoners," and five hundred other persons who had "conspicuously violated the laws of war and The Hague conventions."[13] Prominent among the leaders of public opinion in favor of such prosecutions included Arthur Conan Doyle (author of the *Sherlock Holmes* series);[14] Frederic Harrison (another renowned author); Lord Midleton, a former secretary of state for war;[15] Lord Wrenbury, a highly respected British judge;[16] Lord Morris, former premier of Newfoundland;[17] the Reverend Alfred Gough,[18] a prebendary of St. Paul's Cathedral;[19] and the Reverend Arthur Guttery, president of the National Council of Free Churches.[20] Within the dominions of the British Empire, the acting prime minister of Canada, Sir Thomas White, gave support,[21] as did Prime Minister William Massey of New Zealand.[22]

On 26 October, Lord Finlay, the Lord Chancellor, informed an Inter-Allied Parliamentary Committee that the British government had two aims, one of which was "the punishment of those who could be proved guilty of outrages" and the prosecution of the "offenders would not be mere vengeance; it would be the vindication of international morality." The other aim was reparation.[23]

There were, as always in these things, elements of differing views from those who urged summary political punishment of the kaiser—but there was near unanimous agreement that there had to be some form of punishment.[24] In the end, the government leadership settled on prosecution, rather than summary political treatment.[25]

It would thus be quite wrong to suggest, as has been done, that the British government's determination to prosecute the kaiser resulted merely or mostly from campaign promises to "hang the kaiser," often simplistically attributed to Lloyd George during the British elections of December 1918, ahead of the Paris Peace Conference.[26] Notably, the British government of the day was often criticized in the press for appearing often weak or indecisive in moving in the direction of the prosecution.[27]

On 8 July 2014, the *New York Times* published the obituary of Umaru Dikko, a Nigerian official whose life and times occasioned a major diplomatic row between the British and the Nigerian governments that lasted for two years.[28] Dikko was a minister in a civilian administration that was overthrown by a military coup in December 1983. He fled to London and claimed asylum. The new government wanted him back on charges of embezzlement of massive sums of money. But the Thatcher administration declined extradition, saying he was a political refugee. In

July 1994, his private secretary fortuitously looked outside his home just in time to see him being bundled into a mysterious van that had been parked outside his home in a wealthy London neighborhood. A quick emergency call from her had Scotland Yard put out customs alerts on vessels and aircraft bound for Nigeria. So it was that a Nigerian Airways plane that was getting ready to take off from Stanstead Airport was subjected to closer inspection. As part of the inspection, customs agents insisted on opening a large crate marked "Diplomatic Baggage" addressed to the Nigerian Ministry of Foreign Affairs. They refused to yield to protestations of Nigerian officials that the crate could not be opened on grounds of inviolability of diplomatic baggage. On opening the crate, an anesthetized Dikko was found inside with three men, including an anesthesiologist who was to monitor him during transit to make sure that he did not die during the flight to Lagos. It was alleged that the other two men were Mossad agents who had done the kidnapping. The governments of Nigeria and Israel denied involvement in the plot.

～

In 1919, a similarly serious matter that also ended up a comic flop occurred in the Netherlands, in a failed attempt to kidnap the kaiser and spirit him to Paris to stand trial before the international tribunal that the Allies were contemplating. William Schabas recounts that story in its detail in his excellent book *The Trial of the Kaiser*.[29]

The man at the center of the story was Luke Lea. Although his life's story during the Depression years that followed World War I ended sadly with failed business ventures and imprisonment for fraud,[30] during the war Lea was a colonel in the U.S. Army 114th Field Artillery, a volunteer corps put together from his native Tennessee, which he led in France. Before joining the army to fight in the war, he was a successful business entrepreneur, the owner of the *Tennessean*, a Nashville newspaper; and a U.S. senator representing Tennessee.

Immediately upon the conclusion of the war, Lea's 114th Field Artillery was stationed in Luxembourg as part of the Allied occupation force. As Lea tells the story, though not without some mystery, his eventual adventure started during tea in June 1918 with Prince Arthur, the Duke of Connaught and Strathearn, a highly decorated British soldier who rose to the rank of field marshal but did not fight during World War I.

The duke informed Lea and his colleagues that he was uncle to both Kaiser Wilhelm II and England's King George V. Lea suggests that what prompted him to undertake to kidnap the kaiser was the duke's boast of his relationship with the kaiser and what Lea suspected to be a British design to protect him.[31]

In the ensuing events, Lea assembled a party of eight soldiers of the 114th Field Infantry, including himself. At least four of them were commissioned officers: Colonel Lea, two captains, and one first lieutenant. The group set out from Luxembourg, traversing Belgium, into the Netherlands to kidnap the kaiser from his temporary accommodations at Count Bentinck's castle in Amerongen, near Utrecht.

The plot of kidnapping was eventually foiled—largely, it seems, because a bridge across River Waal had been washed away, thus necessitating the use of a ferry.[32] So it was that the prospect of forcibly abducting the kaiser and zooming off to Paris became a doomed idea, if his abductors had to wait for a ferry to take them back across the river. So, Lea revised his plan. He was now to persuade the kaiser to man up and enter their car and be driven to Paris voluntarily, and face trial with dignity, like a brave man, rather than hide out in the Netherlands in disrepute for the rest of his days.[33] To cut a long story short, the kaiser apparently preferred the latter option, refusing even to meet with Lea and his party when they lied and browbeat their way into Count Bentinck's castle late on a wintry Sunday night on 5 January 1919, surprising the kaiser, his host, and their guests in the middle of a formal dinner.

With their efforts exhausted beyond limp after about two hours, Lea and his party had no choice but to call off the whole attempt finally and leave the place. A platoon of armed Dutch soldiers had arrived and surrounded them, with spotlights and machine guns trained on them. Much was made later about the fact that one of the captains who was with Lea had pilfered an ashtray monogramed with the letters "WI"—which supposedly stood for "Wilhelm Imperator."[34]

It was a diplomatic incident that everyone—especially the Dutch who were fervently courting a visit from President Wilson soon after the war—tried their best to downplay. The burgomaster of Amerongen, who supposedly called the Dutch security forces to intervene and to press the matter of the stolen ashtray, later chose to write the whole thing off as a bet. "Somebody told them they couldn't do it," he said, "and they bet that they could see the Kaiser."[35]

When all diplomatic hell broke loose, Ambassador Whitlock wrote this in his diary: "Very simple! Senator Luke Lee of Tennessee and his joy-riding party, hunting souvenirs, wished to see the Kaiser though why I can't imagine. Sent telegram and letter to The Hague saying that in any event, the visit and the uniforms had been authorised by the Dutch Government through its representative here. What nuisances the traveling souvenir-hunting Americans are! Now for hell a-popping!"[36] Whitlock was the American ambassador in Brussels who had issued the passports that Lea and his colleagues used to travel to the Netherlands. There, of course, may be nothing in the apparent conflict between Lea's initial claim that, during the passport request, he "did not mention [to the ambassador] that Amerongen was a destination."[37] Perhaps the ambassador was merely writing in retrospect and had not been as precise as he might have been.

But the seriousness of the matter was underscored by a military inquiry into the incident. Still in the end, the military authorities decided against a court-martial, closing the book merely as a matter of monumental display of "poor judgment" or as "amazingly indiscreet."[38]

"As an officer of the American Army," the adjutant-general reprimanded Lea, "you had no right whatsoever to present yourself at the chateau of the ex-Emperor without the authority of the President of the United States first obtained.

"Furthermore," he continued, "it should have been apparent to you that the meaning and purpose of your visit *might well have been misunderstood, as indeed it was in some quarters*, and might have entailed the most disastrous consequences, both political and military."[39]

It must of course be taken on good faith that Lea, a lawyer trained at Columbia University who served as a U.S. senator, ran a successful newspaper, and led a regiment as an army colonel, truly did not think of those possibilities before embarking on what some had suggested as "resembling a prank by hyperactive college students addled with drink."[40]

In the end, whatever was the *misunderstanding* "in some quarters" to which the adjutant-general alluded had no demonstrable evidence to back it up—to the extent that it involved any conjecture beyond the theory that Lea was no more than a loose cannon on a juvenile frolic of his own.

In any event, the declared motive of Lea and his colleagues in their abortive attempt to kidnap the kaiser and deliver him to Paris—coincidentally at the same time that the leaders of Allied and Associated Powers were agonizing over how to extract him from the Netherlands—spoke to the global *volksgeist* to prosecute the kaiser.[41]

"We knew the feeling of the soldiers of all the Allies and of the masses of the Allied nations was so bitter," wrote Lea, "that if the Kaiser was surrendered to the chieftain of *any* Allied nation, his trial and punishment would be inevitable. We knew the Kaiser once in the custody of the Allies would be tried before the bar of public opinion of the soldiers and masses of civilization."[42]

The Macdonell Committee

In the United Kingdom, an important aspect of the lawmaking process that culminated in article 227 of the Versailles Treaty, as an expression of *jus puniendi* for violation of international law, commenced in earnest with a Cabinet request for legal advice from the Law Officers of the Crown directed at that purpose. In England, the attorney general and the solicitor general are traditionally referred to as the "Law Officers of the Crown."[43] The Cabinet resolution that requested them to provide a legal opinion on postbellum criminal accountability specifically contemplated the prosecution of the kaiser within its terms of reference. It was worded as follows:

(*a*) To invite the Law Officers of the Crown to examine, from the widest point of view, the question of framing charges against the ex-Emperor of Germany and/or the ex-Crown Prince—

(i) For the crime against humanity of having caused the war; and

(ii) For offences, by one or both, against international law during the war; with a view to bringing home to one or both the responsibility for the acts charged;

(*b*) To invite the Law Officers of the Crown to consider the constitution of a tribunal to try the charges framed

(*c*) To invite the Law Officers to examine with the Foreign Office the practicability of inducing the Dutch Government to hand over the ex-Emperor and the Crown Prince to such a tribunal for trial.[44]

That resolution was thus early documentary evidence of the British government's resolve to reorient international law in the direction of accountability—even of heads of state—for criminal violation of international law.

The Law Officers of the Crown promptly took up the mandate. They, in turn, assembled twenty lawyers[45] to serve as an advisory committee termed the "Committee of Enquiry into Breaches of the Laws and Customs of War," colloquially referred to as the Macdonell Committee, after its chairperson Sir John Macdonell, KC. Some of the members were among Britain's most senior and most eminent international law jurists of the day, and most of them were either King's Counsel or had earned doctorate degrees in law or both. Notable among them were such legal giants as Sir Frederick Pollock, KC (a prolific legal scholar), and Pearce Higgins (soon to be appointed the Whewell Professor of Law at Cambridge University[46]).

Lloyd George described the committee as comprising "a very able and distinguished body of jurists whose names would carry conviction for their knowledge of international law and for their general soundness of judgment."[47] And according to the attorney general, "it would not be possible in this country to form a stronger Committee for the purpose of arriving at a sound conclusion upon such matters."[48]

During the evening of 6 November 1918, the attorney general, Sir Frederick E. Smith, KC, addressed the committee at their inaugural meeting, in Committee Room 5 at the House of Commons. (Soon after, on 14 January 1919, Smith was promoted to the title of Lord Birkenhead, the Lord Chancellor of England and Wales.[49]) He was keen to impress upon the Macdonell Committee the government's views relative to the urgent task at hand. That urgent task involved the British government's intent and determination to correct the glaring deficiency in international law, which left it without sanctions against individuals who violated its norms in gross and criminal ways.

The attorney general began his remarks by characterizing Germany's attitude during the war as a cynical challenge to international law, in light of its obvious weaknesses. And this was a "challenge" that engaged "the whole future" of international law, which until then had "no sanctions" against anyone let alone heads of state who were strong enough to trample upon it. An unrivalled forensic orator in his day,[50] the future Lord Birkenhead wasted no time in getting to the point:

> The general points affecting the whole sanction of Public Law which have been raised by this War are well known to all of you. . . . Our own view is that an aggressive War was forced upon the world by an ambitious and unscrupulous power, and that *the challenge* so developed *involved the whole future of the Public Law of States*. In other words, the challenge which proceeded from Germany meant this, and it meant nothing else: We think that we are strong enough to conquer the world; believing ourselves strong enough to conquer the world we care nothing for all the doctrines of International Law; if we win, and we are convinced that we are strong enough to win, *the inherent weakness of International Law* immediately makes itself manifest, in other words, inasmuch as we shall be the conqueror, *inasmuch as International Law has no sanctions* which it can apply to the conqueror, it is a matter of the most complete indifference to us whether in

the judgment of those, whom by our hypothesis we shall have vanquished, we have broken International Law or not.[51]

He continued to articulate the aching anxiety that the German regime's "challenge" entailed for "the future of international law." According to him, had Germany won the war, which it fought against "the weight of [the] doctrines" of international law, then "public law and the sanctity of treaties would have disappeared in our day and our generation from the world."[52]

The very narrow margins by which that *challenge* was defeated underscored the urgency of considering the steps that must be taken *"for the purpose of re-establishing the authority of International Law."*[53]

Notably, a despondent Lloyd George as secretary of state for war in 1916 once famously confided to Maurice Hankey, "We are going to lose this war."[54] Disastrous British battle experiences such as the Battle of the Somme (where sixty thousand British soldiers lay dead or wounded on the first day alone), Gallipoli, Loos, Arras, and Jutland had inspired this sense of hopelessness. Additionally, the French were hemorrhaged at Verdun, and the Russians were faring no better on the eastern front. Lloyd George's ascension to the post of secretary of war was itself emblematic of the British disasters during the earlier phases of the war. His predecessor in the post, Lord Kitchener, drowned when the warship taking him to Russia, the HMS *Hampshire*, struck a mine and sank in June 1916.[55]

Such was the urgency of establishing the authority of international law to limit warmongering that, after the war, the British government was "determined to reassert, and to reassert under circumstances of the utmost possible notoriety, the authority of those doctrines." That message is clear in the quote set out at length in this endnote.[56]

The British government's determination was channeled in the direction of adjusting international law by bringing into it the same deterrent element of *jus puniendi*: characterized, in Attorney General F. E. Smith's words, by "the presence of punishment—immediate, inevitable" that was a familiar feature of domestic law.[57] This, he said, was to be done *"looking as far as we can* with cool and passionless eyes *into the future of the World."*[58] The *determination* was to ensure that "our children and our grandchildren, and those even who come after them, shall be spared what this generation has gone through."[59]

Thus, *looking into the future of the World*, the British government's declared ambition was to change the sense of war from a source of glory to a source of criminal ignominy. Looking at what the British government was determined to do to deter future wars, it was evident, as F. E. Smith put it, "that the most effective deterrent of all is that *for all ages men* who are tempted to follow the wicked and the bloody path which the Governors of the Central Empires have trodden during the last four years, *shall have present before their eyes, not a picture merely of the brilliant and meretricious glamour of military success, but also the recollection that in this great conflict punishment attended upon crime.*"[60] Notably, in a speech he delivered to the New York State Bar Association in January 1918, Attorney General F. E. Smith had similarly stressed the importance of reforming international law, as an outcome of the war, in the direction of imposing punishment, in order (among other things) that "[p]erhaps no nation, however strong, will ever dare again to dream of aggressive war."[61]

In the course of his remarks to the Macdonell Committee, the attorney general intimated that a similar study was being conducted in France.[62] This was the same information that Lord Curzon was to communicate to his cabinet colleagues during their meeting of 20 November 1918 about his discussions with Clemenceau in Paris.

Steering International Law in the New Direction of Accountability

From various angles, the Macdonell Committee considered the questions arising from their mandate that commenced in earnest on 6 November 1918 (just five days before the formal end of the war on 11 November 1918). The angles included these: What should be the proper forum for any proceedings (i.e., a British court or an international court)? What should be the applicable law (i.e., national law or British law)? And, very crucially, would the kaiser enjoy immunity from prosecution?

Regarding the proper forum (i.e., national or international court), the committee concluded very quickly that an international tribunal should be the better forum.[63] It was to be "composed of Representatives of the Chief Allied States and the United States."[64] A national tribunal should only be a fallback position if it became impossible to establish an international tribunal.[65]

Among the committee's reasons for preferring an international tribunal was their thinking that "on the whole . . . no English Court, administering the ordinary criminal law, would have jurisdiction to try an enemy alien in respect of any, or at all events of the great majority, of the offences in question."[66] The committee further considered that an international tribunal was the less likely to be suspected of national bias. Hence, its decisions "would possess unquestionable authority, which would speak in the name of the conscience of the world, which would help to re-establish and strengthen International Law, *and which in the future would be a deterrent and warning to rulers and highly placed officials who meditated or instigated offences against International Law.*"[67]

Regarding the subject matter of the jurisdiction, the committee referred to the Hague Conventions on the Laws and Customs of War on Land adopted at the first and second Hague Peace conferences—of 1899 and 1907, respectively—and the earlier Geneva Convention of 1864. But they also considered that "laws of humanity" formed part of the subject matter jurisdiction of the international tribunal.[68] This was a function of the Martens Clause[69] that was added in the preambles to the Regulations annexed to the 1899 and 1907 Hague Conventions on the Laws and Customs of War on Land. Named after Fyodor Fyodorovich Martens, the Russian jurist who proposed the text in 1899, the Martens Clause includes within the province of laws and customs of war "the principles of the Law of Nations as they result from the usages established among civilised peoples, from the laws of humanity and the dictates of public conscience."[70]

In recommending an international tribunal as the more appropriate forum to adjudicate questions of international crimes committed as part of World War I, members of the Macdonell Committee were keenly aware that they were recommending an unprecedented mechanism. That, it seemed, was the whole point. And that is the nature of law reforms. International law was being reoriented in a new direction. The committee was also aware of the unprecedented manner of the facts that urged such an unprecedented reorientation.

Notably, Sir Frederick Pollock, KC, a renowned jurist and committee member, spoke to those realities in a memorandum dated 30 December 1918. According to him, "the questions" presented to the committee were "unique in more than one way."[71] In the first place, "[p]recedent is wholly lacking for the facts. Before this war no one thought it possible that a Great Power should issue deliberate and systematic orders for the commission of acts hitherto condemned by the consent and abhorred in the usage of civilised nations."[72]

The idea of an international criminal tribunal was "likewise without precedent," he continued. "History furnishes no example of a tribunal established by several allied States to do justice on offenders against rules and customs equally recognized by all of them."[73] But, Sir Frederick saw an advantage in the fact that, by virtue of its international character, such a tribunal would not be "bound by rules laid down in any one jurisdiction;

so far as the several rules of different nations agree, it may adopt their contents as witness of general consent."[74]

Question of Immunity as Considered by the Macdonell Committee

The Macdonell Committee also had to contend with the critical question of immunity arising from the matter of individual criminal responsibility of a head of state, beyond the issues of the proper forum for the trial and the law that must apply.

On the whole, the committee's opinion that the kaiser must be prosecuted was rendered after a careful consideration of the issue of sovereign immunity. The committee engaged that question, having researched the issue and updated customary international law up to that era. In light of that research, the committee concluded that *"[n]o modern usage establishing such immunity appears to exist,"*[75] given the lack of consistent practice of states according to which it could be said that customary international law posed an obstacle for the prosecution of the kaiser. In the words of the committee:

> It has been urged that the ex-Kaiser, being a Sovereign at the time when the offences charged against him were committed, is and was exempt from the jurisdiction of any Tribunal. This question has rarely been discussed in modern times. Indeed, since the trial of Mary Queen of Scots, and perhaps it may be added, the murder by Queen Christina of Sweden of her chamberlain Monaldeschi at Fontainebleau, it has possessed only an academic interest. In a note are collected the opinions of some of the chief text-writers who have touched the subject. For the most part they do not distinguish between the position of a Sovereign who visits or resides in a foreign country at the invitation or by the permission, express or implied, of its Sovereign, and that of a Sovereign who invades and occupies foreign territory in spite of the resistance of its Sovereign. *For immunity in the latter case there seems to be no authority. Ancient practice was against it. Francis I was imprisoned after the battle of Pavia. No modern usage establishing such immunity appears to exist. In recent times sovereigns have been made prisoners of war, e.g., Napoleon III in 1870 and the Elector of Hesse in 1866. The German Manual of Military Law includes sovereigns among possible prisoners of war; and there seems no reason why, if captured, they should not be treated according as they have or have not violated the laws of war.*[76]

In a separate memorandum titled "Note on Immunity of Sovereigns," Sir John Macdonell (the committee chair) observed that the issue of immunity did engage some academic interest. In that regard, the "point was discussed at length with reference to Mary Queen of Scots, who on her trial pleaded, without success, her rights as a sovereign in answer to the charges against her. In the course of the trial, Sir Christopher Hatton, one of the Commissioners, remarked: '*You say you are a queen; be it so.* But *in such a crime* the *royal dignity is not exempted from answering* neither by the civil nor canon law, *nor by the law of nations.*'! *Such was the opinion of the other Commissioners.*"[77]

Although Macdonell did summarize the disparate treatment of immunity in academic writings, nothing in the review of those writings led him to conclude that immunity was a viable plea as regards the kaiser. There is little doubt that his conclusion on the matter rests on the following passage:

> Probably the opinions of writers on the subject may be thus classified:
>
> (1) Those who state the ancient usage of war as to vanquished sovereigns in all its severity;
>
> (2) those who, like Albericus Gentilis, urge the desirability of exercising moderation and magnanimity in carrying out such usage or rights in regard to defeated Kings and generals;
>
> (3) those who, especially about the time of Louis XIV, seek to exalt the sacrosanct character of the sovereign;
>
> (4) those recent writers who use comprehensive language as to such immunity without having in mind the exact point mentioned in the text.[78]

It may, of course, be noted that Macdonell's observation that "especially about the time of Louis XIV" there were publicists who sought "to exalt the sacrosanct character of the sovereign" may not be unconnected with the historical fact that Louis XIV was the monarch who popularized the expression "*l'état, c'est moi*" ("I am the state").[79]

I pause also to note Macdonell's obvious displeasure with the aptitude of "recent writers who use comprehensive language" to write about immunity, "without having in mind the exact point" of the context of immunity of which they wrote. As discussed elsewhere in this book, the same weakness troubles the scholarship of "recent writers" of our own era. They write expansively about the availability of immunity to heads of state even before international courts, regardless of the context in which the rules of immunity they cite were initially formulated.

In continuing to review and analyze the academic opinions that he classified into the four categories referred to earlier, Macdonell observed,

"It had been the ancient practice to treat with severity leaders of defeated armies." That was an obvious reference to the practice expressed in the Latin slogan *Vae victis!* But on the part of the theoretical writers in the sixteenth and seventeenth centuries, "there was a desire to humanise warfare, especially as to the treatment of prisoners."[80] In that regard, Macdonell cited the example of Alberico Gentili, who enumerated "many examples of Kings who make war being killed or enslaved by their captors. But he pleads for the exercise of humanity towards captured Princes, '*nisi causæ speciales caedem probent.*'"[81]

"Grotius," noted Macdonell, "knows nothing of the special immunity of Kings taken prisoners in war; indeed he cites examples of commanders being put to death. He argues for moderation in the punishment of the vanquished, and enumerates certain classes (e.g., women and children, etc.) which ought to be spared; he does not specially name sovereigns."[82]

Seventeenth-century English writer Richard Zouche, who preferred to write in Latin, did discuss the case of Mary, Queen of Scots. But he offered no conclusions following his discussion on whether one sovereign would in his own territory enjoy jurisdiction over another sovereign.[83]

Macdonell noted that Cornelius Bynkershoek, the classical Dutch jurist, had addressed immunity of foreign sovereigns by analogy to the immunity of ambassadors. But Bynkershoek recommended summary action in the case of a foreign sovereign caught in the act of disturbing the peace in a foreign country. In those circumstances, Bynkershoek denied that there was any usage concerning the sovereign who commits crimes in foreign territory. But Bynkershoek did not write with precision on the matter.[84]

Notably upon a review of Bynkershoek's writing on the subject, four judges of the International Criminal Court's Appeals Chamber noted in 2019 that even in his analogy to ambassadorial immunity, Bynkershoek recognized "certain exceptions to the general rule of immunity, which he awkwardly stated in the terms of the permissibility of arrest and possible infliction of deadly violence [remarkably, Bynkershoek preferred mob action in this respect rather than the due process of law!] when a foreign sovereign commits serious violations of the law in the territory of his or her host."[85]

Samuel von Pufendorf (the famous German jurist) was entirely silent on the topic.[86] But Swiss jurist Emer de Vattel did discuss the subject in his all-time classic on the law of nations, Macdonell noted.[87] But when it came to sparing the sovereign, Vattel expressed himself in terms of praises for belligerents who would spare the life of the sovereign. While adding that such benevolence was not compelled by the law of war, such an obligation arose only when it was possible to take the enemy sovereign prisoner.[88]

It may, of course, be noted that Professor Ferdinand Larnaude and Professor Albert Geouffre de La Pradelle, who effectively served as the French government's counterparts to the Macdonell Committee, noted that Vattel did not in fact exempt sovereigns from punishment for waging unjust war. Larnaude and La Pradelle noted that it was Vattel's conclusion that an unjust war gives no right and how guilty is the sovereign who undertakes it. And having examined the obligations of the sovereign, Vattel settled his position in the following words: "He who does an injury is bound to repair the damage, or to make adequate satisfaction if the evil be irreparable, and even to submit to punishment if the punishment be necessary either as an example or for the safety of the party offended and for that of human society. *In this predicament stands a Prince who is the author of an unjust war.*"[89]

The ambivalence of Lord Phillimore (the latter-day English jurist), when compelled to give a clear answer on the subject, was more curious. Like Bynkershoek, Phillimore recognized that international law did not offer immunity to a foreign sovereign caught in the act of disturbing the peace in another country. Such sovereign may even be killed if violence was required to suppress him. As he put it:

> With respect to Criminal Jurisdiction the foreign sovereign, as a *general proposition*, is exempt from it. *Extreme cases may be put which would make the rule inapplicable.* If, indeed, he should abuse the hospitality of the kingdom, he may be ordered, like a delinquent ambassador, to depart from it without delay. If he should contrive or perpetrate any offence against the welfare or laws of the country in which he is a guest, International Law would warrant the authorities of that country in preventing the commission of the offence, by *placing him under necessary restraint*, and in subsequently demanding satisfaction for the injury at the hands of the country of this delinquent representative. *We may go a step further, and say, that his act of violence may be met by violence, and that if he perish in consequence of the resistance opposed to his unlawful conduct, no maxim of International Law is violated.*[90]

But, Phillimore visibly reared like a horse that ran into a grizzly bear along its path when pressed for an answer regarding the exercise of criminal jurisdiction over the delinquent foreign sovereign by the country whose peace he disturbed. In his words:

> But may the delinquent sovereign, under any circumstances, be rendered amenable to the criminal jurisdiction of a foreign country? *It is difficult in a treatise on law to answer a question which is founded upon the supposition that*

the representatives of the majesty of the law are the criminals to be tried by the law.
If, however, the question must receive a categorical answer, the answer must be in
the negative. The historical precedents which might appear to countenance a contrary
opinion are valueless. Nihil igitur in hoe argumento pro ficues rebus similiter
a gentibus judicatis is the just observation of Bynkershoek. It is obvious,
moreover, that this class of cases is *happily* so rare and the instances cited
are so exceptional in their nature, both from their own circumstances and
from the periods of history in which they happened, that International
Law cannot rely upon them as exponents of usage in this arduous matter, but must guide the enquirer by the reason of the thing applied to the
exigency of each particular occurrence. International Law, like the Civil
Law, must pass by without attempting to bring under exact rules anoma-
lies which sudden emergency may create, or to provide beforehand for all
imaginable contingencies.[91]

Remarkably, Phillimore refused to engage in any meaningful way
with the "historical precedents" of such trials. Rather than demonstrate
the invalidity of those precedents, he merely declared them to be "valueless." And then "happily" finding them "so rare" and "so exceptional," he
landed on a preferential personal opinion that would reject the possibility
that the precedents such as existed suggest an appreciable norm.

Interestingly, his balking at that question has strong influences of the
doctrine of *princep legibus solutus* (the prince is not bound by the law).

Phillimore's overall treatment of the subject only shows that international law was not clear in offering immunity to foreign sovereigns in
every situation. That is to say, contrary to what some like to argue even
in our own time, international law never recognized the idea of *absolute*
immunity of sovereigns from the criminal jurisdiction of each other, notwithstanding any general rule to that effect. If it did, Phillimore would
have cited the necessary rule in support of his preferred personal opinion.

Macdonell was rightly unimpressed by Phillimore's vacillation. "It is difficult to understand," said Macdonell, "why Phillimore arrives at a conclusion adverse to such jurisdiction, if, indeed, he arrives at any conclusion."

"If exemption exists," Macdonell continued, "it must be derived
from express agreement, or implied from usage; and none, it is admitted,
exists."[92]

Ultimately, in Macdonell's view, "The result of an examination of the
authorities, if such can be said to exist, would seem to be that there is no
rule or usage exempting from criminal jurisdiction foreign sovereigns who
have invaded the territory of another sovereign."[93]

For his part, Professor Morgan, the vice chair, similarly considered after a review of the literature:

> It would therefore be the height of pedantry to treat the situation in accordance with precedents; the situation itself is unprecedented. I can see no reason, therefore, for according any immunity to the higher authorities in Germany any more than to the lower. When the Turkish Government ordered the exposure of British subjects on the Gallipoli Peninsula they were informed by the British Government that the authorities who gave the order, and not merely those who executed it, would be held personally responsible. This is a case in point.[94]

The Kaiser Must Be Prosecuted: A Legal Conclusion

It is a matter of interest that Attorney General Frederick E. Smith, KC (the future Lord Birkenhead), had, on 21 November 1918, tasked a special subcommittee—the Special Sub-committee on Law (also chaired by Macdonell)—to consider and report on the desirability of prosecuting the kaiser and the modality of doing so if desirable.[95]

A week later, on 28 November 1918, the Special Sub-committee on Law returned their answer. They reported that prosecuting the kaiser was desirable, not only as "a question of policy" but also a question of necessity "in view of the grave charges" alleged against him. Explaining that view of necessity, the subcommittee reasoned that "the vindication of the principles of International Law, which [the Kaiser] has violated, would be incomplete were he not brought to trial."

Moreover, they continued, "the trial of other offenders might be seriously prejudiced, if they could plead the superior order of a sovereign against whom no steps had been taken."[96] The modalities of his prosecution would entail the international tribunal, as discussed earlier.

It should be reasonable to suppose that the need to establish the Special Sub-committee on Law and the rapidity with which it rendered its opinion in just seven days were necessitated by an Inter-Allied meeting scheduled to take place in London on 1–2 December 1918, between the heads of governments of the Allied powers, for which the delegates arrived on 30 November 1918.[97]

Two days earlier, during the Cabinet meeting of 28 November 1918, the attorney general appeared and presented the report of the Macdonell Committee's Special Sub-committee on Law.[98] Throughout a presentation that Lloyd George described as spellbinding, the attorney general's focus was almost exclusively trained on why the trial of the kaiser was unavoidable for the British government both as a matter of national policy and as a matter of adjusting international law in a manner that would enable the punishment of those who violated its sacred norms.

As Lloyd George summarized the recommendations, "The experts had unanimously recommended a prosecution of the rulers who were responsible for the War."[99] Although, that may be a slight oversimplification of the actual recommendations of the attorney general and the Macdonell Committee, to the extent that the impression is created that there was *unanimous* expert recommendation favoring the prosecution of the kaiser for *starting the war*. Notably, the attorney general did not encourage prosecution of the kaiser on a charge of responsibility for the war. His fear was that a "trial on such a charge would involve infinite disputation," tempting "a meticulous examination of the history of European politics for the past twenty years."[100] Nevertheless, it is generally correct to say that the unanimous recommendations of the attorney general and the committee were insistent that the "ex-Kaiser should be punished"[101] for violation of important precepts of international law. Those important precepts largely entailed war crimes (what international lawyers term *jus in bello*)—meaning crimes committed during a war regardless of who started the war. [Legal questions about who started a war and the circumstances surrounding such questions are termed *jus ad bellum*.]

Speaking to the conclusions arrived at by the experts of the Macdonell Committee, the attorney general informed the War Cabinet that it is "a source of satisfaction to the Law Officers"—meaning the attorney general himself and the solicitor general (then Sir Gordon Hewart, KC)—that the Sub-committee on Law had "unanimously and independently of [the Crown Law Officers] reached the conclusion that the ex-Kaiser ought to be punished," either by way of trial or by way of an extra-judicial resolution—specifically "either to be exiled or otherwise punished in his own person."[102] That course might "be recommended by powerful argument, and I do not myself exclude it,"[103] ventured the attorney general. The committee inclined to the view that the kaiser should be tried.[104]

But, just as quickly as he broached the propriety of the extrajudicial approach, the attorney general moved away from it, training all attention on the greater importance of permitting no immunity for the kaiser.

"As chief Law Officer of the Crown," he declared, "I say quite plainly that I should feel the greatest difficulty in being responsible in any way for the trial of subordinate criminals if the ex-Kaiser is allowed to escape."[105] That was a vital current that animated his opinion, as the bottom line, having invoked the maxim, *"Dat veniam corvis, vexat censura columbas?"* ("How dare you censure the doves yet absolve the perverted raven?"), an allusion to the second of Juvenal's *Satires*, on hypocrisy.[106]

That, of course, was an added emphasis to his earlier pressure upon the conscience of the British government delivered in the following words, "Prime Minister, in my judgment, if this man escapes, common people will say everywhere that he has escaped because he is an Emperor. In my judgment, they will be right. They will say that august influence has been exerted to save him. It is not desirable that such things should be said, especially in these days."[107]

For those inclined to thinking of the eventual rejection of head-of-state immunity as an absent-minded chip in the development of international law, the paradox in the attorney general's observations should be sobering. There, not only was he unambiguous about the need to prosecute the kaiser for the international crimes in question, but more telling is that the reason for prosecuting the kaiser is precisely because of his status as *the emperor*—the individual who played a leading role in the perpetration of those international crimes.

The attorney general's submissions had the effect of melting away any lingering qualms within the Cabinet, regarding prosecuting the kaiser. "It was worthy of note," observed Lloyd George, "that those who expressed doubts at the first discussion were all present on this occasion and all now concurred in the Attorney-General's recommendation. There was not a dissentient voice."[108]

Consequently, "the Imperial War Cabinet carried unanimously the following resolution:—'The Imperial War Cabinet adopted the report presented by the Attorney-General, and agreed that, so far as the British Government have the power, the ex-Kaiser should be held personally responsible for his crimes against international law.'"[109]

Regarding the authority of the Sub-committee on Law that so firmly recommended the kaiser's prosecution, the attorney general observed that "it would not be possible to form a stronger Committee for the purpose of arriving at a sound conclusion upon" the matters tasked of them.[110]

The Inter-Allied Supreme Council Decision to Try the Kaiser

The law reform initiative that would deny immunity to heads of state accused of international crimes received early impetus from the majority of leaders of the Entente states in late 1918. At a meeting of the Inter-Allied

Supreme Council held on 2 December 1918, four days after his Cabinet meeting of 28 November 1918, Lloyd George shared the report and conclusions of the Sub-committee on Law. Clemenceau and Vittorio Orlando, the French and the Italian premiers, respectively, endorsed the resulting position of the British Cabinet.[111]

According to the minutes of that meeting, Clemenceau "said that he thought it would show an immense progress if we could punish the man who was guilty of great historic crimes like the declaration of war in August 1914."[112]

"All the Governments represented here today were proud of the principle of responsibility," he continued sarcastically. "As a rule, it only meant responsibility in newspaper articles and books, which the great criminals of the world could afford to laugh at."[113]

Regardless of his doubts about immediately setting up the League of Nations, he still felt that "[a] great step, however, would have been taken towards international understanding if the peoples of the world could feel that the greatest criminals, such as the ex-Kaiser, would be brought to trial."[114] He therefore supported Lloyd George's proposal "that the ex-Kaiser and his accomplices should be brought before an international tribunal."[115]

With an eye to the future, Clemenceau considered that "people everywhere would be satisfied if this could be done. *They will feel that justice will in future be done in the case of Kaisers and Kings just as much as in the case of common men. If this could be achieved, it would be a magnificent advance and a moral revolution.*"[116]

For his part, Italian prime minister Vittorio Orlando felt constrained to disagree with the reservations earlier hinted at by Baron Sidney Sonnino, his Cabinet colleague and foreign minister. In Orlando's view, the question was "exclusively one of sentiment and it had nothing to do with interests. . . . It was a great question of the universal conscience of mankind. . . . It was a matter of universal sentiment which touched the highest moral laws. We have just witnessed the reaction of the world from a veritable crime against humanity."[117]

Speaking specifically on the matter of leaving it to national jurisdictions to prosecute their own heads of state alleged to have committed international crimes, a matter that evidently preoccupied Orlando in the various discussions he had on the propriety of prosecuting the kaiser, he continued, "There was something to be said in the past for ideas that nations should be responsible for the faults of their Governments, and there were historical instances of this. In the present case, however, we were not dealing with mere blunders, but with crimes, and the ex-Kaiser ought to pay like other criminals. The ex-Kaiser, for example, had decorated, personally, captains of submarines which had come straight back from perpetrating murder. As to the method by which the ex-Kaiser should be brought to book, this was a question of detail."[118]

In the absence of U.S. representatives at the Inter-Allied meeting of 2 December 1918, Clemenceau, Lloyd George, and Orlando took no firm decision regarding the prosecution of the kaiser. Instead, they sent a joint telegram to President Wilson (who could not attend and whose representative, Colonel House, also could not attend due to ill health—possibly due to the flu that had gripped the world in a pandemic) informing him that they were agreed that the kaiser must be tried by an international tribunal.

The four considerations for the idea of the trial included "[t]hat certainty of inevitable personal punishment for crimes against humanity and international right will be a very important security against future attempts to make war wrongfully or to violate international law, and is a necessary stage in the development of the authority of the League of Nations."[119]

At the conclusion of their work, the plenary membership of the Macdonell Committee agreed that the kaiser may not escape without punishment. They were, however, divided on the question of what his punishment should be. The two courses open were (1) "he might be treated summarily and administratively without any trial, in much the same manner as Napoleon was dealt with in 1815," or (2) "he might be tried before a Tribunal."[120] It was considered that the "moral effect of confinement or internment of the ex-Kaiser without a trial would be much less than that of proceedings in which he would be heard and, if found guilty, punished accordingly."[121] The majority of the committee decided on criminal prosecution as the more appropriate course.[122]

Larnaude and La Pradelle: The French Expert Study

In an exercise that approximated the Macdonell Committee inquiry in the United Kingdom, the French government was similarly engaged in an expert study of the question of prosecuting the kaiser.

As noted by Lord Curzon during his 20 November 1918 briefing to his Imperial Cabinet colleagues, the French government had commissioned some of their legal experts to look into the question. That study fell to Professor Ferdinand Larnaude (the dean of the Law Faculty at the University of Paris) and his colleague of the same faculty, Professor Albert Geouffre de La Pradelle. Larnaude was an expert in public law, and La Pradelle an expert in international law. The two dons were assisted by their colleagues Professor Alfred Le Poittevin (an expert in penal legislation and criminal procedure) and Professor Emile Auguste Garçon (an expert in criminal law and comparative penal legislation).[123]

The French Ministry of War published the result of the study by Larnaude and La Pradelle, in a monograph titled *Examen de la responsabilité pénale de l'Empereur Guillaume II.*

It was inconceivable, the study concluded, that the kaiser should enjoy impunity in respect of the crimes attributed to him.[124]

For various reasons, not least of which was the concern about immunity,* the Larnaude–La Pradelle study considered it better to forgo the use of national courts to try the kaiser. Their recommendation was that an international court should be created.[125] Like the Macdonell Committee in England, the Larnaude–La Pradelle study was also alive to the fact that the idea of prosecuting the kaiser before an international court was unprecedented in international law at that time. But they insisted that the solution must be "found." As they put it: "*Il faut trouver un tribunal qui, par sa composition, par la place qu'il occupera, par l'autorité dont il sera investi, puisse rendre le verdict le plus solennel que le monde ait encore entendu*" ("*A tribunal must be found,* which, by its composition, the position it occupies, and the authority with which it is clothed, is able to deliver the most solemn judgment the world has ever heard").[126] That sentiment is strikingly similar to that of the Macdonell Committee: "It seems to us that the trial of the Kaiser ought to be by an International Tribunal, free from national bias, the decisions of which would possess unquestionable authority, which would speak in the name of the conscience of the world, which would help to re-establish and strengthen International Law, and which in the future would be a deterrent and warning to rulers and highly placed officials who meditated or instigated offences against International Law."[127]

"*Il faut trouver une solution,*" continued Larnaude and La Pradelle, "qui permette d'atteindre tous les faits dont il s'est rendu coupable parce

---

* As Larnaude and La Pradelle put it: "The very immunity of a foreign sovereign raises one more difficulty, for it is a rule that this immunity does not permit of his being tried by a municipal camp for an offence against ordinary law" (Larnaude and La Pradelle, "Inquiry into the Penal Liabilities of Emperor William II," 8).

qu'il les a ordonnés en qualité d'Empereur et Roi et de Seigneur de la guerre." ("*A way must be found* to permit all acts of which he has been guilty, because he ordered them as an Emperor and King and War Lord, to be added.")[128] As they saw things, the kaiser must be tried by an international tribunal, because it was only international law that could supply the needed tribunal and the needed solution, as the facts alleged against William II were international crimes: "*Or, cette solution, c'est le droit international seul qui peut nous la fournir. Les faits reprochés à Guillaume II sont des crimes internationaux: c'est par un tribunal international qu'il doit être jugé.*" ("International law alone can supply this way; the facts charged against William II are international crimes; he must be tried before an international tribunal.")[129]

Given the novelty of the solution they proposed, Larnaude and La Pradelle rapturously proclaimed the essence of their study in the memorable words: "*un droit international nouveau est né*" ("a new international law has arisen").[130] *A new international law has emerged.* This theme of a novel approach to international law is repeated several times in their study.[131]

Just as the Macdonell Committee had been careful to account for sovereign immunity of the kaiser, so too did Larnaude and La Pradelle. They considered that the solution they were proposing was entirely consistent with the idea of a *new order* of international law, which contemplated freedom for peoples and their right to self-determination, and a new international order in which responsibility must actionably follow violations. This was a message that, as we will see later, French prime minister Georges Clemenceau was to drive home in his negotiations with his colleagues of the Council of Four at the Paris Conference. Modern law is all about responsibility for violation of the law. Modern law no longer recognizes irresponsible authorities, even at the apex of political power. "*Le droit moderne ne connaît plus d'autorités irresponsables, même au sommet des hiérarchies*" ("Modern law no longer knows irresponsible authorities, even at the top of hierarchies"), they insisted.[132] This was an obvious allusion to the outmoded doctrine of *princep legibus solutus*, which used to hold the king above the law. It is thus an elementary proposition that neither in international law nor in domestic law would it be correct to continue to exempt persons at the top hierarchies of leadership from the commands of law and justice. The German emperor enjoyed all manner of privilege under German law—including immunity from civil suit, honors, and precedence. Under international law, he must assume responsibilities. In conclusion, Larnaude and La Pradelle considered that "irremediable blow would be struck against the new international law if the German Emperor were granted immunity."[133]

The Commission on the Responsibility of the Authors of the War and on Enforcement of Penalties

Respectively armed with the preparatory work done by the Macdonell Committee in London and by professors Larnaude and La Pradelle, the British and the French governments sent delegates to the Paris Peace Conference of 1919 to debate the fate of the kaiser as a critical part of the postwar settlement—with their respective prime ministers Lloyd George and Clemenceau ultimately backstopping the debates. Notably, Larnaude and La Pradelle were part of the French delegation. Similarly, on the British delegation was Sir Ernest Pollock, KC, a member of the Macdonell Committee. By the time of the Paris Peace Conference, Pollock had become the solicitor general of England and Wales. Like a tag team, he and Larnaude would play a decisive role during the debates that ensued at the Paris Peace Conference regarding the kaiser's prosecution.

The work of the conference was divided into many themes.* Each theme was assigned its own commission. One of those themes was responsibility of the authors of the war and enforcement of penalties.[134]

Most relevant for us is the work of the Commission on the Responsibility of the Authors of the War and on Enforcement of Penalties (the "Commission on Responsibilities," for short), as it is their work that drives home the commission's ultimate recommendation that the kaiser must be prosecuted for war crimes—notwithstanding his status as the head of state of Germany at the time of those offenses. It is imperative to remember that this recommendation was the culmination of a deliberate act of lawmaking, the product of a fraught debate in which head-of-state immunity arguments were clearly considered and rejected. It was thus consciously

---

* The themes were the following: (1) League of Nations; (2) Responsibility of the Authors of the War and the Enforcement of Penalties; (3) Reparation of Damage; (4) International Labor Legislation; (5) International Regime of Ports, Waterways, and Railways; (6) Financial Questions; (7) Economic Questions; (8) Aeronautical; (9) Territorial Questions; (10) Control of the Production of Materials of War in Germany and the Disarmament of the German Army; (11) Specification of Materials of War Which May Be Demanded from Germany; (12) Study of the Means of Imposing the Armistice Conditions on Germany; (13) Committee for Drafting of the Military, Naval, and Aerial Clauses in the Treaty with Germany; (14) Morocco; (15) Submarine Cables; and (16) Supreme Economic Council. See U.S. Department of State, "Minutes of the Plenary Sessions of the Preliminary Peace Conference," in *Papers Relating to the Foreign Relations of the United States: The Paris Peace Conference, 1919*, ed. Joseph V. Fuller (Washington, DC: U.S. Government Printing Office, 1946), 3:155.

intended to signal the reform of international law in that direction. It signaled, as Larnaude and La Pradelle had enthused in their study, the birth of a new international law.

⌒

The Commission on Responsibilities held its inaugural meeting on 3 February 1919. Robert Lansing, the U.S. secretary of state, was elected then to preside over the proceedings of the commission.[135]

Following its installation, the commission immediately resolved to distribute its work across three subcommissions: Sub-commission I dealt with the fact pattern of violations committed during the war; Sub-commission II dealt with the legal question of responsibility of the authors of the war (the question of *jus ad bellum*); and Sub-commission III dealt with the legal question of violation of laws and customs of war (i.e., the question of *jus in bello*).[136] It may be recalled that *jus ad bellum* has to do with questions about why and how a war began and who is to blame for starting the war. Was it a just or unjust war? The conception of war as a war of aggression or a crime of aggression comes in here. *Jus in bello* deals with questions of how the war was fought. Did a particular fighter respect the laws and customs of war? In other words, was a given conduct a war crime?

Notably, the critical deliberations and debates of the Commission on Responsibilities were done in the context of the work of Sub-commission III. In addition to being the chair of the main Commission on Responsibilities, it is significant that Lansing was also the chair of Sub-commission III, where those critical deliberations and debates were conducted. The significance of this detail lies in Lansing's sustained opposition to the trial of the kaiser. The second American delegate on the subcommission was James Brown Scott, who was born in Ontario, Canada, but moved to Philadelphia with his parents at the age of ten.[137]

As noted earlier, the British Empire was represented on the subcommission by Sir Ernest Pollock, KC, a member of the Macdonell Committee, who by the time of the Paris Peace Conference had become the solicitor general of England and Wales. At the Paris Peace Conference, he was to alternate with Sir Gordon Hewart, KC, who by now had become the attorney general of England and Wales, when Sir Frederick E. Smith, KC, was moved up to the House of Lords as Lord Chancellor Birkenhead early in January 1919. Pollock and Hewart shared the same spot on both the main Commission on Responsibilities and its Sub-commission III. Hewart, it appears from the record, almost never put in an appearance in the subcommission. That left Pollock with a consistent presence and voice on the subcommission, as the lead representative of the British Empire.

The second British Empire delegate on the subcommission was William Massey, the prime minister of New Zealand. He was not a lawyer by profession, but a farmer popularly known in New Zealand as "Farmer Bill."[138]

Again, as indicated earlier, the representatives of France on the subcommission were the same Dean Larnaude and Professor La Pradelle whose advisory opinion to the French government regarding the kaiser's prosecution was published under the title *Examen de la responsabilité pénale de l'Empereur Guillaume II.*

As the records of the proceedings show, the delegations of France and the British Empire, acting as a tag team, were to be embroiled in a sustained battle of wits with their American counterparts—over the trial of the kaiser.

A Gulf of Empathy

The debates that occurred in the proceedings of Sub-commission III revealed a marked gulf of empathy between the American members on the one side and their European counterparts on the other.

The United States always had a "traditional policy of isolation"[139] toward Europe's frequent wars. It was a tradition of neutrality made easier by their geographic remoteness. That policy guided their initial attitude when the war broke out in 1914. But this was not sustainable throughout. Among the factors suggested as breaking the American resolve against entering the war were frustrating German submarine attacks on Transatlantic merchant shipping. The most notorious of these was the sinking of the *Lusitania* by a German U-boat on 7 May 1915 as the ocean liner was sailing from New York to Liverpool; 128 Americans were among the 1,198 passengers who perished.

The "Zimmermann Telegram" was another major spur of America's entry into the war. It was a coded telegram from the German foreign minister to the German ambassador in Mexico sent on 16 January 1917. It instructed the ambassador to propose an alliance between Germany and Mexico in the event that the United States entered the war on the Allied side. The German offer to Mexico was to help it recover Arizona, New Mexico, and Texas. The decoding of the telegram and its publication enraged public opinion in the United States and helped push it along the path of war with Germany. Two months later, on 20 March 1917,

President Wilson declared war on Germany, backed by a congressional resolution the next day.[140]

It was possible that America's relative remoteness from the war—a remoteness the effects of which were not wholly erased by the factors outlined above—had left them "groping in the dark" at times when they had to join the Peace Conference in Paris.[141] President Wilson, whose role in both the war and the peace that followed made him a darling of Europe, wrote no memoirs to share his thoughts, perspectives, and experiences about the conference that he insisted on attending personally. We are thus left to eke out his mind-set from the secondhand opinions of those who were close enough to him.

By the end of World War I, Colonel Edward Mandell House was widely viewed as one of Wilson's most trusted aides.[142] He was a highly connected rich Texan who received the honorary title of "colonel" from a Texas governor and chose to use it, just in the same way that some people with honorary doctorate degrees choose to use the vocative "Dr."

House's close relationship with Wilson put him at center stage of the dealings at the Paris Peace Conference, often as Wilson's ambassador-at-large. He was closer to Wilson's pulse of things than was Lansing, the secretary of state.

From that vantage point, House was able to begin to convey a gulf of empathy that existed between European statesmen and their American counterparts as regards the war, even at the level of President Wilson himself.

"Until Wilson went to Europe," House wrote, "he did not know how deep and terrible were her wounds, or how close they came to us."[143]

It raises the question whether Wilson himself could truly relate to the extent of the existential threat that Europeans felt the war had entailed to their freedom, or to the harrowing significance of the narrow margins with which that "challenge" was defeated, as Lord Birkenhead so anxiously related it to the Macdonell Committee during their inaugural meeting on 6 November 2018.

It is, therefore, entirely possible that the weight of the European anxieties was largely remote to the American representatives on Sub-commission III. In that regard, certain observations of James Brown Scott, the second American representative on the subcommission, even after the fact of his close encounter with the Europeans on the subcommission may well be revealing.

"Napoleon Bonaparte abdicated and then delivered himself up to the enemy," wrote James Brown Scott. "Not so William of Hohenzollern. He dropped his crown and ran. He fled to Holland, to which country he is apparently more attached than in his earlier years."[144]

"We can ransack the history of the world," Scott continued, "without finding a tragedy in which the hero does not kill himself, is not killed, or does not give himself up in the fifth act, before the curtain falls. Otherwise, the spectators would hiss him from the stage. Were it not for the death of millions of men and the sorrow which hangs over the world and will darken it like a cloud during the lives of those now living, this episode of William of Hohenzollern could more aptly be termed a comedy than a tragedy."[145]

Some may reasonably point to the foregoing commentary as emblematic of the empathic disconnect of the American representatives from their European counterparts on the subcommission. It is enough that the European Allies might have perceived a tendency to trivialize their wrought experiences, given the punctilious legalism that their American counterparts brought to bear in the deliberations of the subcommission. That feeling would be compounded by the tragic paradox of tyranny that Scott's words quoted above reveal. All through history, real tyrants and aspiring ones have often appeared as clowns to those far and safely beyond their physical or psychological grip or both. An American may well see Napoleon from that perspective. But Caligula was not the only tyrant who saw himself as a god. So, too, may their acolytes. But, to the victims, the omnipotence of tyranny would only translate to omnipresent evil even when tyranny doesn't entail "the death of millions of men." And in their minds, it tends to be real.

So it was that Scott, an American representative on the subcommission, might have seen World War I "a comedy rather than a tragedy"—if not "for the death of millions." Unquestionably, the Europeans who had to bury or mourn those *millions* who died could not possibly look beyond that tragedy to find any comedy in the experience.

One of those Europeans was Sir Ernest Pollock, KC, the solicitor general of England and Wales, the future 1st Viscount Hanworth. He lost his only son in the war. Captain Charles Pollock was killed near Moreuil, France, on Easter Sunday, 31 March 1918.[146] He was a twenty-eight-year-old barrister. Leaving a baby son and a young wife behind, he went off to fight in the war that the kaiser unleashed. His father would later appear as the leading voice of the British Empire in the proceedings of the subcommission whose work had to consider whether the kaiser should be prosecuted.

Some may then wonder about the extent to which considerations such as those summarized above should permit Scott to register the following derision of Europeans:

> According to continental practice, a person may be tried in his absence, even in criminal matters. The Allied and Associated Powers did not contemplate this form of procedure. The Government of the Netherlands was to be asked by them to surrender the ex-emperor, in order that he might "be put on trial." Here the hitch occurred. Holland did not want the fugitive, but the rules of hospitality required that he should not be handed over. That little country had too much honor to think of it—more honor than the Allied and Associated Powers which dared to suggest it.
>
> However, the Allied powers were without shame, and asked the Dutch government to surrender the former kaiser, believing, perhaps, that force would prevail where right was lacking.[147]

As a factual detail, it may be pointed out that President Wilson was also instrumental in the proposal to demand that the Dutch must surrender the kaiser. Indeed, he had instructed Lansing to draft the initial demand to be sent to the Dutch government.[148]

But, that detail may pale in light of the principle engaged in the charge that the Allies "were without shame" for asking the Dutch to surrender the kaiser for trial. One could readily see André Tardieu, one of the French delegates to the Peace Conference, deploy the scolding he gave to those who "know nothing of what France has suffered."[149] Scott's derision must resonate as validly as would a derision of Ukrainian demand for Putin's punishment; though as I initially write this (three months after the invasion of Ukraine), the devastation in Ukraine as a result of Putin's war comes nowhere close to what the European Allies suffered by the end of the kaiser's war.

"They should see our ruined towns;" wrote Tardieu, "our devastated fields; our pillaged factories; they should visit our French families mourning 1,400,000 of their dead."[150] Lloyd George agreed. In a comparative war loss analysis, he duly acknowledged the United States as "an associate that had made a truly notable contribution to victory, but whose sacrifices were not comparable to those made by the European States."[151] According to him, the U.S. population at the time was two-thirds larger than that of France, yet America's dead during the war numbered only "60,000, and not one of whose villages had a single shack destroyed by enemy action."[152]

In comparison, "France had lost sacrifices of her sons 1,364,000 dead and 3,740,000 wounded. Of the millions of young men under thirty who went into the line to defend the soil and honour of France, only 50 per cent, ever returned from the battlefield. The War also cost France the equivalent of £8,000,000,000; 4,022 of her villages had been destroyed; 20,000 of her factories ruined and millions of acres of her fertile land rendered uncultivable without complete reconditioning."[153]

The British Empire also suffered heavily. In human costs, it lost nine hundred thousand soldiers, with more than 2 million wounded. In material costs, 8 million tons of its shipping were sunk; and it suffered about £10 billion in economic loss.[154]

Italy also suffered heavy losses. According to Lloyd George, "Italy sacrificed 2,000,000 of her youth in killed and wounded, and although a comparatively poor country, the War cost her seventy milliards of francs."[155]

All that loss and devastation the Europeans attributed to the German kaiser for what was widely seen as his failed "gamble for world dominion."[156]

There was therefore, in European postwar attitude, a determination to exact punishment in a way that should deter future strongmen from similar ventures in Europe or elsewhere, as Lord Birkenhead told the Macdonell Committee at the inception of their work.

It is in that context that the united attitude of the French and the British becomes understandable, in their unyielding stance against the equally uncompromising objections of Lansing and Scott during the debates in Sub-commission III, in relation to the trial of the kaiser.

Round One: Whether to Discuss the Creation of an International Tribunal

Right from the very outset, the proceedings of Sub-commission III bristled with tension. The opening skirmish involved a question about the subcommission's competence to consider and report on the constitution and procedure of an appropriate tribunal for the trial of the offenses to be agreed as deserving of prosecution.

Lansing, the chair of the subcommission, introduced that question, on 25 February 1919, as part of his housekeeping opening remarks concerning what should be in the report that the subcommission must render to the main commission.[157]

Undoubtedly sensing the disparate moods within the subcommission, Pollock, the vice chair, immediately took that early opportunity of housekeeping discussion to plant firmly the flag of the main position of the Allies. "[W]e have got to deal with the question of setting up an international tribunal," he said at once.[158] Recall that the Macdonell Committee in which he had served as a member had concluded that the kaiser must be tried before an international tribunal.[159]

Pollock made sure to underscore to Sub-commission III, at the earliest opportunity, that the outcome of prosecuting the kaiser was "important from the British point of view, because the one demand is that, to take a leading case, the responsibility of the Kaiser, and the outrages committed in the course of the war, the whole of Great Britain demands that he should be tried."[160]

He also made sure that everyone understood that position to be non-negotiable for his government. "And it seems to me *impossible* to hand him over to anything except an international tribunal. On my return, when I was in London last week, this point of view was impressed upon me by those in authority, and the demand that we shall set up a tribunal to try the Kaiser is insistent, and urgent, and I can't possibly neglect it."[161]

In what was to turn out to be a wrestling tag team, Dean Larnaude chimed in support for Pollock. "[W]hat Sir Ernest Pollock says for British opinion," joined Larnaude, "is also true of French public opinion; that it is very anxious about the length of our labour, and especially about the commission which was first set up by the Peace Conference, the Commission on Responsibility for the war."[162]

He hastened to add, however, that while the French have the kaiser "in the foreground" among those they want to hold accountable, the "French public opinion does not concentrate itself on the ex-Kaiser only."[163] Rather, the French do not want to see any of the "other great culprits to escape punishment for criminal acts. Therefore, we do not at all disagree with the British point of view in wishing to see that all culprits,—all those who have committed crimes, whoever they are,—the great chiefs as well as the Supreme War Lord, should be brought before the jurisdiction."[164]

Recalling the views that he and La Pradelle expressed in *Le responsabilité pénale de l'Empereur Guillaume II*, Larnaude reiterated that the contemplated "prosecution should be concentrated before a single tribunal" whose judgment "should resound throughout the whole world which is waiting for a result."[165]

In reply, Lansing contended that looking at the terms of reference for the subcommission he did not see that it spoke of constitution and procedure of an *international tribunal*. It only spoke of the subcommission having the mandate to consider the constitution and procedure of an *appropriate tribunal*.[166] Hence, the question remained to be discussed "as to whether an international or a national tribunal should hear the cases."[167]

With that, Lansing planted an objection he evidently hoped might derail the subcommission from the track of considering the modalities of creating an international tribunal to try the kaiser. "And it was submitted to us, as a sub-commission, simply the question as to whether it should be an international jurisdiction, or whether it should be a national jurisdiction," he said, "and I don't think that this sub-commission can go beyond that. I do not think that they are charged with recommending the constitution or procedure of a tribunal, because if it had been intended it would have been in the mandate received from the commission. I think the commission, as a whole, has reserved that to itself."[168]

The objection provoked an extended discussion during which Pollock and Larnaude stated the common position that the legal possibility of creating an international tribunal for the kaiser's trial fell within the remit of the subcommission—regardless of the forum of the Peace Conference deemed the most appropriate to decide the question.

After the extended discussion, Scott (Lansing's colleague) proposed that all the questions within the subcommission's mandate—including that of the appropriate tribunal—be referred to a smaller drafting committee (comité de rédaction) that would in turn report to the subcommission. The procedure had been followed with salutary effect, he noted, by the other two subcommissions of the Commission on Responsibilities.[169] To that proposal, Pollock and Larnaude expressed no general disagreement, except as to the question of whether it fell within the competence of the subcommission to recommend on the propriety of "setting up" a tribunal. They considered that this particular point had been exhaustively discussed that morning, and thus required bringing to a conclusion by way of an immediate vote.[170]

Dubious as to the trajectory of the discussion, and showing the level of angst in the deliberations, Lansing asked to know where the words "setting up a tribunal" came from as something the subcommission may consider.[171] Pollock riposted to the terms of reference. Riposting back, Lansing pointed out that the term used there "says 'constitution'—that doesn't necessarily mean to 'set up.'"[172]

Quickly parrying back, Pollock pointed out that the precise wording in the terms of reference was "the constitution of a tribunal."

"It means," he explained "we are to consider the setting up—the constitution of a tribunal."

Lansing attempted a tactical retreat. He offered to withdraw the agenda item, to "clear the atmosphere." But Pollock was not appeased. "Well, sir," countered Pollock, "that is not very satisfactory."

"We have discussed it for an hour and a half," he insisted, "and we have made up our minds, I think the most of us, that it is within—we don't want to go back of it. We want to make up our minds, because having discussed it, we want to come to some conclusion, and we don't want to find that withdrawn, and afterwards discussed, on a subsequent day. We come to a meeting in which we must make up our mind, and accept the responsibility."[173]

Clearly outmaneuvered on the point, and no doubt correctly sensing that the subcommission's majority mood was on Pollock's side, Lansing agreed—but with the proviso that he would "have the privilege of filing an adverse memorandum."

"Quite well then," Pollock cut in. "Now, let us decide it is within our jurisdiction to consider the question of the constitution of an appropriate tribunal, such to Mr President's." Pollock was in the disarming habit of referring to Lansing as "Mr. President," especially when he knew he was making life difficult for Lansing or about to do so.

"The constitution and procedure—" Lansing corrected. "—of an appropriate tribunal," Pollock added, completing Lansing's sentence.

"Let us decide that is within our sphere, such to this: Mr President wishes to file a memorandum, indicating, and putting on record his contrary view," said Pollock.[174]

At this point, Scott piped in again—very apologetically, recognizing it to be "bad form"—to reiterate his earlier plea to include that question in the tasks to be delegated to a drafting committee. But he made the tactical mistake of beginning with the rhetorical question: "isn't this really a dispute about words?"[175]

That provided the opening that Pollock needed to bury a slain point.

Protesting Scott's characterization that it was "a dispute over mere words,"[176] Pollock insisted that it was disrespectful to Lansing to characterize as dispute over mere words a matter that Lansing the chairperson had considered "with much deliberation and thought" as to write down and present to the subcommission as part of their agenda for discussion.[177] It would not be correct to suggest that the subcommission had wasted one and a half hours on "a mere difference of words."[178]

As a matter of forensic performance, some may think that Pollock was entitled to drive his advantage home, by ensuring that the point of the debate was definitively settled. Scott, however, was correct in pointing out that there had been a dispute over mere words. But, it was his boss Lansing who raised the matter, insisting that "'constitution' . . . doesn't necessarily mean to 'set up.'"

In view of a late resolution of the Peace Conference, asking them to speed up their work, Pollock argued that the real inefficiency lay with delegating that question to the drafting committee, having them spend time discussing it all over again, and presenting a report on it that would again take up time debating. In the circumstances, he restated his preferred solution of having that particular matter concluded immediately subject to Lansing "putting in his memorandum, indicating the way in which he disagrees."[179]

Lansing responded, "That is all agreed to."[180] But, even at that, Pollock was not prepared to leave any loose ends. "It may have been understood, but it hasn't been agreed to," Pollock retorted.[181]

Then, the Japanese delegate intervened to request a vote on the specific motion as to whether the "Committee on Responsibility for the war" is empowered to propose that an appropriate tribunal should be "set up" to try the contemplated offenses.[182] "As regards the substance," he expressed agreement with "Sir Ernest Pollock's views on the subject."[183] He still asked for an opportunity to vote on that question.

In a final capitulation, Lansing concluded the discussion by expressing his understanding that "it is agreed that the sub-commission has authority to make recommendations as to the constitution and procedure of an international court, with a reservation as to those who will be permitted to file appropriate memoranda on the subject."[184]

And that marked the first cobblestone laid by a multilateral gathering of nations in the direction of a norm that an international court could be created to try persons for international crimes, including heads of state.

It is significant to note, at this juncture, that part of the reasons that the Macdonell Committee considered setting up an international tribunal to try the kaiser was because they believed "that such a Tribunal would be better suited than a National Tribunal for the trial of high officials."[185] Similarly, the Larnaude–La Pradelle study concluded that the reason that the kaiser's responsibility must be adjudged by an international tribunal was because his conducts were in violation of international law and he engaged in those conducts as king and emperor and lord of war.[186]

It is possible that the reorientation of international law in the direction of holding heads of state individually accountable for criminal violations of international law might not have occurred at the Paris Peace Conference had the British and French delegates not insisted that the mandate of Sub-commission III included the authority to consider the matter as something that could be done in international law. That discussion broke the taboo of the subject, given the robustness and tenor of the arguments that were brought to bear.

That decided, the next question was about the composition of the drafting committee.[187] Lansing was given the authority to name the composition of the drafting committee. In what turned out to be a consequential decision for international law, Lansing nominated Larnaude, Pollock, S. Rosental, and Scott to the commission. (As we will see, Pollock was to play a crucial part in drafting the report of the Commission on Responsibilities.) The subcommission then adjourned. They were to meet again on 4 March 1919, after Lansing had proposed that the drafting committee should circulate their draft report ahead of the meeting in which the report would be discussed.[188]

That was the end of round one—the procedural round as it were—of the confrontation between the American representatives and their European counterparts in Sub-commission III, on the question of creating an international tribunal that would try the kaiser.

Round Two: Whether to Create an International Tribunal

One week later, on 4 March 1919, the commission met again for what turned out to be round two of the debates on whether international law should be reformed in the direction of punishing the criminal responsibility of heads of state. It saw more of the same tension.

The meeting opened with Pollock presenting the draft report of the subcommission's Comité de redaction. In doing so, he noted that James Brown Scott helped in drafting the report, as much as he could, while still fully reserving the U.S. position as regards creating an international tribunal.

No doubt sensitive to the American delegation's resistance to the idea of an international tribunal that would try the kaiser, Pollock proposed a compromise solution, if that arrangement would be acceptable to the United States. This entailed the idea of national tribunals sitting together as *haut tribunal* (high tribunal) to try the most important cases. He underscored that, while that arrangement was not the preferred position of the British Empire and the French delegates, they could live with it, if that offered an "opportunity of general accord." But should that scheme prove unacceptable to the U.S. representatives, then the British Empire delegation would insist on reverting to their original position of setting up a straightforward international tribunal.[189] Larnaude expressed full agreement with Pollock.[190]

Lansing greeted the offer with no warmth at all. As he saw it, the basis of jurisdiction over the catalog of offenses being contemplated by the subcommission would be the nationality or the territoriality principles of jurisdiction. In international law, the nationality principle of jurisdiction refers to the jurisdiction a country has to control the fate of its nationals, while the territoriality principle refers to the jurisdiction a country has to control its territory.

Lansing explained the position of the U.S. delegation as follows. In his view, the nationality principle of jurisdiction meant that only the tribunals of the Allied states whose nationals suffered harm should have the jurisdiction to prosecute the offenders: but where a defendant is alleged to have committed harm to the nationals of more than one Allied state, then the national tribunals of those states may in those limited circumstances "unite into a joint tribunal." On that theory, the United States would be "under great embarrassment" to participate in an international tribunal that would try offenses committed before it entered the war.[191]

Notably, along the way, Lansing adverted to his realization that "there is in every country a very decided public opinion in favor of punishing those who are responsible for the abominable acts that have been committed, and for which there is no punishment, but for which some punishment should be devised for the future. The people of the world demand that in some form the judgment of the world should be registered, but at the same time we are all from nations which have a very high reverence and veneration for the law, and for submission to the rules of law. If there is no instrument of justice by which we can operate, we may be helpless, but it does not prevent us from registering our abhorrence of these acts."[192]

The representatives of the other Allied and associated states took turns in expressing disappointment with Lansing's inclination to distance the United States from their need to bring accountability to bear upon the kaiser.

"[S]peaking for the British Empire," a phrase that he would deploy repeatedly in the deliberations, Pollock pointedly observed that between him and Lansing "the difference [was] so great that [they] should be unable to find a basis of agreement on the plan which [Lansing] has put forward."[193]

Among those irreconcilable differences was the consideration that the draft report enumerated a category of cases that, in Pollock's view, would not be readily amenable to the processes of a national tribunal. And the

British government was insistent that such cases must be tried by an international tribunal. For the British government, Pollock stressed, the matter was one of "deep importance."[194]

In the circumstances, he was "quite satisfied that nothing but an international tribunal of commanding power, force, and weight would have the moral position before the world to execute the justice which the entire world demands."[195] Recall that both the Macdonell Committee[196] and the Larnaude–La Pradelle[197] study had put the point approximately in those terms.

And that matter was of "primary and of great importance to Great Britain,"[198] he repeated the emphasis.

That being the case, "the suggestion which Mr Lansing has very kindly made, in order to try and meet us, would not be sufficient to Great Britain. We could not be satisfied with merely trying cases where one or more of the allied nations are concerned. We demand the proposition of justice to the world."[199] In other words, justice administered on an appreciably international basis.

In the result, Pollock withdrew his offer of national tribunals sitting together as one "*haut tribunal*" and returned to his original proposal of a straightforward international tribunal—"a true international court."[200]

When Pollock was done speaking, Larnaude made a very long speech "in the name of France," gently but firmly "taking exactly the same position as the Solicitor-General [Pollock]"[201] that an international tribunal was the correct approach. He urged Lansing to reconsider. Larnaude expressed consternation that the United States would not join in the project of justice after playing a leading role in condemning the atrocities for which the Allies are now seeking to establish an accountability mechanism.[202]

Nikolaos Politis also intervened, after listening to the debates. He was not a member of Sub-commission III, but he had been invited to attend that particular session.[203] He deftly noted that he was not speaking in his capacity as a representative of "a small country, but as a man who had studied law his whole life long" and who was "especially acquainted with steps which must be taken . . . of some form of international justice."[204] Indeed, Professor Politis was no lightweight in the theories and applications of international law. By the time of the conference, he had held professorships at a number of French universities (notably, Aix-en-Provence, Poitiers, and Paris), before being appointed the director general of the Greek Ministry of Foreign Affairs and was the minister of foreign affairs at the time of the Peace Conference. He later gave lectures at the Institut des hautes études internationales de Paris and the Hague Academy of International Law, and he served from 1937 to 1942 as the president of the Institute of International Law.[205]

With fulsome politeness, Politis deftly sought to poke holes in Lansing's arguments. He began by pointing out that "if you want to answer the demands of the public opinion [for justice] which Mr Lansing mentioned," that is achievable "through one means only, and that is an international tribunal."[206] He considered such a tribunal as "the only one qualified" to deliver justice at the "heights of impartiality which is absolutely necessary" in the circumstances for the kinds of transgressions under consideration.[207] Next, he adverted to "the terrible complication of views which would arise in the organisation of national tribunals" along the lines that Lansing had suggested.[208]

In a further argument, Politis pointed out that Lansing's insistence on the nationality principle as the basis of jurisdiction was a throwback to the vengeance theory of justice, according to which justice was to be administered only by the victims of the conducts under adjudication. He argued that the idea was essentially inimical to impartiality, as a cardinal principle in the administration of justice.[209]

That said, Politis raised as an alternative idea the possibility that the international tribunal could be established, with recognition that certain states could be named as entitled to participate in it, while leaving it to individual states to refrain from taking part in the adjudication of certain aspects of the case on grounds that they had not been part of the war when the violations concerning that part of the case had occurred.[210]

Politis's argument was unassailable indeed. It is one thing to allow a state of nationality of victims of atrocity the right to exercise jurisdiction, where there is no other tribunal that may administer justice. It is quite another matter to insist that only such states may adjudicate the wrong in question. It is easy to see how that can raise questions about neutrality in the administration of justice. Indeed, that theory would have made it impossible to have the structures of international justice as we know it, from the Permanent Court of International Court down to the International Court of Justice, to the International Criminal Court, to the ad hoc international tribunals for the former Yugoslavia, Rwanda, Sierra Leone, Cambodia, Lebanon, and Kosovo.

Lansing's objection could come as a surprise to those who might learn that just four short weeks before, he had written a letter to President Wilson (dated 3 February 1919) suggesting a more neutral composition to any international court of justice that would be an organ in the League of Nations that Wilson was proposing. In that letter, Lansing wrote that "a tribunal, on which representatives of the litigants sit as judges, has not proved satisfactory even though the majority of the tribunal are nationals of other countries."[211] To avoid the "undesirable" effects of that phenomenon, he recommended "eliminating arbitrators of the litigant nations."[212] According to that view, international judges should come from states that are neutral to the factual subject matter of the case. It is not easy to reconcile that position with his inclination to withdraw the United States from the proposed international tribunal, on grounds that the United States was not truly a victim state in the war—in other words, the United States should take no part in the administration of justice because it was a neutral state.

The Italian delegate, Mariano D'Amelio, chimed in support for a variant of Politis's idea—D'Amelio's being that the major states should be indicated as having a right to join the international tribunal, while leaving it up to them to abstain from joining the tribunal.[213]

Larnaude found some merit in the Politis formula. Noting that it was not quite the same as what D'Amelio had proposed, Larnaude suggested it as something that the drafting committee could take up if Lansing could agree to it.[214]

Rosental of Romania registered a brief and pointed intervention: An international tribunal must be established.[215]

Confronted with such an overwhelming support for the idea of an international tribunal, Lansing indicated that Larnaude's last proposal could be taken back to the drafting committee to consider if it is agreeable that the drafting committee should take up that proposal.

Yielding to feelings of frustration, Lansing threatened to withdraw Scott from taking further part in the drafting committee, if the Politis idea proved unacceptable, leaving the subcommission to proceed along the lines proposed by Pollock.[216] Lansing's threat to withdraw Scott from the Comité de redaction generated a further stir to already nervy proceedings.

Pollock intervened to say he "should be very sorry to lose [Scott] and his service" on the drafting committee, while making "[him]self plain to Mr Lansing, that certainly speaking for Great Britain, and . . . for other countries, they are quite convinced [that] an international tribunal should be set up" to try the ex-kaiser.[217] He proposed that the drafting committee be shored up by the addition of Politis and D'Amelio. Pollock added that

Scott's name should be kept on the committee, while leaving it up to Scott and Lansing to decide if Scott would actually continue to assist the drafting committee as he was always welcome to do.[218]

In reaction to Pollock's intervention, Lansing announced his regret that Scott could no longer continue to serve on the drafting committee, but that Pollock's suggestion about augmenting the drafting committee with Politis and the Italian delegate D'Amelio would be followed, if that met with the approval of the drafting committee.[219]

Observing that "there seems to have arisen a misunderstanding of an extra-ordinary kind,"[220] Larnaude intervened with a large dose of diplomatic balm to calm Lansing's obviously bristling nerves. Lansing's proposal, he said, was welcomed "with great and general favour."[221] And he begged to thank Lansing "deeply for allowing us to see a way out of the difficulty."[222] Larnaude considered it necessary that the drafting committee should not only study the proposals of Politis and the Italian delegate, "but it should see as to the possibility—to contemplate a limited share of the United States in the international tribunal."[223] Larnaude thus considered "Mr Lansing's proposal as probably being quite right, and welcoming it with enthusiasm."[224] Consequently, he would not understand it as warranted that the drafting committee should be deprived of Scott's services.

Whether the tag team of Larnaude and Pollock was deliberately employing the "good cop / bad cop" strategy is only a matter of conjecture. But Larnaude's last intervention worked. Acknowledging Larnaude's "very generous remarks," Lansing felt "that there is much to be said—very much to be said in favour of Dr Larnaude's remarks."[225] Hence, he considered that the matter should be referred back to the drafting committee, "with instructions to follow, as far as agreement can be reached, [regarding] Dr Larnaude's proposal." In that case, Lansing felt that "the United States should be represented on the drafting committee."[226]

"We should be very glad, indeed, to have Major Brown Scott to assist us," said Pollock. "But Mr Lansing has, I think definitely understood"[227] that the British proposal about setting up an international tribunal "will still be made the matter of discussion and deliberation by the *comité de redaction*, but we should be delighted to have Major Scott, and see how far he can come along with us."[228]

That was the last action in round two of the dogfight between Lansing and Pollock at Sub-commission III. And with that the proceedings were adjourned, with Politis and D'Amelio added to the drafting committee that would consider the proposals made by Larnaude, Politis, and D'Amelio.[229]

At the meeting of the senior American diplomats the next day, Lansing reported of "great difficulties which he had encountered on his sub-committee."[230]

The minutes of that meeting offer a fly-on-the-wall insight into Lansing's state of mind at the time. "It was Mr Lansing's opinion," according to the minutes, "that the British Delegates were not very sincere in their desire to try the Kaiser etc., but merely felt that they had to urge this measure because of a political pledge. The situation was much the same as it had been on the Reparations Committee where both the French and British were trying to accomplish the impossible, knowing that it was impossible, but wishing to place the blame for the failure upon the United States."[231]

As indicated earlier, the theory that America's allies were insincere in seeking to establish an international tribunal to try the kaiser is not borne out by the records of efforts they had expended to achieve those aims. Lansing was in his own peculiar aptitude in opposing those aims. Nothing at all made those aims "impossible" to achieve as he claimed. For one thing, many international criminal tribunals have since been successfully established by the international community. There was no material impossibility about doing so in 1919. Nor was there a material impossibility about trying the kaiser before such a tribunal as he was no longer in power, that being the usual circumstance that practically tends to put powerful men beyond the province of accountability when they are in office. Experiences of Nuremberg,[232] Tokyo,[233] The Hague,[234] Arusha,[*] and Freetown[†] have shown many instances of national leaders being put on trial for international crimes.

Round Three: Trying the Kaiser before an International Tribunal

Round three of the proceedings of Sub-commission III of the Paris Peace Conference saw the battle royal between Lansing on the one hand, and the tag team of Pollock and Larnaude on the other, on the substantive matter of setting up an international tribunal before which not even *heads of state* may be accorded immunity for international crimes. This was the main feature of the meeting of 8 March 1919.

---

[*] Both Colonel Théoneste Bagosora (the effective leader of Rwanda during the genocide) and Jean Kambanda (the prime minister) were tried for international crimes.

[†] Charles Taylor was indicted for trial at the Special Court for Sierra Leone while he was in office as president of Liberia, and eventually tried by the court.

After a few preliminary niceties, Lansing zeroed in on the text of paragraph IV(c) of the revised draft report that the Comité de redaction had produced. In a prior version of the draft, presented to the meeting of 4 March 1919, the text had explicitly focused on the ex-kaiser, reading as follows: "(c) *against the ex-Kaiser himself,* in so far as he ordered or abstained from controlling and mitigating the barbarities committed in many widely separated areas and in many countries."[235] But, as of the meeting of 8 March 1919, the text had been drafted more broadly to say: "(c) *Against all authorities,* civil or military, *however high their position* may have been, without distinction of rank, *including the heads of States,* who ordered, or abstained from preventing, putting an end to, or repressing, barbarities or acts of violence."[236]

Lansing raised two objections against the text. His primary objection was against the phrase "including the heads of States." He saw it as "superfluous and therefore needless,"[237] because the text already contemplated "all authorities, civil or military, however high their position may have been, without distinction of rank."[238]

To that argument he added the following: "Under this article, the President of the United States, or the King of England might be tried for having failed to prevent certain of their soldiers from performing barbarous or atrocious acts. Now, I am not prepared to place the President of the United States in a position like that; but that is the way it reads and I think it is a pretty serious position."[239]

His secondary objection was against prosecuting a commander for "abstaining from preventing, putting an end to, or repressing, barbarities of acts of violence" without requiring that the accused be seen to have had the power to prevent or repress the crime which power he had refused to exercise[240]—in other words, effective control.

As usual, Pollock was ready and quick on the counter.

"Mr President," he began in relation to Lansing's primary objection that the words "including the heads of States" must be deleted, and he moved straight to the heart of the matter: "I am sorry to say that I couldn't accept the report if these words were deleted. To my mind they are not superfluous."[241]

And then he unleashed the flurry, making sure that everyone understood that he was speaking on behalf of the vastness of the British Empire of 1919.

In what must resonate as the main feature of the law reform that resulted from the Paris Peace Conference, in relation to individual criminal responsibility for international crimes, Pollock deployed his main argument for insisting that the words were not superfluous. "I mean on behalf of the British Empire to include the possibility of a charge against the Sovereigns of states," Pollock insisted.

To underscore the clarity of his government's position on the matter, he stressed that the new rule of accountability must apply to all sovereigns of the world.

"And I think," he continued, addressing Lansing directly in that regard, "the view of the United States, which you have expressed quite fairly, and from information which you are now possessed of, is not to include a charge against the Sovereigns of states. And therefore, there is a marked divergence between us. And as I intend, on behalf of the British Empire, we intend—my colleague and myself—that the sovereign of a State should be put on trial. For that reason I think it cannot be said that the words are superfluous, because it is necessary to express what we mean. To make it quite clear, and not to allow anyone to suppose that, by assenting to the deletion of these words, we have agreed to a course which it is not our intention to agree to, and therefore, on behalf of the British Empire I must ask that these words be retained. In that sense these words are not super-fluous. They are intentional and they were put there because I wanted to make our meaning clear. If I mean it, I want to say it."[242]

Undeterred by Lansing's polemic strategy of imagining a president of the United States on trial before an international tribunal, Pollock contin-ued, "I don't think that the danger in which the President of the United States might find himself is one that really is an argument in which we need to dwell upon. If the President of the United States had been in any way guilty, or responsible for the acts which we attribute to William II, I believe the United States would be perhaps the most insistent that the President guilty with such blood guiltiness upon him should be brought to trial. And the mere fact that he happened to be the President of the United States would not protect him from the execration of those persons who elected him to that high and responsible position."[243]

To drive home the range of the logic of accountability that his gov-ernment had in mind, Pollock, KC, the solicitor general of England and Wales, underscored that it wasn't only presidents of the United States that Pollock would be prepared to hold accountable for international crimes.

"In other words," he continued, "a criminal or a guilty person who is responsible for what has happened in the course of the war, be he the President of the United States, or be he the King of England, or the King of any other country, deserves and should receive, not only from the

United States, but from every other country, the condemnation which he ought to receive."[244]

But Pollock was keen to explain that his aim was not to presume sovereign guilt. Everyone accused of a crime must be presumed innocent, unless proved guilty by a court of law. So, too, it must be for sovereigns accused of committing international crimes.

"And on that ground we proceed to ask for the establishment of a grand tribunal. It would be wrong to assume that, in any of these cases, we have prejudged the persons who [may be prosecuted for the violations in question]. What we have said is they ought to be put upon their trial. We don't know what the result of putting them upon their trial would be. We don't say that the sovereigns of States are necessarily, and in fact guilty. But we say that the sovereigns of States ought to be put upon their trial, and in order that if they are found guilty, they shall be properly dealt with."[245]

Having underscored with the utmost clarity that the British government intended to adjust international law in the direction of holding heads of state (regardless of nation) accountable when they are accused of international crimes, Pollock next turned his attention to Lansing's second objection, against the proposal to criminalize a sovereign's omission to prevent violations, without taking into account whether the sovereign had preventive power. Pollock's response was quite straightforward in that regard. He merely explained that the judges would know to acquit if that were so.[246]

And he returned to stress the mood in the "whole of British Empire" to adjust international law to hold heads of state accountable when they commit international crimes.

"[T]here is," he said, "a clear demand throughout the whole British Empire," not only in England or the British Isles, to have criminal charges laid and examined against "persons of the highest authority"—be he a sovereign or not—who failed to exercise the power he had to prevent the atrocities that had been committed.[247] And "therefore we intend to say the sovereigns of states should be placed upon their trial."[248]

Concerned that the discussion was pointlessly going astray, Politis considered that "the whole spirit" of the text at issue was "aimed at enemy persons," even though not stated as such in the text. As that understanding would ease Lansing's concern, Politis suggested that the phrase "belonging to enemy countries" should be systematically reproduced in the appropriate places in the text.[249]

In his intervention, Edouard Rolin-Jaequemyns, the Belgian delegate, approached Lansing's objections in their two separate parts: the first part concerning whether heads of state may be tried at all; and the second part being whether to incriminate criminal omissions as well as criminal acts. Rolin-Jaequemyns had no difficulty with the idea of prosecuting heads of state. This was surely a notable concession, noting that Belgium's King Leopold II, who had died only ten years earlier, had established himself in history as a prime candidate for questions of criminal accountability, given the crimes against humanity attributed to him during his colonial rule in the present-day Democratic Republic of the Congo. He conceived the entire area as his own private colony to exploit. Among other crimes attributed to him, the arms and hands of children, women, and men were amputated because they did not meet rubber production quotas.[250] Generations later, the same method of cruelty was employed in crimes against humanity committed in Sierra Leone.

But while not objecting to trying heads of state as such before international tribunals, Rolin-Jaequemyns did see some concern regarding the second part of Lansing's objection. That was the objection against incriminating omissions.[251] Rolin-Jaequemyns would have difficulty with the idea of prosecuting heads of state who failed to prevent violations. But he would see no objection to prosecuting heads of state "for orders directly given—orders to execute barbarous acts, or acts of violence." According to him, "such Heads of State should be held personally responsible."[252]

In his turn, "on behalf of the French delegation," Larnaude began by "entirely agree[ing] with the powerful argument brought forward by the Solicitor-General [Pollock]."[253]

As far as Larnaude was concerned, the subcommission "[could not] strike off anything whatever in paragraph [IV](c)."[254] He offered that the French delegation had already conceded much in not mentioning the ex-kaiser expressly in the provision, as was done in the first iteration of the draft report. That concession was consistent with the rule against *ad hominem* legislation.

Here, he said, the specific reference to "heads of state" was deliberate, and "for a serious reason."[255] And Larnaude would know. He was on the subcommission's drafting committee. According to him, it was not enough in the circumstances to employ the equivocal formulation of "authorities," as that may allow the kaiser to escape.[256] Larnaude could not agree with the proposal made by Politis.[257] Recall that Politis had proposed making it explicit that what was contemplated was only the prosecution of "persons of enemy countries."

Continuing, Larnaude sought to demonstrate, as Pollock had done, that the idea of prosecuting heads of state was not an abstract idea, as far as they were concerned. They had considered who they meant by heads of state. In seeking to adjust international in the direction of that manner of accountability, they had thought about their own heads of state.

In that regard, Larnaude pointed out that it was a mark of "good faith" on the part of the Entente States to say that "if our sovereigns, or heads of States have ordered such and such criminal acts, let them be brought to trial," he said.

"If we are ready to admit all heads of state whatever may be brought to trial, we strengthen our position. The Entente countries are quite ready to deliver the heads of State into the hands of justice, because they hold that nobody is above justice. This is a great rule in the world of law and right. It is necessary that no man, whatever he may be, even the head of State, should try and take shelter behind the responsibility which is offered to heads of state."[258]

He noted what a remarkable progress it was that even the British were prepared to join in the idea of holding all heads of state responsible for crimes against international law, knowing that their own constitutional law did not permit such a prospect under their domestic law.

Larnaude therefore expressed the opinion that the words "head of state" must be maintained.[259]

Ultimately, Larnaude underscored the law reform value of the proposal that he and Pollock were championing on behalf of their governments. It was a new rule for the whole world. The "horrors felt by all civilised people toward this return to barbarism which we all thought would have been struck out of history" thus made it necessary that "all culprits, whether small or great, and this is the principle of right and law—the principle of equality of all before the law—that all culprits, be they heads of state, or on the last stop of the ladder, should be, I will not say sentenced, but if they are found guilty, should be punished, and receive a punishment which may ultimately be found that they deserve."[260]

The American minutes of the meeting indicated that Lansing directed that an intervention of Mineichirō Adachi of Japan, made in French, should not be interpreted. But the UK notes of the meeting indicated that the Japanese said that until the previous day he was in full agreement with the draft as it stood, but in view of "the Chairman's weighty arguments he would like to reserve his assent."[261]

At this stage of the proceedings, Lansing, the chairperson, considered it useless to continue the debate: for, just as Pollock had indicated that he could not sign the report with the phrase "including heads of state" deleted from the formulation of the accountability clause, Lansing indicated that he could not sign the report with the words left in.[262] So he suggested that "the only possible solution" was to render the report as it was drafted, but with reservation from the U.S. delegation.[263]

Pollock concurred, pointing out that the words in the report were carefully considered and resulted after extended hours of meetings—including long meetings of the drafting committee—in which the objections of the U.S. delegation had been steadfastly pressed and all efforts made to accommodate them, with no further dilution of the text as it was finally presented. In the circumstances, there was no use continuing the debate.[264]

A view from hindsight shows a remarkable faculty of foresight on the part of Pollock and Larnaude, in their insistence on maintaining the specific reference to "heads of state" in the order of individuals who may be held accountable in international law for international crimes. As will become evident, there exists in our own time a string of scholarship that has boldly argued that international law recognizes immunity for heads of state before international tribunals. This is notwithstanding that, beginning with the Charter of the International Military Tribunal at Nuremberg, every founding instrument of an international tribunal has specifically provided that there is no immunity for anyone, including heads of state in particular. One can only imagine how much bolder the immunity-tolerant scholarship would be in the absence of specific language that has clearly and consistently spelled out in all these instruments the norm that "heads of state" do not enjoy immunity.

Round Four: The Debate before the Main Commission— an Attempt to Accommodate Lansing

Round four of the battle occurred on 12 March 1919, during the proceedings of the main Commission on Responsibilities, when it convened to consider and adopt the reports of the three subcommissions. It was the third meeting of the main commission. The first and second meetings took place at the very beginning of the Peace Conference, before the commission broke out to work in subcommissions.

During this third meeting, Pollock was away. "Farmer Bill" Massey, the prime minister of New Zealand, and not a lawyer, was thus left as the only representative of the British Empire.[265]

Having adopted the report of Sub-commissions I and II without incident, the proceedings turned to the report of the typhonic Sub-commission III.[266] Here, Lansing tried a different approach to revisit his battle of wits against prosecuting the kaiser, which he steadfastly fought and lost in Sub-commission III.

Lansing's new approach involved repackaging the same arguments—sandwiched between a declaration of moral condemnation and a proposal to establish an international commission of inquiry that would validate the moral condemnation, but without criminal penalty.

For the top layer of the sandwich, Lansing's draft resolution would declare that "the masters of the Central Powers" had engaged in unjustifiable violation of "international morality and justice," by engaging in a "war of aggression," which had been "inflamed by the passion to possess the territory and sovereignty of others." The resulting "war in magnitude, in waste of life and property, in merciless cruelties and in intolerable woes surpasse[d] all wars of modern times." The evidence of this "moral crime against mankind is convincing and conclusive."[267]

And veering back to a little of his old argument of non-justiciability, Lansing continued, "Restrained by reverence for law which is inseparable from that high sense of justice which is essential to social order, the nations, which have suffered so grievously, may be unable to mete out through judicial channels retribution to the guilty."[268] What this means is that the Allies would declare that the war was an incalculable abomination, but out of a superior sense of justice, the Allies would not prosecute anyone.

The let-off is evident in Lansing's harkening back to proclamations of moral blame. "But the authors of this atrocious war ought not to pass unscathed into history."[269]

What does he propose as the right retribution for the culprits? "They should be summoned before the bar of universal public opinion," he wrote, "to listen to the verdict which mankind passes upon the perpetrators of this greatest crime against the world."[270]

"Therefore," came the flourish in the manner of a holy man performing an exorcism, "in the name of those who sacrificed their lives that liberty might live, in the name of the helpless who endured unspeakable atrocities, in the name of those whose ruined and plundered lands bear witness to the wickedness of the accused, in the name of humanity, of righteousness and of civilisation, an outraged world denounces as infamous and demands the judgment of the ages against Wilhelm of Hohenzollern, once German Emperor and King of Prussia, &c, &c, &c."[271]

But all that was only the top layer of the sandwich. After it came the middle layer. To all intents and purposes, it was the stale meat of immunity that Lansing tried so hard to serve to Sub-commission III. But everyone rejected it then.

With Pollock, his old nemesis, away from the proceedings, Lansing must have found the atmosphere in the room less belligerent to his old arguments.

Lansing's strategy was to propose a text in the report, which would effectively acknowledge that the kaiser enjoyed immunity in international law.

His proposed text would forgo prosecution of the kaiser, "In view of the official and personal influence which the ex-Kaiser possessed and exercised upon the course and conduct of the war, and in view of the immunity from suit and prosecution which a Monarch and Chief of State enjoys according to the municipal law of every civilised country and also according to the Common Law of Nations."[272]

As Lansing saw it, the acknowledgment of immunity was the price to pay for the bottom layer of the sandwich. That bottom layer was a proposal of a commission of inquiry, but with no power to impose punishment. As he presented it, "and lest because of this immunity from judicial process, the ex-Kaiser escape the condemnation which his misdeeds require, the third sub-commission recommends that, instead of attempting to hale the ex-Kaiser before a Court of Justice for which there is no precedent in the accepted Law of Nations, an International Commission of Inquiry be instituted to investigate and to report upon the extent of the responsibility of the ex-Kaiser from the political, legal, and moral point of view for the acts of the German authorities civil and military in violation of the laws and customs of war committed during the course of the war from the first day of August 1914 to the 11th day of November 1918 . . . in order that the public opinion of the world thus enlightened and instructed may anticipate the verdict of history and render the judgment of posterity."[273]

In the nature of things, it is reasonable to assume that the American delegation would have been "working"—or applying "gentle pressure" on—the other delegations, off the record of the proceedings, given the fervor with which Lansing and Scott had pressed their objections against creating an international tribunal and prosecuting the kaiser.

It would also be reasonable to assume that the French and the British Empire delegations would be doing the same in the opposite direction. That is part of the international lawmaking conferences.

It may be assumed that some delegations would have been torn between fidelity to their own position and conscience (which was to create the tribunal and prosecute the kaiser) on the one hand, and accommodating the preferences of the representatives of the United States, an emergent superpower who joined the war and helped end it. What followed Lansing's latest proposal, made in the absence of the indomitable Pollock, reveals this conflicted feeling.

In the absence of Pollock, it was now up to Massey, the non-lawyer, to hold the fort for the position of the British Empire that Pollock had championed robustly all along.

Massey did his best to object to Lansing's recycled proposal to recognize immunity.[274]

Larnaude spoke and expressed frustration with Lansing's latest arguments. As noted earlier, Lansing's latest proposal indicated an intention to abandon the right of prosecuting the kaiser. But the proposal predictably led to the rehashing of variations of the arguments already heard in the context of the proceedings of Sub-commission III.

Larnaude said that France did not accept the idea of abandoning the right to prosecute the kaiser. He explained that a distinction must be made between internal law (where the sovereign head may enjoy immunity in his own state) in contrast to international law (where sovereigns must bear criminal responsibility for violations as would foot soldiers).[275] He expressed astonishment to hear Lansing "advocate that the legal right of the [kaiser] is possibly that he is above the law."[276]

Speaking directly to Lansing's proposal for moral condemnation, Larnaude insisted that "Kings and Emperors are the heads of state, but it was never intended that they should be put above everything else except the risk of incurring moral condemnation."[277] This in effect was a reprising of Clemenceau's derision of moral condemnation during the Inter-Allied meeting in London in early December 1918. As Clemenceau sarcastically put it then, "All the Governments represented here today were proud of the principle of responsibility. As a rule, it only meant responsibility in newspaper articles and books, which the great criminals of the world could afford to laugh at."[278]

It may be enough to summarize Larnaude's reiteration of the responsibility of sovereigns by his observation that it was unacceptable to France "to see the Kaiser and his accomplices are simply taking walks in their golden exile and enjoying perfect immunity" after all the losses and untold suffering that had been inflicted upon France in the course of the war.[279]

All this he said en route to admitting, surprisingly, that he thought they were about to agree to an amendment to the report of Sub-commission III by deleting the phrase "including heads of state" from the much fraught paragraph IV(c) concerning the jurisdiction of the contemplated international tribunal. He indicated that they were doing so "under the gentle pressure exercised by the Delegate of the United States so as to be able to come to an agreement."[280] But, Larnaude expressed confidence that the phrase may safely be deleted because the meaning of the passage as a whole was not in doubt about prosecuting heads of state before international tribunals.[281]

In his turn, Politis began by considering that Lansing was effectively proposing "the principle of irresponsibility of heads of state," which would be "disastrous for law in general and international law in particular."[282]

The meeting adjourned.

Upon resumption on Thursday, 13 March 1919, for the commission's fourth meeting, Politis returned to complete his exposition. In direct contradiction of Lansing's theory that both internal law of civilized countries, as well as international law, recognized immunity of heads of state, Politis countered that the question of responsibility of heads of state does not rest on either internal law or international law.[283]

At the level of internal law, Politis explained, the matter was only a "practical expediency," adopted by the constitutions of various states as a "convenient form" that never prevented domestic systems from prosecuting their heads of state, when it suited them to do so.[284] Therefore, it was impossible to discern an "organic order" in the matter of prosecution of heads of state.[285]

Continuing, Politis observed that "as regards international law, there seems to be fewer obstacles still in the possibility of prosecuting the heads of state."[286] Here, it may be accepted that "immunity is a direct consequence of the independence and the sovereignty of the various states. The practical solution of it is that a country cannot bring for trial before a national tribunal a foreign potentate—a foreign sovereign."[287]

But the situation under consideration did not even contradict that "international practice." By that he meant the "practice" that states had accepted as part of international law. As of 1919, that practice was based on the principle of sovereign equality of states, expressed in the maxim *par in parem non habet imperium* (meaning, no equal may exercise jurisdiction over another). It was an established principle that had a different orientation and a different plane of operation. It operated at the national level, designed to prevent one sovereign power from claiming imperial authority over another.

But that principle did not prevent the creation of an international tribunal. Therefore, as the Macdonell Committee had concluded in their study of the British Empire—as also Larnaude and La Pradelle had concluded in their own study for the French government—Politis also now considered that the solution to trying a head of state lay with establishing an international tribunal.

"What we have to do," he said, to avoid conflict with international practice, "is to establish an international machinery, with the consent which may have to be imposed" upon the countries over whom reigned the head of state in question.[288]

That said, Politis declared that they were "all ready to take a new step towards conciliation by suppressing the words 'heads of state included,'"[289] feeling certain that the context of the entire passage made it unnecessary to refer specifically to heads of state. Recall that this was one of the main points of contention between Lansing (who had earlier pressed for that deletion on grounds that it was "superfluous") and Pollock (who insisted that it was not superfluous having been carefully inserted to leave no doubt at all that sovereigns are also subject to punishment when they are complicit in crimes of international law).

Given Politis's newfound willingness to delete the specific reference to "heads of state" (and here it must be recalled that Pollock was away from this particular debate), Lansing now unsurprisingly expressed much warmth for "Mr Politis's efforts to bring into harmony what seemed to be the very conflicting views of the delegates in the Commission" and for having "done so with very great adroitness."[290]

Larnaude intervened in the same "spirit of conciliation" that had always animated him, he said. He would concur in the proposal offered by Politis, provided that the proposal has the consequence that the American delegates would withdraw their remaining objections.[291]

Massey haltingly expressed evident discomfort with the amendment now being proposed, arguing that if it be unnecessary to specify heads of state, then it is harmless to leave it in.[292]

$\sim$

Farmer Bill Massey's point was indeed an astute one. Lansing had fought a sustained battle of wits to delete a phrase he thought was "superfluous."

Taking the opposite position, Pollock found the phrase not superfluous. To Pollock, the phrase was of immense value, and so much so that he would not approve a document that didn't have the phrase in it. In those circumstances, the equity of the debate must fall on Pollock's side, for whom the phrase was a deal breaker. It was not on Lansing's side, as his objection was that the phrase was merely superfluous.

The equity of the argument falls this way: if Lansing was right, then no harm would have been done in retaining the superfluous words. In the task of construing legal documents, one could always ignore words and phrases that are clearly superfluous. But if Lansing was wrong, then great harm would have been done in deleting the words that were not superfluous after all.

It is a different matter of course, if Lansing's real objection was against the idea of prosecuting heads of state. And there are reasons to consider that as his real concern. Notable in that regard was his difficulty imagining a president of the United States on trial before an international criminal tribunal for an international crime committed by a subordinate. Also notable was his reliance on the U.S. Supreme Court decision in the *Schooner Exchange* case. It was a civil case where the Supreme Court decided in 1812 that the doctrine of sovereign equality of states prevented a U.S. federal court from adjudicating the suit of two Americans seeking to recover what they claimed was their vessel that Emperor Napoleon's naval forces had seized and converted into a French war ship.

But those considerations must then put a lie to Lansing's argument that the reference to "heads of state" was merely superfluous. That, of course, would present a different problem—one of false pretenses and hidden motives—to the basis upon which Politis and Larnaude eventually succumbed to the pressure to delete the reference: that being Lansing's insistence that the words were superfluous. Would they have agreed to the deletion if Lansing had been forthright in maintaining that his real motive for insisting on the deletion was his philosophical opposition to the idea of prosecuting heads of state before an international tribunal? Given Larnaude's and Politis's arguments before and after that heads of state are not immune from the jurisdiction of international criminal tribunals, it is evident that they might not have agreed to delete the reference to "heads of state" as persons to be included within the scope of jurisdiction of an international court.

Round Five: Non-Immunity "Expressly and Firmly" Restated

When the fifth meeting of the main commission convened at 11:00 a.m. on 14 March 1919, Lansing could not attend. He had gone to receive President Wilson whose arrival in Paris had been delayed. In the result, Scott was representing the American delegation alone. Politis took the chair.[293] Pollock remained absent.

With Massey as the only person now speaking against the deletion of the phrase "including heads of state,"[294] an amended text was put to the vote with the phrase deleted.[295] There were ten votes for the amendment, none against, with the United States abstaining.[296]

After the vote, Massey realized he, too, had voted for it. He said that he thought the voting was in relation to another word that had also been altered in the text. He explained that he was waiting for an opportunity to vote on the proposal to delete the phrase "including heads of state." He thus requested to have the words reinserted into the text. But he was told it was too late, as the voting had already taken place to delete the words. He was, however, allowed an opportunity to explain his vote and to record a vote against the amendment that had already passed.[297]

Upon further discussion later, Larnaude reassured Massey "expressly and firmly" that the deletion of the phrase "including heads of state" was not intended at all to recognize immunity for heads of state. Quite the contrary, Larnaude reassured Massey, the wording of the particular text "makes it clear that heads of state should be brought to trial."[298] Massey said that as long as that was clearly stated on the record, then he would be satisfied to leave things as they were.[299]

Then, Scott voted against the entire amendment.[300] His reason? Although the amendment to delete the phrase "including heads of state" was in accord with the position of the American delegation, there was a second amendment that was voted down—this was the proposal to delete criminal responsibility of a superior who omitted to prevent or suppress violations.[301] Consequently, the American delegation reserved their position in relation to that part of the report of the commission.[302]

Round Six: British Delegation on Progressive Development of International Law for Accountability of Heads of State

The seventh meeting of the commission, which began on Monday, 17 March 1919, was the sixth and final round of the saga concerning head-of-state immunity. Pollock stormed back into the fray.[303] He wasted no time in revisiting the essence of the resolution and amendment that Lansing proposed during the meeting of 12 March 1919 and how they under-scored the stark difference between Lansing's position (which was that international law had been cast as he found it in 1919 and could not be altered) and that of Pollock and his European colleagues (which was that international law could always be adjusted to meet the exigent needs and anxieties of the community that it serves).

Pollock made clear that the British Empire and the other Allies were engaged in the process of developing international law, through the oppor-tunity afforded by the Peace Conference. Pollock felt a special need "to call attention to the remarkable speech of M Politis on Thursday last."[304] Pol-lock was referring to the main commission's fourth meeting of Thursday, 13 March 1919, during which Politis had, among other things, observed that there was no rule of international law that would obstruct the creation of an international tribunal to try heads of state for international crimes.

With that as his springboard, Pollock then drove home the deter-mination of the Allies to develop international law in the direction being considered and debated all along in the proceedings of both Sub-commission III and now in the main Commission on Responsibilities.[305] What did he mean by "the law"? he asked. "Law is the settled practice which by evolution and development comes when a large body of opin-ion in a State, by Act of Parliament, or by the changes introduced from time to time, improves, alters and develops the law. Law is not some-thing incapable of development. The law in France, in the days of Louis XIV, is not the same as it is today. The law in the British Empire is not the same as it was in the days of Henry VIII. And we regard the occa-sion of the Peace Conference, with its association of, I think I am right in saying something like fifteen or sixteen countries—as an opportunity when these countries, in accord with the traditions and principles of law, may bring up to date the duties which now arise from the settled opinion of civilised States."[306]

The British Empire believed, Pollock continued, that "for the peace of the world, it is right we should bring to trial those who are responsible for such unconscionable breaches of the principles of humanity which have been committed." That was the "root difference between your views, Sir, and mine," Pollock addressed Lansing.[307]

With that, Pollock pivoted back to the matter of the phrase "includ-ing heads of state," which was deleted from paragraph IV(c) of the Sub-commission III report. He hinted delicately that the deletion had occurred while he was absent.

Insisting on the importance of the phrase to his delegation, he declared, "We could not allow, at the right time, when the *Comité de Redaction* brings up the report, we could not allow those words in Paragraph 'C' to remain as 'authorities or persons' or 'personalities' or whatever it is. We must include those words 'including the heads of state.' And for this reason. We have here a number of distinguished jurists sitting around the table—men of high position, not only in their own countries, but in the world at large, and they know quite well, if you want to use in drawing up a legal document, you want to use an expression— you ought to use an expression which is apt, and which will be understood by lawyers."[308]

Then he explained how a rule of statutory construction called the *ejusdem generis* rule may preclude heads of state from liability from the class of persons who may come within the term "authorities" as was the expression left following the amendment that deleted the phrase "including heads of state." *Ejusdem generis* rule is a rule of construction that limits a specific statutory provision to things or persons of the same kind or class as that which is clearly identified in the provision.

Pollock feared that the *ejusdem generis* rule might preclude sovereigns or heads of state from the applicable meaning of "authorities." The concern, as he explained it, arises because all authority derives from the sovereign or the head of state. That understanding could conceivably be construed as placing the sovereign or head of state above the class of persons clearly accepted as "authorities" who are ordinarily known to be subject to criminal responsibility.[309]

Thus, to leave out the words "head of state" when there was no difficulty in using the expression would, in Pollock's view, place him and the eminent jurists in the commission "in a position in which they might be derided in all countries, and by all lawyers." The derision might come in the manner of other lawyers asking the distinguished jurists in the room, "What do you mean? If you meant heads of state, you ought to have had the courage to say it. There was no necessity to use cryptic or different [he might have meant "diffident"] language on so simple a point."[310]

Following the inability of the delegates to close the remaining gap between the United States and the Allies, Lansing was finally constrained to declare failure.

"We have been labouring here for six weeks," Lansing said. "Everybody has endeavoured to find a formula that would harmonise irreconcilable differences. We have failed. Frankly, we have failed.

"The United States," he continued, "went as far as it could without surrendering what it considered fundamental principles. I am quite sure that every other member of the Commission has gone as far as he could to reach a common ground. I say we have failed. It is not a failure from lack of desire, or lack of effort. It is simply that our views no more mingle than oil and water. And I consider, therefore, that the wise course to pursue is for the Commission, at the present time, to vote on this report of the Third Commission. And that the United States dissent from Articles IV and V, and file a minority report on that subject."[311]

Following that declaration of failure by Lansing, Pollock then asked that the report of Sub-commission III be returned to the original state in which the Allies would have wanted it, since they had modified the report in ways that they did not like in hopes of securing the "adhesion of the United States." As those concessions did not persuade the United States to join the Allies, and the United States was going to file its dissenting report in any event, the right course, in the circumstances, would be for the report to be reverted to what it was before the latest spate of amendments, among which was the deletion of the phrase "including heads of state."[312]

Lansing agreed.[313]

In the ensuing vote in the main commission, on the adoption of the report of Sub-commission III, eight national delegations voted to adopt the report—with the phrase "including heads of state" reflected in section IV(c) regarding whom the international tribunal may try—while two (being the United States and Japan) voted against.[314]

The Final Report of the Commission on Responsibilities

A close study of the final report of the Commission on Responsibilities, with particular regard to violations of laws and customs of war, carries a strong impression of Sir Ernest Pollock's fingerprints. This was so not only as regards his membership in Sub-commission III's Comité de redaction (together with Scott, Larnaude, Politis, and D'Amelio) but also as regards his collaboration with Rolin-Jaequemyns (of Belgium) as the rapporteurs of the final report of the main Commission on Responsibilities.

Larnaude testified to the dominant role that Pollock played in the drafting. Larnaude rendered that testimony as he diplomatically but firmly proposed that Pollock should join Rolin–Jaequemyns (whom Lansing had proposed) as rapporteur.

"[W]e have the honour to approve the choice of the Reporter General as suggested by Mr Lansing. It is quite natural to choose the representative of the country that had suffered the most—the representative of Belgium," Larnaude began tactfully.

"But it is also right," he continued, "to state the main part of the work, especially the work accomplished by this Third-Committee [*sic*][315] has been done, thanks to the efforts of the British Delegation."

"I therefore beg," he firmly pressed, "that the name of Sir Ernest Pollock should be added to the name of M Rolin-Jaequemyns, and should be included in the final report. It would be simply an injustice—a crime not to, as the British Delegation has introduced a report so valuable and so full of ideas, it should also have the honour. I therefore think that M Rolin-Jaequemyns, for whom I have the greatest respect, will not think his merits are diminished by adding the other name—the name of the Solicitor-General, Sir Ernest Pollock."[316]

Both Rolin-Jaequemyns and Lansing concurred. Lansing took the opportunity to also add the name of D'Amelio as the third rapporteur, so that French, English, and Italian speakers are represented on the team of rapporteurs.[317]

⌒

Chapter I of the main commission's report dealt with responsibility of the authors of the war, in the sense of commencement of a war of aggression or *jus ad bellum*. In this regard, the commission found that not only did the Central Powers—i.e., Germany and its allies—commence a premeditated war of aggression, they had also deliberately worked to defeat all the reconciliatory proposals and repeated efforts of the Entente Powers to avoid war.[318]

Chapter II of the report was a catalog of violations of the laws and customs of war, *jus in bello*. The violations were grouped under the following thirty-two heads, mostly proscriptions in the Hague Conventions of 1907 regulations on the Laws and Customs of War on Land.[319] They were the following:

1. murders and massacres; systematic terrorism;
2. putting hostages to death;
3. torture of civilians;
4. deliberate starvation of civilians;
5. rape;
6. abduction of girls and women for the purpose of enforced prostitution;

7. deportation of civilians;
8. internment of civilians under inhuman conditions;
9. forced labor of civilians in connection with the military operations of the enemy;
10. usurpation of sovereignty during military occupation;
11. compulsory enlistment of soldiers among the inhabitants of occupied territory;
12. attempts to denationalize the inhabitants of occupied territory;
13. pillage;
14. confiscation of property;
15. exaction of illegitimate or of exorbitant contributions and requisitions;
16. debasement of the currency, and issue of spurious currency;
17. imposition of collective penalties;
18. wanton devastation and destruction of property;
19. deliberate bombardment of undefended places;
20. wanton destruction of religious, charitable, educational, and historic buildings and monuments;
21. destruction of merchant ships and passenger vessels without warning and without provision for the safety of passengers or crew;
22. destruction of fishing boats and of relief ships;
23. deliberate bombardment of hospitals;
24. attack on and destruction of hospital ships;
25. breach of other rules relating to the Red Cross;
26. use of deleterious and asphyxiating gases;
27. use of explosive or expanding bullets, and other inhuman appliances;
28. directions to give no quarter;
29. ill treatment of wounded and prisoners of war;
30. employment of prisoners of war on unauthorized works;
31. misuse of flags of truce; and
32. poisoning of wells.

Chapter III then dealt with immunity of heads of state, under the general theme of "personal responsibility" for those violations. Here, the report began by indicating that there were "grave charges" that must be investigated and prosecuted in a court against a number of persons.

In those circumstances, the commission desired to "state expressly that in the hierarchy of persons in authority *there is no reason why rank, however exalted, should in any circumstances protect the holder of it from responsibility* when that responsibility has been established before a properly constituted tribunal. *This extends even to the case of heads of state."*[320]

To make their meaning perfectly clear, the commission engaged the argument of head-of-state immunity. "An argument has been raised to the contrary based upon the alleged immunity, and in particular the alleged inviolability, of a Sovereign of a State," the report continued. "But this privilege, where it is recognised, is one of practical expedience in municipal law, and is not fundamental. However, even if, in some countries, a Sovereign is exempt from being prosecuted in a national court of his own country the position from an international point of view is quite different."[321]

That text was obviously inspired by the argument made by Politis to that effect on 12 March 1919, which had much impressed Pollock. So, too, the following further passage of the report: "We have later on in our Report proposed the establishment of a High Tribunal composed of judges drawn from many nations, and included the possibility of the trial before that Tribunal of a former Head of a State with the consent of that State itself secured by articles in the Treaty of Peace. If the immunity of a Sovereign is claimed to extend beyond the limits above stated, it would involve laying down the principle that the greatest outrages against the laws and customs of war and the laws of humanity, if proved against him, could in no circumstances be punished. Such a conclusion would shock the conscience of civilized mankind."[322]

Continuing on that note, the report considered along the same lines as both the Macdonell report and the Larnaude–La Pradelle study had done, "In view of the grave charges which may be preferred against—to take one case—the ex-Kaiser, the vindication of the principles of the laws and customs of war and the laws of humanity which have been violated would be incomplete if he were not brought to trial and if other offenders less highly placed were punished. Moreover, the trial of the offenders might be seriously prejudiced if they attempted and were able to plead the superior orders of a Sovereign against whom no steps had been or were being taken."[323]

In conclusion, said the report, "All persons belonging to enemy countries, without distinction of rank, including Chiefs of States, who have been guilty of offences against the laws and customs of war or the laws of humanity, are liable to criminal prosecution."[324]

In chapter IV of the report, the commission dealt with the question of "constitution and procedure of an appropriate Tribunal." Their recommendation in this part concerns both violations in the orders of *jus ad bellum* (starting a war of aggression) and *jus in bello* (violations committed in the course of the war or violations of the laws and customs of war). Regarding the prosecution for violations of *jus ad bellum*, the commission concluded that there should be no charges brought for *starting* the war. The rationale for this was that the proceedings would be too drawn out and may even prove embarrassing for many of the governments whose states had fought against Germany.* Indeed, the kaiser himself had intimated that much embarrassing information might be unearthed in the archives of the governments of many of those states.† In that connection, the commission merely proposed the following: "It is desirable that for the future penal sanctions should be provided for such grave outrages against the elementary principles of international law."[325]

But as regards "violations of the laws and customs of war and of the laws of humanity" (*jus in bello*), the commission proposed that prosecutions should be undertaken in both national courts and in an international tribunal.

In relation to national prosecutions, the report acknowledged what was an accepted understanding in international law: "Every belligerent has, according to international law, the power and authority to try the individuals alleged to be guilty of the crimes of which an enumeration has been given in Chapter II on violations of the laws and customs of war, if such persons have been taken prisoners or have otherwise fallen into its power. Each belligerent has, or has the power to set up, pursuant to its own legislation, an appropriate tribunal, military or civil, for the trial of such cases. These courts would be able to try the incriminated persons according to their own procedure, and much complication and consequent delay would be avoided which would arise if all such cases were to be brought before a single tribunal."[326]

This is an early acknowledgment of a practice that seems to elude many jurists of the modern era, regarding the jurisdiction of courts to prosecute

---

* As it was put in the Macdonell Committee report: "to the inclusion of this charge there are several objections, not the least important of which is the fact that it might involve a prolonged examination of the whole political situation, the political difficulties and controversies preceding August 4th, 1914, and, indeed, the entire political history of Europe for some years before that date. It might be difficult to set limits to such enquiries, and the effect of entering upon it might be to distract attention from the grave and much more precise charges." Regardless of that objection, the Committee voted by a narrow majority (4–3) to include the charge. See "First Interim Report Presented to Sir Frederick E. Smith, KC, His Majesty's Attorney General," 97.

† As Kaiser Wilhelm II was later to observe in his memoirs, "[N]o tribunal in the world can pronounce a just sentence before the state archives of all the nations participating in the war are thrown open, as has been done, and is still being done, by Germany. Who, after the unprecedented judgment of Versailles, could still summon up optimism enough to believe that the Entente nations would place their secret documents at the disposal of such a tribunal?" Wilhelm II, *The Kaiser's Memoirs—Wilhelm II, Emperor of Germany 1888–1918*, trans. Thomas R. Ybarra (New York: Harper, 1922), 294.

officials of foreign states. This blind spot is particularly implicated in the positions of those opposed to draft article 7 of the International Law Commission's proposed draft articles on Immunities of State Officials from Foreign Criminal Jurisdictions. The draft article identifies certain international crimes—including war crimes—as conducts in relation to which officials of states enjoy no immunity from the criminal jurisdictions of one another.

Beyond the jurisdiction of national courts to try foreign soldiers, the report of the Commission on Responsibilities continued to contemplate trial before an international tribunal. In that regard, the report observed that there remained "a number of charges . . . (c) Against all authorities, civil or military, belonging to enemy countries, *however high their positions* may have been *including the heads of state*, who ordered, or, with knowledge thereof and with power to intervene, abstained from preventing or taking measures to prevent, putting an end to or repressing, violations of the laws or customs of war (it being understood that no such abstention should constitute a defence for the actual perpetrators)." For persons belonging to that category—in addition to two other categories—the report considered that "a High Tribunal is essential and should be established."[327]

A Review of the Memorandum of the U.S. Commissioners

The American and Japanese delegations filed memoranda of reservations that were appended to the report as Annexes II and III. The memorandum of the U.S. commissioners—that being Lansing and Scott—reprised the objections they made in the course of the deliberations of the Commission on Responsibilities and its Sub-commission III, against creating an international tribunal and trying the kaiser. The U.S. commissioners insisted that the only trials that might be conducted should be limited to trial of suspect soldiers of the Central Powers before the national courts of Entente States. Beyond that, "moral sanctions only"—not criminal prosecution—was permissible at the international stage, "however iniquitous and infamous and however terrible" the conduct in question.[328]

In their memorandum, Lansing and Scott noted that the Entente commissioners had recognized the wisdom of this approach in relation to responsibility for starting a war of aggression (*jus ad bellum*), but they refused to extend the same forbearance to responsibility for violations of laws and customs of war (*jus in bello*).

Lansing and Scott imputed motives for what they saw as inconsistency. As they put it, "this inconsistency was due in large measure to a determination to punish certain persons, high in authority, particularly the heads of enemy states, even though heads of state were not hitherto legally responsible for the atrocious acts committed by subordinate authorities."[329]

The imputation of motives, rooted in complaining against the Allied commissioners' "determination to punish" even heads of state, was curious. First, because the Allied commissioners had clearly expressed their concern that prosecution for a war of aggression would involve a sprawling litigation that would drag out the proceedings and take them to unknown directions. Also because the Allied commissioners never hid their determination to prosecute the kaiser. But that determination presents no contradiction with giving up litigation on the *jus ad bellum* angles (with which the American commissioners agreed) while insisting upon prosecution for *jus in bello* violations. This is because a determination to punish is an omnibus idea that can accommodate prosecuting certain crimes while not prosecuting others implicated in the same transaction. In the administration of national criminal justice, prosecutors make that discretionary call all the time. In other words, the "determination to punish" would comfortably motivate a determination to prosecute the *jus in bello* violations, even though a decision was made to drop the case of *jus ad bellum* violations.

Lansing and Scott restated their objection against the reference to "laws of humanity" or "principles of humanity" employed in the commission report as a companion phrase to "laws and customs of war;"[330] the Allies' determination to prosecute the kaiser—abjuring immunity—which Lansing and Scott considered as available in international law;[331] and that to subordinate a head of state to prosecution before an international tribunal (rather than leaving him or her answerable to his or her national forum) was to "den[y] the very conception of sovereignty."[332]

Lansing and Scott agreed, however, with the commission's majority that "'every belligerent has, according to international law, the power and authority to try the individuals alleged to be guilty of the crimes' constituting violations of the laws and customs of war, 'if such persons have been taken prisoners or have otherwise fallen into its power.' The American representatives are likewise in thorough accord with the further provisions that 'each belligerent has, or has power to set up, pursuant to its own legislation, an appropriate tribunal, military or civil, for the trial of such cases.' The American representatives concur in the view that 'these courts would be able to try the incriminated persons according to their own procedure.'"[333]

Indeed, Lansing and Scott accepted that "in case of acts violating the laws and customs of war involving more than one country, the military tribunals of the countries affected may be united, thus forming an international tribunal for the trial and punishment of persons charged with the commission of such offence."[334] Lansing and Scott "believed that the nations should use the machinery at hand, which had been tried and found competent, with a law and a procedure framed and therefore known in advance, rather than to create an international tribunal with a criminal jurisdiction for which there is no precedent, precept, practice, or procedure."[335]

In the light of these admissions, Lansing's and Scott's objection (about which they "felt very strongly"[336]) against creating an international tribunal of the kind contemplated by the Allies, because there was no precedent for it in international law, becomes surprising in light of the Americans' insistence that only the states concerned may be eligible to administer justice in such situations.

The objection was surprising because of the pedantry of the distinction between, on the one hand, the Allies creating an international tribunal at large (to which Lansing and Scott objected) and, on the other hand, the Allies who suffered harm uniting their military tribunals to form "an international tribunal" (which Lansing and Scott recommend).

It is true that the difference between the two scenarios would be that the membership of the former tribunal (which Lansing and Scott rejected as an idea) would be open to judges whose states might not have been affected by the violations, in terms of the territoriality of the incidents or the nationality of the victims. Whereas the membership of the latter tribunal (which Lansing and Scott propose) would exclusively consist of judges from the affected states.

But one would have thought that such a difference between the two arrangements must involve the enhanced element of impartiality of the former kind of tribunal (which Lansing and Scott rejected), as Politis had argued during the deliberations of Sub-commission III. The psychological appeal of that element of impartiality should have overcome the need for Lansing and Scott to object against the tribunal's creation. After all, as noted earlier, Lansing had specifically advised Wilson to ensure that any court of justice to be created as an organ of the League of Nations must be composed of judges who come from states not implicated in the transaction that was the subject matter of the dispute under adjudication. It is not easy to see why neutrality would be a valued feature in an international court of justice forming part of the League of Nations yet a disadvantage for an international criminal tribunal that the Allies were proposing to try the kaiser.

Needless to say, the administration of modern international criminal justice has put Lansing and Scott on the wrong side of history. Many international criminal tribunals—such as the International Criminal Court, the International Criminal Tribunal for Rwanda, the International Criminal Tribunal for the former Yugoslavia, and the Special Court for Sierra Leone—have been established in arrangements that contemplate at least the predominate membership of judges who come from states that were not affected by the conflict in question.

As regards the rule against retrospective law and the absence of precedent, it should be noted that the sole authority upon which Lansing and Scott rested their strong objection against the creation of an international criminal court that would try the kaiser was the U.S. Supreme Court judgment in *U.S. v. Hudson.* From that judgment, Lansing and Scott quoted the following dictum in support of their objection: "the legislative authority of the Union must first make an act a crime, affix a punishment to it, and declare the court that shall have jurisdiction of the offence."[337]

Hence, argued Lansing and Scott, "The American representatives know of no international statute or convention making a violation of the laws and customs of war—not to speak of the laws or principles of humanity—an international crime, affixing a punishment to it, and declaring the court which has jurisdiction over the offence."[338]

But the *Hudson* case was inapposite. Let us take a closer look and see why. It involved an attempt to bring sedition charges, in the U.S. Federal Court, against the defendants who had published an allegation in a Connecticut newspaper—the *Currant*—claiming that the U.S. president and Congress had secretly gifted $2 million to Napoleon Bonaparte for leave to enter into a treaty with Spain. The question for determination was whether the U.S. *federal court* had jurisdiction to hear the case as a common law crime of sedition against the sovereign. The U.S. Supreme Court said no. The important thing to keep in mind for now is that the U.S. *federal court* is not the only jurisdiction that can exercise criminal jurisdiction in the United States. In fact, *superior courts of the states* were exercising criminal jurisdiction (including common law criminal jurisdiction) in the United States, in their capacity as *common law* courts, before the federal court system was created under the Judiciary Act of 1789. That nuance is vital in a proper understanding of the *Hudson* case.

For present purposes, it is not necessary to dwell on the relative dis-similarities between the facts of that case (denigration of the sovereign in a manner likely to invite popular opprobrium) versus the egregious violations of laws and customs of war during World War I. It is enough that Lansing's and Scott's invocation of the dictum quoted above offers an unfortunate misunderstanding of what was decided in *Hudson*.

For one thing, Lansing and Scott gave the impression that the case stands for the proposition that no court may try a criminal case if the crime charged had not been written down ahead of time in a penal statute (*nullum crimen sine lege*). That is wrong. The Supreme Court did recognize expressly that state courts in the United States could have jurisdiction for common law crimes. A defining feature of "common law crimes" was that they were typically not written down in a penal statute; they had rather been distilled from the judicial pronouncements of superior courts in Eng-land from immemorial customs that the people accepted as law.

The Supreme Court's point was rather that jurisdiction of that kind might only be exercised by *state courts*, which are descendants of superior courts of England. Common law jurisdiction may not be exercised by *federal courts*, because federal courts are creatures of federal legislation. As such, federal courts derive their jurisdiction not from common law but from the statute that gave them that jurisdiction. That is to say, no federal statute gave the federal courts jurisdiction to try any one for crime of sedi-tion against the sovereign. So, the federal court could not exercise that jurisdiction. Hence, the defendants could not be tried in the federal court for a charge framed in those terms, though the crime might be a common law crime.

And that brings us to the second mistaken impression left by Lansing and Scott, in light of the dictum they quoted from *Hudson*. That dictum was made in the context of the Supreme Court's reasoning on the constitutional question presented in the case, involving distribution of powers within the U.S. federal system. In that arrangement, the powers of the federal gov-ernment (comprising the president, the U.S. Congress, and U.S. federal courts) "are made up of concessions from the several states—whatever is not expressly given to the former, the latter expressly reserve. The judicial power of the United States [i.e., the federal government] is a constituent part of those concessions—that power is to be exercised by courts organized for the purpose, and brought into existence by an effort of the legislative power of the Union."[339] Thus, with the exception of the U.S. Supreme Court that derives its authority directly from the Constitution, all other courts created by the federal government "possess no jurisdiction but what is given them by the power that creates them, and can be vested with none but what the power ceded to the [federal government] will authorize them to confer."[340] It is against that background that the Supreme Court pronounced that the "legislative authority of the Union,"[341] meaning the U.S. Congress, "must first make an act a crime, affix a punishment to it, and declare the court that shall have jurisdiction of the offence."[342]

In that sense, *Hudson* is not truly a general authority for *nullum crimen sine lege*, than it is a requirement that a federal court cannot exercise jurisdiction that the Constitution has reserved to the state courts. Lansing and Scott were mistaken in relying on it. Pollock, on the other hand, was correct in reminding Lansing that, in England, superior courts have jurisdiction over common law crimes[343]—as no doubt do U.S. state courts, as one could deduce from *Hudson*.

Indeed, at the time Lansing and Scott were making their objection on the basis of *Hudson*, there was an earlier judicial precedent, *Respublica v. De Longchamps*, from the U.S. Supreme Court, sitting per Oyer and Terminer in Philadelphia. The case involved an assault upon a diplomat. In its judgment, the court recognized the jurisdiction of the courts of Pennsylvania to punish violations of the law of nations, which is part of the *common law* of that state that applied without prior statutory proscription of the impugned conduct as a domestic crime.[344] According to the Supreme Court, the law of nations so violated "in its full extent, is part of the law of this State, and is to be collected from the practice of different Nations, and the authority of writers."[345]

A further evolution that put the Allied commissioners on the sounder side of history, to the detriment of Lansing and Scott, is the imposition of criminal responsibility on superiors who fail to prevent or suppress international crimes that they knew, or ought to have known, that their subordinates were committing or about to commit.[346] This was one of the objections pressed by Lansing and Scott in their memorandum of objection.[347]

For their own part, the Japanese delegation attached as Annex III a brief memorandum of reservations, generally shadowing in a short outline essentially the same reservations that Lansing and Scott had laid out in detail.[348]

The Final Decision of the Council of Four on the Kaiser's Trial

The final report of the Commission on Responsibilities was presented to the Preliminary Peace Conference on Saturday, 29 March 1919.[349]

Three days later, on Tuesday, 1 April 1919, Lloyd George prompted the Peace Conference's steering authority, the Council of Four (also known as "The Big Four") to discuss the report. The prompt came toward the end of a meeting during which many other difficult items of the broader Peace Conference had been discussed.

"We also have the report on the question of responsibilities that we could consider here," Lloyd George began. A quick repartee with Wilson followed, showing Wilson's initial hesitation about trying the kaiser. After all, Wilson's secretary of state, Robert Lansing, had been intransigently opposed to the idea of trying the kaiser. As will be seen in a cover note dated 4 April 1919, with which Lansing submitted the U.S. commissioners' memorandum of reservations to Wilson for approval, Lansing indicated that he had discussed with Wilson "some days ago" the "attitude which we had taken on the Commission on Responsibilities" and that Wilson had "approved of it." Lansing "pursued the same policy to the end and the memorandum is the result."[350]

It was thus unsurprising that once Lloyd George prompted the discussion of the report of the Commission on Responsibilities, Wilson had been primed with an initial position.

"I have a word to say on this subject," said Wilson. "Charles I was a contemptible character and the greatest liar in history; he was celebrated by poetry and transformed into a martyr by his execution. The same for Mary Stuart, whose career was not in the least exemplary."

"Concerning Mary Stuart," Lloyd George retorted, "the poetry could be explained otherwise: she was a very seductive woman."

"Napoleon who—by different methods, I concede—tried, exactly like the German Emperor, to impose his domination upon the world, was surrounded by legend because of his captivity at Saint Helena," Wilson countered.

"It wasn't only Saint Helena that created the Napoleonic legend," shot back Lloyd George. "I would like to see the man responsible for the greatest crime in history to be punished for it."[351]

"He has drawn universal contempt upon himself," Wilson said, bringing the conversation back to the kaiser. "Isn't that the worst punishment for a man like him?"[352]

With those preliminary exchanges about the report, the Council of Four adjourned the matter for the day, which was to be taken up more intensely in at least two further meetings.

∽

The Council of Four's meeting at 4:00 p.m. on 2 April 1919 opened with a preliminary matter of agreeing to the text of a telegram to be sent to Poland's minister of foreign affairs about the need for Poland and Ukraine to agree to a truce between them regarding Eastern Galicia, pending the discussion of an armistice under the auspices of the Paris Peace Conference.[353]

After that, Lloyd George launched straight back into the discussion of the report of the Commission on Responsibilities. "I would like to discuss the question of responsibilities with you," he began.

"Our commission declared itself against bringing to trial those who are in different degrees responsible for the declaration of war," he said. "Personally, I regret this decision, but I accept it."

Alluding to why accountability of sovereigns for wars of aggression would be a deterrent against such wars in future, Lloyd George continued, "In my opinion, if we could hold the high and mighty men who unleashed such a scourge—the greatest of all—responsible for this greatest of all crimes, there would be less danger of war in future."[354]

And then, Lloyd George turned the discussion in the direction of violations of laws and customs of war, prosecution for which a majority of the commission had recommended.

"On the other hand," he said, "responsibility has been admitted for the violation of treaties which caused death of millions of men. The same for acts against individuals, atrocities of all sorts committed under orders, the kidnapping of girls for forced prostitution, the destruction of ships on the high seas by submarines, leaving ships' crews in boats hundreds of miles from shore. In the text of the treaty, we will demand that the enemy acknowledge our right to judge these crimes and promise to deliver the culprits to us. We must also have the right to demand the production of all German documents which would be necessary for the tribunal's use. Finally, the commission proposes the establishment of a court of justice in which all the belligerent nations, great and small, would be represented, and which would pronounce judgments."[355]

Given the context of the discussion, being an informal gathering of the heads of government of the four leading nations, there would be occasional imprecision in the use of language. For instance, there was no evidence at this stage that the Central Powers had "admitted" any wrongdoing, given the occurrence of the word in Lloyd George's introduction of that agenda item. He must be taken, in the context, to be referring to the Commission on Responsibilities. This is in the sense that they had *accepted*—and recommended—the idea of prosecution for violation of laws and customs of war, notwithstanding their recommendation against prosecution for the war of aggression.

Following Lloyd George's introduction of the topic, Wilson spoke next, doing his best to start on the positive note of common grounds between the majority of the Allied commissioners and their American colleagues.

"You know that the representatives of the United States signed a minority report," he began. "I believe certain recent proposals, such as the one renouncing prosecution of authors of the war, bring them a little closer to your advisers than before."[356]

On a certain view, Wilson was correct in noting that the advisors of both the French and the British governments had earlier advocated prosecution for not only war crimes but also the crime of aggression—before the Peace Conference. Notably, in the report to the British government, members of the Macdonell Committee had (albeit by a very narrow 4:3 margin) also recommended prosecuting the kaiser for starting the war, in addition to a unanimous agreement to prosecute him for war crimes.[357] Larnaude and La Pradelle, in their study conducted for the French government, had also essentially recommended prosecuting the kaiser for starting the war.[358]

But Wilson was careful not to overstate the common ground. The agreement of the commissioners against the aggression crime prosecution did no more than bring the two sides only "a little closer." Beyond that, there remained a huge gulf of entrenched positions between the U.S. commissioners and their Allied counterparts on the matter of prosecution for war crimes.

The task of the Council of Four, at the stage, was to try at their level to bridge that gulf. To their credit, they ultimately did, following a period of intense deliberations that culminated in Wilson himself drafting the initial text of article 227 of the Versailles Treaty that called for the prosecution of the kaiser, despite Lansing's best efforts to dissuade Wilson from that outcome.

The story of how Wilson and his colleagues on the Council of Four closed that gulf and settled the terms of article 227 is told in the next chapter of this book. It is enough for now to capture a notable effort on Lansing's part to encourage Wilson to oppose the idea of prosecuting the kaiser.

In that regard, Lansing submitted his memorandum of reservations to Wilson for approval under cover of a note dated 4 April 1919, the text of which is reproduced here:[359]

THE SECRETARY OF STATE
OF THE UNITED STATES
OF AMERICA

Hotel de Crillon, PARIS
April 4, 1919

My dear Mr. President:

I regret very much to ask you to examine so long a document as the memorandum of reservations by the United States to the report of the Commission on Responsibilities, but as the matter is one of high policy I think that it should have your entire approval before it is filed.

You will recall that some days ago at a meeting of the Commissioners in my office I told you of the attitude which we had taken on the Commission on Responsibilities and that you approved of it. We pursued the same policy to the end and the memorandum is the result.

It is unfortunate that it could not be abbreviated, but in view of the points made in the Commission's report and the popular favor with which it will be received we could not do otherwise than explain fully the reasons for our objections to it.

The British and French were simply determined that the Kaiser should be tried by a high tribunal, the former because of promises on the hustings, the latter because the French members of the Commission had previously written a monograph in favor of his trial and punishment (done, I am informed, at Clemenceau's instigation).

Popular sentiment in the United States, as far as I can judge from letters and newspapers, is in sympathy with the judicial trial and punishment of the Kaiser. There is general clamor for vengeance and for physical punishment regardless of legal right or the fundamental principles of jurisprudence. The memorandum of the United States enclosed with the Report of the Commission will probably excite in America and elsewhere severe criticism, but I have felt that to take any other attitude than the one taken would be to advocate international "Lynch law."

The Commission's Secretariat asked for the memorandum yesterday evening in order that it might be printed so that the report could be filed by Monday noon next with the General Secretariat. This I could not do, as I felt that you should read and approve the memorandum before the United States was committed to it.

In view of this I hope that you can return the memorandum to me at the earliest possible moment with such changes and suggestions as you may see fit to make. My regret is that I feel compelled to burden you at this time with this paper and to ask for its immediate consideration.

Faithfully yours
[signed, Robert Lansing]

Enclosure:

Lansing's note to Wilson reveals much that is interesting about Lansing's attitude and motivation. For one thing, it is unclear as to the point at which he had received Wilson's approval to press the objections that he and Scott had pressed in the deliberations of the Commission on Responsibilities and Sub-commission III. In that regard, the note to Wilson only asserts that "some days ago" at a meeting in Lansing's office in Paris, "that [Lansing] told [Wilson]" of the attitude that Lansing and Scott "had taken" on the Commission on Responsibilities "and that [Wilson] approved of it." What is not clear from the letter or from available research is whether Lansing had fully given Wilson *advance* briefing as to the position that Lansing and Scott were going to take before they took those positions, or whether Wilson was only briefed *after* Lansing had already embarked upon that course at the commission. In other words, did they bring Wilson along, before they started pressing their objections at the deliberations of the commission, or did they try and bring Wilson along only after they started pressing their objections, thus presenting him with a fait accompli?

More important, perhaps, is that the letter does not suggest that Lansing's position during the deliberations of the Commission on Responsibilities and its Sub-commission III had a similar background of in-depth study and reflection that the British and the French positions notably had.

It is instructive that, in light of a popular clamor in the United Kingdom, France, the United States, and around the world for the trial of the kaiser, the British and the French governments commissioned their eminent jurists to study the legal feasibility and desirability of such a trial. The Macdonell Committee, which undertook the British study, comprised some of the most distinguished jurists in their country.

That familiarity breeds contempt is a fact of life. It may be understandable, then, that the familiarity of working with Larnaude and La Pradelle in a commission and subcommission that Lansing presided over might have taken the mystique out of the study that Larnaude and La Pradelle wrote for the French government. But Larnaude and La Pradelle had collaborated with some of their fellow professors at the Paris University Law Faculty in producing that study.

There is no record of a similar study done ahead of time, in support of the position that Lansing and Scott took. The only record of the American position was the dogged objection of Lansing and Scott during the deliberations of the commission and subcommission and elsewhere, based merely on their personal predispositions* and opinions on the law. Often, those opinions and predispositions were driven by assumptions and arguments that were always readily rebuttable, as has already been seen.

Lansing's note of 4 April 1919 to Wilson reveals more assumptions and arguments that were simplistic. One of them is the imputation of motives for the British and the French positions. As Lansing put it in the letter, the British position resulted from "promises on the hustings." This was a long-standing view on his part. Notably, during a meeting of the American delegates on 5 March 1919 when White, Colonel House, and Herter were present, Lansing expressed his "opinion that the British Delegates were not very sincere in their desire to try the Kaiser etc., but merely felt that they had to urge this measure because of a political pledge."[360]

Similarly, in his note of 4 April, he also denigrated the French position as having resulted from a monograph written by Dean Larnaude and Professor La Pradelle at Clemenceau's "instigation." That is to say, Dean Larnaude and Professor La Pradelle might not have exercised their academic or intellectual independence; according to Lansing, they could only be seen as having Clemenceau put them up to it.

Perhaps worse was the dismissal of the British position as resulting from electoral campaigns of the mid-December 1918 election. Lansing does not indicate in the note that he was aware—if he was, he did not bother to acknowledge—that a body of eminent British jurists (the Macdonell Committee) had conducted the study that informed the legal position of the British position.

---

* Notably in a meeting of the U.S. delegates on 4 March 1919, Lansing informed his colleagues (Ambassador Henry White, General Tasker H. Bliss, and Christian A. Herter) of what was transpiring in Sub-commission III, regarding the determination of the British and French to try the kaiser before an international tribunal. "He explained that he was in rather an uncomfortable position in this matter as he stood alone against the other representatives on the Commission against having the Kaiser tried by a tribunal. He was willing to have a court of inquiry pass upon the case, but was not willing to let it go further. General Bliss and Mr. White agreed that a court of inquiry might in this connection bring out some useful information in regard to the obscure beginnings of the war, but that the actual trial of the Kaiser could not take place before a tribunal." See U.S. Department of State, *Papers Relating to the Foreign Relations of the United States 1919: The Paris Peace Conference, 1919*, 11:92.

And finally, Lansing registered the exaggerated claim that the British and the French insistence upon creating an international tribunal before whom the kaiser must be tried was akin to an "international lynch law." It was an unnecessary caricature, of course.

More than that, the derision did not accurately reflect the fact that he had acknowledged during the debates in the Commission on Responsibilities and Sub-commission III that violations of laws and customs of war would be punishable within the domestic legal systems of most states, implicating a general principle of law recognized by modern nations. The only thing that was truly new was to promote that norm to the international stage, particularly through the creation of an international tribunal to try the cases as a joint effort of states.

Here again, we see how developments during our own time retroactively belie the objection of Lansing and Scott on the point. Indeed, many a modern international criminal tribunal was established and given jurisdiction to prosecute conducts recognized as international crimes, only after an episodic event during which those international crimes were committed. This was the case with the international criminal tribunals for the former Yugoslavia, for Rwanda, and for Sierra Leone.

THE LEGISLATIVE SCOPE   6
OF ARTICLE 227

Professor William Schabas—a cherished friend of mine—is an eminent jurist with an impressive record of important publications, including the excellent book *Trial of the Kaiser*. For that book, the world of scholarship owes him a great debt of gratitude for his labor of mining, summarizing, and distilling into a contemporary and readily available volume disparate primary historical documents on the Paris Peace Conference that are buried deep in government archives and other places that are not easily accessible to the average person.

As to certain aspects of Schabas's subjective interpretation of those documents, however, it is possible to see things differently. Professor Claus Kreß of the University of Cologne, another eminent international criminal law scholar, correctly did just that in relation to the following opinion from Schabas: "[J]udges at the International Criminal Court have cited the Commission's Report to support arguments that Heads of State have no immunity before international tribunals. This is surely overstating things."[1]

As reasons for this demurrer, Schabas immediately points to "the importance of the dissenting views and the total neglect of the Report by the real lawmakers, the Council of Four."[2] In disagreeing with Schabas and insisting that the International Criminal Court (ICC) judges were right in identifying article 227 as original repudiation of immunity in international criminal law, Kreß recalled, first, that Robert Lansing and James Brown Scott (the American representatives on Sub-commission III) did not dissent at all as to the unavailability of immunity *ratione materiae*. Without diving too deep into the pool of legal arcana, immunity *ratione materiae* generally refers to the immunity that the official of one state might enjoy in another state for acts performed on behalf of his or her state in that official capacity. The other kind of immunity that is usually mentioned, also in favored Latin, is immunity *ratione personae*. This refers to immunity that a limited number of officials enjoy in their personal capacity: people like heads of state, ministers of foreign affairs, and diplomats (and members of the diplomatic household) while the diplomat is at his or her designated duty station.

Kreß's allusion here is to the fact that Lansing and Scott had conceded that their considerations of immunity—based on the 1812 judgment of the United States Supreme Court in the case of the *Schooner Exchange*,[3] the usual authority for the proposition that sovereigns are presumptively exempt from the jurisdictions of one another—"do not apply to a head of a state who has abdicated or has been repudiated by his people."[4] Though their dissent[5] rested more strongly on the grounds of their understanding of the rule against retroactivity[6] and criminal omission.[7] Similarly, Lansing and Scott also never objected to the institution of national war crimes proceedings. Quite the contrary, they saw it as an appropriate recourse, as envisaged by article 228 of the Versailles Treaty.[8] Furthermore, that Lansing and Scott registered a dissent on behalf of the United States, in Subcommission III, on grounds of immunity *ratione personae* of the ex-kaiser cannot override the fact that the representatives of France and the United Kingdom made no distinction at all between the two kinds of immunity as they led the majority of the subcommission in rejecting immunity.[9]

Indeed, to Kreß's response to Schabas the following may be added. First, assuming even that Lansing's and Scott's immunity objections were not in the end erased by their own president as was the case, Schabas's demurrer still implied a highly doubtful proposition in the process of decision-making. It would stand for the hypothesis that the principle of majority must be ignored when a decision is arrived at by vote following a failure of consensus. Very narrow majorities have carried the day in all manner of decision-making—from judicial decisions to national elections to referendums. In contrast, the majority decision that rejected immunity in Sub-commission III was not slim. It was a majority of 8:2 (counting by countries).[10] In other words, an overwhelming majority of 80 percent rejected immunity—including immunity for heads of state. In so repudiating immunity, no distinction was made between immunity *ratione personae* and *ratione materiae*.

In offering his demurrer, Professor Schabas did not identify an accepted rule of law that required ICC judges to ignore the 8:2 majority outcome as an event to be taken into account in judicial reasoning.

Indeed, at the very same Paris Peace Conference, there had been at least two other instances where a matter of interest to the Americans was resolved by a vote. One was on Woodrow Wilson's own motion for Geneva to be the seat of the League of Nations, which was adopted by a majority vote.[11] Perhaps even more significant was that Wilson's proposal to mention the Monroe Doctrine (a cherished American foreign policy doctrine) in the Covenant of the League of Nations[12] was adopted by a bare majority of one vote.[13]

The one baffling story that came out of the same Paris Peace Conference concerned Japan's proposal that a racial equality clause (or an appropriate formulation that would accommodate the idea) should be inserted into the preamble to the League of Nations Covenant, such as the "principle of equality of nations and the just treatment of their nationals."[14]

The proposal was notoriously opposed by delegations from the British Empire—including by Australian prime minister Billy Hughes who was famous for his uncompromising racist "White Australia" dogma (meaning that only white immigrants were welcome in Australia).[15] Apparently, he was "willing to admit the equality of the Japanese as a nation, and also of the individual man to man." But, to him, the line must be drawn at their immigration to Australia. "It is not that we hold them to be inferior to ourselves," he was reported to have said, "but simply that we do not want them. Economically, they are a perturbing factor, because they accept wages much below the minimum wage for which our people are willing to work." (It may be noted that Hughes used to be a trade union organizer.) "Neither do they blend well with our people," he continued. "Hence we do not want them to marry our women."[16]

For his part, British foreign secretary Arthur Balfour could not accept that "a man from Central Africa was created equal to a European."[17]

Wilson, the leader of the American delegation, left a legacy of disheartening racism that even supported the Ku Klux Klan.[18] These included introducing segregation into the U.S. federal public service.

Against the pressure to drop the racial equality clause at the Paris Peace Conference, Japan insisted on pressing the proposal to a vote. Eleven delegations voted in favor and seven against.[19] But, presiding over the proceedings was Wilson. And he ruled that the proposal did not carry, despite the outcome of the vote. Explaining the decision, to the chagrin of the majority who voted, Wilson ruled, only after the fact of voting, that the proposal required unanimity. It was bare-faced chicanery that has been charitably described as "dexterity."[20] What, then, is the purpose of allowing a proposal to go to a vote, if the outcome of the exercise would not determine the question voted upon?

༄—

Much more could be said against Professor Schabas's undervaluing of article 227 on grounds of "the importance of the dissenting views," although the orientation of that appraisal of importance was not explained. Assuming, as we must, that the allusion could not possibly be a reference to the comparative intellectual statures of the commissioners who voted on either side of the issue,* we are then left with the national stature of the United States in 1919. It is not necessary to get into comparisons of stature between the British Empire alone versus the United States in 1919—let alone the combined statures of the British Empire, France, and all the other countries who comprised the majority that rejected immunity for heads of state at the Peace Conference.

It is enough to say that Schabas's demurrer would be hard to sustain as it stands. First, it would effectively nullify the legitimacy of every international initiative that the United States did not support. This would include the Rome Statute and the greater majority of human rights instruments (from the Convention on the Elimination of All Forms of Discrimination against Women to the Convention on the Rights of the Child). Still, it may not be necessary to dwell on this consideration, given the next one.

Second, one subtle yet highly significant point that is often missed in the story of immunity at the Paris Peace Conference is that President Wilson ultimately erased in effect the objection of Lansing and Scott regarding immunity of the kaiser for prosecution before an international tribunal. Consequently, there was no *dissent* from the *United States* as such that was left standing on that particular point. This was the inescapable effect of Wilson's eventual agreement that the kaiser must be prosecuted on the basis of article 227 of the Versailles Treaty. And Wilson himself

---

* There is no reasonable view upon which it can be supposed that the combined intellect of Lansing and Scott outweighed all the jurists who had lined up behind the view that the kaiser enjoyed no immunity. These would include Sir Ernest Pollock, KC (solicitor general of England and Wales, later to become Viscount Hanworth, Master of the Roll); Sir Gordon Hewart, KC (attorney general of England and Wales, later to become Lord Hewart, Lord Chief Justice); Lord Birkenhead, LC (Hewart's predecessor as attorney general); Britain's big-wig jurists that served on the Macdonell Committee (including Sir John Macdonell, KC, himself and Sir Frederick Pollock, KC); and Dean Ferdinand Larnaude and his colleague Professor Albert Geouffre de La Pradelle and their colleagues at the University of Paris Law Faculty.

drafted the initial text.[21] That affected the so-called "American objection" in two ways. The more immediate effect was that it could no longer be said that the United States objected to or "dissented" from article 227 that Wilson himself had drafted. Beyond that, there was the further constructive effect that, in drafting a provision that permitted the prosecution of the kaiser, Wilson effectively expunged from the process whatever had remained of the effects of the so-called "American objection" that Lansing and Scott had left on the record—even with a possible earlier approval of Wilson—against the prosecution of the kaiser. All these were in addition to the fact the objection of Lansing and Scott was effectively academic, since that objection and Japanese delegates' (comprising only two national votes) were too slim to perturb the decision of the commission's majority (comprising eight national votes).

Although this is not determinative of the significance of Wilson's reversal of the objection against prosecuting the kaiser, it may still be noted as a matter of detail that Wilson did not embrace the argument of inviolability of heads of state as a ground of the Lansing–Scott objection. To be noted in this regard is that Wilson had rejected as resting "on a ridiculous principle"[22] the Japanese basis for the objection against prosecuting heads of state—because the Japanese were understood to have founded the objection on the divine right of their emperor.[23] Wilson was keen to distance himself from that ground of the objection, even though David Lloyd George unequivocally informed him that the "Japanese principle is the English principle."[24] And, Lloyd George added, "All we want to do is to punish those responsible, whoever they may be."[25]

But to make sure that Wilson understood that the office of the President of the United States was contemplated in the decision to prosecute the kaiser, Lloyd George informed Wilson that Lansing's objection had been founded in part on concerns of setting a precedent that might come back to haunt the U.S. president in future.[26] Pollock had earlier informed Lloyd George that such was the motivation for Lansing's objection.[27] To that, Wilson replied, "I don't believe that." And then he went on to discuss who had the power to declare war in the United States.[28]

So, what must matter in the final analysis of the lasting effects of the objections of Lansing and Scott was not that they made and pressed the objection, but that their president did not sustain their objection in the end. Notably, Lansing himself had to accept that the "Constitution of United States confines to the President the absolute right of conducting the foreign relations of the Republic."[29] In a manner of speaking, then, by accepting that the kaiser must be tried, Wilson had effectively overruled or withdrawn the objection of Lansing and Scott against the trial of the kaiser. It is not unreasonable, even if speculative, to take that eventuality into account as a factor in the overall irritation that Wilson displayed toward Lansing in general and Lansing's legal punctilios in particular, an attitude that Lansing amply discussed in his bitter memoirs of the Peace Conference.*

What was surprising was that influential scholars might have compounded what was surely an oversight of not being sufficiently sensitive to the foregoing considerations, by stating a demurrer in the terms that article 227 of the Versailles Treaty does not count for much because of "the importance of the *dissenting* views." Notably, Professor Schabas made that argument notwithstanding that he had elsewhere recognized that Wilson's eventual acceptance of the prosecution of the kaiser and proposing the text of article 227 was "a great personal humiliation" for Lansing "given the opposition to any trial of the Kaiser that he had stubbornly maintained throughout the sessions of the Commission on Responsibilities."† Schabas

---

* In a particularly poignant passage, Lansing recalled a specific meeting with Wilson, during which "the President took up the provisions of his original draft of a Covenant, which was at the time in typewritten form, and indicated the features which he considered fundamental to the proper organization of a League of Nations. I pointed out certain provisions which appeared to me objectionable in principle or at least of doubtful policy. Mr. Wilson, however, clearly indicated—at least so I interpreted his words and manner—that he was not disposed to receive these criticisms in good part and was unwilling to discuss them. *He also said with great candor and emphasis that he did not intend to have lawyers drafting the treaty of peace.* Although this declaration was called forth by the statement that the legal advisers of the American Commission had been, at my request, preparing an outline of a treaty, a 'skeleton treaty.' In fact, the President's sweeping disapproval of members of the legal profession participating in the treaty-making *seemed to be, and I believe was, intended to be notice to me that my counsel was unwelcome.* Being the only lawyer on the delegation I naturally took this remark to myself, and I know that other American Commissioners held the same view of its purpose" (Lansing, *The Peace Negotiations*, 107).

† See Schabas, *Trial of the Kaiser*, 195. Wilson's reversal of Lansing's objection in this regard was acute, given that Lansing himself had confessed that there was no way that he could have found a compromise without abandoning "fundamental principles." He presented that dilemma both in his declarations at the commission and in his dissenting opinion to the commission report. At the commission, he said this: "I quite agree with the Dean [Larnaude] that it is useless to continue this discussion. We have been laboring here for six weeks. Everybody has endeavored to find a formula that would harmonize irrecon[cil]able differences. We have failed—frankly, we have failed. *The United States went as far as it could without surrendering what it considered fundamental principles.* I am quite sure that every other member of the Commission has gone as far as he could to reach a common ground. I say we have failed. It is not a failure from lack of desire, or lack of effort. It is simply that our views no more mingle than oil and water, and I consider, therefore, that the wise course to pursue is for the Commission, at the present time, to vote on this report of the Third Sub-Commission, and that the United States dissent from Articles IV and V, and file a minority report on that subject." Excerpt from the "Minutes of Meeting of 17 March 1919," Commission on the Responsibility of the Authors of the War and the Enforcement of Penalties," Paris Peace Conference doc. no. 181.1201/7, U.S. National Archives Microfilm Publications, microcopy no. 820, roll 141, vol. 115, doc. 403, 11, para. 3 (emphasis added). And in the eventual dissenting report that the U.S. representatives filed, the same sentiment is repeated as follows: "From the first of these, held on February 3, 1919, there was an earnest purpose shown to compose the differences which existed, to find a formula acceptable to all, and to render, if possible,

correctly observed that it is generally accepted that it was the Americans who ultimately "budged" on the matter of trial of the kaiser, when Wilson relented.[30] The effect, then, was that there was no "dissenting views" to speak of in relation to article 227, if that reference was to the position of the United States. The American president himself drafted the text, yielding to the relentless insistence of Georges Clemenceau and Lloyd George that the kaiser must be tried.[31]

The second ground of Schabas's demurrer rests on "the total neglect of the Report by the real lawmakers, the Council of Four." This is a difficult assertion to understand. First, the discussion of the Council of Four began with Lloyd George raising the item in the following words, during their meeting in the afternoon of 2 April 1919: "I would like to discuss the question of responsibilities with you. Our commission declared itself against bringing to trial those who are in different degrees responsible for the declaration of war. *Personally, I regret this. But, I accept it.*"[32] The point here, as correctly noted by the editors of the notes of Paul Mantoux (the Council of Four's official interpreter),[33] is that their Commission on the Responsibility of the Authors of the War and on Enforcement of Penalties made two recommendations regarding prosecution. The first recommendation was unanimously against prosecution of those alleged to have *started* a war of aggression (the *jus ad bellum* recommendation).[34] Instead, the conference should issue a formal condemnation of the violation of the neutrality of Belgium and Luxembourg, set up a special mechanism as might be considered necessary to deal with it, and indicate that it was desirable to criminalize such violations in future.[35] The second recommendation was to proceed with the prosecution of those alleged to have committed *atrocities* during the war by violating the laws and customs of war (the war crimes or *jus in bello* recommendation).[36] The latter recommendation was adopted by a majority of eight votes, against the dissenting votes of the delegates of two states (the United States and Japan).[37]

Once Lloyd George indicated that he *regretted*—but *accepted*—the *jus ad bellum* recommendation, the Big Four's discussion about prosecuting the kaiser proceeded in earnest and concentrated on the *jus in bello* recommendation. On that basis, it is difficult to understand Professor Schabas's

---

a unanimous report. That this purpose failed was not because of want of effort on the part of any member of the Commission. *It failed because, after all the proposed means of adjustment had been tested with frank and open minds, no practicable way could be found to harmonize the differences without an abandonment of principles which were fundamental.* This the representatives of the United States could not do and they could not expect it of others": Commission on the Responsibility of the Authors of the War and on Enforcement of Penalties, "Report Presented to the Preliminary Peace Conference, 29 March 1919," 128 (emphasis added).

contention that the Big Four had "totally neglect[ed] the Report" of the commission.[38]

It may be noted that after all the preliminary thrust-and-parry about prosecuting the kaiser according to the *jus in bello* recommendation, Wilson proposed a formulation of article 227 that was broad enough to accommodate even the *jus ad bellum* prosecution, as discussed below. It thus makes it difficult to characterize that outcome of the Big Four's deliberations as implicating a *total neglect* of the recommendation against that course. The more charitable view of it would be a certain level of fuzziness* that can set in during discussions on discrete points, in the course of sustained and difficult negotiations of very large and complex issues involving numerous angles with global orientations and implications, which confronted the Big Four at the Paris Conference.

And on the specific question of *immunity*, it would be particularly incorrect to suggest that the Big Four—i.e., Clemenceau, Lloyd George, Vittorio Orlando, and Wilson—"*totally* neglect[ed] the Report" of the commission. Despite the strenuous objections of Lansing and Scott, the commission's majority report specifically rejected immunity for the kaiser. They insisted that he must be prosecuted—because no one should enjoy immunity, not even heads of state.[39] Not even their own and not even the president of the United States. Article 227 is a direct testament of the Council of Four's rejection of immunity for the kaiser, according to the recommendations of the majority of the commission.

In addition to Lloyd George's indication of the direct link between article 227 and the report of the commission, when he prompted the discussion of the Big Four on it during their meeting of 2 April 1919, perhaps the clearest other evidence of that direct link is to be found in Appendix IV to the 11:00 a.m. meeting of the Big Four on 1 May 1919 at Wilson's residence in Paris.† The appendix is the first draft of the four articles that became articles 227, 228, 229, and 230 of the Versailles Treaty. The link is evident in the title of the appendix stated as follows: "*Draft Clauses Prepared by the Drafting Committee of the Peace Conference, on Instructions*

---

* Notably, at some point during the deliberations of the Big Four on 8 April 1919, the discussions veered back to the invasion of Belgium, as a violation of the guarantee of its neutrality. And Clemenceau interjected, "The Germain Emperor must be tried. The violation of the law in the case of Belgium was so flagrant that the conscience of the peoples will not be satisfied if that act were treated in any other way than as a crime against public law" (see Mantoux, *Deliberations of the Council of Four*, 189). But it was clear in the context of this discussion, involving the majority recommendation to proceed with prosecutions for violations of laws and customs of war (*jus in bello*), it did not signal a clear intention to reject the first recommendation against prosecution for *jus ad bellum*.

† Notably, Orlando was absent from this particular meeting, possibly part of the period he was engaged in a walkout on the Big Four because of their refusal to grant the concessions he wanted for Italy.

Received from the Council of the First Delegates of the Powers with General Interests *after Consideration of Report of the Commission*" (emphases added). In other words, the Council of Four read the commission's report, and then instructed the drafting committee to draft the provisions that are now articles 227–30. The outcomes of both processes are the same: the kaiser must be prosecuted; he was to enjoy no immunity.

⁂

It is true that the Council of Four had struggled to formulate the crimes for which the kaiser must be prosecuted, after Wilson finally agreed that he must be prosecuted. The struggle resulted from finding a formulation that would work for Wilson. It may be tempting to take a cynical view of the dilemma in terms that Wilson was anxious to be seen to leave something for Robert Lansing, his secretary of state, whom Wilson had to disappoint following Lansing's robust public objection (in front of the whole world) against prosecuting the kaiser, an objection that Lansing evidently thought he had Wilson's support and approval in pressing.

The more charitable view must be that Lansing's legality argument did make an impression on the Council of Four. The argument had, in fact, resonated strongly enough with Wilson and Orlando that it required a turbo-charged vocal pushback from Clemenceau to beat it down.

Lansing's concern was this: Up until the Peace Conference, international law had not indicated that violation of international law was a criminal offense for which any punishment had been laid down.[40] He also objected that the idea of an international tribunal to try such violations was unknown to international law.[41] Additionally, he objected against the trial of a head of state for the same reasons. There was no real dispute as to the factual propositions upon which Lansing's objections were founded. The dispute was as to what should be done. The Allied majority wanted to create the precedents that were missing, using the Versailles Treaty. Lansing insisted on the opposite outcome. As he saw it, using the Versailles Treaty to do those things for the first time directly raised concerns about violation of the rule against retroactive application of law also known as the principle of legality or the rule of *nullum crimen sine lege*.

It is not necessary now to review at length the correctness of Lansing's objections on the point. It is enough to say this: Given that he had admitted that international law had recognized, as did national law, the right of states to prosecute enemy soldiers for war crimes,[42] the question thus engaged as to whether "general principles of law recognized by civilized nations"—even then a recognized source of international law[43]—should not have formed a confident basis for the prosecution before an international tribunal.

But, taking Lansing's objection at its highest, for the time being, his point was that the condemnation of the kaiser could go no higher than the level of *morality*. For, to seek recourse to criminal law would violate the principle of legality. While not overly impressed by Lansing's objection on grounds of *immunity*, Wilson was more concerned about violating the principle of *legality*.[44] Consequently, after yielding to the insistence of Clemenceau and Lloyd George that the kaiser must be prosecuted, Wilson sought a formulation that might achieve that outcome, while still respecting the principle of legality. To that end, Wilson's formula was to introduce into the draft of what became article 227 the terminology of "international morality and the sanctity of treaties" and "high international policy." Lansing might have been the original inventor of the phrase "international morality and the sanctity of treaties."[45] In an apparent effort to meet the Allied commissioners part way, he awkwardly suggested that the kaiser could be referred to a *political tribunal* or international commission of inquiry for violation of "international morality and sanctity of treaties," but not before a tribunal of law for criminal conduct.[46] That was the central message of a proposal he made to the Commission on Responsibilities[47] during their meeting of 12 March 1919, amply echoed in the memorandum of reservations appended to the report of the commission.[48]

Consequently, once Wilson agreed that the kaiser must be tried, there ensued much handwringing about whether to prosecute him for crimes or for breach of international "morality." In the end, as indicated earlier, Wilson sought to work into the design of article 227 a formula that would accommodate the Allies' insistence that the kaiser must be prosecuted, while minimizing the concerns about the principle of legality. So, it was decided (a) that the kaiser must be tried "for supreme offence against international morality and the sanctity of treaties"; (b) in deciding the case, the adjudicating tribunal would be "guided by the highest motives of international policy, with a view to vindicating the solemn obligations of international undertakings and the validity of international morality"; (c) the tribunal was to be composed of five "judges"; and (d) it would be the tribunal's "duty to fix the punishment which it considers should be imposed." In other words, the kaiser was to be *punished*, following a trial before a *tribunal* (with no indication that it would be anything other than a court of law) that was given the discretion to decide what that punishment might be.

An earlier draft of article 227 that reflected Wilson's formulation contained language to the effect that the kaiser's trial was "not for an offence against criminal law," inserted right in the middle of the first clause, which read as follows: "The Allied and Associated Powers publicly arraign William II of Hohenzollern, formerly German Emperor, not for an offence against criminal law, but for a supreme offence against international morality and the sanctity of treaties."[49]

But, during the meeting of the Big Four (minus Vittorio Orlando) at 11:00 a.m. on 1 May 1919, Lloyd George informed that both his solicitor general (Sir Ernest Pollock) and the attorney general had criticized the phrase "not for an offence against criminal law, but," on grounds that it "might possibly be construed as an admission on the part of the Allied and Associated Powers that the German Emperor had not committed any offences against criminal law." Consequently, Lloyd George proposed that the phrase be omitted from the final version. Apparently with no argument at all, "President Wilson agreed." Thus, it was agreed that the first clause should simply read as follows: "The Allied and Associated Powers publicly arraign William II of Hohenzollern, formerly German Emperor, for a supreme offence against international morality and the sanctity of treaties."[50] That is how the clause reads now.

The text of article 227 provoked uncharitable commentary. Emblematic of such reactions was Billy Hughes, the sharp-tongued trade union leader who became Australia's prime minister. "They started out to vindicate 'international morality' and then dropped to 'international policy,'" he was reported to have complained during a meeting of the British Empire delegation that reviewed the earlier draft. "We would never get a conviction under them. They would make us ridiculous and cover us with confusion."[51] Criticism of the provision continued even into recent years.[52]

＊

It is always easier to criticize the outcome of difficult work than to do the work better. Anyone who has ever done such difficult work, even at the national level let alone before a varied and global community, will verify that.

It is in the nature of these things that, when the legislator is done drafting a legal instrument and has left the stage, it falls to prosecutors and judges to apply their creative minds to give a treaty the interpretations that it can reasonably bear, to achieve its object and purpose.

From that perspective, a proper analysis of the eventual text of article 227 indicates that, as the very first precedent of its kind, it was ample for purposes of an international criminal prosecution. And Lloyd George was correct when he said, "I think that what the President proposes will cover *all* of the violations of international law that we want to *punish*."[53]

The kaiser was to be prosecuted for a "supreme offence." That notion pointed at once to both "international morality" and to "sanctity of treaties" as well as to "vindicating the solemn obligations of international undertakings." There will be no reasonable dispute that the "treaties" and "obligations of international undertakings" indicated in the provision would include in the foreground the 1907 Hague Convention (IV) on the Laws and Customs of War on Land and the Regulations annexed to it, upon which the work of Sub-commission III focused. Germany was a party to that treaty:[54] having signed it upon adoption on 18 October 1907 and ratified it on 27 November 1909. Its violation, allegedly on the orders or willful condonation of the kaiser, would surely anchor a charge of "supreme offence . . . against sanctity of treaties" and the failure to discharge "solemn obligations of international undertakings."

That is to say, even as they struggled to find a suitable formulation, Wilson and his colleagues still managed to come up with a text that is functionally equivalent to punishing "grave breaches [to the Geneva Conventions of 1949]," speaking in the language of the 2020s.

For added value, the phrases "supreme offence . . . against sanctity of treaties" and "solemn obligations of international undertakings" also would certainly accommodate the obscure 1839 Treaty of London and the 1867 Treaty of London that guaranteed neutrality for Belgium and Luxembourg, respectively,[55] as well as the 1907 Hague Convention (V) Respecting the Rights and Duties of Neutral Powers and Persons in Case of War on Land.[56]

In any event, the Big Four's struggle in formulating article 227 does not obscure the fact that the Paris Peace Conference did ultimately agree that the kaiser was to enjoy *no immunity* from prosecution before the international tribunal. That was the adjustment that the French and the British governments had deliberately set out to achieve at the Paris Peace Conference; that was what their jurists fought for in the deliberations of the Commission on Responsibilities and its Sub-commission III; and that was what they unambiguously achieved in the text of article 227 of the Versailles Peace Treaty.

ᐁ

Here, now, I'll offer a word or two about Lansing's objections. In Paris, Lansing objected strenuously and numerously. Lansing knew that he had fallen out of favor with Wilson by the time they got to Paris and throughout their stay.[57] Lansing would have been intensely conscious of the fact that the diplomatic gossip mill would have informed his interlocutors of his depressed relationship with his president.[58] And he perceived that the "whole [American] delegation, the President included, lost prestige and influence" with the other delegates due to Lansing's view that the U.S. delegation (because of Wilson's way of doing things) had gone to the Peace Conference without a plan, direction, or coordination.[59] In those circumstances, it is difficult to avoid wondering to what extent his numerous objections implicated a skidding ego grappling for traction. The minutes of the meetings of Sub-commission III and of the main Commission on Responsibilities and the dissenting report he filed gave his objections a shotgun feel. It is a mistake that young barristers are taught to avoid in the courtroom. Numerous objections give a tedious air to advocacy. They irritate their audience, though professionalism requires them to be endured politely, rather than help their cause.

Some of Lansing's objections were truly pedantic and short sighted. Take, for instance, his extensive exegesis against the reference to "offences against humanity" when, he insisted, the mandate was to inquire about violations of the "laws and customs of war."[60] We may ignore the fact that "*offences* against humanity" is another way of saying "*crimes* against humanity," a very familiar notion in contemporary international law. Still, there are many who would consider that (as of 1919) the entire corpus of the laws and *customs* of war—or international *humanitarian* law or *jus in bello*—flowed out of the stream of humanity: much in the same way that John Westlake correctly observed that "the train of observable resemblances" rather than "arbitrary definition" does lead to "the final meaning of law."[61]

That certain concrete norms might have been distilled from that stream and codified in discrete provisions of a treaty should not have validated the level of sustained objection that Lansing deployed against a residual reference to the same stream beyond the specific norms. If that consideration was not sufficiently clear from the 1868 Declaration of St. Petersburg (the text of which is set out in this endnote[62]) it surely would have been abundantly clear from the preamble to the 1907 Hague Convention (IV) Respecting the Laws and Customs of War on Land,* which also specifically included the Martens clause† captured in it. Why hold up proceedings of an important conference with an objection on the point?

Lansing's story of his fraught relationship with Wilson is remarkable for Lansing's predisposition for insistent objections. He often gave the impression of a wiser minder anxious to save those under his charge—including President Wilson—from themselves.[63] One interesting objection he appeared to have pushed with Wilson, apparently to his own ultimate detriment, was the objection that Wilson should not put in a personal appearance at the Peace Conference. Lansing's reasons were not on substance but, rather, that personal appearance would be detrimental to Wilson's prestige and dignity. Lansing could have argued, but did not, that it would be unsafe for the president to be sailing across the Atlantic to Europe so soon after the war, given the danger posed by floating mines.[64] But the result of Wilson's nonappearance would make Lansing the head of the American delegation at the conference. Wilson took time out to reflect on the objection, and he reverted to Lansing after some days.[65] Lansing's objection seemed too strongly formulated in terms, whether or not he verbalized them to Wilson in those terms. When he first got wind of Wilson's decision to be in Paris personally, he felt *"very strongly* that it would be a *grave mistake."*[66] And after about a week, on 18 November 1918, Wilson went to Lansing's house and personally informed Lansing that he had made up his mind to go to Paris.[67] Lansing suggests that he did not argue with the president,[68] though he does admit in another context that "petty influences" can "warp" attitudes more than one may care to admit.[69] Whether Wilson's rejection of his advice about traveling to Paris was a "petty influence" that warped Lansing's attitude toward Wilson remains to be seen.‡ It is enough to note that after the President

---

* Notably, the convention was "[a]nimated by the desire to serve, even in this extreme case, the *interests of humanity* and the ever progressive needs of civilization" (emphasis added).

† As the original iteration of that clause reads in the preamble to that convention: "Until a more complete code of the laws of war has been issued, the High Contracting Parties deem it expedient to declare that, in cases not included in the Regulations adopted by them, the inhabitants and the belligerents remain under the protection and the rule of the principles of the law of nations, as they result from the usages established among civilized peoples, from *the laws of humanity*, and the dictates of the public conscience" (emphasis added).

‡ Apparently, there were others. In her memoirs, for instance, Mrs. Wilson took care to tell the story of the occasion in Paris when Henry White made a request of her. White was a former U.S. ambassador to France during Teddy Roosevelt's administration, whom Wilson had taken to Paris as one of the American commissioners. He used the ruse of giving Mrs. Wilson a guided tour of some of the historic places in Paris. During the tour, White engaged the more serious purpose of needing

left Lansing's home, Lansing wrote a note to himself, saying: "I am convinced that he is making *one of the greatest mistakes of his career* and will
imperil his reputation. I may be in error and hope that I am, but *I prophesy
trouble in Paris* and *worse than trouble here. I believe the President's place is here
in America.*"[70] Lansing records that their differences of opinion on this
matter were the beginning of Wilson's "loss of confidence" in Lansing's
"judgement and advice, which became increasingly marked during the
Paris negotiations,"[71] ultimately ending up with Wilson seeking Lansing's
resignation with a note that Lansing complained against as conveying
"manifest imputation . . . that I had advised him wrongly and that, after
he had decided to adopt a course contrary to my advice, I had continued
to oppose his views and had with reluctance obeyed his instructions."[72]
It was an imputation that Lansing strongly denied,[73] even as he eviscer-
ated Wilson in his memoirs of the Paris Peace Conference, notably in the
books *The Big Four and Others of the Peace Conference* and *The Peace Negotiations: A Personal Narrative*. Wilson's note to Lansing, dated 11 February
1920, demanding resignation, read as follows:

> While we were still in Paris, I felt, and have felt increasingly ever since,
> that you accepted my guidance and direction on questions with regard to
> which I had to instruct you only with increasing reluctance. . . .
> [. . .] I must say that it would relieve me of embarrassment, Mr. Sec-
> retary, the embarrassment of feeling your reluctance and divergence of
> judgment, if you would give your present office up and afford me an
> opportunity to select someone whose mind would more willingly go along
> with mine.[74]

Lansing resigned the following day.[75]

Now, why would Wilson insist on attending the Peace Conference
instead of leaving Lansing to attend as head of the American delegation?
The answer is only a matter of conjecture since Wilson did not tell the
story himself. The obvious picture would suggest a man determined personally to seize a historic moment presented to him to remake the world

---

to inform the First Lady of "a few jealousies and sore spots in the Commission to which, I think, by
a word to the President, you can bring balm. The first one is that Lansing is terribly sore because the
[American commission's] meetings the President attends are held in Colonel House's suite instead of
his. Since he is the Secretary of State, forgive me if I say I think he is right; for he is being ignored.
Also all the newspaper men, in quest of information, are told by Gordon Auchincloss to see his father-
in-law, Colonel House. I told Mr White that these things were so small I was sure they had never
entered the President's mind, but that I knew he would appreciate his thought in telling me of them,
and he would look into them. 'Yes,' Mr White answered, 'they are small things, but Lansing is a small
man, and sometimes personal vanity makes or mars the success of large affairs.'" See Bolling Wilson,
My Memoir, 225–26.

according to his own vision of a new world order. After all, the best way to do something a particular way is to attend to it personally.

It is also possible that the president was keenly aware of Lansing's proclivity for pedantic objections as a factor that may not augur well in great historic moments such as the Peace Conference. We may recall Wilson's speech to the International Law Association in which he reproached international lawyers for thinking out international law "a little too much . . . in the closet."[76] We also recall Lansing's complaint about Wilson's summary dismissal of another of Lansing's objections to a draft article to the Versailles Treaty proposed by Wilson, saying "with great candor and emphasis that he did not intend to have lawyers drafting the treaty of peace."[77] Lansing and others present apparently interpreted Wilson as meaning he would not allow *Lansing* to draft the peace treaty.[78] Wilson was known to think very little of Lansing toward the later part of their relationship, which spanned the period of the Paris Peace Conference. Notably, Colonel House once memorialized Wilson's deprecation of Lansing in terms that "Lansing was the most unsatisfactory Secretary in his Cabinet; that he was good for second place but unfitted for the first. That he had no imagination, no constructive ability, and but little real ability of any kind."[79] In that connection, it has been noted that Wilson's lack of faith in Lansing had often resulted in Wilson's reversal of policy initiatives that Lansing had launched in the name of Wilson's administration.[80]

Many will understandably consider Wilson's poor opinion of Lansing as stemming from the strong differences of opinion between the two men.[81] But, it is also the case that much of Lansing's objections during the proceedings of both the Commission on Responsibilities and its Subcommission III often came across as objections from someone who appreciated the law from a very narrow perspective. Also to be recalled is Lloyd George's dismissive views of Lansing as "a mere cypher—an amiable lawyer of good standing and of respectable abilities but of no particular distinction or definite personality. He just did what he was told, and was never told to do very much. He was not of the true faith; his 'Memoirs' show that he had not assimilated into his system the Decree of Infallibility."[82]

Indeed, in the course of the work of the Commission on Responsibilities, Lansing was able to play amply into the hands of those who held a poor view of him as not a very creative lawyer, notwithstanding that he might have been a fairly successful lawyer; after all, there are many very successful lawyers who represented rich corporations in real estate and corporate transactions or litigation in which forensic success could come from dismissing claims against rich clients on grounds that the cause of action was "unknown to law" or without precedent.

Take, for instance, his insistence that no international tribunal might be created—let alone one that would try the kaiser—because no precedents existed for such an outcome. No doubt, Lansing and Scott thought that a brilliant argument. But they never stopped to ponder about the phenomenon of precedents, how they become so and who creates them, and in what circumstances. It never occurred to them that it is human beings like them who create precedents. They were content to do no more than apply precedents created by other people who came before them. Their argument was never that though they recognized that they could create a new precedent, the occasion did not sufficiently warrant creating one. To the contrary, they recognized—as Lansing's proposals of 12 March 1919 amply showed—the unprecedented egregiousness of the violations that were animating their European colleagues to create a new precedent. But the sole argument of Lansing and Scott was simple. They found no precedent from an earlier time that could be used; therefore, they felt helpless to do anything. And they said as much in Lansing's proposed amendment of 12 March 1919. It is difficult to see such an attitude in any other light than in Wilson's reproach of Lansing as a lawyer with limited imagination.

In a postmortem of the process, Lansing considers that a "different" outcome might have resulted had Wilson "adopted the customary method of negotiation through commissioners"—which meant in effect that Lansing, as U.S. secretary of state with *full powers* to negotiate the treaty, would have been the head of the U.S. negotiators—"instead of pursuing the unusual and in fact untried method of participation."[83] It is highly doubtful that the "different" outcome that Lansing alluded to might have been a positive one, had he attended the Peace Conference as the head of the U.S. delegation with full powers.

Wilson's determination to attend at Paris personally and take matters of moment into his own hands might have had particular regard to the incidence of other large egos at the Peace Conference (notably Lloyd George and Clemenceau) that needed to be worked with more amenably by someone ranking higher than they and not lower (as Lansing was as a foreign minister) in diplomatic protocol. Here, the information is noted about the tendency of Lloyd George to avoid situations where he was left to debate important decisions with Lansing, without Wilson there.[84]

It is more likely that the answer to why Wilson decided to attend the Paris Peace Conference personally entails a complex mix of considerations including the foregoing. Whatever the case, it seems clear by now that there might not have been an article 227 of the Treaty of Versailles had Wilson not attended the conference, where he overrode Lansing's trenchant objection against prosecuting the kaiser and drafted the provision himself. There was also the further consideration that there might not have been a Versailles Treaty at all without that provision, as Lloyd George subtly threatened.[85] No doubt some pundits might view that as salutary, given the intense criticisms that had been heaped upon the treaty after the fact. That, of course, is a pointless consideration, as there were some who thought the treaty didn't go far enough.[86] No doubt many more would have criticized the complete failure to conclude a treaty at all, had that been the case.

DUTCH REFUSAL TO SURRENDER THE KAISER 7

ollowing intense international pressure, the Nigerian government, on 29 March 2006, arrested a latter-day warlord, Liberia's former president Charles Taylor, from his place of asylum in Nigeria. They then transferred him for trial at the Special Court for Sierra Leone, an international tribunal of the modern era.[1]

Eighty-six years earlier, the government of the Netherlands steadfastly rebuffed more intense pressure from the Allied and Associated Powers, who had requested the Dutch authorities to arrest and surrender Kaiser Wilhelm II, the original "lord of war," so that he might stand trial before the international tribunal contemplated in article 227 of the Treaty of Versailles.[2]

Following his defeat at the end of World War I, the kaiser went into exile in the Netherlands during the night of 9 November 1919.[3]

In a statement to the Staten Generaal (the Dutch parliament) on 21 November 1918, Prime Minister Charles Ruijs de Beerenbrouck acknowledged the ex-kaiser's presence in the Netherlands. According to the statement, Count Bentinck "tendered the Castle of Armerongen" to house the ex-kaiser at "the express request of the Dutch Government." The "character of the asylum offered the ex-Emperor differs in no way from that enjoyed by refugees for centuries," the prime minister insisted. "The offering of asylum is a trait deeply rooted in the spirit of liberty and tolerance of the Dutch people, and in the course of our history refugees of humble and of high position, as well as princes, have benefited by it."[4]

The sentiment regarding a national tradition of safe haven for asylum seekers is certainly understandable. But it overstates things to say that the asylum afforded the ex-kaiser "differs in no way" from that offered to everyone else throughout the ages. For one thing, it would be difficult to suppose that the Dutch government would request members of their national aristocracy to offer up their castles for every other refugee who sought asylum in the Netherlands. Nor would it be the case that the Dutch Ministry of Foreign Affairs would post a diplomat to every obscure Dutch village where asylees were located, to manage the government's interest in a particular refugee's presence in the village.[5]

Also overworked has been the suggestion that it was fidelity to Dutch laws (of hospitality) and the country's long tradition of affording safe haven for political refugees that explained the Dutch government's attitude of resistance to deliver up the ex-kaiser to the Entente powers for his trial. There was much greater nuance to the circumstances. Even a subtext to the prime minister's statement to the parliament contains elements of exceptions. Notably, the prime minister was careful to add this qualifier: "National interests might demand that the exigencies of the case should outweigh humanitarian considerations and historical traditions."[6] There is indeed much room for exceptions in that regard. To be noted in that connection was the significance of early intelligence from John W. Garrett, the U.S. ambassador in The Hague.

"In the course of a conversation with the Minister for Foreign Affairs," Garrett informed in his dispatch of 10 December 1918, "it became evident that he wished me to understand that Holland would welcome the solution of its difficulties caused by the presence of the ex-Emperor. He seemed to realize the danger that his presence in the country might be to Holland, but it was evident that he feared that a demand might be made by the United States and the Allies calling for such action or couched in such terms as to threaten the honor of Holland and make it difficult to concede the demand, however much the Dutch might be inclined to meet it favourably."[7]

Professor William Schabas has suggested that "[h]ad the Kaiser's surrender been demanded immediately upon signature of the Treaty of Versailles, the Dutch might have complied."[8] Noting that the treaty was signed on 28 June 1919, the hypothesis of an early successful demand of the kaiser's surrender would stand on even stronger grounds had the demand been made during the period of Garrett's diplomatic note in December 1918, at the height of the anxiety that the dispatch above indicates as vexing the Dutch government—when the prime minister indicated that the "exigencies of the case" might present "national interests" that "should outweigh humanitarian considerations and historical traditions." Notably, it was about then—specifically on 2 December 1918 during the Inter-Allied meeting of the heads of the Entente governments in London—that David

Lloyd George raised the question of making the demand of the Dutch government to surrender the kaiser. But Clemenceau suggested that they should await the arrival of Woodrow Wilson,[9] who was not represented at the meeting because his emissary in Europe, Colonel House, was seriously unwell in Paris. In a resulting telegram of the Entente heads of government to Wilson, they expressed the hope that Wilson would be supportive of the idea of prosecuting the kaiser and of requesting the Dutch government to surrender him.[10] A note to file dated 6 December 1918 indicated that the assistant secretary of state, William Phillips, spoke to Wilson about the contents of the telegram. Wilson said that under no circumstances would he express a position on the matter at that time. The matter could be taken up when he arrived in France, he insisted.[11]

It is a fair supposition that the eventual hardening of the attitude of the Dutch government against the Entente demand for the kaiser's surrender was emboldened by a combination of resistance to foreign bullying and the fact that the shifting winds of politics had resulted in the attrition of the ranks and the resolve of the Entente powers, following their initial momentum to prosecute the kaiser.[12]

There is a suggestion or understanding that a "lukewarm but opportunistic President Wilson" had combined with "the resolute and unyielding Secretary of State, Robert Lansing" to obstruct the prosecution of the kaiser.[13] Half of that proposition is not supported by the available evidence. Whatever Wilson's real motive might have been for ultimately agreeing to the prosecution of the kaiser, there is no evidence to support the proposition that he had remained "lukewarm" from that point on. The fact that he had initially been impressed by Lansing's objection to the prosecution, and was sympathetic to it and might have given approval at first, does not mean that he remained lukewarm to the idea of prosecution after he had agreed to it. Indeed, the evidence pointed in the opposite direction.

A significant factor in the eventual dooming of the prospect of the prosecution, as part the phenomenon of the attrition of the ranks and the resolve of the Entente powers on the project, is accounted for by President Wilson's unsuccessful battle in the U.S. Senate for the ratification of the Versailles Treaty that also contained article 227. It gave Lansing the opportunity of actionable retribution—which apparently he could not resist—against an idea he had vigorously objected to, notwithstanding that President Wilson did eventually show real commitment to the idea, once he came around to agreeing finally that it was the right thing to do.

In the meeting of the Supreme Council (comprising the Big Four plus Japan), at 4:00 p.m. on 25 June 1919, with Italy represented by Foreign Minister Baron Sonnino (Orlando having resigned as prime minister of Italy on 19 June 1919) and the Japanese foreign minister Baron Makino representing his country, Lloyd George suggested to his colleagues that the trial of the kaiser should take place in some Allied country removed from those where resentment of the kaiser was naturally the most acute. He suggested that either Great Britain or the United States would be the most advantageous from this point of view. It was thus clear that the obvious aim of Lloyd George was to avoid conducting the trial in France. Wilson suggested that the trial should not take place in any great city.[14] Georges Clemenceau needed to consult his colleagues on the subject and would give a reply on the following day.[15]

Later, during the same meeting, Wilson himself said that "the hour was approaching when some demand would have to be made to Holland in regard to the surrender of the Kaiser." He was anxious to avoid making the demand in a manner that would embarrass the Dutch sense of hospitality. Lloyd George was keen to stress that "a new principle was involved in this Treaty." According to him, this was in the sense that a great crime had been perpetrated against the nations of the world. It had taken five years to bring this question to fruition, and the Allies could not afford to allow Holland to stand in the way. Wilson agreed that, while there was a moral obligation upon Holland to surrender the kaiser, the Allies should nevertheless make it as easy as possible for the Netherlands. Clemenceau said he would be surprised if Holland objected. At Wilson's suggestion, it was ultimately agreed that Robert Lansing, in his capacity as the chairperson of the Commission on Responsibilities, should be asked to draft the text of the needed demand to the Netherlands for consideration of the council.[16]

During their meeting of the next day, 26 June 1919 at 11:00 a.m., Wilson read out the text of the draft letter Lansing prepared for eventual delivery to the Dutch government. A discussion ensued in reaction to Lansing's suggestion in his cover memo advising that the delivery of the letter to the Netherlands should be withheld until the ratification of the treaty. Having complimented the draft letter as "a very able document," Lloyd George questioned the wisdom of delaying its dispatch until the ratification of the treaty.

In the context of the discussion, Lloyd George recalled the information he had provided to his colleagues upon arrival: that he had received intelligence that morning to the effect that the German crown prince, to whom the Netherlands had also granted asylum, had fled his place of asylum in

Holland and had been seen driving to the east (Germany borders the Netherlands to the east) in a motorcar in the company of a German staff officer. Lloyd George presumed that the crown prince's flight must be for mischief making. The fact that the crown prince had gone with a staff officer might have aroused suspicion that there was some conspiracy. Lloyd George had learned from newspaper reports that an attempt was being made by the German military to undermine the Versailles Treaty. He thus wondered whether it was safe to leave the kaiser in the Netherlands. He had often thought that action ought to have been taken before on this matter.

But Wilson questioned whether action could be taken before ratification of the Peace Treaty. Lloyd George considered that action could be taken ahead of ratification, on the grounds of public safety. If the kaiser reached Germany, a dangerous situation might arise. It might facilitate renewal of war. Wilson said he did not dispute the concern. He only wanted to be sure that there was a valid legal basis for the contemplated action. Clemenceau said that the demand could be based on the escape of the crown prince and the danger of renewing the war if the kaiser escaped.

Wilson considered that it would be sufficient to approach the Dutch government immediately with urgent representations, urging them to ensure that the kaiser did not leave the country. In Wilson's view, both the kaiser and the crown prince had the right to leave the country if they wished, but in view of the imminent signature of the Peace Treaty, he thought that Holland would have the right to refuse their departure.

While the correctness of the first part of Wilson's opinion (that the kaiser and the crown prince had the right to leave the Netherlands if they wished) was open to question on the basis of the law of neutrality, which, as shown below, imposed certain obligations upon a neutral state (which the Netherlands was during World War I), he was certainly correct as regards the second part (that the exigent circumstances of war permitted the Dutch to restrict that right). The council members did not advert to any specific norm of international law in their discussion. Lloyd George said that he would put the matter on the ground of the volatile state of Germany: the escape of the crown prince and the danger to the peace of the world if the kaiser reached Germany.

The Hague Conventions provided a specific norm on the point. According to article 11 of the 1907 Hague Convention (V) Respecting the Rights and Duties of Neutral Powers and Persons in Case of War on Land, to which both the Netherlands and Germany were parties as of 1919, "A neutral Power which receives on its territory troops belonging to the belligerent armies shall intern them, as far as possible, at a distance from the theatre of war. It may keep them in camps and even confine them in fortresses or in places set apart for this purpose. It shall decide whether officers can be left at liberty on giving their parole not to leave the neutral territory without permission."

Clemenceau suggested—and it was agreed—that Arthur Balfour (the British foreign secretary) should be asked to draft a dispatch to the Dutch government, asking them to take precautions to prevent the departure of the kaiser. It was also agreed that Lansing's draft dispatch to the Dutch government demanding the kaiser's delivery should be immediately approved, so that it might be used when the occasion arose. Japanese foreign minister Makino reserved his assent to the draft dispatch until he had had an opportunity to study it more closely. Once more, Clemenceau asked for more time to consider his final assent to the proposal to try the kaiser in England.[17]

Wilson, Lloyd George, and Clemenceau met again in the afternoon—at 4:00 p.m.—without the Italian and Japanese representatives. The note Balfour prepared was provisionally approved. Clemenceau agreed to deliver the note, once finalized, to the Dutch government on behalf of the conference.[18]

When the Supreme Council next met at noon on 27 June 1919, with Sonnino and Makino present again, the Balfour draft note was presented again for their benefit (noting that they were absent at the meeting of the afternoon of 26 June 1919 when the note was provisionally approved). Makino proposed one typographic suggestion—changing a sentence that said the kaiser "*is* a potentate" to "*was* a potentate" (emphasis added). The amendment was approved, along with the text. It was agreed that the telegram should be published in the morning papers on Sunday, 29 June 1919. Makino also agreed to the text of the letter drafted by Lansing for delivery to the Dutch government at the appropriate time.[19]

On the next day, 28 June 1919 at 11:00 a.m., the Supreme Council received new information that the crown prince had not escaped after all from the Netherlands. Perhaps it was a false alarm. For that reason, it was agreed that the note Balfour drafted would not be published in the newspapers, but would still be dispatched to the Dutch government only.[20]

A notable phenomenon in the circumstances of the Allied states' determination to prosecute the kaiser was a surfeit of German officials who were prepared to replace the kaiser as the defendant in any resulting prosecution. During the Supreme Council's afternoon meeting on 28 June 1919, Clemenceau requested Paul Mantoux (the official interpreter to the Supreme

Council) to read the English translation of a letter of 25 June 1919 from Theobald von Bethmann Hollweg (the German chancellor from 1906 to 1917),[21] begging the Allied and Associated Powers "to direct against [his] person the procedure which they propose to initiate against His Majesty the Emperor."[22] According to him, under the German constitutional law, Bethmann Hollweg, as former chancellor of the Empire, bore "the exclusive responsibility for political acts of the Emperor during [his] tenure of office." On that basis, he placed himself at the disposal of the Allied and Associated Powers.[23]

Wilson rejected the premise of Bethmann Hollweg's offer. That premise was the suggestion that the German constitution was similar to that of Great Britain or France, according to which the head of state was only ceremonial, with executive authority resting only on the prime minister.[24] Wilson understood that the chancellor of the German Empire was under the direct control of the kaiser. So, Bethmann Hollweg's interpretation was not acceptable to Wilson. It was eventually agreed that the reply to Bethmann Hollweg's letter should express the recognition of the Allied and Associated Powers of the spirit in which the offer was made, but should state that Bethmann Hollweg's interpretation of the German constitution could not be accepted.[25] It was further evidence of Wilson's support for the kaiser's trial, and rejecting any strategy that preserved immunity for him.

On 28 June 1919, Clemenceau duly delivered to the Dutch the note that Balfour had drafted for the council. It was a blunt communication. The Allied and Associated Powers expressed perturbation by "the rumours which have been repeatedly spread of late regarding the eventuality" that the crown prince of Germany, who was a high-ranking officer in the German army, "should in violation of the laws of war escape from the neutral country in which he [was] interned"—that being the Netherlands. On that premise, the note sternly warned the Netherlands that "[t]o allow this escape would be an international crime which could not be pardoned to those who would have contributed to it through their negligence or their complicity." Continuing, the note said that the "Allied and Associated Powers are convinced that these considerations will spontaneously commend themselves to the Government of the Netherlands." In an artful play at ironic charity, the note communicated the desire of the allies to add that in case the Netherlands "felt that in the present circumstances the safe keeping of the ex-Emperor carries with it responsibilities more irksome

than [the Netherlands] is in a position to assume the Allied and Associated Powers are disposed to assume this burden and thereby relieve a neutral state of an ungrateful task which it has not sought but the execution of which constitutes a most weighty obligation."²⁶

The Dutch were not impressed. And their reply was reciprocally blunt. In his note of 1 July 1919, Harman van Karnebeek, the Dutch minister of foreign affairs, informed that the "admonition" of the Allied and Associated states had "painfully surprised" the Dutch government, given especially that the note "according to its terms [was] only based on rumours." The Dutch government, the reply informed, was "conscious of its international obligations" and "equally conscious of not having failed to fulfill them." In conclusion, the minister informed the Allied and Associated Powers that, concerning the subject matter of the note verbale, the Dutch government "must reserve to itself the free exercise of its sovereignty as to the rights which belong to it and the duties incumbent upon it."²⁷

Following the exchange between Clemenceau and Karnebeek, of which the U.S. embassy in The Hague was fully aware, Franklin Mott Gunther, the U.S. chargé d'affaires in The Hague, had a meeting with Karnebeek in the afternoon on 10 July 1919. During the meeting, Gunther did his best to avoid the subject of the ex-kaiser. But Karnebeek brought it up, making sure to underscore the comfort that the Dutch government took in the knowledge that Lansing considered the prosecution of the ex-kaiser as unlawful in international law. According to Gunther, Karnebeek "added that he had been much interested in reading the memorandum [of reservation] concerning the ex-Kaiser prepared by Mr Lansing and Doctor Scott and in thus becoming acquainted with [the American] attitude." In that connection, Karnebeek informed Gunther that the Dutch would never consent to an action that was unlawful in the view they shared with Lansing.²⁸ More plainly understood, they would not be surrendering the ex-kaiser.

∽

In a related development, Karnebeek had a lengthy discussion with the British chargé d'affaires in The Hague about the ex-kaiser. His purpose was to drive home "the ridiculous position in which Clemenceau's communication might place" the Allied and Associated Powers should they "really want to get the ex-Kaiser." In that connection, Karnebeek rubbed in the fact "that he knew of [from] Mr Lansing's memorandum that the American Government was not in accord with the policy [of the kaiser's trial] being pursued."[29] All this is to say that the Dutch government had formed the view that "the American Government" was against prosecuting the kaiser.

In the fog of the circumstances, coupled with the fact that the communication to the Dutch government was handled by Clemenceau (as the president of the Peace Conference) on behalf of the Allied and Associated Powers, Karnebeek may not have known that President Wilson was fully in accord with both the idea of prosecuting the kaiser and the demand made to the Dutch to surrender him for trial. That is to say, by the time of that demand for surrender, the only Americans to speak of who were "not in accord" with the idea of the kaiser's prosecution were U.S. secretary of state Lansing and James Brown Scott. Their boss, President Wilson, was fully in accord with the trial and the surrender of the kaiser for that trial.

On 7 December 1919, Gunther wrote to Lansing, informing him that Karnebeek confided in Gunther that the demand of the Allied and Associated Powers for the surrender of the ex-kaiser was imminent. Karnebeek inquired whether Gunther was also aware of that development. Gunther answered in the negative.[30] If the Dutch government had all along been operating on the assumption that their resistance to surrendering the ex-kaiser had the tacit support of the U.S. State Department, in light of Lansing's memorandum of reservation, Lansing's reply to Gunther's telegram of 7 December 1919 removed all mystery from the situation.

Lansing's earlier instruction to Gunther had favored a "non-committal attitude in this matter," to avoid questions about America's "good faith" by their allies.[31] What "good faith" did Lansing have in mind to preserve at first? Might it be his understanding that President Wilson was now in agreement with the trial of the kaiser and his surrender for that purpose, though Wilson was running into political difficulty obtaining the U.S. Senate's approval of the Versailles Treaty?

But, by Lansing's reply of 13 December 1919, he was effectively directing Gunther to spell out to the Dutch that the U.S. State Department was not in support of surrendering the ex-kaiser for trial. First, Lansing informed Gunther that the State Department "was without information in this matter."[32] Lansing's claim was at least curious that his department was without information on the matter as of December 1919. This is considering that it was Lansing himself who produced, at Wilson's direction, the first draft of the communication, back in June 1919, eventually to be sent to the Dutch government, the dispatch of which he advised to be delayed until the ratification of the treaty. Next, Lansing conveyed a set of information and instruction for Gunther's "information and guidance."[33]

In that connection, Lansing repeated the text of a telegram that was sent to the U.S. Mission in Paris on 27 November 1919, saying: "In view of the failure of the Senate to ratify the treaty the President feels that you should withdraw immediately the American representatives on all commissions growing out of or dependent on either the Peace Conference or the treaty."[34] It was indeed a fair and prudent position. What was questionable was what Lansing added beyond that. First, he added the following positions from the State Department, "Until the Senate takes some action the *Department* proposes to express no opinion concerning questions arising under the terms of the treaty except those in which it may interest itself because of the necessity to protect American interests" (emphasis added).[35] Again, a fair position.

But Lansing's next instruction to Gunther went beyond the strict logic of the two foregoing points of information. "Following out the policy above indicated," Lansing wrote, "the United States *will not at present support* any demand for the extradition of the ex-Kaiser or participate in any way in his trial should it occur."[36] In ordinary life, let alone in the ultrasensitive world of diplomacy, there is a radical difference between the formulations "At this time, we are *not in a position* to oppose or support *x*" versus "We *will not support x* at this time."

More telling, perhaps, is that as of the time of those instructions from Lansing to Gunther in December 1919, President Wilson was in the grip of debilitating ill health. He suffered an apparent cerebral stroke in early October 1919,[37] and as of February 1920, "the President apparently was not fully in command of the executive branch of the government."[38] In the meantime, Lansing was laboring under allegations of disloyalty toward Wilson in connection with aspects of the Treaty of Versailles that Lansing had advised Wilson against, eventually leading to Wilson's demand for Lansing's resignation.[39] Wilson's brother-in-law and confidant wrote of how Wilson held no personal grudges against others or his aides with whom he parted ways on account of differences of opinion. "There was nothing to get excited about. The case of Mr Lansing was different; there he felt there had been duplicity, and that he would not forgive."[40]

Mrs. Edith Wilson plaintively recalled Lansing's negative attitude toward her husband, ranging from lack of support to outright betrayal. She complained that amid all the complexities that Wilson had to deal with during the Peace Conference, "[her] husband stood practically alone—with very lukewarm support from some of his own Commission, such as Lansing,"[41] who "had been a hindrance rather than a help."[42] What is more, Mrs. Wilson wrote of Lansing's outright betrayal. In that regard, she complained that he was the first person to raise questions about President Wilson's "disability," during Wilson's bout of ill health, with the aim of forcing the president from office by reason of impairment of mind.[43] "As soon as the President became ill," Mrs. Wilson wrote, "Mr Lansing started agitation to put his Chief out of office. He began calling the heads of other Departments to his office to confer on the direction of public affairs."[44] It was the latter conduct that eventually led President Wilson to write to Lansing, on 7 February 1920, formally accusing him of usurpation of a presidential prerogative, among other things.[45] In reply, Lansing tendered his resignation, which Wilson promptly accepted.[46]

It is not clear whether Lansing's undermining of Wilson's agreement to both the trial and the surrender of the kaiser would have been part of the compost of what Wilson felt to be acts of betrayal and disloyalty from Lansing. But, all told, it would be difficult to avoid that conclusion.

It is not unusual to encounter commentary in the literature alleging that the public profession of the leadership of Allied governments for the kaiser's trial was something of a *tour de passe-passe*, a jiggery-pokery, on the

Figure 7.1.   *Punch,* January 21, 1919

part of the Allies who did not really wish to prosecute the kaiser. A *Punch* cartoon of 21 January 1919 makes that point (see figure 7.1). It shows an Allied policeman in conversation with a Dutch damsel with the kaiser apprehensively chopping wood (his renowned pastime) a little distance behind her. "So, you say you'd like me to surrender the Ex-Kaiser?" inquired the woman. "Well, ma'am," replied the policeman, "I didn't go so far as that. I only *asked* for him."[47]

Such allegations would not be entirely fair to what the record showed of the attitude of Allied leaders. Indeed, available evidence does not reveal much else that the Allied and Associated leaders could reasonably have done to demonstrate a serious commitment toward prosecuting the kaiser. Such available evidence includes, but is not limited to, the serious work of the Macdonell Committee, the Larnaude–La Pradelle study, the intense debates within the Commission on Responsibilities, and the intense exchanges during the deliberations of the decision-making bodies of the Paris Peace Conference.

One more effort of the last kind is seen from the records of the meeting of the Supreme Council held at 4:00 p.m. on 16 January 1920—six days after the Versailles Treaty came into force. The Supreme Council, now only comprising Lloyd George, Clemenceau, Hugh Wallace (U.S. ambassador to London), Mr. Nitti (Italy), and Mr. Matsui (Japan), each with their secretaries, considered the final text of communication to be sent to the Dutch government. It fell to Matsui to read out the text (though he was seeing it for the first time). Wallace indicated that as the United States did not ratify the treaty, the issue did not concern him, and Lloyd George stated that Wallace should not participate in the discussion. Matsui indicated that he was not in a position to approve the text of the document without instruction from his government. Clemenceau indicated that the communication must be delivered to the Dutch by 6:30 p.m. that evening, and so could not wait for Matsui's consultation with his government.[48]

The text of the communication to the Dutch government is set out in full below, in light of its importance in the early practice of states in relation to the question whether a head of state enjoyed immunity before international courts in relation to international crimes:

Paris, January 15, 1920.

Note to the Queen of Holland Demanding the Delivery of the Kaiser for Trial

The Powers, *in communicating herewith to the Government of the Queen the text of Article 227* (certified copy annexed hereto) of the Peace Treaty with

Germany, which was put into force on January 10, 1920, have, at the same time, the honor to advise that *they have decided to enforce the provisions of that Article without delay.*

Consequently, the Powers address the official request to the Government of the Netherlands for the surrender to the Allies of William of Hohenzollern, ex-Emperor of Germany, in order that he may be put on trial.

As the persons residing in Germany against whom complaint has been lodged by the Allied and Associated Powers must be surrendered to them in compliance with Article 228 of the Treaty of Peace, the ex-Emperor, if he had remained in Germany, would have been surrendered under the same conditions by the German Government.

The Dutch Government is aware of the unassailable reasons which *imperatively demand that the premeditated violations of international treaties, as well as systematic disregard of the most sacred rules of international law, suffer, irrespective of persons, no matter of how high position, the penalties* provided for by the Peace Congress.

The Powers call attention, *among other crimes, to the cynical violation of the neutrality of Belgium and Luxembourg, the barbarous and merciless hostage system, the mass deportations of populations,* [page 888] *the carrying away of the young women of Lille, torn from their families and thrown defenceless into the most promiscuous environment, the systematic devastation without military justification of entire territories, the unrestricted submarine warfare including the inhuman abandon of victims on the high seas, the innumerable acts committed by the German authorities against non-combatants in contempt of the laws of war, etc. The responsibility for all these acts, at least the moral responsibility, lies with the supreme chief who* commanded and *who took advantage of his power to break, or to permit to be broken, the most sacred rules of the human conscience.*

The Powers cannot conceive that the Dutch Government could consider the tremendous responsibility of the ex-Emperor with less disapproval than they themselves.

Holland would not be fulfilling her international obligations if she refused to join the other nations within the means at her disposal in carrying out or at the very least in not hindering the punishment of the crimes committed.

In addressing this request to the Government of the Netherlands, *the Powers deem it their duty to dwell especially on the particular character of this request. It is the duty of the Powers to insure the execution of Article 227 without being held back by argumentation,* because the case under discussion does not fall within the lines of a public accusation of a fundamentally legal nature, but is an act of high international policy, imposed by the conscience of the universe, for which the procedure was provided in order to give the accused such guarantees as have never been known before in international law.

The Powers are convinced that Holland, a country that has always asserted its respect of Law and its Love of Justice, and which, among the first, asked for a place in the League of Nations, will not attempt to help cover with her moral authority, violations of the essential principles of the solidarity of nations, all equally interested in preventing the return of a similar catastrophe.

The people of the Netherlands have the highest interest in not appearing to protect or to shelter the principal author of these crimes on their territory, and in facilitating the trial which the voices of millions of victims demand.[49]

As is clear from the text of the document, not only did the Allies indicate in article 227 of the Treaty of Versailles that the kaiser must be prosecuted before an international court, the communication also shows clearly that the Allies were pressing their demand in earnest for the surrender of the kaiser so that he might be prosecuted in furtherance of that provision.

The Rule of Non-Refoulement

The Dutch government enjoys current reputation as a great promoter of international law. Its capital city, The Hague, is held out as the "City of Peace and Justice."[50] These are well-deserved reputations. For that reason, there would be those who would wish the Dutch government to have taken a different decision in 1919 and surrendered the kaiser for his criminal trial before an international criminal court. That would no doubt have been a resonant event in legal history, heralding a new dawn in international law and international relations.

But, as a matter of international law, the Dutch refusal to surrender the kaiser to the Entente powers is a reasonably defensible position. It was correct of the latter to have known not to force the issue. Here is why. The Netherlands was a neutral country during World War I. The rules of international law concerning rights and duties of neutral states reasonably encompassed the right of the Dutch to grant asylum to the kaiser.* The pressure on the Dutch to surrender the kaiser came dangerously close to

---

* It may be noted in this regard that the Institute of International Law adequately captured that norm in their *Oxford Manual* (1880): "It is universally admitted that a neutral State cannot, without compromising its neutrality, lend aid to either belligerent, or permit them to make use of its territory. On the other hand, considerations of humanity dictate that asylum should not be refused to individuals who take refuge in neutral territory to escape death or captivity. Hence the following provisions, calculated to reconcile the opposing interests involved": see the commentary preceding article 79. It may be noted that the authority of the *Oxford Manual* lies in its value as a distillation of customary international law as understood at the time. The manual's authors indicated that value as follows: "Rash and extreme rules will not, furthermore, be found therein. The Institute has not sought innovations in

pressuring the Dutch to violate what in present-day terminology would be called the rule of *non-refoulement* in international law of asylum. This is the rule that prevents an asylum state from handing a refugee over to the people from whom he was fleeing—or sending him back to such a place where he might suffer harm.[51] It is true that this principle finds its clearest expression in the Refugee Convention of 1950.[52] No claim may be confidently made that, as of 1919, when the Dutch were resisting the pressure to surrender the kaiser, the *non-refoulement* principle had attained the "constant and uniform usage practised by the States in question" standard laid down in the *Asylum Case* as the test of customary international law.[53] But sympathy for that argument—in support of a successful bullying of the Dutch into surrendering the kaiser to the Allies—might have registered to modern sensibilities just as feebly as sympathy would embrace the denial of moral guilt for a foul conduct merely because it took place before society had the good sense to abjure it formally.

A Historic Failure?

The Dutch refusal to surrender the kaiser for trial, thus defeating his prosecution, has led some to view article 227 of the Versailles Treaty as something of a historical failure. In his very important work on the politics of the Allied efforts to prosecute the kaiser, James Willis commented that Lloyd George's "single most important error was disregarding President Wilson's readiness to dispose of the problem of the kaiser in the first days of the Paris Peace Conference."[54] Willis's point rests in the claim that Wilson's preference was for the Allied leaders to deal with the problem of the kaiser using a summary political decision to send him to exile as happened to Napoleon Bonaparte, but that Lloyd George insisted on sending the question to the Commission on Responsibilities to study the idea of prosecuting the kaiser as a legal question.

From the perspective of development of international law, it is a highly misconceived criticism to say that Lloyd George was mistaken in rejecting the political solution, insisting on sending the question for a considered study by legal experts.

Here, it must be kept in mind that there was nothing at all remarkable about the political solution of sending deposed leaders into exile—except that such a disposition was every bit the same thing as punishing someone without the due process of law. Recall that banishment or transportation

---

drawing up the 'Manual'; it has contented itself with stating clearly and codifying the accepted ideas of our age so far as this has appeared allowable and practicable."

(in the sense of sending someone away to a place of punishment, or a penal colony, such as Australia originally was) was a form of punishment for a criminal offense. So, it was an unremarkable solution because, long before Napoleon, such political measures—even including summary executions—had been visited upon deposed heads of state.

"Finding a safe haven for ex-leaders is a practice that goes back to ancient times," wrote Tom Geoghegan. "Greek tyrant Peisistratus was ousted from office in Athens and exiled to northern Greece, where he gathered an army to once again conquer the city." Notably, "Scottish monarchs in the Middle Ages were often exiled to France, united by the so-called Auld Alliance and their common enemy, England."[55]

Beyond the many exiles of Peisistratus (the first of which was around 556 BCE),[56] the very long list of exiled leaders include, but are not limited to, Piero "Otto" Orseolo, the Doge of Venice (exiled in Byzantium in 1026);[57] George Terter I of Bulgaria (exiled in Byzantium in 1292);[58] Muhammad XII of Granada (exiled in Morocco in 1492);[59] Piero de' Medici of Florence (exiled in Venice in 1494);[60] Antonió I of Portugal (exiled in France in 1580);[61] Charles II, "The Merry Monarch" of England (exiled in France in 1651);[62] James II (exiled in France in 1688);[63] Agustín de Iturbide, or Agustín I of Mexico (exiled to Tuscany in 1823);[64] Charles X of France (exiled in England in 1830);[65] Antonio López de Santa Anna of Mexico (exiled in Cuba and other countries in 1845);[66] Constantine I of Greece (exiled in Switzerland in 1917);[67] and Ferdinand of Bulgaria (exiled in Germany in 1918).[68] And the period after World War I also saw similar political methods. For instance, Emeka Odumegwu Ojukwu, the secessionist leader of Biafra, went into a long exile in Côte d'Ivoire in 1969 at the end of the Nigerian civil war;[69] Idi Amin of Uganda went into exile in Saudi Arabia in 1979 following his defeat in the war with Tanzania;[70] the last Mohammad Reza Shah Pahlavi of Iran fled into exile in Egypt in 1979;[71] and Yahya Jammeh of Gambia escaped to Equatorial Guinea in 2017.[72] Samuel Doe of Liberia was tortured and summarily executed in 1990 upon capture by rebels during one of Liberia's civil wars,[73] as was Muammar al-Qaddafi of Libya.[74]

Indeed, a quick internet search will reveal that history had known no less than fifty instances before 1919 when deposed leaders were forced into exile.

That it would have been easier or more convenient to do the same for the kaiser in 1919—which was more or less the case given his abdication and exile to the Netherlands—should not give it a heightened normative value.

But the novel course that Lloyd George set out to carve out in 1919, at the Paris Peace Conference, was to change international law: to subject heads of state to the judicial process on charges of committing crimes of atrocity. He could not have achieved that by following the usual, more convenient political process of summary banishment or even execution. He needed to bring the legal consideration of the matter to bear. By insisting on that course, he achieved much in the development of international law, notwithstanding that it did not produce the immediate result of prosecuting the kaiser. It was an important precedent, by breaking the taboo of untouchability of supreme national power, the development indicated new possibilities in international law, by reorienting it along the lines of the norms of international law contemplated in article 227 of the Treaty of Versailles: the prosecution of a head of state or head of government before an international criminal tribunal where the plea of immunity would not be allowed. That development has served international law quite well in recent decades, the culmination of which has been jurisprudence such as the *Jordan Referral re Al-Bashir* appeals judgment of the International Criminal Court, and the earlier jurisprudence of the Appeals Chamber of the Special Court for Sierra Leone in *Prosecutor v. Charles Taylor* to a similar effect, consistent with several earlier pronouncements of the International Criminal Tribunal for the former Yugoslavia saying the same thing.

THE LEIPZIG LETDOWN   **8**

In putting up their stiff objection against the trial of the kaiser before an international criminal tribunal, Lansing and Scott relied heavily on the claim of need to respect the sovereignty of states. As they put it: "the people of every independent country are possessed of sovereignty, and that that sovereignty is not held in that sense by rulers; that the sovereignty which is thus possessed can summon before it any person, no matter how high his estate, and call upon him to render an account of his official stewardship; that the essence of sovereignty consists in the fact that it is not responsible to any foreign sovereignty; that in the exercise of sovereign powers which have been conferred upon him by the people, a monarch or head of state acts as their agent; that he is only responsible to them; and that *he is responsible to no other people or group of people in the world.*"[1]

The U.S. Supreme Court in *Trump v. U.S.* (2024) eventually dispelled the claim that in the existence of sovereignty, national systems can be trusted to hold their own heads of state to account, thus obviating the need for accountability in international law. Still, Lansing and Scott's absolute conception of sovereignty was truly surprising on the part of any serious international lawyer. For one thing, it is normatively incompatible with the idea of international law as a rules-based order that demands real accountability at any level. In other words, international law becomes entirely pointless if those who violate its tenets in ways that injure other people are held "responsible to no other group of people in the world." What is the point of law, then, when those whose conduct it regulates are not accountable to those who share an interest in having the law respected?

James W. Garner, a renowned World War I–era American international relations scholar delivered a sensible repudiation of the absolute theory of sovereignty, in the wake of the creation of the League of Nations for better coordination of international relations.

"Among the traditional political conceptions which in recent years have become the object of almost irreverent attack," he began, "is that which ascribes the quality of absolutism to that often elusive, but ever present, double-faced creation of the jurists which bears the name of sovereignty."

"Text-writers," he continued, "sometimes in unqualified terms, still persist in claiming for it the unrestricted supremacy which was attributed to it in an age when its wielders everywhere were absolute monarchs; but an increasing number, less influenced by legal theories than by realities, see in it only the ghost of personal monarchy, as Hobbes characterized it, 'sitting crowned on the grave thereof.'"[2]

Garner considered that "the term is not only inapt, unscientific and confusing, but the notion itself is misleading and even dangerous since it gives rise to illusions and creates a mentality which has often proved to be an obstacle to the maintenance of peace and the advancement of the common interests of states. The pretended 'prerogative' of sovereignty has often been invoked to justify national conduct which was in violation of rights of other states and the common interests of the society of states."[3]

Citing precedents, Garner pointed out that states had relied on claims of sovereignty to forbid navigation through rivers that course through several territories including their own, to exclude foreign aircraft from flying above their territories, to forbid the transmission of radio telegrams through the air above their territory, to confiscate the property of aliens, and to repudiate debts due to foreign bondholders.[4]

"An almost superstitious attachment to the theory and the disinclination to abate a jot or tittle of the substance," he continued, "has been the chief obstacle to the organization of the world for the promotion of common economic interests and the establishment of safeguards for the maintenance of the general peace."[5]

It is instructive that the absolute conception of sovereignty that Lansing and Scott asserted was only in relation to heads of state. For Lansing and Scott had no objection to the idea that states have a right to prosecute soldiers on the opposite side of the war. As already noted, Lansing and Scott expressly conceded that such jurisdiction may be exercised. As they put it:

The American representatives, however, agree . . . that "every belligerent has, according to international law, the power and authority to try the individuals alleged to be guilty of the crimes" constituting violations of the laws and customs of war, "if such persons have been taken prisoners or have otherwise fallen into its power." The American representatives are likewise in thorough accord with the further provisions that "each belligerent has, or has power to set up, pursuant to its own legislation, an appropriate tribunal, military or civil, for the trial of such cases." The American representatives concur in the view that "these courts would be able to try the incriminated persons according to their own procedure."[6]

The foregoing concessions are uncontroversial as correct statements of international law. They become remarkable only because of events such as the curious controversy that, in 2017, attended draft article 7 of the International Law Commission's Draft Articles on the Immunity of State Officials from Foreign Criminal Jurisdiction. The draft provision rejects immunity of state agents from the criminal jurisdiction of foreign states in relation to war crimes and other international crimes.[7] The commentators who opposed the draft article 7 appeared not to have been aware that, as far back as 1919, Lansing and Scott had accepted that states always had the right to prosecute enemy soldiers for war crimes.

Lansing's and Scott's objection was only in relation to prosecuting heads of state before any external forum.

Perhaps the greater surprise was that Lansing and Scott thought it a serious argument that nations should be systematically trusted to hold their own citizens accountable for international crimes, let alone their own heads of state. The "futility" of that expectation was recalled by Robert H. Jackson during his opening statement at the trial of the major war criminals before the International Military Tribunal at Nuremberg on 21 November 1945. "Either the victors must judge the vanquished," said Jackson, "or we must leave the defeated to judge themselves.

"After the first World War," he noted, "we learned the futility of the latter course."[8]

Jackson's allusion was to the national trials that the Allies left Germany to conduct at the German Supreme Court at Leipzig, the Reichsgericht, as part of the eventual settlements of World War I. That "futility," as Jackson described it in 1995, was all but eventually brought home in the United States in 2024 by the U.S. Supreme Court in *Trump v. U.S.*

᠊᠊᠊᠊᠊᠊᠊᠊᠊᠊᠊᠊᠊᠊᠊᠊᠊

The background to the Leipzig story, it may be recalled, was that article 228 of the Versailles Treaty required Germany to recognize the right of the Allies to prosecute German nationals accused of war crimes. To that end, Germany was required by the provision to "hand over to the Allied and Associated Powers, or to such one of them as shall so request, all persons accused of having committed an act in violation of the laws and customs of war, who are specified either by name or by the rank, office or employment which they held under the German authorities."

But in the end, German authorities proved unwilling to surrender their own nationals to the Allies for prosecution. Instead, the Germans moved quickly to pre-empt that imposition by passing national legislation under which Germany would prosecute its own nationals at the Reichsgericht in Leipzig.[9]

In the circumstances, as the Allies were establishing the list of suspects for their article 228 prosecution, the German authorities interceded with them on 25 January 1920, with a fervent offer to allow the Leipzig prosecutions to substitute the prosecutions contemplated in article 228 of the Versailles Treaty. Though initially skeptical of the offer, the Allies ultimately relented,[10] notwithstanding that, under the terms of article 228, "any proceedings or prosecution before a tribunal in Germany or in the territory of her allies" would not offset the right of the Allies to prosecute Germans suspected of war crimes.

On 3 February 1920, the Allies forwarded a rather limited list of nine hundred suspects to Baron von Lerner, the Reichstag leader and head of the German delegation to the Paris Peace Conference.

The Allied list included Field Marshal Paul von Hindenburg and General Erich Ludendorff, the two generals who co-commanded the Eighth Army. Hindenburg was a German war hero who fought in both the Austro-Prussian War and the Franco-Prussian War. He retired in 1911, but was called back into service at the start of World War I, where in addition to co-commanding the Eighth Army, as field marshal, he was also the chief of general staff. His rampant use of submarine warfare was generally believed to have been one of the dominant factors that drew the United States into the war, resulting ultimately in Germany's defeat. He eventually served as the second president of Germany, during the Weimar Republic that followed the abdication of Kaiser Wilhelm II. Hindenburg was the German president who appointed Adolf Hitler the chancellor of Germany on 30 November 1933, after Franz von Papen had assured Hindenburg that he (Papen as deputy chancellor) could control Hitler.[11] His name on the list of war criminals that the Allies wanted to prosecute in 1920 was indeed a big deal then.

Other big names on the Allied list were Field Marshal August von Mackensen; Admiral Alfred von Tirpitz; Albrecht, the Duke of Wurttemberg (field marshal of the German Fourth Army in the Ardennes and the last Wurttemberger crown prince, as Kaiser Wilhelm II had no son of his own to succeed him); Prince Rupprecht of Bavaria (commander of the German Sixth Army in Lorraine); and Theobald von Bethmann Hollweg (he was imperial chancellor when the war started and remained in the post during much of the war).[12]

When Lerner saw the list, he returned it to Alexandre Millerand who, on 20 January 1920, succeeded Georges Clemenceau as the French premier and the president of the Paris Peace Conference. Rather than transmit it to his government, Lerner resigned in protest. It was the first sign of things to come. Millerand was thus constrained to send the list directly to the chancellor of Germany. In a further sign of the German disinclination to prosecute their nationals in good faith, their government informed the Allies that the demand upon them to prosecute men held in high esteem as national heroes was politically problematic in the extreme for the government.[13]

From the perspective of accountability, the outcome of the Leipzig proceedings was very disappointing to many observers and commentators. A representative assessment appears as follows:

> The net result of the trials was that out of a total of 901 cases of revolting crimes brought before the Leipzig Court, 888 accused were acquitted or summarily dismissed, and only 13 ended in a conviction; furthermore, although the sentences were so inadequate, those who had been convicted were not even made to serve their sentence. Several escaped, and the prison warders who had engineered their escape were publicly congratulated. . . . Criminals were honoured as heroes, and the German people learned that not only could crimes be committed with impunity, but that it paid to be a criminal.[14]

It is interesting to note that even the leading advocates of immunity of heads of state before international criminal courts do accept that the reason that "attention has been paid to the possibility of subjecting state agents to prosecution in foreign domestic courts or in international courts" is because "states often fail to institute domestic prosecution of their own officials and agents alleged to have committed international crimes."[15]

The Leipzig letdown was clear proof of that phenomenon, and proof that Lansing and Scott—and Vittorio Orlando to a lesser extent—were barking up the wrong tree when they contended that accountability for international crimes was to be left to national jurisdiction. But Leipzig showed the world a good way to leave justice a neglected orphan in the territory of national sovereignty. At Nuremberg, the Allies refused to repeat the mistake.

LONDON CONFERENCE   **9**
OF 1945

Twenty-six years after the Paris Peace Conference of 1919, there was another conference to clean up the normative dross left by another war. At the conclusion of World War II, the Allies were, as noted earlier, determined to avoid repeating the Leipzig mistake of leaving it to Germany to prosecute their own nationals accused of violations of norms of international criminal law. U.S. chief prosecutor Robert H. Jackson alluded to that lesson when, during his opening statement at the Nuremberg trial, he noted the "futility" of leaving Germans to judge themselves.[1]

Unlike at Paris in 1919, in 1945, the Americans were at the vanguard of seeking accountability of Nazi leaders before an international tribunal. Chief among the targets for prosecution was Adolf Hitler, the head of state of Germany.

As World War II raged on, Allied leaders made sure to communicate their determination to prosecute the nationals of Axis powers suspected of atrocities. U.S. president Franklin D. Roosevelt communicated that determination in a series of statements.

In a press statement of 21 August 1942, he put Axis powers on notice "that the time will come when they shall have to stand in courts of law in the very countries which they are now oppressing and answer for their acts."[2] On 7 October 1942, he issued a press statement announcing the intention of his government and that of the British government to establish a United Nations Commission for the Investigation of War Crimes for purposes of the "just and sure punishment" of "the ringleaders for atrocities."[3] During a radio broadcast of 12 October 1942, his Fireside Chat no. 23, he informed as follows:

> The United Nations have decided to establish the identity of those Nazi leaders who are responsible for the innumerable acts of savagery. As each of these criminal deeds is committed, it is being carefully investigated; and the evidence is being relentlessly piled up for the future purposes of justice.
>
> We have made it entirely clear that the United Nations seek no mass reprisals against the populations of Germany or Italy or Japan. But the ring leaders and their brutal henchmen must be named, and apprehended, and tried in accordance with the judicial processes of criminal law.[4]

In their response of 14 October 1942, the Soviet government endorsed the message of President Roosevelt's Fireside Chat no. 23. In their note verbale to that effect, Soviet foreign minister Vyacheslav Molotov communicated his government's position in the following words:

> The Soviet Government is in agreement with the declaration of Mr. Roosevelt, President of the United States of America, made in his speech of October 12th, on the question of punishing the Nazi leaders concretely responsible for countless acts of brutality, i.e., that the clique of leaders and their cruel accomplices must be *mentioned by name, arrested* and *tried according to the criminal code*.[5]

Continuing, Molotov announced the names of those his government had in mind to arrest and prosecute "according to the criminal code."

"The whole of mankind knows the names and bloody crimes of the leaders of the criminal Hitlerite clique," he wrote. They were "Hitler, Goering, Hess, Goebbels, Himmler, Ribbentrop, Rosenberg and other organizers of German brutalities from among the leaders of Fascist Germany."[6]

In a press statement of 30 July 1943, President Roosevelt enthused that the "wheels of justice have turned constantly since those [prior] statements were issued and are still turning."

No doubt mindful of the kaiser's escape to the Netherlands at the end of World War I, Roosevelt warned neutral countries against similarly granting asylum to Mussolini, Hitler, and Tojo, thereby allowing them "to escape their just deserts."[7]

"There are now rumors," he said, "that Mussolini and members of his Fascist gang may attempt to take refuge in neutral territory. One day Hitler and his gang and Tojo and his gang will be trying to escape from their countries. I find it difficult to believe that any neutral country would give asylum to or extend protection to any of them."[8]

In remarks made on 24 March 1944, President Roosevelt continued to lament "the wholesale systematic murder of Jews of Europe" that continued "unabated every hour." In that connection he considered it "fitting that we should again proclaim our determination that none who participate in these acts of savagery shall go unpunished.

"The United Nations have made it clear," he continued, reiterating his earlier statements, "that they will pursue the guilty and deliver them up in order that Justice be done."

Indicating that the range of potential accused would comprise leaders and followers, Roosevelt stressed that the "warning applies not only to the leaders but also to their functionaries and subordinates in Germany and in the satellite countries."[9]

He warned that "[a]ll who share the guilt shall share the punishment."

"Hitler is committing these crimes against humanity in the name of the German people," Roosevelt continued, naming the primary suspect in the crimes he insisted must be punished.

And he asked all Germans and all those under Nazi domination to "show the world by his action that in his heart he does not share these insane criminal desires."[10]

⌒

The Declaration of Atrocities, part of the Moscow Declaration of 1943, was another renowned medium through which the Allied determination for punishment was communicated. The Declaration of Atrocities was signed by President Roosevelt, UK prime minister Winston Churchill, and Soviet premier Joseph Stalin. It communicated the commitment of the Allies, on behalf of thirty-two states then organized as the "United Nations," to subject to the judicial process "those German officers and men and members of the Nazi party who have been responsible for or have taken a consenting part in . . . atrocities, massacres and executions," evidence of which had been received by the Allies.[11]

As the London Conference was in progress during the summer of 1945, to organize the prosecution of Nazi atrocities, the Allies' determination to prosecute Axis war crimes suspects was reiterated in article VI of the Potsdam Declaration of 1945 in which the Allies "reaffirm[ed] their intention to bring [the major] criminals to swift and sure justice."

In addition to the various statements of President Roosevelt made during the war, it was clear that, even ahead of the London Conference and through it, the Allies had their eyes firmly trained on the punishment of the Nazi leadership—including Germany's head of state Adolf Hitler.

ↄ—

Regarding the Allied resolve to prosecute the leadership of Germany, it is notable that while Justice Jackson was considering acceptance of his appointment as the U.S. representative to the London Conference, the U.S. government provided him with a copy of the "Yalta Memorandum" as a "statement of the position already taken by the Government" on the matter of punishment of the alleged war criminals.[12] The memorandum was a joint document of Secretary of War Henry Stimson, Secretary of State Edward Stettinius Jr., and Attorney General Francis Biddle dated 22 January 1945—a good three months before the war ended in Europe on 8 May 1945 and eight months before it did for Japan on 2 September 1945. At that time, Hitler was alive and the head of state of Germany. He would not die until 30 April 1945.[13]

The document was called the "Yalta Memorandum"—occasionally the "Crimean Proposal"—because "it had been prepared to guide President Roosevelt when he attended the Yalta Conference,"[14] also known as the Crimean Conference, from 4 to 11 February 1945 where Churchill, Roosevelt, and Stalin discussed the reorganization of Germany and Europe in anticipation of the conclusion of the war.

Regarding the "crimes to be punished," it was contemplated in the Yalta Memorandum that the "criminality of the German leaders and their associates does not consist solely of individual outrages, but represents the result of a systematic and planned reign of terror within Germany, in the satellite Axis countries, and in the occupied countries of Europe," dating as far back, at least, as 1933 "when Hitler was first appointed Chancellor of the Reich."[15]

And the leadership of the Third Reich were unremarkably identified as primary "criminals to be punished," in the following words: "The outstanding offenders are, of course, those leaders of the Nazi Party and German Reich who since January 30, 1933, have been in control of formulating and executing Nazi policies."[16] In addition to the Nazi leaders, the other criminals to be punished were the operational organizations that the Nazi leaders "created and utilized" for purposes of "carrying out the acts of oppression and terrorism which their program involved." Chief among these were the Gestapo, the elite Schutzstaffel (SS), and the Sturm-abteilung (SA; also known as the Stormtroopers or the "Brown Shirts").[17]

Leaving no doubt that the contemplated criminals were Hitler and his colleagues at the top and that what was contemplated was their criminal prosecution, the Yalta Memorandum noted as follows:

> After Germany's unconditional surrender the United Nations could, if they elected, put to death *the most notorious Nazi criminals, such as Hitler or Himmler*, without trial or hearing. *We do not favor this method.* While it has the advantages of a sure and swift disposition, it would be violative of the most fundamental principles of justice, common to all the United Nations. This would encourage the Germans to turn these criminals into martyrs, and, in any event, only a few individuals could be reached in this way.
>
> *We think that the just and effective solution lies in the use of the judicial method.* Condemnation of these criminals after a trial, moreover, would command maximum public support in our own times and receive the respect of history. The use of the judicial method will, in addition, make available for all mankind to study in future years an authentic record of Nazi crimes and criminality.[18]

Against that background, it was recommended in the memorandum that the "German leaders" and the organizations employed by them, notably the Gestapo, the SA, and the SS, "should be charged both with the commission of their atrocious crimes, and also with joint participation in a broad criminal enterprise which included and intended these crimes, or was reasonably calculated to bring them about."[19]

⌒

On 23 April 1945—seven days before Hitler died—another important document that revealed the mind-set of the Allies was delivered by Sir Alexander Cadogan (the permanent undersecretary in the UK Foreign Office) to Judge Samuel Rosenman, White House counsel. The British aide-mémoire reveals that it was a foregone conclusion within the British government that Hitler (Germany's head of state) and Mussolini (Italy's head of government) must be punished by death. The only question left for debate was how that punishment was to be exacted: summary extrajudicial execution or death penalty following conviction by a judicial tribunal. His Britannic Majesty's Government ("HMG") addressed the matter as follows:

> H.M.G. assume that it is beyond question that *Hitler* and a number of arch-criminals associated with him (including *Mussolini*) *must*, so far as they

fall into Allied hands, suffer the penalty of death for their conduct leading up to the war and for the wickedness which they have either themselves perpetrated or have authorized in the conduct of the war. *It would be manifestly impossible to punish war criminals of a lower grade by a capital sentence pronounced by a Military Court unless the ringleaders are dealt with equal severity.* This is really involved in the concluding sentence of the Moscow Declaration on this subject, which reserves for the arch-criminals whose offences have no special localization treatment to be determined in due course by the Allies.[20]

Passing upon that basic assumption that Hitler and Mussolini and their associates *must* suffer the sentence of death, the aide-mémoire then addressed the question of the most appropriate process for that outcome. There is little question that the British government was debating the American position as communicated in the Yalta Memorandum that the most appropriate manner of punishment was through the judicial process. In that regard, the British government argued as follows:

> It being conceded that *these leaders must* suffer death, *the question arises whether they should be tried by some form of tribunal claiming to exercise judicial functions, or whether the decision taken by the Allies should be reached and enforced without the machinery of a trial.* H.M.G. thoroughly appreciate the arguments which have been advanced in favour of some form of preliminary trial. But H.M.G. are also deeply impressed with the dangers and difficulties of this course, and they wish to put before their principal Allies, in a connected form, the arguments which have led them to think that execution without trial is the preferable course.[21]

Training its analysis on Hitler, the rest of the document laid out why it was better to subject him to summary execution than to criminal prosecution. The primary consideration, it was contended, revolved around this question: "[W]hat is the real charge which Allied people and the world as a whole makes against Hitler?"[22]

The answer was this: "It is the totality of his offences against the international standard which civilised countries try to observe which makes him the scoundrel that he is."[23]

That being the case, the argument continued, an indictment and trial of "these offences in the manner that is necessary for reasons of justice in a criminal court"—and the determination of Hitler's fate "on the conclusion reached by the tribunal as to the truth of this bundle of charges and the adequacy of the proof"—would make the judicial process "exceedingly long and elaborate."[24]

Just to be sure, the aide-mémoire elaborated upon the anticipated features of Hitler's trial, according to the ordinary judicial process that carried that risk of a very long trial:

> He, of course, must have in such a trial all the rights properly conceded to an accused person. He must be defended, if he wishes, by counsel, and he must call any relevant evidence. According to British ideas, at any rate, his defence could not be forcibly shut down or limited because it involves a great expenditure of time. There is nothing upon which British opinion is more sensitive in the realm of criminal procedure than the suspicion that an accused person—whatever the depths of his crime—has been denied his full defence.[25]

All of which is to say, the British government accepted it as an elementary proposition that Hitler must suffer capital punishment. Their argument, rather, was to get straight to that result without the complication of a criminal prosecution.

The farthest consideration from HMG's mind—assuming it ever occurred to them—was to grant Hitler any reprieve merely because he was a head of state who enjoyed immunity. But, as will be seen, the Allies had occasion to address the issue of immunity head-on, even before the London Conference of 1945.

As of the time of the Yalta Conference in 1945, President Roosevelt was in declining health.[26] On the afternoon of 12 April 1945, two weeks before the commencement of the San Francisco Conference, which he had convened for the formation of the United Nations, Roosevelt suffered a massive cerebral hemorrhage while sitting for a portrait. He died within a few hours.[27]

At the time of Roosevelt's death, the White House counsel, Judge Rosenman, was in England trying to persuade the United Kingdom to proceed with the trial of war criminals as outlined in the Yalta Memorandum.[28]

On the margins of the San Francisco Conference that commenced on 23 April 1945 and lasted until 26 June 1945, now with President Harry S. Truman as the convenor, Rosenman continued his effort to rally the Allies for war crimes prosecution according to the Yalta Memorandum. By this time, the U.S. government representatives, working with Justice Jackson, had distilled the Yalta proposal down to a draft protocol, which Rosenman and a team of U.S. government representatives took to San Francisco, to canvass with foreign ministers Molotov (Soviet Union), Anthony Eden (UK), and Georges Bidault (Provisional Government of France), as the basis of an agreement for the war crimes prosecution.[29]

One striking clause in the draft protocol was Clause 10, which precluded immunity in the following words:

> The parties to this Agreement declare that any defense based upon the fact that the accused is or was the head or purported head or other principal official of a state is legally inadmissible, and will not be entertained by any tribunal before which charges brought pursuant to this Agreement are tried.[30]

The draft protocol was accompanied by a U.S. government memorandum dated 30 April 1945, which the U.S. government presented to its allied interlocutors at San Francisco, responding to the position and arguments presented in the UK aide-mémoire of 23 April 1945. The American memorandum of 30 April (the "San Francisco" Memorandum) was, in effect, a robust legal brief.

In the San Francisco Memorandum, the U.S. government reiterated their argument that the preferred method of determining guilt and exerting punishment must be the judicial process—and not "political action." For, such action "would be violative of concepts of justice, which the freedom loving United Nations accept and, on that account, would be distasteful and inappropriate."[31]

"No principle of justice," the memo argued, "is so fundamental in most men's minds as the rule that punishment will be inflicted by judicial action."[32]

That said, it was stressed, once more, that in the judicial proceedings contemplated for the "Axis leaders" or "Nazi leaders"[33]—more specifically, "Hitler and his associates"[34] or "Hitler and the other Axis leaders . . . being tried"[35]—the procedure would "exclude any defense based upon the fact that the accused is or was the head or purported head or other principal official of a state."[36]

Thus, the international law reform value of prosecuting "Hitler and the other Axis leaders" was specifically highlighted in the San Francisco Memorandum, precisely in the same sense that motivated the insistence of Georges Clemenceau and David Lloyd George that Kaiser Wilhelm II must be prosecuted after World War I. In insisting that the avenue of prosecution must be followed—and that summary extrajudicial execution must be rejected—the San Francisco Memorandum reasoned as follows: "Punishment of war criminals should be motivated primarily by its deterrent effect, by the impetus which it gives to improved standards of international conduct and, if the theory of punishment is broad enough, by the implicit condemnation of ruthlessness and unlawful force as instruments of attaining national ends."[37]

Recalling how extrajudicial summary executions can lead to "disastrous results" when such outcomes are perceived to have been "dictated by politics and not by fundamental principles of law and justice," the San Francisco Memorandum stressed, once more, the deterrent value of prosecuting Hitler and the Axis leaders:

> If Allied actions are soundly conceived, however, there exists *an opportunity to mark up an important step in the obtaining of future world security.* Punishment following a judicial determination, in which a number of nations participate, to the effect that the alleged violations of international law have occurred, *will certainly induce future government leaders to think before they act in similar fashion.*[38]

The San Francisco discussions did not produce definite action immediately in San Francisco. But it helped to coalesce the Allies in the direction of a unified acceptance of criminal prosecution pursuant to definite agreement to be worked out later[39] in London—rather than go down the route of extrajudicial summary execution.

On 2 May 1945, President Truman formally designated Justice Jackson as the U.S. representative and chief counsel in the preparation and prosecution of charges of atrocities and war crimes "against the leaders of the European Axis powers and their principal agents and accessories."[40]

It bears stressing that the focus of that designation signaled the commitment of the United States to prosecute "leaders of the European Axis powers" for international crimes. It was an element of state practice of the United States on the international plane.

Notably, that was the second time that a U.S. president had indicated a commitment to prosecute the leadership of a state for international crimes. The first time was during the Paris Peace Conference in 1919, when President Wilson did the following things: (1) eventually agreed with Clemenceau and Lloyd George that the kaiser must be prosecuted; (2) produced the first draft of article 227 of the Versailles Treaty in his own hand, for purposes of effectuating that prosecution; (3) supported the plan to submit demands to the Dutch government to deliver up the kaiser to the Allies, so that he would be prosecuted according to article

227 of the Versailles Treaty; and (4) instructed Secretary of State Robert Lansing to prepare the draft note to the Dutch government making that demand.

༄

The reflective reader may wonder why it was that accountability—even of heads of state—before international tribunals was so readily accepted as a feature of the Nuremberg trials agreed to at the post–World War II London Conference, in contrast to the spirited debate the idea generated at the Paris Peace Conference at the end of World War I. The answer does not invite involved cogitation. Without excluding the inscrutable factor of circumstances, it is enough to accept that at the right place and the right time, individuals can steer the ship of circumstances positively or negatively in defining ways. It took the arrival of Mikhail Gorbachev to end the first Cold War and the arrival of Vladimir Putin to start what many agree is a second Cold War. Donald Trump brought general turmoil to the American presidency, hallmarked by not only an insurrection against the American constitutional order, but also efforts to erode the international rule of law including an unbridled coercion against the International Criminal Court (ICC) complete with imposition of "sanctions" against the ICC's chief prosecutor through an Executive Order. Upon Joe Biden's arrival in office, his administration immediately used a reverse Executive Order to remove the measures that Trump had imposed against the ICC chief prosecutor, finding ways to cooperate with the court. Such is the difference that personalities can make in defining ways in the affairs of nations and in international relations.

One person whose appearance on the world stage made a world of difference in international law reform efforts to ensure accountability—including of heads of state—for serious international crimes was U.S. Supreme Court justice Robert H. Jackson, who was appointed by President Truman as U.S. representative and chief prosecutor for the efforts to prosecute the Nazi war criminals.

༄

In his new position as the U.S. representative, Jackson traveled to London on 22 May 1945, at the direction of President Truman, to try and organize the effort to prosecute the European Axis leaders and their associates and accomplices.[41]

During Jackson's meetings in London with his British interlocutors, Viscount Simon, the Lord Chancellor, unsurprisingly informed Jackson that "the United Kingdom Government had become convinced of the desirability of proceeding along the general lines outlined in the American proposal."[42] In other words, the United Kingdom was now fully on board that punishment would follow the judicial process—not the extrajudicial execution that HMG had earlier urged. The reversal of position was unsurprising, because the earlier British aide-mémoire that favored extrajudicial execution was conveyed by Cadogan, and neither he nor his political superior, Winston Churchill (a former soldier), was a trained lawyer. It must be presumed that they could not have related to the innate qualms that U.S. secretary of war Henry L. Stimson and attorney general Francis Biddle—both Harvard-educated lawyers—might have felt on reading the UK aide-mémoire of 23 April 1945 that summarily and unequivocally contended in less than four pages that the more sensible recourse for the Allies to follow was extrajudicial execution. But, in May 1945, Jackson was meeting with the cream of the British legal establishment, who, it must be presumed, must have cringed at the proposal in Cadogan's aide-mémoire.

In another aide-mémoire dated 3 June 1945, the UK government formally communicated their agreement in principle to employ the judicial process on the general basis of the draft agreement proposed by the U.S. government, offering London as the most suitable venue to begin the negotiations for a final agreement.[43] Hence, the London Conference of 1945 was convened.

∽

On 6 June 1945, Jackson wrote a report to President Truman, updating him on the progress made at the London Conference, the position taken on important elements of the Axis leaders prosecution project, and the reasons for those positions.

Jackson's report addressed such crucial questions as immunity due to official position, the criminality of aggressive wars, and the role of precedents in the growth of international law.

Jackson addressed the matter of the official position of *immunity* from both sides of the accountability coin, beginning with the head side of the coin, which concerns the question of immunity of heads of state, and ending with the tail or subordinate position side of the coin.

Immunity of heads of state was an "obsolete doctrine,"[44] Jackson declared without hesitation. "There is more than a suspicion that this idea is a relic of the doctrine of the divine right of kings. It is, in any event, inconsistent with the position we take toward our own officials, who are frequently brought to court at the suit of citizens who allege their rights to have been invaded."[45]

"We do not accept the paradox," Jackson insisted in the sublime flourish of his argument, "that legal responsibility should be the least where power is the greatest. We stand on the principle of responsible government declared some three centuries ago to King James by Lord Chief Justice Coke, who proclaimed that even a King is still 'under God and the law.'"[46]

And from the tail side of the immunity coin—that being the perspective of the subordinate state agent—Jackson observed that the doctrine of head-of-state immunity logically embraces the defense of superior orders. It is to the effect that "orders from an official superior protect one who obeys them."[47]

The combined implication of head-of-state immunity and superior orders defense would amount to a complete failure of accountability for anyone. "Society as modernly organized," observed Jackson, "cannot tolerate so broad an area of official irresponsibility."[48]

While there may be cases of superior orders that may result in diminished responsibility, if in the given circumstances the subordinate was left no room for discretion; there should be no such diminished responsibility where the subordinate had enough room for discretion or where he was an enthusiastic participant in the crime that he was prompted to commit by what was only an apparent order.[49]

∽

Regarding the criminality of the crime of aggression, Jackson indicated that the American position, driven by "the common sense of justice," will be relatively simple, nontechnical, and uncomplicated by "sterile legalisms developed in the age of imperialism to make war respectable."[50] From that perspective, it was doubtless the case that "the crime which comprehends all lesser crimes, is the crime of making unjustifiable war."[51]

The criminality of war is readily seen in the light of the apparent criminality of the conducts that necessarily define war: "calculated series of killings, of destructions of property, of oppressions."[52] These acts "unquestionably would be criminal except that International Law throws a mantle of protection around acts which otherwise would be crimes, when committed in pursuit of legitimate warfare."[53] In Jackson's view, it is only that pursuit of legitimate cause for warfare that separates belligerency from piracy and brigandage for which international law had always allowed universal criminal jurisdiction. That is to say, in the absence of a legitimate cause, an armed conflict becomes an enterprise as criminal as piracy and brigandage—or even worse.

In his classic text on war and peace written circa 1625, Hugo Grotius, reputed to be the father of international law, explained that there was a distinction between just and unjust war in international law.[54] But by the nineteenth and early twentieth centuries, the prevailing views in international law had abandoned that distinction, in the effect that wars of aggression were no longer considered illegal let alone criminal.[55]

In the process of explaining how international law reverted to the original idea of repudiation of unjust war, Jackson invoked the faculty and right of law reform in international law—in other words, the right that every generation has to develop or adjust international law to meet the exigencies of its own time. "International Law," wrote Jackson, "is more than a scholarly collection of abstract and immutable principles."[56]

"It is," he continued, "an outgrowth of treaties or agreements between nations and of accepted customs. But every custom has its origin in some single act, and every agreement has to be initiated by the action of some state."[57]

⌒

From that exordium, Jackson got to his main point. "Unless we are prepared to abandon every principle of growth for International Law, we cannot deny that our own day has its right to institute customs and to conclude agreements that will themselves become sources of a newer and strengthened International Law."[58] Such innovations and revisions in international law, Jackson observed, "are brought about by the action of governments designed to meet a change in circumstances."[59] This is much the same process on the international plains as the growth process of common law in its own domestic sphere.[60]

Hence, Jackson was not impressed by any concern about "lack of precedent" for the proposed Nuremberg international trial.[61]

Considering the focus of that trial on the crime of aggression, Jackson recalled the progression of international law in that direction, which occurred after World War I. There was "a marked reversion to the earlier and sounder doctrines of International Law," which, as articulated by Grotius, repudiated unjust wars. This reversion resulted from "the shock to civilization" that World War I had occasioned.[62]

On the resulting state of international law Jackson observed, "By the time the Nazis came to power it was thoroughly established that launching an aggressive war or the institution of war by treachery was illegal and that the defense of legitimate warfare was no longer available to those who engaged in such an enterprise."[63]

Hence, Jackson contended to Truman, "It is high time that we act on the juridical principle that aggressive war-making is illegal and criminal."[64]

Jackson's report—together with a statement indicating Truman's approval—was released to the media by the White House, widely published across Europe, and accepted by other governments as an official statement of the American position and the basis for further negotiations on the Charter of the Military Tribunal at Nuremberg.[65]

NORMS OF NUREMBERG **10**

Charter and Judgment

Upon the conclusion of the London Conference of 1945, the representatives of the Allied powers signed an agreement to which was annexed the Charter of the International Military Tribunal for Nuremberg.

In what was the first code of applied norms of international criminal law, the Charter provided, among other things, for the following: that crimes against peace (in other words, wars of aggression), crimes against humanity, and war crimes were liable to prosecution in international criminal law; that an international criminal tribunal would be the forum for the prosecution; and, that heads of state and heads of government were subject to prosecution before the international criminal tribunal with no immunity available to them.

As regards the crimes over which culprits bore individual criminal responsibility, article 6 of the charter provided as follows:

> The Tribunal established by the Agreement referred to in Article 1 hereof for the trial and punishment of the major war criminals of the European Axis countries shall have the power to try and punish persons who, acting in the interests of the European Axis countries, whether as individuals or as members of organizations, committed any of the following crimes.
>
> The following acts, or any of them, are crimes coming within the jurisdiction of the Tribunal for which there shall be individual responsibility:
>
> (a) Crimes against peace: namely, planning, preparation, initiation or waging of a war of aggression, or a war in violation of international treaties, agreements or assurances, or participation in a common plan or conspiracy for the accomplishment of any of the foregoing;

(b) War crimes: namely, violations of the laws or customs of war. Such violations shall include, but not be limited to, murder, ill-treatment or deportation to slave labour or for any other purpose of civilian population of or in occupied territory, murder or ill-treatment of prisoners of war or persons on the seas, killing of hostages, plunder of public or private property, wanton destruction of cities, towns or villages, or devastation not justified by military necessity;

(c) Crimes against humanity: namely, murder, extermination, enslavement, deportation, and other inhumane acts committed against any civilian population, before or during the war, or persecutions on political, racial or religious grounds in execution of or in connection with any crime within the jurisdiction of the Tribunal, whether or not in violation of the domestic law of the country where perpetrated.

Leaders, organizers, instigators and accomplices participating in the formulation or execution of a common plan or conspiracy to commit any of the foregoing crimes are responsible for all acts performed by any persons in execution of such plan.

In his report to President Truman, Robert H. Jackson had repudiated the notion of immunity for heads of state, insisting that it was legal facility that would be precluded from the Nuremberg Charter. That promise was kept by virtue of article 7, which provided as follows: "The official position of defendants, whether as Heads of State or responsible officials in Government Departments, shall not be considered as freeing them from responsibility or mitigating punishment."

Without a doubt, the Nuremberg Charter was a more effective and complete realization of what the Allied and Associated Powers had sought to do in 1919 through certain novel provisions, introduced for the first time in international law through the Versailles Treaty, particularly article 227.

⌒

The Charter of the International Military Tribunal was not the only instrument immediately after the post–World War II period that stated the norms indicated above. Indeed, two other instruments did the same thing. The first was Control Council Law no. 10, which the condominium authority of the four Allied powers adopted. Its purpose was to establish a uniform legal framework in Germany for the prosecution (within the

Allied zones of occupation) of war criminals and other similar offenders, other than those dealt with by the International Military Tribunal.

Article II(1) of Control Council Law no. 10 repeated the same stipulation of crimes that were set out in article 6 of the Charter of the International Military Tribunal. And in the same way that article 7 of the Charter precluded immunity for heads of state and of government, so, too, did Control Council Law no. 10 in article II(4)(a) preclude immunity for such individuals. "The official position of any person," it said, "whether as Head of State or as a responsible official in a Government Department, does not free him from responsibility for a crime or entitle him to mitigation of punishment."

Similarly in the Far East, General Douglas MacArthur, the supreme commander of the Allied powers at Tokyo, created an International Military Tribunal for the Far East (IMTFE), whose mandate was to try the wartime leadership of Japan, using the model of the International Military Tribunal at Nuremberg (IMTN). Once more, the Charter of the IMTFE, in article 5, reprised the same stipulation of crimes that were stipulated under article 6 of the Charter of the IMTN. Regarding immunity, article 6 of the IMTFE Charter provided—although in slightly different language but to the same effect—that the official position would not free the accused from responsibility.

In the result, the IMTN tried all the surviving leaders of the Third Reich; Hitler had escaped that fate through his suicide toward the conclusion of the war. The crime of aggression was a primary charge in the IMTFE trial. All but only three of the twenty-two accused Nazi leaders were convicted at the IMTN trial. For its part, the IMTFE tried the entire membership of the Japanese wartime cabinet, including Hideki Tojo (the prime minister when Japan entered the war), who was convicted and executed. The only high-profile figure of the Axis powers who escaped prosecution was Japan's emperor, Hirohito. That circumstance invites some commentary.

International law rejects the idea of immunity from accountability on grounds that the suspect is a head of state. International law does not presumptively impose criminal liability on a suspect, on the bare theory that a "nation's supreme secular and spiritual authority [must bear criminal] responsibility" for international crimes perpetrated by agents of the state.[1]

As a historical footnote, it may be noted that neither the emperor of Germany during World War I nor the emperor of Japan during World War II claimed entitlement to such immunity in international law, insisting that they should not be prosecuted. As a practical matter, however, the two men had very different attitudes as regards the prospect of facing justice. The kaiser chose to escape to the Netherlands and claim asylum when Germany lost World War I. Once secure in exile, he refused to surrender himself to justice,[2] a predisposition he only underscored, as we saw earlier, when Colonel Luke Lea, the American bounty hunter, personally went to his asylum residence in Amerongen to urge him to surrender himself manfully to justice.

Emperor Hirohito, on the other hand, it seems, had a very different approach. When his country lost the war, he did not flee into exile. Nor did he hide from justice. Indeed, when the surviving members of his wartime Imperial Cabinet were arrested for trial before the Tokyo Tribunal, the emperor went to General Douglas MacArthur, the supreme commander of the Allied powers in the Pacific and offered himself for trial, as his country's sovereign, in lieu of his compatriots who had been arrested for trial. As MacArthur recalls the emperor's words, "I come to you, General MacArthur, to offer myself to the judgment of the powers you represent as the one to bear sole responsibility for every political and military decision made and action taken by my people in the conduct of war."[3]

The emperor must have known at the time that there was insistent political demands in the United States for his prosecution.[4] But MacArthur saw the matter differently.

It is unsurprising that there has been much debate about the decision to spare Emperor Hirohito prosecution at the Tokyo Tribunal.[5] Political rationales have understandably received the lion's share of the arguments against prosecuting him. According to these related rationales, General MacArthur needed to retain the emperor on the Chrysanthemum Throne to help facilitate an orderly postwar transition of Japan, especially in light of the reform of its governance that MacArthur wanted to make; the prosecution of the emperor, let alone the expected capital punishment in the end, would unleash extensive popular revolt that would make the country practically ungovernable;[6] and the Soviet Union, who wanted the prosecution of the emperor,[7] was exactly hoping for such a popular revolt in hopes of a communist takeover,[8] thereby turning Japan red as was the case in China, or half of both Germany and Korea.[9]

Lawyers will regret that those political considerations have tended to obscure the forensic problem, which is that none of the literature in the debate has revealed a sustainable theory of the case, let alone credible supporting evidence, needed to prosecute the emperor. Some of the best arguments made for the emperor's prosecution include the allegation that "tons" of contemporaneous records of the wartime Imperial government had been destroyed or falsified as the Japanese capitulation and its U.S. occupation became imminent.[10] The implied argument seems to be that among those destroyed documents might have been evidence inculpating the emperor.[11] That may well be so. But such speculation does not supply the needed evidence that would speak to the emperor's guilt, given also the reasonableness of a competing inference that the destroyed records might have done no more than deepen the guilt of Prime Minister Tojo and his cabinet colleagues who were actually tried by the Tokyo Tribunal.

Beyond the question of evidence, strong arguments have been made that all that was done on behalf of the Japanese state was done in the name of the emperor. War was declared in his name, the business of government was conducted in his name, and soldiers fought and died in his name and committed atrocities in his name. And the Japanese people are deeply loyal to the emperor.[12]

But the fact that all those propositions are true affords no credible theory of a criminal responsibility for the monarch of any nation. Emperor Hirohito's guilt could not lie in the mind-set represented by the following bare assertion: "as Emperor and acknowledged head of state, Hirohito cannot sidestep war guilt. He is a part of, and must be considered an instigator of, the Pacific War."[13] What is required is evidence of the monarch's actual complicity in criminal conduct.

David Lloyd George once pointed out to Woodrow Wilson that the original idea of legal immunities of the British monarch in the domestic realm shared the same divine origins as that of the Japanese monarch.[14] There is reason to believe that the two sovereigns share much more than that in common. For instance, the business of the British government is also conducted in the name of its reigning monarch. The national anthem is a unitary ode to the monarch complete with a declaration of "long to reign over us." The government of the day is formally known as "HMG" (meaning "His [or Her] Majesty's Government").[15] The British prime minister meets regularly with the monarch for updates on governance, during which the monarch "has a right and a duty to express her [or his] views on Government matters."[16] And at the opening of every parliament, the monarch actually reads the "King's [or Queen's] Speech," in his (or her) own words.[17] It is drafted by the government in power, in which government policies and activities are laid out and defended. The monarch plays a role in the making of laws. Though the monarch's role is "purely formal," he or she "has the right to be consulted, to encourage and to warn through regular audiences with her [or his] ministers."[18] The British monarch is the commander in chief of the armed forces.[19] On enlistment, soldiers in the British Army, the Royal Air Force, and the Royal Marines are required by law to take an oath of allegiance to the monarchy as head of the armed forces; although by convention the Royal Navy is the only branch of the military not required to swear any oath on enlistment.[20] Also significant is that the British monarch is the only authority with the power to declare war.[21] Indeed Queen Elizabeth's father, King George VI, was the authority that declared war on Germany in 1939.[22]

But these considerations are not known to detract from the constitutional theory that the British monarch only reigns, but does not rule. It is not easy to see how the situation was different for Emperor Hirohito.

An argument usually made or implied in support of the thesis that Emperor Hirohito was not merely a figurehead (under the Meiji Constitution of the period) is that it took his intervention—including an unprecedented public broadcast—for Japan to surrender. As the argument goes, he should have done that sooner, especially so to end atrocities committed by Japanese soldiers in the theater of war. The trouble with that argument, especially in relation to the war crimes committed by Japanese soldiers, is the presumption that he ordered them; or that he knew about them, or having known about them did nothing to stop them.* There is no known evidence of any of that. But, more broadly, it is not persuasive to argue that the circumstances of his unprecedented act of direct and open intervention in the government of his country on that particular occasion—devastating atomic bombs had been dropped on two Japanese cities with a threat made to drop more—should be normalized as the minimum threshold of impetus for the emperor's direct and open intervention in government. It is expected that any admittedly

---

* The risk of erroneous presumption of responsibility upon a commander was once unwittingly demonstrated in a story told in MacArthur's own memoirs. Intent on ensuring that Japan could never be in a position to build atomic bombs, the U.S. government destroyed certain Japanese cyclotrons as part of the demilitarization of Japan following its American occupation. As the instruments were merely harmless scientific equipment incapable of repurposing to military use, *their destruction provoked outrage* even within the American scientific community, with the president of the Massachusetts Institute of Technology leading the protest. The official American storyline had indicated MacArthur as having given the order to destroy the instruments, presumably in his capacity as the supreme commander of the Allied forces in the Pacific. But, in his memoirs, MacArthur informed that he had given specific orders against destruction of the instruments. Eventually, the secretary of war admitted that the order to destroy the instruments had come directly from his office in Washington, DC, but that it "went without his personal cognizance, that it was a mistake, and that the matter should have been reported to him." See MacArthur, *Reminiscences*, 286–87.

ceremonial monarch whose subjects hold in awe would in those circumstances break the unprecedented tradition that required him to be seen and not heard. He may speak to his proud people and spur them to resist until death, even take their own lives (as some cult leaders have done), or he may urge them to "endure the unendurable" condition of surrender, knowing that his people in such desperate times are likely to heed his call. The emperor did the latter. That circumstance furnishes no persuasive evidence of criminal responsibility.

Pitted against the foregoing considerations, especially the general lack of evidence of his complicity in crimes,[23] was a constitutional culture that required that the emperor only be seen and not heard; the fact that a militaristic faction had a stranglehold on a government[24] in relation to which the emperor only reigned but did not really rule;[25] and the fact that the militarist faction attempted a coup[26] against the emperor to prevent his direct *broadcast to the Japanese* people to urge acceptance of surrender.

In any event, beyond the legal considerations reviewed above, there is also something of a poetic justice in the non-indictment of the Japanese emperor, whose hand is not directly implicated in the commission of atrocities, when compared to the fact that the president of the United States (also reputedly) ordered the dropping of atomic bombs on Hiroshima and Nagasaki,[27] with no serious questions asked about accountability for those acts.

AFFIRMATION OF THE NUREMBERG NORMS **11**

The judges of the International Military Tribunal for Nuremberg (IMTN) were from the United Kingdom, the United States, France, and the Union of Soviet Socialist Republics. The British judges were Lord Justice Lawrence (president of the tribunal) and Justice Birkett (alternate judge); the American judges were Francis Biddle and Judge John J. Parker (alternate judge); the French judges were Professor Donnedieu de Varbres and R. Falco (alternate judge); and the Soviet judges were Major-General I. T. Nikitchenko and Lieutenant-Colonel A. F. Volchkov (alternate judge).

Twenty-four of the highest-ranked surviving leaders of the Third Reich were indicted for trial before the tribunal. Two of the twenty-four defendants—Robert Ley and Gustav Krupp von Bohlen und Halbach—were never tried. The former committed suicide while in detention awaiting trial, and the latter was declared unfit on humanitarian grounds to stand trial due to mental and physical frailty.

For the remaining twenty-two defendants, the judgment of the Nuremberg Tribunal was delivered on 1 October 1946, after 216 court sessions. Three defendants were acquitted, and nineteen were convicted. The majority of the convicts, twelve, were sentenced to death: Hermann Göring, Joachim von Ribbentrop, Wilhelm Keitel, Ernst Kaltenbrunner, Alfred Rosenberg, Hans Frank, Wilhelm Frick, Julius Streicher, Fritz Sauckel, Alfred Jodl, Arthur Seyss-Inquart, and Martin Bormann (who was tried *in absentia*). Three received life sentences: Rudolf Hess, Walter Funk, and Erich Raeder. Four received terms of imprisonment ranging from ten to twenty years: Baldur von Schirach (twenty years), Albert Speer (twenty years), Constantin von Neurath (fifteen years), and Karl Dönitz (ten years).[1] The three acquitted defendants were Hjalmar Schacht, Franz von Papen, and Hans Fritzsche.

The Soviet judge, Major-General Nikitchenko, entered a dissenting opinion against the three acquittals and the life imprisonment of Rudolf Hess. In his view, those were "unfounded" verdicts and sentences. According to him, Hess should have been sentenced to death.[2]

The death sentences were never carried out against Hermann Göring and Martin Bormann, as the former had committed suicide while awaiting his execution and the latter was tried in his absence.

The remaining ten were hanged on 16 October 1946.[3]

On 11 December 1946—ten weeks after the delivery of the Nuremberg judgment on 1 October 1946—the General Assembly of the newly established United Nations (UN) adopted resolution 95(I), "affirm[ing] the principles of international law recognized by the Charter of the Nürnberg Tribunal and the judgment of the Tribunal." In the same resolution, the General Assembly mandated its Committee on the Codification of International Law "to treat as a matter of primary importance plans for the formulation . . . of the principles recognized in the Charter of the Nürnberg Tribunal and in the judgment of the Tribunal." This was to be done "in the context of a general codification of offences against the peace and security of mankind, or of an International Criminal Code."

Let's recall the important history of resolution 95(I). It was an initiative of the United States[4] traceable to President Harry S. Truman's[5] response to Judge Francis Biddle (the U.S. judge on the Nuremberg Tribunal) who had submitted a report to the president—at the president's request—making precisely the recommendations that were eventually reflected in General Assembly resolution 95(I).

Judge Biddle's report is particularly revealing in more ways than one. For one thing, Biddle was attorney general to President Roosevelt, and together with Henry L. Stimson (as secretary of war) and Edward R. Stettinius Jr. (as secretary of state), he had helped formulate the U.S. policy for the prosecution of war criminals. Under certain professional codes of conduct, questions might have been raised as to whether a potential conflict of interest might not have prevented him from also sitting as a judge at that prosecution. Then again, it was precisely that interest that ironically gave him a special perspective on U.S. policy in the prosecution. Second, being part of that policy, Biddle was well placed to understand Truman's own desire for a new world order according to international law and justice. We will study Judge Biddle's report a little later. But it may be more convenient, for now, to consider the key messages of President Truman's letter to him responding to that report.

Truman was clear that the Nuremberg proceedings ushered in a new order of international law. As he put it, Nuremberg "blazed a new trail in international jurisprudence and may change the course of history."[6] As the historical records make clear, an elementary feature of the new trail being blazed was that even heads of state must be held accountable—enjoying no immunity—when they commit international crimes. Truman recognized that.

According to Truman's letter, the more concrete key features of that new international order included the affirmation that aggressive war is an international crime; and that there will be accountability for those who criminally violate norms of international law. "When the Nurnberg Tribunal was set up," he wrote, "all thoughtful persons realized that we were taking a step that marked a departure from the past."[7] The past that was being abandoned was one that entailed no accountability for wars of aggression, and such expectations of accountability were inconceivable for heads of state.

"An undisputed gain coming out of Nurnberg," he continued, "is the formal recognition that there are crimes against humanity."[8]

And directly addressing the crime of aggression, he wrote, "I hope we have established for all time the proposition that aggressive war is criminal and will be so treated."[9]

Even at the level of logic, the idea of making aggressive war a crime necessarily implies the individual criminal responsibility of those who initiate such wars. And those are persons in a position of effective political and military leadership of their state. Anything else would be to normalize the perverse reality that leaders of nations are always spared the extreme hazards of the wars of aggression that they unleash. The first order of that reality is, of course, that political leaders initiate wars in which only soldiers, not the politicians, will fight and die. Making wars of aggression a crime in international law should not similarly mean that only the soldiers and not their leaders will be prosecuted for the crime.

With prescient vision for what eventually materialized in 1998 on the adoption of the treaty known today as the Rome Statute, which has now codified the crime of aggression, Truman considered—possibly in hopes of influencing that eventual outcome—that the advances made through the process of Nuremberg could be consolidated as part of an international project of codifying the crime of aggression. Such a codification would, in his view, foster a tendency toward global peace. "That tendency will be fostered," he said, "if the nations can establish a code of international criminal law to deal with all who wage aggressive war."

"The setting up of such a code," he continued in his letter to Biddle, "as that which you recommend is indeed an enormous undertaking, but it deserves to be studied and weighed by the best legal minds the world over. It is a fitting task to be undertaken by the governments of the United Nations."[10]

Truman hoped that the United Nations would, in line with Biddle's proposal, "reaffirm the principles of the Nurnberg Charter in the context of a general codification of offenses against the peace and security of mankind."[11]

In those observations, President Truman was largely echoing the sentiments that Judge Biddle had expressed in his report. Biddle's report was not spontaneous. When Biddle, on returning from Nuremberg, conferred with Truman, the two men could have exchanged ideas and interesting musings—verbally—about a new world order and left it at that. But no. President Truman specifically asked Biddle not only to submit to him a report on the work of the Nuremberg Tribunal but also to "make recommendations for further action."[12] Biddle obliged and submitted a report.

☙

In his report, Biddle drove home the message that the Nuremberg process had reformed international law at least in the direction of holding heads of state accountable for international crimes. One of those international crimes was the crime of aggression. What needed to happen next was that the international community should affirm those ideas, sharpen the definition of aggression, and establish an international criminal court for purposes of enforcement.

In distilling the essence of the judgment of the IMTN, he considered it of "great importance for a world that longs for peace" that "the Judgment has formulated, judicially for the first time, the proposition that aggressive war is criminal, and will be so treated."[13]

Together with that development came the related development that rejected immunity. The "official position of defendants in their government is barred as a defense. And orders of the government or of a superior do not free men from responsibility, though they may be considered in mitigation."[14] Noting that rejection of the pleas of "sovereign immunity" and superior orders, in relation to the confirmation of the norm that a war of aggression is an international crime, Biddle was not so naïve as to consider that "men with lust for conquest will abandon war simply because the theory of sovereign immunity cannot be invoked to protect them when they gamble and lose; or that men will ever be discouraged from enlisting in armies and fighting for their country, because military orders no longer can justify violations of established international law."[15]

"But the Judgement of Nurnberg does add another factor to those which tend towards peace. War is not outlawed by such pronouncements, but men learn a little better to detest it when as here, its horrors are told day after day, and its aggressive savagery is thus branded criminal. Aggressive war was once romantic; now it is criminal. For nations have come to realize that it means the death not only of individual human beings, but of whole nations, not only with defeat, but in the slow degradation of decay of civilized life that follows that defeat."[16]

Against that background, Biddle made some proposals about how to consolidate the advances of Nuremberg (or Nürnberg, as it is alternatively spelled). "The conclusions of Nürnberg," he observed, "may be ephemeral or may be significant. That depends on whether we now take the next step."

"It is not enough," he continued, "to set one great precedent that brands as criminal aggressive wars between nations. Clearer definition is needed. That this accepted law was not spelled out in legislation did not preclude its existence or prevent its application, as we pointed out in some detail in the judgment. But now that it has been so clearly recognized and largely accepted, the time has come to make its scope and incidence more precise."[17]

Biddle then proposed what eventually was done in the Rome Statute of the International Criminal Court. "In short," he wrote, "I suggest that the time has come to set about drafting a code of international criminal law."[18]

"To what extent aggressive war should be defined," he continued, "further methods of waging war outlawed, penalties fixed, procedure established for the punishment of offenders I do not consider here. Much thought would have to be given to such matters."[19]

"But certain salutary principles have been set forth in the Charter, executed by four great powers, and adhered to, in accordance with Article 5 of the Agreement by 19 other governments of the United Nations. Aggressive war is made a crime—'planning, preparation, initiation or waging of a war of aggression.'"[20]

In that regard, Biddle recalled that they had in the judgment pointed out that criminal acts are committed by individuals, not by those fictitious bodies known as nations, and law, to be effective, must be applied to individuals.[21]

Hence, Biddle suggested "that immediate consideration" be given to drafting an international criminal code, to be adopted, after the most careful study and consideration, by the governments of the United Nations. In the meantime, "time is therefore opportune for advancing the proposal that the United Nations as a whole reaffirm the principles of the Nürnberg Charter in the context of a general codification of offences against the peace and security of mankind. Such action would perpetuate the vital principle that war of aggression is the supreme crime. It would, in addition, afford an opportunity to strengthen the sanctions against lesser violations of international law and utilize the experience of Nürnberg in the development of those permanent procedures and institutions upon which the effective enforcement of international law ultimately depends."[22]

☙

Shortly before the declarations in his response letter to Judge Biddle, President Truman had foreshadowed the value that the Nuremberg proceedings held for the world, in charting a "path along which agreement may be sought" in securing global peace. He did so in his first address to the General Assembly of the newly formed United Nations, delivered on 23 October 1946—three weeks after the Nuremberg judgment that was delivered on 1 October 1946.

"No nation wants war," Truman began. "Every nation needs peace." He insisted that "peoples of all countries must not only cherish peace as an ideal but they must develop means of settling conflicts between nations in accordance with the principles of law and justice."[23]

He recognized, however, that it is easier to get people to agree upon peace as an ideal than to agree upon principles of law and justice or to agree to subject their own acts to the collective judgment of mankind. He insisted, nevertheless, "that the path along which agreement may be sought is clearly defined. We expect to follow that path with success."[24] In that regard, he observed that many "members of the United Nations have bound themselves by the Charter of the Nuremberg Tribunal to the principle that planning, initiating or waging a war of aggression is a crime against humanity for which individuals as well as states *shall be tried before the bar of international justice.*"[25]

The statements of Truman and Biddle, as recounted above, form part of the state practice of the United States. Indeed, Truman must have intended Biddle's report to have that effect not only in calling for the report but also in describing it as "an historic document."[26]

ℓ⁓

On 24 October 1946, the day after President Truman's speech, Trygve Lie, the first UN secretary general, followed in the same vein of underlining the significance of the Nuremberg precedents. In his "Supplementary Report on the Work of the Organization" for the General Assembly, he stressed the "decisive significance" of crystallizing the Nuremberg principles "as a permanent part of . . . international law."[27]

He noted that under its newly adopted Charter, the United Nations is charged with the duty of encouraging the progressive development of international law and its codification. "The Nuremberg trials have furnished a new lead in this field."[28] Continuing, he noted, as did Truman, that Nuremberg was the first time in history that, through cooperation between nations founded on democracy and the rule of their people, "it has been possible to agree on the establishment of an international court to judge war criminals and the leaders of a people which have brought a war upon mankind."[29] The observation serves its value of correctly underscoring the Nuremberg trials as the first time that an agreed upon international tribunal actually functioned and prosecuted the political leadership of a nation. Strictly speaking, though, the first time an agreement was reached for such a purpose was in article 227 of the Versailles Treaty.

"Eleven of the most evil men in modern times have been judged according to international laws by an international court," he wrote.[30]

But the important normative results of that process at Nuremberg needed to inform the progressive development of international law from then on. "In the interests of peace and in order to protect mankind against future wars," Trygve Lie wrote, "it will be of decisive significance to have the principles which were employed in the Nuremberg trials and according to which the German war-criminals were sentenced, made a permanent part of the body of international law as quickly as possible."[31]

Why? Because of the dawning of a new order of international law, according to which those who commit international crimes must be punished. "From now on," he said, "the instigators of new wars must know that there exists both law and punishment for their crimes. Here we have a high inspiration to go forward and begin the task of working toward a revitalized system of international law."[32]

〜〇〜

It was against that background that the General Assembly adopted resolution 95(I) on 11 December 1946, affirming the principles of international law recognized in the Charter of the Nuremberg Tribunal and in the judgment of that tribunal.

The next year, on 21 November 1947, the General Assembly also adopted resolution 177(II): directing the United Nations International Law Commission to prepare "a draft code of offences against the peace and security of mankind, indicating clearly the place to be accorded to the principles" of international law recognized in the Charter of the Nuremberg Tribunal and in the judgment of that tribunal.

But it must be stressed that the UN General Assembly's affirmation of the principles of international law recognized in the Charter of the Nuremberg Tribunal and in the judgment of that tribunal in resolution 95(I), and recalled in resolution 177(II), were no perfunctory footnotes in UN history. They have a real normative value in the development of international law.

For one thing, there is general agreement that "it is not just the practice of States which contributes to the development of customary rules. The practice of international organizations can do so too."[33]

There may be a discussion about whose practices are implicated in actions of the international organizations—specifically the UN—that contribute to the development of international law. M. H. Mendelson observed that to "a varying extent, intergovernmental organizations participate in international relations in their own name, and not that of the members who constitute them. As such, they are subjects of international law who play their own part in the law-making process."[34]

On the other hand, he insists that the adoption of resolutions, notably by the UN General Assembly, "is more helpfully understood as a form of action by the member States of the organization. In voting for or against a resolution which has something to say about international law—and not all do—States are engaging in a form of State practice and/or are manifesting their subjective attitude (consent or belief) about the rule in question."[35]

That is a sensible understanding of the default value of UN General Assembly resolutions or indeed the decision of any other multilateral gathering of states, whatever other value the specific action of an international organization may have.

The view of the value of such multilateral decisions as indicating the practice of states and their subjective mind-set as law oriented should be clear from the following picture. It will be difficult to track the conduct of individual states as to what they have done and their mind-sets in relation to a specific point of emergent international law. It will be difficult to get the various states to take up a specific point and address it in their individual strides: perhaps their leaders have other problems to tackle that they consider more important or pressing; perhaps the particular matter bears no direct relevance to their national interests; and perhaps they lack special technical expertise or experience to attend to the matter on their own without helpful insight from other states who may have greater experience or expertise. But the coming together of states in a multilateral forum to rub minds on a discrete point of international law compels all states to devote the needed attention to the subject and focus their minds on it in a coordinated way, within precisely the same time line. In that sense, there is no better way than resolutions of international organizations to gauge state practice and "their subjective attitude (consent or belief) about the rule in question."[36]

It is in that light that the UN General Assembly resolutions 95(I) and 177(II) must be seen in the affirmation of principles of international law recognized in Nuremberg.

The ILC's Formulation of Nuremberg Principles

The International Law Commission (known for short as the "ILC") is a subsidiary organ of the UN General Assembly. It is composed of lawyers, mostly university professors, with a mandate to assist the General Assembly in its own mandate of progressive development of international law and its codification, pursuant to article 13(1)(a) of the UN Charter.

Established in 1947, the first set of assignments that the second session of the UN General Assembly gave to the ILC, as set out in resolution 177(II) of 21 November 1947, included these: "(a) Formulate the principles of international law recognized in the Charter of the Nürnberg Tribunal and in the judgment of the Tribunal, and, (b) Prepare a draft code of offences against the peace and security of mankind, indicating clearly the place to be accorded to the principles mentioned in sub-paragraph (a) above."

Notably, that mandate was a redirection of the same task that the General Assembly originally gave to the Committee on the Codification of

International Law pursuant to the same resolution 95(I) of 11 December 1946 in which the General Assembly affirmed the principles of international law recognized in the Charter of the IMTN and in the judgment of the tribunal. But in the course of debate, the committee considered it more appropriate for the task to be referred to the ILC, whose establishment was then under consideration. The General Assembly accepted the report and recommendation of the committee to that effect; hence the tasks were transferred to the ILC according to resolution 177(II).[37]

The ILC approached its task following the order outlined in the resolution. Accordingly, they began with the formulation of the principles of international law recognized by the Charter of the IMTN and in the judgment of the tribunal. They would attend to the codification task later.

☙

It may be recalled that, in their judgment, the IMTN made pronouncements on the substance of international law that it applied. Among such pronouncements was that the Charter of the IMTN was "not an arbitrary exercise of power on the part of the victorious Nations, but in the view of the Tribunal . . . it is the expression of international law existing at the time of its creation; and to that extent is itself a contribution to international law."[38]

More substantively, it may be recalled that some of the more defining principles enunciated in the Charter of the IMTN included, but were not limited to, the notion that a war of aggression is an international crime (article 6), and that the "official position of defendants, whether as Heads of State or responsible officials in Government Departments, shall not be considered as freeing them from responsibility or mitigating punishment" (article 7).

It may also be recalled that the tribunal was confronted with the defendants' plea that wars of aggression were acts of state in relation to which the accused state officials and agents were protected by the defense of sovereign immunity. The tribunal dismissed the arguments. They reasoned, among other things, that "[t]he principle of international law, which under certain circumstances, protects the representatives of a state, cannot be applied to acts which are condemned as criminal by international law. The authors of these acts cannot shelter themselves behind their official position in order to be freed from punishment in appropriate proceedings."[39] In that connection, the tribunal applied article 7 of the Charter, which provided: "The official position of Defendants, whether as heads of State, or responsible officials in Government departments, shall not be considered as freeing them from responsibility, or mitigating punishment."[40]

And the tribunal further observed that "the very essence of the Charter is that individuals have international duties which transcend the national obligations of obedience imposed by the individual state. He who violates the laws of war cannot obtain immunity while acting in pursuance of the authority of the state if the state in authorizing action moves outside its competence under international law."[41]

Upon taking up their task of formulating the principles of international law—such as the foregoing—recognized in the Charter and judgment of the IMTN, a debate ensued about the precise scope of the ILC's task. Was the ILC to accept without question that what the authors of the Charter and the judgment described or assumed to be principles of international law were indeed so? Or was the ILC free to question the validity of any such declared or assumed principle? That debate was evident in the interventions of two prominent members of the ILC: Emile Sandström and Ricardo Alfaro.

Sandström thought it helpful to consider the significance of the term *formulate* as employed in resolution 177(II). Did it invite the ILC to analyze and critique the principles of international law supposed as such in the Charter and the judgment in order to determine their conformity with international law? Or was the ILC merely to transcribe from the Charter and the judgment what was stated as principles of international law, and accept them officially as such? He considered the second interpretation the better of the two, given that the General Assembly had *already affirmed* what was stated in the Charter and the judgment as *principles of international law*. In the circumstances, argued Sandström, it was not open to the ILC to embark upon a course of analysis that might lead them to contrary conclusions.[42]

For his part, Alfaro believed that the question was very clear. The ILC had no mandate to enter upon the inquiry on whether the principles indicated in the Charter and the judgment were in conformity with positive international law as it existed before the Charter and the judgment.

At any rate, he insisted, any innovation in the charter and the judgment would pose no difficulty for him, as such an incident would belong to the domain of the progressive development of international law that was indeed part of the ILC's mandate to formulate. It is in that vein appropriate for the ILC to formulate as such innovations as the principle of individual criminal responsibility for crimes against peace, war crimes, and crimes against humanity.[43]

In the end, the ILC decided that "since the Nürnberg principles had been affirmed by the General Assembly, the task entrusted to the Commission by paragraph (a) of resolution 177(II) was not to express any appreciation of these principles as principles of international law but merely to formulate them."[44]

It was on the foregoing basis that the ILC formulated a set of seven principles[45] of international law recognized in the Charter and judgment of the IMTN. They are as follows:

PRINCIPLE I

Any person who commits an act which constitutes a crime under international law is responsible therefor and liable to punishment.

PRINCIPLE II

The fact that internal law does not impose a penalty for an act which constitutes a crime under international law does not relieve the person who committed the act from responsibility under international law.

PRINCIPLE III

The fact that a person who committed an act which constitutes a crime under international law, acted as Head of State or responsible government official, does not relieve him from responsibility under international law.

PRINCIPLE IV

The fact that a person acted pursuant to order of his Government or of a superior does not relieve him from responsibility under international law, provided a moral choice was in fact possible to him.

PRINCIPLE V

Any person charged with a crime under international law has the right to a fair trial on the facts and law.

PRINCIPLE VI

The crimes hereinafter set out are punishable as crimes under international law:

(a) *Crimes against peace:*—(i) Planning, preparation, initiation or waging of a war of aggression or a war in violation of international treaties, agreements or assurances; (ii) Participation in a common plan or conspiracy for the accomplishment of any of the acts mentioned under (i).

(b) *War crimes:*—Violations of the laws or customs of war which include, but are not limited to, murder, ill-treatment or deportation to slave labor or for any other purpose of civilian population of or in occupied territory; murder or ill-treatment of prisoners of war or persons on the Seas, killing of hostages, plunder of public or private property, wanton destruction of cities, towns, or villages, or devastation not justified by military necessity.

(c) *Crimes against humanity:*—Murder, extermination, enslavement, depor-tation and other inhumane acts done against any civilian population, or persecutions on political, racial, or religious grounds, when such acts are done or such persecutions are carried on in execution of or in connec-tion with any crime against peace or any war crime.

Leaders, organizers, instigators, and accomplices participating in the for-mulation or execution of a common plan or conspiracy to commit any of the foregoing crimes are responsible for all acts performed by any persons in execution of such plan.

PRINCIPLE VII

Complicity in the commission of a crime against peace, a war crime, or a crime against humanity as set forth in Principle VI is a crime under inter-national law.

Moving from substantive content (regarding the proscription of conducts) to general principles, we may begin from the terminal two Nuremberg principles—Principle VI and Principle VII.

Principle VI is a distillation of the substantive contents of international criminal law in the outlines mapped out in the Charter of the IMTN. It was on that basis that the surviving Nazi leaders were prosecuted at Nuremberg. Notably, according to the principle, it was crystallized as a norm that war of aggression is a crime in international law, under the umbrella of crimes against peace,[46] alongside crimes against humanity and war crimes. In their commentary on this principle, the ILC noted that the IMTN "made a general statement to the effect that its charter was 'the expression of international law existing at the time of its creation.'"[47]

Principle VII deals with complicity in international crimes. The point of Principle VII is to make complicity in international crimes punishable conduct. Notably, the ILC considered that, in relation to the assessment of the criminal responsibility of individual Nuremberg defendants, the tribunal appeared to have applied general principles of criminal law regarding complicity.[48]

But from the substantive proscription of conduct (the subject matter of Principles VI and VII), we may now return to the matter of general principles. According to the ILC, the Nuremberg trial established the international law principle of individual criminal responsibility for international crimes. The ILC expressed it as Principle I: "Any person who commits an act which constitutes a crime under international law is responsible therefor and liable to punishment." And that principle is consolidated in Principle II by the rejection of any eventuality in which the domestic law that ordinarily regulated the life of the accused might have been either silent or contradictory on the principle that liability to punishment attends international crime.

Perhaps, above all else, one of the more profound principles of international law recognized in Nuremberg is Principle III. It is a principle that started its trek on the plains of international law in 1919. This was in the manner of the revolutionary attempt to prosecute Kaiser Wilhelm II (emperor of Germany and king of Prussia) before an international criminal court, pursuant to article 227 of the Treaty of Versailles. It may be recalled that at the Paris Peace Conference of 1919, the Commission on the Responsibility of the Authors of the War and on the Enforcement of Penalties cleared the path for article 227 of the Versailles Treaty, by recommending that "a High Tribunal is essential and should be established" to try "all authorities, civil or military, belonging to enemy countries, however high their positions may have been including the heads of state, who ordered, or, with knowledge thereof and with power to intervene, abstained from preventing or taking measures to prevent, putting an end to or repressing, violations of the laws or customs of war (it being understood that no such abstention should constitute a defence for the actual perpetrators)."[49]

In 1945, the principle that started its journey in article 227 of the Versailles Treaty completed its journey by virtue of article 7 of the Charter of the Nuremberg Tribunal, which precluded immunity for even heads of state. And in 1950, the ILC formally formulated that emergent norm as Principle III: "The fact that a person who committed an act which constitutes a crime under international law, acted as Head of State or responsible government official, does not relieve him from responsibility under international law."

On the other side of that coin is the plea of superior orders, which was also ruled out at Nuremberg as not amounting to an absolute defense to criminal charges, pursuant to article 8 of the Charter of the IMTN. That principle is now enshrined in international law as Nuremberg Principle IV: "The fact that a person acted pursuant to order of his Government or of a superior does not relieve him from responsibility under international law, provided a moral choice was in fact possible to him."

The ILC's Draft Codes of Crimes (Offenses) against Peace and Security of Mankind

It may be recalled that, in addition to the task of formulating the principles of international law recognized in the charter and the judgment of the Nuremberg tribunal, the second task that the General Assembly gave to the ILC by virtue of resolution 177(II) was to prepare a draft code of offenses against the peace and security of mankind, indicating clearly the place to be accorded to the principles of international law contemplated in the first task.

Pursuant to that mandate, the ILC produced two sets of draft codes. The first was the Draft Code of Offences against the Peace and Security of Mankind produced in 1954. The second was the Draft Code of Crimes against the Peace and Security of Mankind produced in 1996, updated to take into account the comments and observations that UN member states made to the 1954 draft.

The ILC did its best to infuse the Nuremberg Principles into the texts of both the 1954 and the 1996 drafts.

The 1954 draft (an earlier and slightly longer version of which was first published in the 1951 yearbook of the ILC) contained only four articles. Article 1 provided that the offenses outlined in it "are crimes under international law." But more than that, "the responsible individuals shall be punished." This reflects Nuremberg Principle I.

Largely reflecting Nuremberg Principle VI, article 2 of the 1954 draft code enumerated what those international crimes are. The list began with aggression and kindred crimes. (See clauses [1] to [8] of article 2.) Interestingly, the 1954 draft code also reflected the basic elements of the crime of genocide in clauses (10) and (13) of article 2, but failed to call the crime explicitly by its name "genocide." An effort was also made to account for crimes against humanity in clause (11) and war crimes in clause (12).

The significance of articles 1 and 2 of the 1954 draft code is that they captured the conducts that international law had, as of the Nuremberg proceedings, evolved to recognize as criminal. Those conducts were duly reflected as criminal in the Nuremberg Principles of international law. This is the case not only as regards genocide (for which a special convention was adopted in 1948) but also for the crime of aggression, which the international community started viewing as a crime since the conclusion of World War I. The same goes for crimes against humanity. All of these conducts were implicated as criminal in the Charter and judgment of the IMTN. And they all were captured for the world in the Nuremberg Principles.

Nuremberg Principle III is reflected in the same place in the draft code of 1954: that is in article 3. The "fact that a person acted as Head of State or as responsible government official," it said, "does not relieve him of responsibility for committing any of the offences defined in this Code." And, finally, the draft concluded with article 4, which imported the same bar against the plea of superior order that Nuremberg Principle IV prohibits, if it was possible for the subordinate to avoid compliance with the order.

As indicated earlier, following the ILC's submission of the report to the General Assembly, UN member states were invited to provide comments and observations. Notably, states did not generally quarrel with the draft code to the extent of what it provided. More specifically, states did not generally disagree with the reflections of Nuremberg Principles III and IV in the draft code. Rather, the general complaints of states were to the effect that the draft code did not go far enough in reflecting the fuller range of what had been accepted as international crimes since the Nuremberg period. The absence of apartheid from the list of international crimes was seen as a serious omission. Some states also wanted the crime of genocide to be spelled out more clearly in the code. As well, there was a general feeling that the draft code should have indicated the judicial forum for the enforcement of these norms, lest it becomes, as Chile's representative put it, "nothing more than an expression of lofty moral sentiments by the international community with little or no practical effects on the conduct of those committing them."[50]

Against that background, the General Assembly adopted resolution 36/106 of 10 December 1981, inviting the ILC to resume its work of formulating a draft code of offenses against peace and security, taking into account the comments and observations of states, and also inviting more states to give their comments and observations.

The result was the much more elaborate draft code of 1996, under the revised title of Draft Code of Crimes against the Peace and Security of Mankind. While the 1954 draft had only four articles, the 1996 draft had twenty. The 1996 draft code was work in progress at the ILC, shepherded by Senegalese jurist Doudou Thiam as special rapporteur, since

1981 when the UN General Assembly requested the ILC to resume work on the project.

The ILC adopted the draft code on first reading on 12 July 1991 which it then submitted to the General Assembly in its report of that year.[51] While further revisions were made to what became the 1996 draft code, following comments and observations received from UN member states and Switzerland (which was then not a UN member state),[52] the basic content of the 1996 draft code did not vary in substance from the 1991 version of the draft that was submitted to states for comments and observations.

Once more, all the important Nuremberg Principles are reflected in the text of the 1996 draft code. Notably, draft article 1(1) explained that all the crimes set out in the draft code are crimes against peace and security of mankind. And draft article 1(2) provided that "[c]rimes against the peace and security of mankind are crimes under international law and punishable as such, whether or not they are punishable under national law." Draft article 2(1) restated the principle of individual criminal responsibility for the crimes. Draft article 2(2) provided uniquely that "[a]n individual shall be responsible for the crime of aggression in accordance with article 16"— just to be sure that the matter is beyond reasonable debate. Draft article 2(3) restated the norm of individual criminal responsibility for the crimes of genocide, crimes against humanity, and war crimes—set out in articles 17, 18, and 20, respectively.

As was the case with article 7 of the IMTN Charter, draft article 7 of the 1996 Draft Code similarly provided that the "official position of an individual who commits a crime against the peace and security of mankind, even if he acted as head of State or Government, does not relieve him of criminal responsibility or mitigate punishment." It is the same principle captured in Nuremberg Principle III.

A striking significance of the reiteration of these norms in the 1996 Draft Code of Crimes is that the ILC was encouraged to repeat them following the comments and observations of states to the 1954 draft code that contained the same norms. None of the member states of the UN raised any objection to either the substantive contents of the 1954 draft code in general, with particular regard to the principle that heads of state or heads of government enjoy no immunity when accused of committing an international crime or complicit in its commission.

It may, of course, be noted that the United Kingdom raised an interesting question concerning immunity in the context of the 1996 Draft Code of Crimes. As the report of their intervention put it, "It is obviously important for the effective implementation of the Code that officials, including heads of state or government, are not relieved of criminal responsibility by virtue of their official position." The United Kingdom did not object to the norm in question, nor did they point out any specific rule of international law that accorded immunity to heads of state in the context of international crimes, such as were tried at Nuremberg and Tokyo. Nevertheless, continued the report of the UK observations, "the Commission has failed to address . . . the possible immunity of such officials from judicial process. The Commission should consider the immunity from jurisdiction to which officials may be entitled under international law, and the relationship of this draft to existing rules on the subject."[53]

It was a pedantic concern that might have adequately answered itself in the very exordium of the question, which recognized that "it is obviously important for the effective implementation of the Code that officials, including heads of State or Government, are not relieved of criminal responsibility by virtue of their official position."[54]

Indeed, that concern was amply addressed by previous efforts at the international level in which the British delegation played a leading role, beginning at the Paris Peace Conference of 1919, where the British delegation was enabled by the legal opinion of the leading British jurists of the day in insisting that the kaiser must be prosecuted before an international tribunal where the plea of immunity will be unavailable. It may be recalled that the British solicitor general, Sir Ernest Pollock, KC (the future Viscount Hanworth MR), played a foremost role in drafting the report of the Commission on Responsibility of the Authors of the War and on the Enforcement of Penalties. In the relevant part, the report read as follows:

> In these circumstances, the Commission desire to state expressly that in the hierarchy of persons in authority, there is no reason why rank, however exalted, should in any circumstances protect the holder of it from responsibility when that responsibility has been established before a properly constituted tribunal. This extends even to the case of heads of states. An argument has been raised to the contrary based upon the alleged immunity, and in particular the alleged inviolability, of a sovereign of a state. But this privilege, where it is recognized, is one of practical expedience in municipal law, and is not fundamental. However, even if, in some countries, a sovereign is exempt from being prosecuted in a national court of his own country the position from an international point of view is quite different.
>
> We have later on in our Report proposed the establishment of a high tribunal composed of judges drawn from many nations, and included the possibility of the trial before that tribunal of a former head of a state with the consent of that state itself secured by articles in the Treaty of Peace.

If the immunity of a sovereign is claimed to extend beyond the limits above stated, it would involve laying down the principle that the greatest outrages against the laws and customs of war and the laws of humanity, if proved against him, could in no circumstances be punished. Such a conclusion would shock the conscience of civilized mankind.[55]

Consequently, British prime minister David Lloyd George was instrumental in the decision of the Paris Peace Conference that the kaiser must be prosecuted before an international tribunal, with no immunity available to him. That decision was memorialized in article 227 of the Versailles Peace Treaty.

Similarly in 1945, the British government was a leading member of both the Nuremberg Charter that precluded immunity in article 7 and the prosecutorial effort that prosecuted Grand Admiral Dönitz, who served as the head of state of Germany following Hitler's suicide.

Against that background, the *immunity* question that the British delegation raised in relation to the Nuremberg Principle III as reflected in the 1996 Draft Code of Crimes was adequately answered in Poland's comments and observations. "The provisions of this article," noted the report of Poland's observations, "do not recognize any kind of immunity with respect to the position or office of an individual who commits a crime, including for heads of State or Government."

"It is a serious but logical and reasonable limitation of the full immunity of heads of State," the observations continued. "Their immunity cannot be such as to put them beyond the reach of criminal responsibility for crimes against the peace and security of mankind."[56]

Indeed, the ILC ably responded to the UK query in its 1996 report to the General Assembly. On that occasion, the commission explained: "The absence of any procedural immunity with respect to prosecution or punishment in appropriate judicial proceedings is an essential corollary of the absence of any substantive immunity or defence. It would be paradoxical to prevent an individual from invoking his official position to avoid responsibility for a crime only to permit him to invoke this same consideration to avoid the consequences of this responsibility."[57]

POST-NUREMBERG ADMINISTRATION OF INTERNATIONAL CRIMINAL JUSTICE

12

I n the immediate period following the Nuremberg proceedings, there were no further prosecutions before international tribunals. In the meantime, as indicated in the preceding chapter, the Nuremberg Principles were being woven into the fabric of international law through the efforts of the International Law Commission (ILC).

It would not be until the early 1990s that these principles would be called into service. But eventually they were, during the course of the work of the International Criminal Tribunal for the former Yugoslavia (ICTY) and the International Criminal Tribunal for Rwanda (ICTR), both of which the UN Security Council created in 1993 and 1994, respectively. And in 2002, the UN secretary general, under the authority of the Security Council, entered into an agreement with the government of Sierra Leone, establishing the Special Court for Sierra Leone (SCSL).[1]

It must be noted that Nuremberg Principle III, which rejects head-of-state immunity, is reflected with clarity in the statutes of each of these tribunals. "The official position of any accused person," they uniformly provide, "whether as Head of State or Government or as a responsible Government official, shall not relieve such person of criminal responsibility nor mitigate punishment."[2]

Consequently, each tribunal tried persons who were, or acted in the position of, head of state or head of government. The ICTY tried Slobodan Milošević, the former president of Serbia. He was indicted while in office[3] and died in the course of his trial.[4] The ICTR tried both Théoneste Bagosora[5] and Jean Kambanda.[6] Bagosora was the acting head of state of Rwanda during the genocide committed there following the death of President Juvénal Habyarimana when his plane was shot down on 6 April

1994, and Kambanda was the prime minister. The SCSL tried Charles Taylor, the president of Liberia, for his complicity in the Sierra Leone civil war and the atrocities committed in the course of that war.[7]

⌒

The trial of Charles Taylor by the SCSL gave a particular profile to the question of head-of-state immunity, because of a specific challenge that his defense counsel mounted against the case in that regard.

The SCSL confirmed the indictment against Charles Taylor on 7 March 2003, while he was still the president of Liberia, and an arrest warrant was issued on that date. The indictment and arrest warrant were formally unsealed on 12 June 2003. Taylor stepped down as president of Liberia on 11 August 2003.[8]

As a preliminary objection, his defense counsel attacked the validity of his indictment. The challenge was motivated by arguments, including that the "Indictment against Charles Taylor was invalid due to his personal immunity from criminal prosecution. Further, the timing of the disclosure of the arrest warrant and indictment on 12 June 2003 was designed to frustrate Charles Taylor's peace-making initiative in Ghana and cause prejudice to his functions as Head of State."[9] It was additionally contended that the "Special Court's attempt to serve the indictment and arrest warrant on Charles Taylor in Ghana was a violation of the principle of sovereign equality."[10] In the outcome, his counsel's application sought (1) orders quashing the indictment, arrest warrant, and all consequential orders; and (2) interim relief restraining the service of the indictment and arrest warrant on Taylor.

But the Appeals Chamber of the SCSL dismissed the challenge, reasoning that "the principle seems now established that the sovereign equality of states does not prevent a Head of State from being prosecuted before an international criminal tribunal or court."[11]

Notably, the SCSL Appeals Chamber had exercised its powers to appoint two professors of international law—Philippe Sands from the United Kingdom and Diane Orentlicher from the United States—as *amici curiae* in the appeal.[12] The Appeals Chamber also received submissions from the African Bar Association.[13]

As the Appeals Chamber understood him, Sands had submitted as follows, among other things: "In respect of international courts, international practice and academic commentary support the view that jurisdiction may be exercised over a serving Head of State in respect of international crimes. Particular reference may be had to the *Pinochet* cases and the *Yerodia* [aka *Arrest Warrant*] case."[14] This is entirely correct. But "[i]n respect of national courts a serving Head of State is entitled to immunity even in respect of international crimes."[15] This was not an entirely correct view that the majority of the judges of the International Court of Justice (ICJ) expressed in the *Yerodia* case. The ICJ was confronted with the question whether international law permitted Belgium to prosecute a former foreign minister of the Democratic Republic of the Congo before Belgian courts. The ICJ majority declared that they had "been *unable to deduce . . .* that there exists under customary international law any form of exception to the rule according immunity from criminal jurisdiction and inviolability to incumbent Ministers for Foreign Affairs, where they are suspected of having committed war crimes or crimes against humanity."[16] Writing extrajudicially in relation to the main pronouncement in the *Yerodia* case, Antonio Cassese was quick to fault the judgment of the ICJ majority in their "[inability] to deduce" that customary international law recognized no immunity in foreign *national courts* in relation to international crimes. He supplied some of the modern examples where immunity was not recognized in foreign national courts in prosecutions of international crimes.[17] It goes without saying that the *inability* of the jurists on the majority of the ICJ bench to "deduce" the point of customary international law on the matter does not gainsay the *ability* of other jurists of equal stature to deduce that point of customary international law. Cassese was a leading authority in international criminal law during his lifetime. He served as president at both the International Criminal Tribunal for the former Yugoslavia and the Special Tribunal for Lebanon.

My own research additionally supports that of Cassese to the effect that there are further strong and numerous data that favor the proposition that customary international law recognizes no immunity for state officials when prosecuted in foreign national courts for international crimes.[18]

On the part of Professor Orentlicher, the Appeals Chamber of the Special Court summarized her submissions as follows. Taylor's incumbency of office as head of state when he was indicted was not a consideration that rendered that indictment invalid on grounds of personal immunity or "procedural immunities accorded to head of State in international law."[19] Nor did he enjoy immunity in relation to international crimes committed as part of his official functions (immunity *ratione materiae*, as international lawyers call it), such that he could not be prosecuted even as a former head of state. Orentlicher submitted that in the *Arrest Warrant* case, the International Court of Justice had made a distinction between "the law applicable in the case of an attempt by a national court to prosecute the foreign minister of another State, from the rule embodied in statutes of international criminal tribunals." And for purposes of that distinction, "the Special Court is an international court and may exercise jurisdiction over incumbent and former heads of state in accordance with its statute."[20]

In their own submissions addressing the challenge against the validity of the indictment, the African Bar Association submitted that Taylor enjoyed no immunity from prosecution in respect of the international crimes charged against him. In support of their submission, they made "reference to the case of *United States of America v Noriega*, the *Pinochet* case, the *Milosevic* case, the 1993 World Conference on Human Rights and the Rome Statute of the ICC."[21]

⌒

As part of the unbroken string of international law instruments that captured the Nuremberg Principles, the UN General Assembly midwifed the adoption of the Rome Statute of the International Criminal Court (ICC) in 1998,[22] in which the Nuremberg Principles are reflected in a thoroughgoing way, including by way of enumerating the substantive crimes of genocide, crimes against humanity, war crimes, and the crime of aggression.[23]

⌒

The circumstances of world affairs and the opportunity they afforded for the creation of the ICC in 1998 are not always fully appreciated. That timing and those circumstances may be described as a lucid moment in time given the distrust amid the Cold War that preceded that time. The 1990s presented the world a period of positivity and possibilities rarely witnessed in the often-demoralizing conditions of global geopolitics, which play out in the micro-climate of the UN Security Council whose work is infamously defined by the veto power—and where some of its wielders seem ever ready and willing to use it more often than others to block accountability for international crimes.

The ICC was created within just a five-year window of time during which the UN Security Council had managed to create two ad hoc international criminal tribunals: one for the former Yugoslavia (in 1993) and the other for Rwanda (in 1994)—to bring accountability for the violations, including ethnic cleansing, that were committed in the former Yugoslavia, and the genocide that had been committed against Tutsis in Rwanda.

Some of the heady hallmarks of the immediately preceding period had been the policies of glasnost and perestroika in the Soviet Union that permitted the collapse of the Iron Curtain and the associated demolition of the Berlin Wall. That period also saw the abolition of the apartheid regime in South Africa and the associated release of Nelson Mandela from a lifetime of political imprisonment.

As fate would have it, that lucid moment of the 1990s lingered just long enough to permit the ICC finally to be created in an international conference in Rome in July 1998. This came after extended periods of moribund efforts to create a permanent international criminal court immediately after the Nuremberg experiment of 1945–1946. As soon as it started, it quickly became an abandoned project—a wishful thinking at best—in the following decades, due to the Cold War.

Perhaps the significance of the lucid moment of the 1990s that saw the creation of the ICC may be better appreciated if one considered that the other time—much to their credit—that France, Russia (then the Union of Soviet Socialist Republics), the United Kingdom, and the United States—four of the P5 members of the eventual UN Security Council—had agreed to create an international accountability mechanism was at the London Conference of 1945, regarding the Nuremberg proceedings that were to address the atrocities committed in Europe during World War II.

Of particular note was the agreement of the negotiators of the text of the Rome Statute—the founding treaty of the ICC—to reflect Nuremberg Principle III in article 27 of the Rome Statute, which provides as follows:

1. This Statute shall apply equally to all persons without any distinction based on official capacity. In particular, official capacity as a Head of State or Government, a member of a Government or parliament, an elected representative or a government official shall in no case exempt a person from criminal responsibility under this Statute, nor shall it, in and of itself, constitute a ground for reduction of sentence.
2. Immunities or special procedural rules which may attach to the official capacity of a person, whether under national or

> international law, shall not bar the Court from exercising its
> jurisdiction over such a person.

The formulation of article 27 invites brief commentary. There is no mystery to its different formulation, as compared to the text of the actual ILC formulation of the same principle, which has also been reflected in the texts of the ICTY, the ICTR, and the SCSL statutes seen earlier.

As already shown, Nuremberg Principle III is adequately understood in its context, and against the background of its historical provenance, as precluding immunity to the judicial process. Poland correctly reflected that understanding, as indicated in its comments to the 1996 Draft Code of Crimes, which captured the principle.[24]

Nevertheless, it was wise of the drafters of the Rome Statute to cast Nuremberg Principle III in a formulation that addressed the issue raised by the UK comments to the 1996 Draft Code of Crimes.[25] Article 27 of the Rome Statute is thus informed by a drafting practice known as *ex abundanti cautela*—drafting motivated by extreme caution to rule out a perceived concern or risk. As long as the intendment of a provision is not diluted, there is no harm in framing it in a formulation that forecloses a needless debate on a point of law even if the cautious formulation is ultimately superfluous. A point astutely and correctly put by New Zealand's prime minister, "Farmer Bill" Massey, at the Paris Peace Conference on 13 March 1919.

⌒

In 2007, the UN Security Council established a special tribunal for Lebanon in an effort to ensure accountability for the attack of 14 February 2005 in Beirut, which resulted in the death of former Lebanese prime minister Rafik Hariri and others. As the jurisdiction of the tribunal was over the national laws of Lebanon and not over international crimes (genocide, crimes against humanity, war crimes, and the crime of aggression), the Nuremberg Principle III was not accounted for in the statute of the tribunal.

⌒

The circumstances of Lebanon may be contrasted with those of East Timor, where pursuant to authority conferred by the UN Security Council resolution 1272 (1999) of 25 October 1999, the UN Transitional

Administration in East Timor (UNTAET) enacted its Regulation 2000/15 on 6 June 2000, establishing within the District Court in Dili special judicial panels with exclusive jurisdiction over serious crimes. The jurisdiction of the panel as conferred had a decided central focus on international crimes—i.e., genocide, war crimes, crimes against humanity, and torture[26]—in addition to murder and sexual violence proscribed in the national criminal code.[27]

Undoubtedly as a result of the jurisdiction of the panel over those conducts that have been accepted as international crimes as part of the Nuremberg Principles and reflected in the ILC Draft Codes—and reflected in the statutes of the ICTR, ICTY, and the ICC—the UNTAET Regulation 2000/15 similarly reflected Nuremberg Principle III in its provisions, following the formulation employed in the Rome Statute. In that regard, section 15.1 provided as follows:

> 15.1 The present regulation shall apply equally to all persons without distinction based on official capacity. In particular, official capacity as a Head of State or Government, a member of a Government or parliament, an elected representative or a government official shall in no case exempt a person from criminal responsibility under the present regulation, nor shall it, in and of itself, constitute a ground for reduction of sentence.
>
> 15.2 Immunities or special procedural rules which may attach to the official capacity of a person, whether under national or international law, shall not bar the panels from exercising its jurisdiction over such a person.

In 2015, the government of Kosovo established a Specialist Chamber and a Specialist Prosecutor's Office, pursuant to an exchange of letters between the government and the European Union.[28] It followed a Council of Europe Parliamentary Assembly Report of 2011 containing allegations of inhuman treatment of people, enforced disappearances of people, and illicit harvesting and trafficking in human organs.[29]

These crimes were allegedly committed between 1998 and 2000, during the turbulent transition period following independence from Yugoslavia and the stabilization of the country by the intervention of the international community. According to the basic law of the Specialist Chamber, the crimes over which the tribunal was given jurisdiction included both international crimes (i.e., crimes against humanity and war crimes specified in articles 13 and 14) and crimes under Kosovo law (article 15). Notably, as regards the international crimes, article 16(1)(b) of the basic law of the tribunal enacted Nuremberg Principle III, precisely in the same text as it was enacted in the ICTY and the ICTR statutes: "the official position of any accused person, including as Head of State or Government or as a responsible Government official, shall not relieve such person of criminal responsibility nor mitigate punishment."

๑

The foregoing boils down to this: Since 1919, when the leaders of Allied and Associated Powers resolved to prosecute the kaiser of Germany before an international criminal tribunal, with no absolving immunity recognized on account of his position as head of state at all material times, that same anti-immunity norm of international law—in relation to international crimes—has been consistently repeated in all the international prosecutorial efforts that have followed. It was so during the Nuremberg era. It has been so in all international prosecutorial efforts to prosecute international crimes since then, and up until now at the ICC.

That this anti-immunity norm is now a usual, customary, or standard feature of international law is the very essence of *customary international law*. In other words, customary international law does not recognize immunity for anyone including heads of state charged with international crimes before international courts and tribunals.

DIVINE RIGHT OF KINGS   **13**

"History is all about changing times and changing ideas," wrote the authors of a book of world history for children. "Long ago, for example, slavery was an accepted part of everyday life. The ancient Egyptians made slaves of their prisoners. So did the Greeks, the Romans, the Aztecs, and many others. But today, people all over the world know that slavery is wrong."[1]

That, too, is true of the idea that a human being can commit whatever atrocity that pleases him against his fellow human beings, as Emperor Caligula routinely did two thousand years ago. He claimed that he could do whatever he pleased without legal accountability, because he was the emperor of Rome.[2]

As demonstrated in this book, the repudiation of immunity of heads of state for international crimes, in the processes of an international court, is a distinct feature of change in ideas that started at the Paris Peace Conference of 1919. Notably, the representatives and heads of government of Allied and Associated Powers—including Woodrow Wilson—decided from then on that even heads of state who engage in conduct repudiated as criminal in international law must be held personally accountable.

That is to say, the international lawmakers of the period did not allow the idea of immunity of heads of state or heads of government to enter the stream of administration of international criminal law and justice at the source of that stream, when its channels were first hewn after World War I.

As President Wilson said at the time, the processes of development of international law do not always produce instant results in the intended way. They take time to settle. He fully spoke to that theme during a dinner speech he delivered to the International Law Association in Paris in May 1919, following the Council of Four's agreement to prosecute the kaiser.

"You cannot in human experience rush into the light," he said. "You have to go through the twilight into the broadening day before the noon comes and the full sun is on the landscape; and we must see to it that those who hope are not disappointed, by showing them the processes by which that hope must be realized—processes of law, processes of slow disentanglement from the many things that have bound us in the past. You cannot throw off the habits of society immediately any more than you can throw off the habits of the individual immediately. They must be slowly got rid of, or, rather, they must be slowly altered. They must be slowly adapted, they must be slowly shapen to the new ends for which we would use them. That is the process of law, if law is intelligently conceived."[3]

That may well describe the journey of both the idea of administration of international criminal justice and the preclusion of head-of-state immunity from that process. Beginning at the end of World War I, both ideas finally solidified into actionable form after World War II, by virtue of the Charter of the International Military Tribunal in Nuremberg.

⌒

U.S. Supreme Court justice Robert H. Jackson, on secondment to the Nuremberg process, emerged as the preeminent champion of both ideas in the immediate aftermath of World War II. Jackson's particular distaste for the idea of immunity of heads of state was evident in his June 1945 report to President Harry S. Truman. There, Jackson deprecated immunity as suspiciously reflecting the idea of the divine right of kings.

"There is more than a suspicion that this idea is a relic of the doctrine of the divine right of kings," he chided. "It is, in any event, inconsistent with the position we take toward our own officials, who are frequently brought to court at the suit of citizens who allege their rights to have been invaded."[4]

But Jackson was not the only anti-immunity statesman who linked head-of-state immunity to the doctrine of the divine right of kings. Both President Wilson and Prime Minister David Lloyd George also made that connection. Wilson had sought to distance himself from the idea of head-of-state immunity, on the basis of his understanding that the Japanese disinclination to prosecute the kaiser[5] rested on what Wilson described as the "ridiculous principle" of the divinity of the emperor.[6] But Lloyd George quickly pointed out that the notion of immunity of the British monarch was similarly linked to the divinity of the monarch. The "Japanese principle is the English principle," said Lloyd George.[7] That notwithstanding, he added, "All we want to do is to punish those responsible, whoever they may be."[8]

The logic of that insistence is apparent. An important reason that international law feels constrained to intervene to proscribe atrocities is because of the complicity—if not the agency—of heads of state or heads of government in their perpetration. Notably, it is the leadership of government that typically initiates wars of aggression, as Putin demonstrated to the world in real time in 2022. So, too did the leadership of Germany unleash World War I and World War II in 1914 and 1939 when they invaded Belgium and Poland, respectively. So, if international law is finally going to intervene and punish such conduct as a crime, by bringing the international community's *jus puniendi* to bear, the objective will become pointless if the same heads of state or heads of government whose conduct inspired the intervention are precluded as a class from the scope of the contemplated liability while their underlings are punished.

☌

The concern of Jackson, Lloyd George, and Wilson that immunity of heads of state is traceable to the doctrine of the divine right of kings has demonstrable basis in history.

It may be noted, to begin with, that when the U.S. Supreme Court in the *Schooner Exchange* case conducted relevant research and concluded that foreign sovereigns enjoyed immunity in each other's courts, the principle of *rex non potest peccare* (the king can do no wrong) or *princep legibus solutus* (the king is above the law) was alive and well. It had to be because most of the world's heads of state were royalty then. We know this as of 1812, because the "Nomenclature of the Sovereigns and Rulers of States Represented at the Peace Conference" in The Hague in 1899 is a good indication. Of the twenty-five states represented, all were monarchies, except four—France (a former kingdom), Mexico (a former colony of a kingdom), Switzerland, and the United States (a former colony of a kingdom).[9]

The idea that monarchs were immune from the law because they were above it is traceable to the Middle Ages and earlier. When France's Louis XIV famously declared "*l'etat, c'est moi*" during the seventeenth century, he was not declaring an original idea.

The stoic philosopher Seneca wrote to that effect with greater flourish in 55 CE in *De Clementia*, his desperate plea for clemency from Emperor

Nero. Seneca had hoped to serve the purpose of a mirror of conscience for Nero, thereby revealing the emperor to himself as the alpha and omega far better served by the benevolence of clemency than by imperious severity.

"I of all mortals," groveled Seneca, desperately suggesting how the emperor should see himself, "have found favour with Heaven and have been chosen to serve on earth as *vicar of the gods*. I am the arbiter of life and death for the nations; it rests in my hand what each man's fortune and state shall be; by my lips Fortune proclaims what gift she would bestow on each human being; from my utterance peoples and cities gather reasons for rejoicing; without my favour and grace no part of the wide world can prosper; all those many thousands of swords which my peace restrains will be drawn at my nod; what nations shall be utterly destroyed, which ones transported, which shall receive the gift of liberty, which have it taken from them, what kings shall become slaves and whose heads shall be crowned with royal honour, what cities shall fall and which shall rise this is my jurisdiction."[10]

The idea of royal divinity preceded the reign of Nero. In the annals of creative cruelty, no tyrant rivalled the monstrosity of Nero's maternal uncle Emperor Caius Caesar, known better by his nickname "Caligula,"[11] who reigned from 37 to 41 CE.[12] When Antonia, his grandmother, counseled moderation, he duly replied: "Remember that all things are lawful for me."[13]

And just as Louis XIV was not content to see himself merely as embodying the sovereignty of the state, but was the state itself, Caligula had not been content to see himself merely as embodying the divinity of royal power. He saw himself as a god in his own right.[14] But, as often happened to tyrants whose excesses were beyond the restraining power of the law, the only alternative left to the people would be to hasten his death by assassination. So it was that the "mad and riotous career" of Caligula was terminated after three years.[15] An enduring lesson even in our times for those who counsel immunity for heads of state beyond the rule of law.

❧

Several popes of the Middle Ages formally consecrated the idea of the "divine right" of monarchs into a doctrine of secular life, through the Christian faith that once predominated life in Europe. St. Gregory the Great, a prolific scholar, enjoyed a special renown in the propagation of the doctrine.[16]

Their ready authority for the doctrine was primarily the biblical portrayal of the king in the Old Testament as the "Lord's Anointed," which was the ultimate moral of the story of the relationship between David and King Saul, as the story is told in the first book of Samuel.[17]

In the story, David kills the giant Goliath with one sling shot. As Goliath is the champion of the forces arraigned against King Saul's forces in which David and the king himself are warriors, David's slaying of Goliath quickly makes him a popular hero and a rising political superstar in the kingdom of Saul. Consumed with jealousy of David who is generally expected to become king eventually, Saul plots to kill him. David is aware of the plot, thanks to Saul's children—Princess Michal who is married to David and Prince Jonathan who is his very close friend—who warn David of Saul's machinations. In one of the more famous episodes of the plot, David is forced to dodge a spear throw from Saul, as David plays his lyre in hopes of soothing Saul's troubled soul. (In addition to being a highly skilled warrior, David is also an accomplished harpist.) Saul's spear impales the wall. The need for safety eventually drives David to abandon his post as the captain of Saul's personal security detail and flee. In the ensuing manhunt that Saul personally leads to catch and kill David, Saul engages in a ruthless massacre of people—including an entire city of priests—he suspects of aiding David's peripatetic flight.[18] On one of the manhunts through the wilderness of Engedi, Saul temporarily drops his guard and enters a cave to relieve himself. He does not know that David and his men are hiding in the deeper recesses of the same cave. David stealthily creeps up and cuts off a piece of cloth from the corner of Saul's robe and retreats, much to the chagrin of David's own men who had earlier enthused, "This is the day the Lord spoke of when he said to you, 'I will give your enemy into your hands for you to deal with as you wish.'" But David will have none of that if it meant regicide. Even the mere act of cutting off a piece of Saul's robe is too trying for his loyal conscience. "The Lord forbid that I should do such a thing to my master, the Lord's anointed, or lay my hand on him; for he is the anointed of the Lord," says David to his men, forbidding them to attack Saul, who safely leaves the cave after he is done relieving himself, unaware of his close call.[19]

There are also similar refrains in the New Testament, notably in the epistles of St. Paul and of St. Peter. Writing to the Romans, St. Paul enjoins as follows in chapter 13:

[1] Let everyone be subject to the governing authorities, for there is no authority except that which God has established. The authorities that exist have been established by God.

[2] Consequently, whoever rebels against the authority is rebelling against what God has instituted, and those who do so will bring judgment on themselves.

[3] For rulers hold no terror for those who do right, but for those who do wrong. Do you want to be free from fear of the one in authority? Then do what is right and you will be commended.

[4] For the one in authority is God's servant for your good. But if you do wrong, be afraid, for rulers do not bear the sword for no reason. They are God's servants, agents of wrath to bring punishment on the wrongdoer.

[5] Therefore, it is necessary to submit to the authorities, not only because of possible punishment but also as a matter of conscience.[20]

Similarly in chapter 2 of his first epistle, St. Peter issues the following exhortations to the faithful:

[13] Submit yourselves for the Lord's sake to every human authority: whether to the emperor, as the supreme authority, [14] or to governors, who are sent by him to punish those who do wrong and to commend those who do right. . . . [17] Show proper respect to everyone, . . . fear God, honour the emperor.

[18] Slaves, in reverent fear of God submit yourselves to your masters, not only to those who are good and considerate, but also to those who are harsh. [19] For it is commendable if someone bears up under the pain of unjust suffering because they are conscious of God. [20] But how is it to your credit if you receive a beating for doing wrong and endure it? But if you suffer for doing good and you endure it, this is commendable before God.[21]

St. Gregory the Great has been credited with the clearest articulation of the doctrine of the divine right of rulers within Christendom. But the foundations of the idea as put forth in the writings of St. Peter and St. Paul, as indicated above, ought not to be underestimated. St. Peter was the first pope, and St. Paul was the first apostolic scholar with prolific output. They both taught their followers to obey secular political powers, however harsh the reign, for every authority came from God.

In time, Ambrosiaster (an anonymous writer whose real identity at various times was attributed to St. Augustine or St. Ambrose) described the monarch as commanding revered station as the "Vicar of God" on earth. But that was only the monotheist version of the same "vicar of the gods" moniker that Seneca had employed in *De Clementia* to describe Nero Caesar in the year 55 CE. "*Rex enim adoratur in terris quasi vicarius Dei. Christus autem post vicariam impletam dispensationem adoratur in cœlis et in terra*," Ambrosiaster insisted. That is to say, the king is in the image of God as the bishop is in that of Christ.[22] Then, again, the occurrence of the "vicar" cognomen is unsurprising in context, given the word's meaning as representative or deputy.

‹∽

The thinking, it seems, started life along the lines that "Government" is a sacred institution, serving the purpose of a divine remedy for human sins. In that arrangement, the ruler becomes God's representative on earth and, as such, must be obeyed in the name of God. The theory always ran the risk of development into the conception of the ruler as "the absolute and irresponsible representative of God, who derives his authority directly from God, and is accountable to God alone for his actions."[23]

Particularly telling in the conception of the divine right of the ruler in absolute terms is the strain of reasoning that held that even bad rulers must be endured—for they are part of penitence of citizens for their own transgressions against God. St. Irenaeus, the bishop of Lyon during the second century, was a big apologist for the notion that people get the rulers they deserve. He once insisted that God gives rulers to citizens as expiation for their sins, with evil rulers being the punishment for transgressions—the veritable instrument of God's punishments.[24] St. Augustine expressed the same idea during the fourth century,[25] as did Sigebert of Gembloux, speaking on behalf of the clergy of Liège in 1103 CE.[26]

A minority of progressive ecclesiastical scholars, notably St. Isidore and St. Ambrose and their followers, did their best to distinguish the just ruler who should retain his throne as king, as opposed to the tyrant who should not.[27] But their views met with opposition from the Gregorian school who insisted that, while it is true that some rulers may be tyrants, "yet the king was answerable only to God, that there was no authority which could judge him, and that the subject must therefore submit even to injustice and oppression, looking only to the just judgment of God to punish the oppressor and to defend the innocent."[28]

From its original provenance in the Middle Ages and earlier, the idea that a temporal ruler is a representative of God, whose authority may in no circumstance be resisted, persisted well into the sixteenth century. Martin Luther, the leader of the Reformation movement, was renowned to have thrown his weight behind the idea.[29] It has been urged that Luther's views on the matter deserve noting, no doubt because of the man's considerable influence, notwithstanding "that Luther was not a systematic political thinker, that indeed he can hardly be described as a political thinker at all."[30] It might not have occurred to Luther—or he might not have cared—that his very Reformation movement contradicts the idea that under no circumstance may the temporal ruler be resisted, because he or she is God's representative on earth. The Reformation movement was pursued by its leaders and adherents in defiance of the day's powers that be, who did not want the Reformation[31]—except, of course, King Henry VIII who desired the annulment of his marriage to Catherine of Aragon, which the pope would not grant him.

Like Gregory the Great, Luther was much impressed by the representation of the king as the "Lord's Anointed," in the Old Testament.

In an apologia Luther wrote in the summer of 1525 defending the harsh and violent methods that the feudal aristocracy had employed earlier in May against the Great Peasants' Revolt, Luther posited that there are two kingdoms: the spiritual kingdom and the temporal kingdom. The former is a kingdom of grace and mercy, while the latter is of wrath, judgment, and punishment. The temporal kingdom has the sword, he wrote, because its purpose is to coerce the wicked and defend the godly. The ruler thus represents the wrath and rod of God.[32]

In Luther's view, the Great Peasants' Revolt manifested an ill-conceived desire for equality, a clamoring that was a vain effort to convert the spiritual kingdom into the earthly one. It was an impossibility, in his view, because the temporal kingdom could not exist without inequality. The earthly kingdom, Luther insisted, must account for the different realities on the spectrum of freedom and status. Some people must be free and others in bondage; some will be feudal lords, and others will be serfs; and there will be rulers and there will be subjects.[33]

In short, according to Luther, it is the duty of citizens to submit to the earthly authority—*Die Obriegkeit*—at all times. This is so even in cases of tyranny, as the relationship between David and Saul revealed. God is the only power with authority to judge and punish the tyrant.[34]

In England, the sixteenth-century thought leaders of the Protestant Reformation movement also conveyed the same doctrine as Luther. Two leading figures in that regard were William Tyndale and Robert Barnes.

In his book *The Obedience of Christian Men* (1628), Tyndale stood on the authority of St. Paul's message in the book of Romans to contend, "Heades and governors are ordeined of God, and are even the gift of God, whether they be good or bad. And, whatsoever is done unto us by them, that doth God, be it good or bad. If they be evill, why are they evill, verily, for our wickednesse sake. . . . Therefore doth God make his scorge of them, and turn them unto wild beastes to avenge himself of our unnaturall and blind unkindnesse, and of our rebellious disobedience."[35] Since rulers are ordained by God and are God's gift—whether good or bad—to the Christian citizens, the duty of citizenship, therefore, is only one of acceptance. For "[a] Christian man in respect of God, is but a passive thing, a thing that suffereth only and doth nought."[36]

Ultimately for Tyndale, the monarch is above all temporal law. He can do as he pleases—right or wrong—he is accountable only to God.[37]

According to R. W. Carlyle and A. J. Carlyle, commenting on Tyndale, "It would be difficult to find any stronger declaration of the conception that the king holds by Divine Right an absolute and unqualified authority, that he is above law and not under it, that all appeal to constitutional tradition is empty and void, that all resistance to his authority, however reasonable the cause for this might be, is an offence against God, and the authority which he has given to the king."[38]

Barnes, in his turn, also stipulated the citizen's duty of absolute submission to the monarchy—however unjust and unlawful the monarch's conduct.[39]

Robert Filmer had a very low tolerance for democracy and individual liberty. To him it was a "vulgar" tenet to say that "[m]ankind is naturally endowed and born with freedom from subjection, and at liberty to choose what form of government it please, and that the power which any one man hath over others was at first bestowed according to the discretion of the multitude."[40]

It is one thing to tolerate such a view propagated by those who hung onto it so dearly, on the basis "that it prodigally distributes a portion of liberty to the meanest of the multitude, who magnify liberty as if the height of human felicity were only to be found in it, never remembering that the desire of liberty was the first cause of the fall of Adam." It is quite another matter to allow the clamor for democracy and individual liberty to assume the "perilous" dimension of saying that "the people or multitude have power to punish or deprive the prince if he transgress the laws of the kingdom."[41]

Such a "vast engine of popular sedition"[42] called for a restatement of the doctrine of the divine right of kings in the most robust terms. Filmer did just that in his book *Patriacha*, posthumously published in 1680, though the manuscript had been completed before his death in 1653.[43]

Patriarcha is indeed an unmitigated restatement of the doctrine of the divine right of monarchy, according to which the monarch ruled by the will of God. The ruler's authority was beyond the powers of the citizens to challenge or question. Perhaps the uniqueness of Filmer's take on the doctrine entailed his premise that a ruler's power was fundamentally patriarchal or paternal in character, akin to the relationship that a father has to his family—in the conception of that relationship in Filmer's days. As such, the relationship between the ruler and the subject was natural or derived from God. Conversely, the father's authority over his family was akin to that of a king over his kingdom. Filmer sought to validate his thesis by arguing that God had given to Adam authority over his children. Such authority was not merely that of a father over his children, but that of a king over his subjects.[44]

In his famous *Commentaries on the Laws of England*—an eighteenth-century venture—William Blackstone served up all the usual fictions that lawmakers and interpreters employ to short-circuit difficult problems. From the English perspective, sovereignty presents one such problem. Can you have sovereignty for the ruler in any circumstance where the ruler is subjected to any kind of inquiry on the allegation that the king has done some wrong? The resolution of that dilemma required some fiction—though Blackstone does not identify these legal devices as fictions—to the effect that the law is "incapable of distrusting those whom it has invested with any part of the supreme power." This is because "wherever the law expresses its distrust of abuse of power, it always vests a superior coercive authority in some other hand to correct it." That is a notion that "destroys the idea of sovereignty."[45]

But, fictions, as they come, rarely come alone. Once you construct one fiction, you need to construct other fictions to prop up the first. And thus came in the fiction of "absolute perfection" of the monarch. "Besides the attribute of sovereignty," Blackstone informs us, "the law also ascribes to the king, in his political capacity, absolute *perfection*. The king can do no wrong."[46] Blackstone rightly calls that an "ancient and fundamental maxim." We earlier saw the genesis of the maxim in the Middle Ages, and we shall return to it presently. But given the categorical manner of the maxim, Blackstone felt compelled to explain it. And that, too, called more fictions into service.

The ancient and fundamental maxim, explained Blackstone, "is not to be understood, as if everything transacted by the government was of course just and lawful, but means only two things. First, that whatever is exceptionable in the conduct of public affairs, is not to be imputed to the king, nor is he answerable for it personally to his people; for this doctrine would totally destroy that constitutional independence of the crown, which is necessary for the balance of power in our free and active, and therefore compounded, constitution. And, secondly, it means that the prerogative of the crown extends not to any injury: it is created for the benefit of the people, and therefore cannot be exerted to their prejudice."[47]

The second explanation must have made sense to Blackstone for him to have deployed it. But others may see it as nonsensical. The first is more tolerable; but only to the extent that it is understood in the sense of the observations of Frederick Pollock and William Maitland that the "mere amount of the business that is performed in the king's name but without his knowledge does not demand any . . . feat of jurisprudence" to create legal fictions that absolve him from legal responsibility for every wrong done in his name. "A great prelate or a palatine earl will like the king have many high placed officers, stewards, chancellors, treasurers and the like, who will do very many acts in his name, judicial acts and governmental acts, of which in all probability he will hear no word."[48]

But if that is what was originally meant by the "ancient" maxim that "the king can do no wrong"—and origins of the maxim in the supposed divinity of the monarch may well contradict Blackstone's explanation—it requires only to say more modestly that the king is not vicariously liable for all the wrongs of his servants, rather than the extravagant claim that "the king can do no wrong." And when he commits some error with his own hands, then others must bear the blame, because of the doctrine of "absolute perfection" of the monarch.

But the extravagant claim really soared in the further commentary of Blackstone. "The king, moreover, is not only incapable of doing wrong," he wrote, "but even of thinking wrong: he can never mean to do an improper thing: in him is no folly or weakness. And, therefore, if the crown should be induced to grant any franchise or privilege to a subject contrary to reason, or in any wise prejudicial the commonwealth, or a private person, the law will not suppose the king have meant either an unwise or an injurious action, but declares that the king was deceived in his grant; and thereupon such grant is rendered void, merely upon the foundation of fraud and deception, either by or upon those agents whom the crown has thought proper to employ."[49]

All this made sense to Blackstone, "For the law will not cast an imputation on that magistrate whom it entrusts with the executive power, as if he was capable of intentionally disregarding his trust: but attributes to mere imposition (to which the most perfect of sublunary beings must still continue liable) those little inadvertencies, which, if charged on the will of the prince, might lessen him in the eyes of his subjects."[50]

Entirely unimpressed, Professor A. V. Dicey—who was Blackstone's successor to the Vinerian chair of jurisprudence at Oxford University—succinctly spoke to many a Blackstone claim. "It has but one fault," Dicey wrote; "the statements it contains are the direct opposite of the truth."[51]

Although Dicey was specifically addressing other aspects of Blackstone's claims, the refutation is valid also as regards the theory of royal impeccancy according to which the king is "incapable of doing wrong" or "ever thinking wrong" or "[even] mean[ing] to do an improper thing." Human experience has grown weary of kings and other sovereign heads plotting and committing genocide, torture, and other crimes against humanity—let alone wars of aggression. The victims can accept that the sovereign head will enjoy attributes of preeminence that do not violate human rights, such as those that are evident in Blackstone's understanding of "royal dignity," which he expressed as follows:

> First, then, of the royal dignity. Under every monarchical establishment, it is necessary to distinguish the prince from his subjects, not only by the outward pomp and decorations of majesty, but also by ascribing to him certain qualities, as inherent in his royal capacity, distinct from and superior to those of any other individual in the nation. For, though a philosophical mind will consider the royal person merely as one man appointed by mutual consent to preside over many others, and will pay him that reverence and duty which the principles of society demand, yet the mass of mankind will be apt to grow insolent and refractory, if taught to consider their prince as a man of no greater perfection than themselves. The law therefore ascribes to the king, in his high political character, not only large powers and emoluments which form his prerogative and revenue, but likewise certain attributes of a great and transcendent nature; by which the people are led to consider him in the light of a superior being, and to pay him that awful respect, which may enable him with greater ease to carry on the business of government. This is that I understand by the royal dignity.[52]

Even here, "royal dignity," as conceived in those words, feels only two alphabets away from "royal divinity" but for the explicit reference to God in the fuller explanation of the latter idea. Then, again, Blackstone, as hard as he tried to explain the king's infallibility in practical, temporal terms—recall his two explanations for the proposition that the king can do no wrong—was ultimately incapable of weaning his own updated hypotheses from the original doctrine of the divine right of kings. The clues are evident not only in his allusion to the "mere imposition (to which the most perfect of sublunary beings must still continue liable) those little inadvertencies, which, if charged on the will of the prince, might lessen him in the eyes of his subjects." The opposite of those *sublunary beings* that must still continue to be liable is that *divine being* that must not be similarly imposed upon with "those little inadvertencies," which will lessen him in the eyes of his subjects.

What is more, the primary authority for Blackstone's commentary on royal dignity was the same maxim that was originally used to support the supremacy of the king: "*Rex est vicarius et minister Dei in terra: omnis quidem sub eo est, et ipse sub nullo, nisi tantum sub Deo.*"[53] When Blackstone relied on it to support the sovereignty of the king, it had precisely the same meaning that Seneca, Gregory the Great, Ambrosiaster, Luther, and others put on it in the Middle Ages, when the maxim that the king can do no wrong was originally fashioned. Translated in English, the words say this: "The king is the vicar and the minister of God on earth; everyone is under him, and he is under none but only under God."

In the end, the doctrine of procedural immunity that entails exemption for heads of state from accountability are recycled modern versions of precisely the same ideas that originated in the Middle Ages as the doctrine of the divine right of kings. Jackson expressed that *suspicion* in 1945. William Holdsworth had effectively confirmed that suspicion earlier in 1938, in his explanation of the origins of sovereign immunity, in his important work on the history of English law. In his words:

> Most procedural privileges originated at an early period in the history of the common law. Some of them represent relatively primitive legal ideas. Others represent a period in legal history when the relation of the King and the law, to the courts, and to his judges was very different from the relations which were established as the result of the great Rebellion and the Revolution. All of them were worked up into a rigid set of rules in

the atmosphere of the most technical part of English law—the law of procedure and pleading. Thus, the medieval rule that no lord could be sued
in his own court gave rise to the rule that no action lay against the King
in his own courts. But it soon became evident that some remedy must be
given to a subject damaged by the acts of the Crown; and so a complicated
and inadequate set of remedies was evolved. Right down to the end of
the seventeenth century, the fact that the courts of law were the King's
courts, and the fact that the judges were the King's judges, gave the King
large powers of control: and these large powers of control possessed by an
immortal and infallible King, who was accepted as the head and representative of the state, strengthened the tendency of the judges to give the
King all sorts of remedies which were not open to the subject, all sorts of
exemptions from the ordinary rules of pleading, and all sorts of procedural
privileges. The judges gained independence and security of tenure at the
Revolution but the special remedies, exemptions, and procedural privileges, which had originated in the Middle Ages and had been developed
and elaborated in the sixteenth and seventeenth centuries, remained.[54]

In other words, even when, eventually, the English legal system gradu-
ally started chipping away at the doctrine of the divine right of kings and
started allowing suits to be filed against the king, other procedural obstacles, called royal prerogatives, were devised to impede those inroads. This
led Francis Bacon to exclaim, "In the pleadings and proceedings of the
king's suits, what a garland of prerogatives doth the law put upon them!"[55]

"This garland," observed Pollock and Maitland, "is not woven all at
once and some of its flowers were but buds in the days of Henry III. But
our main point must be that there is as yet little in the law of procedure
to suggest that the king is other than a natural person, nothing to suggest
that he has two capacities. He enjoys the same privileges whether the
matter under discussion is what we should call 'an act of state' or whether
it is a private bargain. And, after all, the grandest of his immunities is no
anomaly."[56]

There, Pollock and Maitland tell us that the king's immunity from
legal proceedings in "his own court"—that being the height of the king's
immunities—is not surprising. Why? As was Holdsworth's observations,
Pollock and Maitland also observed that the king could not be compelled
to answer in his own court. But that was also "true of every petty lord of
every petty manor." It was only "an accident" that there happened to be
in this world no court above his court.[57]

All this is to say that it is beyond reasonable doubt that the idea of
immunity of heads of state traces its beginnings straight to the notion of

the divine right of kings. And Robert H. Jackson was right in thinking so in 1945.

A Global Cartel of Impunity

It may, of course, be possible to explain the idea of foreign sovereign immunity from the post-Westphalian fictions of equality of nations, sovereignty of nations, and a mutual understanding of noninterference in the internal affairs of other nations.

But even so, the composite rationales employed to justify immunity—among equals none may sit in judgment over another, immunity is necessary to avoid hindrances to functions of rulership, etc.—must at some point provoke difficult questions about the unseemly effect of that particular fiction. In other words, is there more than a hint of corruption in the idea of sovereign immunity, as understood creed of reciprocity? Did it become a global cartel of impunity? Under the arrangement of immunity, sovereigns must leave each other alone, as they engage in self-sustaining conduct (even if criminal) without mutual judicial scrutiny, as long as each steers truly clear of each other's domain. "As long as you don't attack me," the thinking may go, "I'll look the other way and not intervene when you are accused of a crime, especially within your realms, if you promise the same in my turn. We can use whatever means necessary to perpetuate ourselves in power in our respective domains. But all bets are off once you attack me. In that case, we shall fight a war and, well, *Vae victis!*"

The plot ran aground not only during World War II, but even earlier in World War I when the conduct of one head of state directed and occasioned great brutality at other states and their own populations. It was an overreach that unraveled the bargain.

This phenomenon comes to mind from the text of the summations of Lord Birkenhead (Attorney General Sir F. E. Smith, KC, as he then was) to Lloyd George and his Imperial Cabinet on 28 November 1918, laying out the case for a British government policy decision to punish the kaiser. As he put it, after summarizing some of the atrocities alleged against the kaiser: "Prime Minister," said the attorney-general, "in my judgment, if this man escapes, common people will say everywhere that he has escaped because he is an Emperor. In my judgment, they will be right. They will say that august influence has been exerted to save him. It is not desirable that such things should be said, especially in these days."[58]

It is generally understood that Lord Birkenhead's delicacy had a different orientation: The ex-kaiser was the grandson of Queen Victoria and first cousin of the reigning British monarch, King George V. The attorney general's hint was clear enough in the heady days of post-Bolshevik revolution—which toppled King George's other first cousin, Czar Nicholas II, another of Queen Victoria's grandsons, in Russia the year before and was threatening Europe and much of the wider world at large. In those broader uncertain circumstances that included a strong public clamor in England for the trial of the kaiser, it was "not desirable" that the "common people" of England be allowed to speculate that the man who had brought so much violent misery to them and inspired strong anti-Prussian feelings had escaped punishment because "august influence ha[d] been exerted to save him." It may be a different specific concern. Yet, it is related to the concern about a phenomenon that some members of the public may view as a cartel of impunity that is consistent with the idea of sovereign immunity.

TIMES, THEY ARE A-CHANGIN'

14

W e see from the last chapter that all manner of legal artifacts were employed to maintain the immunity of kings from earthly accountability. Over time, a doctrine of immunity that started its journey as a substantive theory of immunity, according to which the king could do no wrong, was ultimately buttressed by a procedural accompaniment, equally effective in ensuring immunity. That procedural accompaniment insisted that the king could not (for practical reasons) be sued in any event.

The original substantive argument that the king could do no wrong was driven by the fiction of the king as God's vicar on earth, thus imbuing him with divine rights that placed him above all earthly powers within his realm. God his master was the only entity entitled and fit to sit in judgment over him—and it was, almost always, a "him." The procedural argument was based on the practical consideration that the courts of the realm were the king's courts and he could not be sued in them. Likewise, not even a minor feudal lord of the manor could be sued in his own court. But the king had a stronger claim to immunity on that basis. This, it was argued, was because the king could not compel himself. As George Stuart Robertson put it in 1908, "It has been supposed to be due to the idea that 'the King by his writ cannot command himself.'"[1] That, of course, is a subtle way of saying that the king was the head of the executive branch of government—that was his main job—with the prerogative of means of enforcement of the law, including judgments of courts of law: he would not employ those means against himself. William Blackstone was less subtle on that point. He observed that no suit or action could be brought against the king, even in civil matters, because no court could realistically exercise powers over him. "For all jurisdiction implies superiority of power: authority to try would be vain and idle, without an authority to redress; and the sentence of a court would be contemptible, unless that court had power to command the execution of it: but who, says Finch, shall command the king?"[2]

So remained the state of the law through 1908, when, according to Robertson, "[n]o action lies against the Crown at the suit of a subject. Whatever the origin of this fact, there is no doubt that it forms part of the existing law."[3] The status quo remained up to at least 1936, when William Holdsworth observed that the procedural bars placed against judicial accountability of the king, such as were developed in the Middle Ages, still remained essentially in place in one guise or another, "badly need[ing] revision."[4]

In the United Kingdom and much of the world that comprised its empire, that revision began in earnest in 1947 with the British Parliament's passage of the Crown Liability Act. It was the culmination of an effort begun in 1921 by Lord Chancellor Birkenhead.[5]

It is not necessary to read too much into the fact that Lord Birkenhead was the same Frederick E. Smith, KC, who, as attorney general of England and Wales, insisted on the accountability of the kaiser at the end of World War I, commissioning the Macdonell Committee to inquire into the project's feasibility. Nor should we overinterpret the fact that his effort to reform the Crown liability law in England began in 1921 (two years after World War I) and materialized in 1947 (two years after World War II).

But there is much significance in the fact that the U.S. Supreme Court rendered their classic judgment on sovereign immunity back in 1812—long before the British law reform of 1947. That classic judgment was in the *Schooner Exchange* case.[6] The judgment resulted from a civil suit brought in the U.S. federal court—not an international court. The issue for determination was whether two American citizens, John McFaddon and William Greetham, could regain possession of a vessel they claimed was theirs. It had earlier been commandeered in the name of Emperor Napoleon and converted into a warship of France on 30 December 1810 during its voyage from Baltimore, Maryland, to St. Sebastian, Spain, a voyage that began on 27 October 1809. Months later, the vessel was brought into the port of Philadelphia for repairs due to storm damage. McFaddon and Greetham seized the opportunity and brought proceedings in the U.S. federal court on 30 August 1811 to recover the ship. The district court declined to exercise jurisdiction. The Circuit Court of Appeal reversed.

On further appeal, the U.S. Supreme Court reversed the circuit court decision and reinstated the judgment of the district court. Chief Justice John Marshall delivered the judicial pronouncement that has become the precedent often relied upon to argue that foreign sovereigns are exempt from the jurisdictions of one another.

Notably, the judgment of the Permanent Court of International Justice (PCIJ) in the *Lotus* case[7] stands in significant opposition to the reasoning in the *Schooner Exchange* case.

For present purposes, the value of the *Lotus* case is simply for the lesson it teaches about how customary international law develops from the practice of states. It teaches the need to avoid confusing grapefruits for oranges. A norm that has developed to solve a specific problem may not readily serve an appreciably different situation, even though the two situations may look alike on a casual view.

In *Lotus*, France had protested Turkey's exercise of criminal jurisdiction over Lieutenant Demons, a French citizen, for a maritime collision that occurred outside the territory of Turkey, involving boats of both nations. The PCIJ considered that the case cast in relief the "very nature and existing conditions of international law."[8] In the end, the PCIJ held, among other things, that there is "the necessity of ascertaining whether or not under international law there is a principle which would have prohibited Turkey, in the circumstances of the case before the Court, from prosecuting Lieutenant Demons. *And moreover . . . this must be ascertained by examining precedents offering a close analogy to the case under consideration; for it is only from precedents of this nature that the existence of a general principle applicable to the particular case may appear. . . .* The Court therefore must, in any event, ascertain whether or not there exists a rule of international law limiting the freedom of States to extend the criminal jurisdiction of their courts *to a situation uniting the circumstances of the present case.*"[9]

On the authority of the *Lotus*, which requires "a close analogy" between the case pending before a judge and the circumstances that inspired the norm urged as applicable, it then stands to reason that the plea of immunity of heads of state or of other state officials before an international criminal court may not, as a matter of customary international law, readily derive from the *Schooner Exchange* case, which involved the question of immunity from the jurisdiction of the U.S. Federal Court for the District of Pennsylvania. That is to say, the *Schooner Exchange* case did not offer "a close analogy to the case under consideration" before an international criminal court. Put differently, the *Schooner Exchange* case did not involve, as it was put in *Lotus*, "a situation uniting the circumstances" of the average case before an international criminal court.

༄

But anachronism will still remain an issue, even assuming the factual appositeness of the *Schooner Exchange* case relative to the average case before an international criminal court. Here, the question arises: Does it matter that the *Schooner Exchange* judgment was rendered in 1812? The anachronism is that, in the era of 1812, the rule in much of the world was that the king could do no wrong (*rex non potest peccare*). And just as important, the king could not be sued in *his* own court, so he was effectively above the law (*princep legibus solutus*). Legal publicists agreed that, at its height, the idea that the courts of the realm were the king's courts had real connotations. "When Bracton says that were the king strong enough he would do all justice in person," Frederick Pollock and William Maitland inform us, "he means what he says. Far at all events from him is the thought that the king may not sit as the active president of his own court. King Henry sits as such and important cases will be adjourned if he be not present. Justices have been fined for proceeding in the king's absence."[10] It may also be recalled that King Solomon's legend for unrivaled wisdom came from his judicial functions.

༄

That then brings us to the sovereignty implications of subjecting the king to the judicial processes of his own courts. As we shall see, the notion of *sovereignty* is one of the cardinal legal artifacts constructed by jurists of old to exempt rulers from accountability to their own people. And as we have seen, sovereign immunity from the legal process was derived from the idea of the divine right of kings.

It is said that the elevation of Kaiser Wilhelm I into the title of "emperor" of Germany impressed Queen Victoria so very much that she asked her private secretary in 1873, "why have I never officially assumed this title?" She got her wish shortly thereafter after Benjamin Disraeli became prime minister in 1874. He sponsored the passage of the Royal Titles Act (1876), the entire point of which was to add the title of "empress of India" to Queen Victoria's formal style.[11]

It may be helpful to consider Blackstone's telling explanation for why the British monarch's far-flung colonial "realm [was] declared to be an *empire*, and his crown *imperial*, by many acts of parliament."[12]

With palpable petulance, Blackstone remarked, "Formerly there prevailed a ridiculous notion, propagated by the German and Italian civilians, that an emperor could do many things which a king could not . . . and that all kings were in some degree subordinate and subject to the emperor of Germany or Rome. The meaning therefore of the legislature, when it uses these terms of *empire* and *imperial*, and applies them to the realm and crown of England, is only to assert that our king is equally sovereign and independent within these his dominions, as any emperor is in his empire; and owes no kind of subjection to any other potentate upon earth."[13] The direct implication is "that no suit or action can be brought against the king, even in civil matters, because no court can have jurisdiction over him."[14]

It is in those circumstances that the law recognized "the person of the king as sacred" even when his reign "be completely tyrannical and arbitrary," because "no jurisdiction upon earth has power to try him in a criminal way; much less to condemn him to punishment."[15]

At this point in his commentary, Blackstone made an observation that lends a better appreciation of the import of sovereign immunity in international law, in the relations between equal states, founded on the doctrine *par in parem non habet imperium* (there is no dominion in relations among equals).

"If any foreign jurisdiction had this power," Blackstone stated, referring to the power to sit in judgment over an alien king, "as was formerly claimed by the pope, the independence of the kingdom would be no more; and, if such a power were vested in any domestic tribunal, there would soon be an end of the constitution, by destroying the free agency of one of the constituent parts of the sovereign legislative power."[16]

The last proposition is hopelessly exaggerated hyperbole—obviously belied by modern precepts of the rule of law in many countries. Nowadays, the law imposes civil liability on the sovereign in domestic law. And throughout history, it is not unknown for people to try their own heads of state for criminal offenses.[17] There are historical instances of subjection of heads of state to the death penalty.* And the states in question still survived.

---

* Lady Jane Grey, Queen of England, was executed in 1554 following conviction for high treason; Charles I suffered the same fate in 1649, despite his own insistence that no earthly court had jurisdiction to try him; so, too, were Louis XVI of France and his wife Marie Antoinette in 1793. See *Encyclopaedia Britannica*, s.v. "Lady Jane Grey, Queen of England," last updated 8 March 2024, https://

There is no state whose existential circumstances are conjoined with that of any human being who is a citizen of the state during his or her own lifetime, which life will come to an end at some point. Cemeteries are full of the bones of people once thought indispensable—some of them heads of state—that lie beneath as gardeners tend the greens above. Similarly, upon the end of reign of one head of state or government for any reason—loss of election or imprisonment—another would be found to replace him or her.

More interesting, perhaps, is the first part of Blackstone's point in the passage quoted above. Recall his argument that "the independence of the kingdom would be no more" if a foreign power were to exercise the power to subject the king to criminal trial and punishment. That argument had a resonant implication in an era—long before 1947—when the law was reformed in the common law world to allow tort lawsuits against the domestic sovereign. A cardinal premise of the precept was that the local courts were seen as courts of the domestic monarch for whom judges acted as mere delegates or agents. In those circumstances, to subject a foreign king to stand trial in the court of his peers was to diminish both the independence of the foreign king and that of his realm.

Blackstone gave that concern an appreciable political realism by his allusion to the imperial claims that "Rome" and the Germans once made against other kingdoms. That was an obvious allusion to the Holy Roman Empire that held sway in much of Europe since the coronation of Charlemagne in 800, until the Peace of Westphalia of 1648 signaled its sunset following the Thirty Years' War.

The Holy Roman Empire was a political arrangement that centered around Germany and the neighboring Frankish regions, ruled mostly by German emperors predominantly of the Hapsburg lineage. The pope, physically situated in Rome, was the spiritual head of the empire. Under the arrangement, other kings or princes (numbering hundreds) still had their realms—many of them styled "principalities"—but they did so under the suzerainty of the emperor who was also the king of his particular kingdom (the metropolis). The accession to the imperial throne was by way

www.britannica.com/biography/Lady-Jane-Grey; *Encyclopaedia Britannica*, s.v. "Charles I, King of Great Britain and Ireland," last updated 21 February 2024, https://www.britannica.com/biography/Charles-I-king-of-Great-Britain-and-Ireland; *Encyclopaedia Britannica*, s.v. "Louis XVI, King of France," last updated 5 March 2024, https://www.britannica.com/biography/Louis-XVI; and "Marie Antoinette, Queen of France," last updated 10 March 2024, https://www.britannica.com/biography/Marie-Antoinette-queen-of-France

of an election in which the other kings (or regnant princes) within the Holy Roman Empire were designated as the "electors." At the time, the election process paralleled that for the pope, which remains in place today. Cardinals, known as "the princes of the church" elect a fellow cardinal who then becomes both the pope and the bishop of Rome. In a parallel process, the other temporal princes within the Holy Roman Empire acting as "electors" elected one of their peers as the Holy Roman emperor.

In the heyday of the Holy Roman Empire, the pope and the emperor asserted dominion over the vast expanse of Christendom. It was an ambition in which the pope, through the spiritual allure and superstition, had an advantage over the emperor. But in an era in which wars of aggression were permissible for any ruler able to fight them, the hinted claims of the Holy Roman emperor to global hegemony were always a serious threat to the territorial and political independence of other states. Hence, the allusion in Blackstone's commentary.

Even kingdoms such as the British and the French, who managed to remain outside the immediate political orbit of the Holy Roman Empire, still took spiritual direction from the pope, as the spiritual head of their own kingdoms. This was pursuant to the formula that validated the divine right of kings, by the doctrine of the necessity of two kingdoms of God on earth that must work hand in hand: the temporal kingdom headed by a king and the spiritual kingdom headed by the pope. That arrangement came to an end for England during the reign of Henry VIII. He wanted an annulment of his marriage to Catherine of Aragon, whom he blamed for not bearing him a male heir, so he could marry the much younger Anne Boleyn. But Pope Clement VII refused to grant the annulment. Hence, Henry VIII embraced the Reformation movement, terminated England's spiritual fealty to the Vatican, and established a breakaway Protestant denomination called the Church of England, of which he proclaimed himself the head in 1534.[18]

But power was also starting to crumble from within the Holy Roman Empire. The Peace of Westphalia, which concluded the Thirty Years' War in 1648, was an important catalyst in the demise of the Holy Roman Empire.

One of the principal causes of the Thirty Years' War was the determination of the Holy Roman emperor, Ferdinand II, to suppress religious minorities, particularly the Reformation movement, thus provoking armed resistance from the Protestants within Bohemia and Austria.[19] Ferdinand II was both the king of Bohemia and the Holy Roman emperor.

After thirty years of exhausting war—in which not only religious but also territorial, dynastic, and commercial rivalries were brought to bear[20]—peace was finally concluded in the two German cities of Münster and Osnabrük. Together, the two treaties are known in international relations as the "Peace of Westphalia."[21]

Among its legacy claims was the notion of sovereignty of states. This stipulated that from then on every state party to the treaty was to have sovereignty over its internal affairs, such "that they never can or ought to be molested therein by any whomsoever upon any manner of pretence."[22] The treaty also reaffirmed and incorporated by reference the earlier Peace of Augsburg (1555), which not only established the principle of *cuius regio, eius religio* (the religion of the ruler was to be that of the state) but also established that freedom of worship was guaranteed for religious minorities.[23]

Sovereignty thus conceived spelled the beginning of the end of the formal authority of both the Holy Roman emperor and the pope over the states party to the Peace of Westphalia. The pope protested with great vehemence and issued a papal bull denouncing the treaty. But he was cooly ignored by rulers who were exhausted from fighting a bloody and drawn-out war. The Holy Roman Empire was eventually dissolved as such on 6 August 1806, when Francis II laid down the imperial crown,[24] leaving the residual essence of the entity to carry on as Germany, which was always its main constituent entity to begin with.

But the orientation of the idea of sovereignty as contemplated in the Peace of Westphalia entailed its own contexts. On one hand, the treaty contemplated that the united ideals of two men—the emperor and the pope—held secular and religious sway over the multiple principalities that comprised the Holy Roman Empire. In other words, it was an empire after all—in which the emperor and the pope were respectively seen as God's and Christ's vicars on earth and whose diktats must be obeyed as such. The notion of sovereignty as introduced in the Peace of Westphalia was animated by the negative outcomes of that kind of vertical hegemony, one telling evidence of which was Ferdinand II's determination to restore in absolute terms the authority of Roman Catholicism within his domain. That authority was being eroded by the Reformation movement.

On the other hand, the Peace of Westphalia also contemplated sovereignty on the horizontal axis of international relations (i.e., relations at the state-to-state level).[25] This was in the sense of states trampling upon the territorial integrity of one another, by engaging in wars of aggression motivated by religious sympathies, commercial interests, territorial acquisitions, hegemonic domination, and so on—all of which motivations were implicated in the Thirty Years' War. International law retains the ideal of sovereignty in that sense, even codifying it as a central feature of the United Nations' law and policy (see article 2 of the UN Charter).

Taken in the round, however, the prevailing contexts of the Peace of Westphalia should not dictate an absolutist understanding of sovereignty relative to international law. International relations as conceived among European nations as of 1648 did not entail the repudiation of the twenty-first-century vision of a *multilateral* clearinghouse arrangement—ultimately underwritten by the international judicial process—which would meaningfully reconcile conflicting interests, rights, and obligations for states and persons (natural and legal)—as a substitute to resort to war. There is quite simply nothing in the Peace of Westphalia that supports such a repudiation.

Indeed, the opposite is true. There are many provisions in the Peace of Westphalia—notably articles 5, 7, 17, 30, 41, 46, and 132—that contemplated settlement of international disputes, notably through arbitration and adjudication—rather than war. Article 132 in particular contemplated judicial punishment and sentence for anyone who would violate the Peace of Westphalia, "being an Infringer of the publick Peace," so that its settlements "shall have its full effect."

And for his part, Jean Bodin, the original doctrinarian of sovereignty, as explained in his classic *Les six livres de la république* (1576), did not conceive the doctrine in such absolutist terms as would set it up against international law of the time, let alone as we know it today.

Bodin, a man of his own times, was vexed by the War of Religion that was driving France to the brink of disintegration. The conflict was symbolized by the violent encounters between the Catholic majority and the Protestant minority that the Huguenots represented. The St. Bartholomew's Day massacre of 1572—genocidal by today's standards—was emblematic of that violence.

Bodin was thus anxious to ensure an "indivisible sovereignty." This was in the nature of one central, strong authority—that being the king—who would ensure the safety and security of the state. According to Bodin, those imperatives transcended religious differences.[26] Bodin's theory of the absolute obedience to one authority within the realm—the monarch—found expression in the doctrine of sovereignty. Within the national domain, such a conception of sovereignty is defined by such an absolute authority of a king to govern his people. Bodin conceived that authority as indivisible, in the sense that sovereignty did not permit supreme power to be distributed between the king, on the one part, and the estates, parliament, or other authority within the realm.[27]

Bodin was also appreciably perturbed by the broader context of the turbulent circumstances of the Holy Roman Empire's regional shadow that waxed and waned.[28] Although he remained a Catholic formally, he was a known critic of the policies and aptitudes of the pope and the Holy Roman emperor, thus warranting some speculation that Bodin might have been a closet Huguenot.[29] Perhaps, the explanation of his critical attitude toward the pope and the Holy Roman Empire might be his belief that the safety and security of the state was more important than religious allegiances.

But even as sovereignty in Bodin's conception meant the concentration of all political power in one absolute, supreme authority within the realm, he still insisted on certain exceptions. Sovereignty meant that the king was not bound by the positive law laid down by himself or his predecessors: but the king was at the same time bound by the constitution, natural law, and the *law of nations*, as well as by covenants between him and his subjects and *covenants between him and other sovereigns*.[30]

Nevertheless, motivated by the doctrine of the divine right of kings, as well as by concerns about anarchy within the realm, Bodin insisted that it is not for the king's subjects to punish him for violating the constitution and natural law. It was between God and the king's conscience.[31] While this did not fully address what would happen when the king violated international law or obligations to other sovereigns, it was the case that international law of the time, as expounded by Hugo Grotius, fully recognized such violations as just causes for war between nations,[32] an entitlement Bodin evidently did not allow the subjects of a king who violated his civic compact. Claims of entitlement to fight just wars were all well and good until the brutal Thirty Years' War came along. Having exhausted themselves fighting just such a bloody war for three decades at least, continental European states finally thought it more sensible to allow in the Peace of Westphalia (concluded more than seventy years after the publication of Bodin's *Six livres*) that anyone who violated that treaty would be treated as "an Infringer of the publick Peace," liable to punishment and sentence, so that the treaty "shall have its full effect."

This all boils down to recognizing that there are real implications for the idea of sovereign equality of states and political independence, in an arrangement in which a head of state cannot be proceeded against in his own court, because conceptions of his supremacy or sovereignty (as Bodin would conceive the idea) effectively placed that king above his own court.

The logic of that arrangement must then preclude subjecting a second head of state (i.e., the head of state of another country) to the jurisdiction of the courts seen as an emanation of the powers of the first head of state whose supremacy has placed him above his own court. The antithesis to the idea of equality of sovereigns is plain enough to see.

But that concern disappears when it is accepted that heads of state can be proceeded against in their own courts, like anyone else. In those circumstances, it cannot be said that the notion of sovereign equality is negated—for all heads of state are equally subjected to the jurisdiction of any national court, including their own. What generates the concern of inequality is when one head of state is placed above the courts that another head of state is subjected to. There may, of course, remain some lingering awkwardness about proceedings against a foreign head of state in a national court that was not his or her own. But such awkwardness is just that. It has no juristic significance.

At the international level, the considerations are markedly different. Proceedings before international courts and tribunals are not proceedings before the national courts of any head of state, as Bodin and jurists of his time had defined sovereignty. They are proceedings before forums in which no credible theory can sustain the outcome or process as one that negates the doctrine of equality *between* states. (See further discussion in the epilogue of this book dealing with certain confusions in legal scholarship on this point.) Beyond the consideration that the international court belongs to no sovereign as such, it is also the case that all heads of state of the court's founding treaty are equally subject to the jurisdiction of the international court in question. Again, it is accepted that criminal proceedings can be trying for the defendant's ego. It will certainly be more so for heads of state. But, that concern has no juristic significance.

In conclusion, it is a long time from the Middle Ages, when the prevailing doctrine was that the king was both above the law and the master of the courts of his realm, thus according him immunity from the processes of the courts of his domain. But it has long since been accepted in the modern era that the head of state is subject to the laws and courts of his country. That resolves the concern about sovereign inequality.

Additionally, when the doctrine of the divine right of kings generated their exemption from the rule of law in their own realms, there was no multilateral international order that mediated relations between states in the same way as now, using the compulsory jurisdiction of international courts beyond arbitration as a substitute for use of force to settle international disputes. Compulsory international adjudication beyond arbitration was a twentieth-century idea.[33]

Also, the international order did not directly recognize rights and duties for individuals in a way that also required objective mediation using international mechanisms. That, too, is a post-1945 eventuality.

Now the foregoing realities signal changed times that make head-of-state immunity an entirely anachronistic idea in the processes of an international criminal court that has jurisdiction in a particular case. As international practice has firmly established since 1945, there is no place for such immunity in the twenty-first century.

THE RIGHT TO PEACE: **15**
A NEW ORDER OF
ACCOUNTABILITY

Peace is the most important global public good. . . . War
brings death, human suffering and unimaginable destruction.
—Antonio Guterres

In his observation quoted in this chapter's epigraph, the United Nations secretary general sets up the zero-sum value of war relative to peace. It should not be a profound observation in the twenty-first century. But there it is—still sounding so profound. And that says so much about the human condition.

In my view, the invasion of Ukraine occurred partly because the international community has not managed—or has not resolved—to make wars of aggression sufficiently risky (at the personal level) for the world's "lords of war," to use the terminology used by Lloyd George, Clemenceau, Larnaude, and Lapradelle to describe Kaiser Wilhelm II.

As a matter of good faith, Russia's invasion of Ukraine should change that calculation. This can be done by enhancing the legal hazards of war—not only at the more familiar level of criminal prosecution but also at the level of civil liability that remains largely beyond our consciousness. Both strategies are easy enough to design, but their realization depends only on the political will of the international community: the good faith.

As a matter of the accountability imperatives, how can we make aggressive wars—or those fought with unconscionable brutality—more legally hazardous to their authors and accomplices, from the angles of both criminal and civil liability? I examine that question immediately below.

Wars as the Traditional Driver of Growth of International Law

Perhaps we may ask why it became necessary to engage this discussion about enhancing the legal hazards of war in the period following Russia's invasion of Ukraine.

It became necessary because of an overwhelming outrage against a war of invasion that fueled feelings to do something against wars of aggression. But no one seemed really sure of what to do. In a cascade of umbrage, Western governments froze assets within their domains that belonged either to the Russian government or to wealthy Russians pejoratively termed "oligarchs," wondering what to do with them in the end.

⌒

In reflecting upon what to do, when what to do may involve new adjustments to international law, it helps to keep in mind that armed conflict has been the greatest driver of the development of international law. There's always the temptation for some to see something of a salutary relationship between war and civilization—in this case, international law. According to that view, war becomes a chief enabler of international law.

But a workable analogy may be that of the struggle between a boa constrictor and its prey. The snake wraps itself around its prey and tightens its grip with every movement the prey makes. That's what international law tries to do to war.

Some may see that as perhaps too optimistic a view of the abilities of international law. But consider these:

1648: *Peace of Westphalia.* Often seen as the recognizable starter for contemporary international law, it resulted from the Thirty Years' and the Eighty Years' wars in Europe that spanned the period between 1568 and 1648.

1856: *Paris Declaration.* Often seen as the first international instrument that sought to codify both the principle of neutrality and the proscription of privateering or mercenary activities during war, it resulted from the Crimean War (1853–1856).

1863: *The Lieber Code.* The code was the first attempt to codify (albeit at the national level) the essential elements of the law and customs of war at an early stage. It resulted from the American Civil War (1861–1865).

1864: The first edition of the *Geneva Convention.* The convention resulted in the creation of the Red Cross Society and the recognition of the need to provide care and succor to sick and wounded soldiers. It resulted from the brutality of the Second Italian War of Independence that Henry Dunant (a Swiss businessman) witnessed in the Battle of Solferino in 1859.

1868: *St. Petersburg Declaration.* This declaration was the first international instrument that sought to make war more humane. It indicated the principle that the weakening of the enemy—rather than total annihilation and wanton cruelty—is the only legitimate aim of war; it laid down the principle against use of weapons that inflict unnecessary suffering that would make peace more difficult to achieve. The declaration resulted from the discovery of munitions that would inflict unnecessary suffering.

1899 and 1907: *First and Second Hague Peace Conferences.* There were, of course, extensive international law instruments that resulted from the First and Second Hague Peace Conferences, in 1899 and 1907, respectively. They resulted from the many wars that had blighted life in Europe.

1919: *Paris Peace Conference.* The conference produced the Versailles Treaty and the Covenant of the League of Nations. The former (in article 227) laid down the unprecedented idea that heads of state could be prosecuted before international tribunals as a requirement of international law, with no scope at all for the plea of sovereign immunity. The latter instrument introduced for the first time the idea of a standing international organization with universal remit, to try and foster peace between nations and limit their inclination to make war. Both instruments resulted from World War I.

1945: The conclusion of World War II harbingered a number of developments including the following: (1) the Charter of the International Military Tribunal for Nuremberg and the Charter of the International Military Tribunal for the Far East; they not only unequivocally recognized aggressive war as a crime in international law, but similarly confirmed unequivocally that heads of state and heads of government may be prosecuted before an international tribunal as a requirement of international law, and that the plea of immunity does not apply; (2) the creation of an updated version of a standing international organization—the United Nations—to replace the League of Nations as the global clearinghouse of efforts to maintain international peace and security and the improvement of the human condition all over the world; (3) the adoption of the Universal Declaration of Human Rights, in recognition for the first time that human beings are beneficiaries of rights conferred directly upon them by international law; (4) a new international crime—genocide—was nominated for concerted global action in the eponymous Convention on the Punishment and Prevention of the Crime of Genocide; and (5) the twin project of formulating an international code of crimes and creating a permanent international criminal court to enforce that code.

1991 to 1994: The Balkan wars and the Rwandan civil war resulted in the UN Security Council's creation of two ad hoc international criminal tribunals—for the former Yugoslavia and for Rwanda. In doing so, the United Nations, through its Security Council, repeatedly reiterated the norm that heads of state are not immune to prosecution before an international tribunal.

The events in the former Yugoslavia and in Rwanda, which resulted in the creation of two United Nations ad hoc international criminal tribunals in 1993 and 1994, respectively, also inspired renewed impetus for the creation of a permanent court that eventually produced the International Criminal Court (ICC) in 1998.

A further by-product of the events in the former Yugoslavia and Rwanda was the development of the doctrine of Responsibility to Protect (R2P) declared at a UN World Summit in 2005. The doctrine insists that sovereignty entails much more than vaunting rights for rulers, purportedly in the name of their states, with accountability to no one. Sovereignty also entails responsibility to protect the domestic population. The failure to discharge that responsibility would justify the intervention of the international community, coordinated by the United Nations.

ᘒ

The foregoing is a nonexhaustive outline of the appreciable ways that armed conflict has enabled the growth of international law.

And then in 2022, another wretched war was unleashed, animating much global rage against wars of aggression, which not only visit death and destruction upon innocent victims but also general hardships on the world at large.

It is never a good policy to waste energy generated by rage. The better strategy would be to channel all such rage into a productive outcome. Such an outcome should be another adjustment to international law. This is in the manner of enhancing the legal risks—criminal and civil types—in ways that must perturb those who would launch aggressive or unconscionably brutal wars.

Enhancing the Risk of Criminal Prosecution

At the start of Russia's invasion of Ukraine, the Rome Statute and the ICC comprised the only standing global mechanism against international crimes in general, and the crime of aggression in particular.

Yet much more could be done from the perspective of enhancing the risk of criminal prosecution for the crime of aggression. This could be achieved by amending the Rome Statute in the following ways. First, there is a need to cover the gap that exists in article 15*bis*(5). The gap now excludes persons (or territories) of non–ICC member states from the aggression jurisdiction of the ICC, except when the UN Security Council refers the situation to the ICC prosecutor for investigation and prosecution. That gap can be covered by deleting article 15*bis*(5), given the fact that the use of the veto power will obstruct the Security Council from referring a situation to the ICC when a permanent member of the Security Council or a client or ally of such a state is implicated in the conduct that needs to be referred to the ICC.

Second, there is a need to expand the avenues for United Nations referrals of situations to the ICC prosecutor, when the overall interest of justice for humanity sorely cries out for such referral. Currently, only the Security Council is recognized under article 13(b) of the Rome Statute as the UN organ that may refer a situation to the ICC. But it is possible to amend the Rome Statute, also to recognize the General Assembly as a source of UN referral to the ICC using the General Assembly's "Uniting for Peace" procedure, which allows the General Assembly to step in and act when the veto power has been immorally used to block the Security Council from discharging its functions in the interest of the UN. At the barest minimum, under the proposed amendment, the General Assembly could recommend such referral to UN member states. In the outcome, the ICC would have an operable basis possibly to exercise jurisdiction resulting from a specific General Assembly resolution that makes the referral directly or recommends that member states should make it jointly or severally.

And the third strategy for enhancing the risk of criminal prosecution for the crime of aggression involves extending liability for the crime beyond persons in a position to direct the military or political actions of a state, as is now the case. It will be necessary to extend criminal responsibility for aggression also to lower-level soldiers. It means that they, too, should be prosecuted for the crime of aggression. This will encourage rank-and-file soldiers to refuse to obey orders to fight wars of aggression: thus putting pressure on any head of state or head of government conceiving of a war of aggression.

These amendments need not be made as a package. Beginning with the first recommendation as the easiest to make, any of the other two or both will significantly enhance the risk of criminal liability for the crime of aggression. It will add layers of deterrence against the crime.

And the great prospect of enhancing that risk through the amendments lies in the fact that it is entirely up to the member states of the Rome Statute to resolve to make the indicated amendment. It requires no input from the United Nations, let alone veto power from any member of its Security Council.

Enhancing the Risk of Civil Liability

In addition to adjusting international law by enhancing the risk of criminal prosecution for the crime of aggression, there is also much scope in making adjustments on the civil liability side of international law.

As the world groped for ways to adjust international law after World War I to deter future wars, Professor Coleman Phillipson (a member of the British delegation to the Paris Peace Conference) thought that the main problem to which statesmen and their nations should devote themselves was how to fortify international law "by such potent sanctions as will make its violation not merely dishonourable, but *unprofitable*."[1]

The invasion of Ukraine has once more sent the world to the drawing board of international law to explore ways of making wars of aggression "unprofitable" for those who wage or aid them.

Beyond enhancing the hazards of criminal prosecution as indicated above, the strategy of suppressing future crimes of aggression will be significantly boosted by directly exposing aggressive warmongers—and their accomplices—to the risk of personal civil liability, universally.

This can be accomplished in the specific manner of adopting an international covenant that specifies peace as an actionable fundamental human right.

I suggest one strategy in particular that can be employed to enforce international law directly by means of national law and domestic legal processes, a valuable strategy that compensates for the renowned weakness of international law in the execution of its own commandments.

The scheme of the new treaty can be arranged as follows. First, it will begin with the declared premise that all peoples, nations, and persons (natural or legal) have a fundamental and inalienable right to peace. The premise should be noncontroversial, for there is seldom a fundamental human right internationally recognized as such that could be enjoyed meaningfully in the absence of peace.

Second, the foregoing premise will then be the basis for enumerating the acts that would amount to breach of the right to peace, with specific focus on wars of aggression. Those acts would obviously include the following: (1) acts of aggression as defined and explained in the United Nations General resolution 3314 (XXIX) of 14 December 1974; (2) the launching of sustained internal violent conflict or acts of terrorism by any group of persons in violation of international law; and (3) complicity or aiding and abetting the conducts indicated in (1) and (2) above including by furnishing the logistics or material assistance to any such conduct.

Third, it won't be enough to stop at declaring peace as a fundamental human right and indicating what would amount to a violation of that right. In light of the doctrine expressed in the maxim *ubi jus ibi remedium* (where there is a right, there is a remedy), it will be necessary to spell out the consequences of such a violation. Here, it will be necessary to provide for a right to reparation, and the modalities of actualizing it. The right to reparation would be given to all peoples, nations, and persons (natural or legal) who suffer damage as a result of a breach of their right to peace. The right to reparation may be claimed against any person (natural or legal), entity, government, or state responsible for the breach or who aids and abets it.

Fourth, the forum for claims for reparation would be any existing or future multilateral, regional, or national court or human rights adjudicatory body with jurisdiction to make the award of reparation contemplated in the covenant. In that regard, each state party to the covenant should be required to take such measures as may be necessary to establish its jurisdiction over claims of reparation contemplated in the covenant, especially when the asset or property of the parties and accomplices to any breach of the right to peace is located within the state. This is how national laws and domestic legal processes will be used to enforce international law in this particular respect.

Additionally, states parties to the covenant on the right to peace will be required to cooperate in the execution of any foreign judgment for reparation against any asset or property of any state or person or their accomplices adjudged liable for a breach of the right to peace, wherever such assets or property may be found, without regard to considerations of sovereign immunity.

It is in these circumstances that the question of what to do with frozen assets (such as those frozen by many Western governments at the beginning of Russia's invasion of Ukraine) answers itself. In any future war of aggression, following the adoption of a covenant on the right to peace, assets frozen in such circumstances can remain frozen pending the determination of the claims of victims of wars of aggression. The frozen assets can be used to satisfy those claims.

What the Right to Peace Does Not Forbid

Past efforts to recognize the right to peace ran into opposition from a number of states who were concerned that the right to peace may be construed in a manner so broad as to impinge upon the right of states to individual or collective self-defense. Businesses engaged in arms manufacture and trade have also been concerned about the implications of such a right to their commercial interests.

The imperfections of life must commend a sensible compromise. To begin with, there is no intrinsic incompatibility between the fundamental right to peace and the right of a state to individual or collective self-defense as recognized in international law. This includes the right of a state to avail itself of appropriate industry, methods, or means of self-defense. That is to say, the right to peace does not automatically stand against the interests of corporations who manufacture and sell weapons that will enable states to engage in self-defense.

But what the right to peace will—and does need to—stand against would be the selfish interests of businesses inclined to *continue* to replenish the ways and means of aggressive wars, by selling weapons and other means of perpetuating an ongoing war of aggression, when they ought to know that the weapons and means they provide are being used to further acts of aggression or unconscionably brutal wars.

As of the time of writing this book, there remains a large room for the growth of international law in ways that will constrain the space for wars of aggression as a pernicious global phenomenon. Beyond the bleakness of the invasion of Ukraine, the resulting possibility of development of international law in the needed respect represents a silver lining. The negative global passion unleashed against that war should be harnessed into a positive force for good in that respect, as had happened in other past wars that occasioned the growth of international law.

The enhancement of the risks against wars of aggression beyond criminal liability, especially by accentuating the strategy of civil claims, will make wars of aggression personally costly to the pocketbooks of the authors and accomplices of wars of aggression. The outcome will be to give those culprits an extended food for thought on whether they truly need to wage a particular war of aggression before they do.

CONCLUSION

In the preceding chapters, we have seen how international law evolved to its present condition, in which it rejects immunity for heads of state when charged with international crimes before an international criminal court. The march of that evolution started in 1919, immediately after World War I. The rejection of head-of-state immunity was made more robust in 1945, immediately after World War II. And it crystallized during the period after World War II, not only through the work of the International Law Commission (ILC) on behalf of the United Nations (especially in their formulation of the Third Nuremberg Principle as well as two draft codes of crimes against the peace and security of mankind, all which reject head-of-state immunity) but also in the international instruments through which the international community created various international tribunals (notably for the former Yugoslavia, for Rwanda, and for Sierra Leone). All of these instruments have rejected immunity for heads of state. The same rejection of immunity is repeated in the Rome Statute of the International Criminal Court. It is important to stress that the occurrence of that norm in the Rome Statute is not a new idea. It was, at the adoption of the statute in 1998, an idea that had been repeated in every relevant multilateral instrument of international law since 1919. That process of repetition is a well-known method through which international law is created.

Ultimately, it is difficult to miss this irony. Any argument for immunity of heads of state is effectively a protest against the judicial process however demonstrably impartial, even at an international tribunal.

But with the judicial process eliminated, the "political" process becomes a real, remaining option. The latter process is adequately captured by James Brown Scott in his apt observation that "Napoleon Bonaparte abdicated and then delivered himself up to the enemy. . . . We can ransack the history of the world, without finding a tragedy in which the hero does not kill himself, is not killed, or does not give himself up in the fifth act, before the curtain falls."[1] Stripped of the double negatives, the proposition is that the final act in those tragedies usually shows the leader committing suicide, being summarily executed, or surrendering himself to his opponents for whatever exactions they may impose.

It may not be necessary to rely on the allusion to dramatic fiction to highlight the political point. It is enough that historical facts abound for instances where popular passion, comeuppance, or sheer convenience has led to the summary execution or banishment of a deposed almighty tyrant with no pretense of a judicial process. Such was the fate of Napoleon Bonaparte, Benito Mussolini, Idi Amin, Muammar al-Qhaddafi, and Yahya Jammeh, among others. In 1919, there were many who advocated for summary exile-imprisonment (or worse) of the kaiser without a judicial inquiry, as was the fate of Napoleon. Notable among them were Lord Curzon, a minority of the Macdonell Committee, and even the Crown Law Officers at some initial point. But Georges Clemenceau and David Lloyd George insisted on a judicial process as more consistent with the rule of law. Similarly in 1945, a strong case was made for a "political treatment" of the Axis leaders—specifically meaning their summary execution. Notably, Sir Alexander Cardogan and a faction of the successive administrations of President Roosevelt and President Truman were of that view. That was one of the pillars of rough treatment that U.S. treasury secretary Henry Morgenthau contemplated for Germany in the notorious plan named after him.[2] But U.S. war secretary Henry L. Stimson and the rule of law advocates within the administrations prevailed in their urge for the judicial process.[3]

The international judicial process that Clemenceau and Lloyd George urged in 1919, which became a reality in the Nuremberg experiment, has since become part of the mainstream of international law. One would hope that those who protest against the international judicial process can see its real advantages from the perspectives of fairness and justice even for the accused. For that point, it is not possible to improve upon Robert Jackson's typically eloquent argument:

> For these defendants, however, we have set up an International Tribunal and have undertaken the burden of participating in a complicated effort to give them fair and dispassionate hearings. That is the best-known protection to any man with a defense worthy of being heard. If these men are the first war leaders of a defeated nation to be prosecuted in the name of

the law, they are also the first to be given a chance to plead for their lives in the name of the law. Realistically, the Charter of this Tribunal, which gives them a hearing, is also the source of their only hope. It may be that these men of troubled conscience, whose only wish is that the world forget them, do not regard a trial as a favor. But they do have a fair opportunity to defend themselves—a favor which these men, when in power, rarely extended to their fellow countrymen. Despite the fact that public opinion already condemns their acts, we agree that here they must be given a presumption of innocence, and we accept the burden of proving criminal acts and the responsibility of these defendants for their commission.[4]

The advantages of the due process of the law that Jackson outlined in the above quote come in the manner of independent judges who are determined to resist the pressure and clamor to convict accused persons—regardless of the evidence—to please popular opinions on questions of guilt and innocence. That judicial determination to do justice has resulted in the acquittal or discharge of high-profile defendants whom popular opinions had already convicted of the crimes alleged against them. Notably, of the 92 people indicted at the International Criminal Tribunal for Rwanda (ICTR), 14 were acquitted (more than 10 percent), and two of the indictments were withdrawn prior to trial.[5] At the International Criminal Tribunal for the Former Yugoslavia (ICTY), 161 persons were indicted: 18 were acquitted, and 20 had their indictments withdrawn.[6]

High-profile examples of such outcomes include the cases of Laurent Gbagbo, Charles Blé Goudé, William Ruto, Jean-Pierre Bemba, Ante Gotovina, Gratien Kabiligi, and Augustin Ndindiliyimana. Those who think they are doing heads of state a favor by insisting that they must enjoy immunity, only need to consider whether what they would wish for their intellectual (or even professional) clients is the eventual fate of Mussolini, Muammar al-Qaddafi, or Samuel Doe (of Liberia), and many other tyrants who came to a hard and humiliating end, and there were no legal scholars to take up their cause (even posthumously). Imagine such a fate for Laurent Gbagbo, Charles Blé Goudé, Jean-Pierre Bemba, Ante Gotovina, Gratien Kabiligi, Augustin Ndindiyilimana, and all the former defendants who were acquitted of the charges against them following trials by independent international courts.

It is helpful to recall that, in answering the question about the raison d'être of international law, Matti Koskenniemi reminded us that international law "provides the shared surface—the only such surface—on which political adversaries recognize each other as such and pursue their adversity

in terms of something shared, instead of seeking to attain full exclusion—
'outlawry'—of the other."[7] In other words, "international law, in all its
imperfections must be allowed a continued role as an avenue for orderly
expression and resolution of grievances: to deny the powerless (with no
real access to justice) one excuse to resort to less than legitimate means of
settling scores with the powerful."[8]

～2～

Ever since H. L. A. Hart[9] and Ronald Dworkin[10]—together with Joseph
Raz,[11] John Finnis,[12] Alf Ross,[13] and many more—gave them contemporary prominence, debates about the relationship between morality and law
have troubled the discipline of legal philosophy. Does law as command
from its giver to the subject sustain its own legitimacy? Or does morality
serve as the compass of law's legitimacy?

Such questions no doubt come to mind in any debate concerning the
propriety of the immunity of heads of state from accountability before
international courts for the criminal kinds of gross violations of human
rights. How could international law truly withhold accountability from
heads of state reasonably believed to have committed, say, murder or torture against innocent civilians on a widespread or systematic basis, let alone
those suspected of genocide?

Those are truly important questions that those who favor the so-called
"natural law"—essentially meaning common sense—side of legal philosophy are allowed to ask. No doubt, answers that satisfy the sensibilities of
natural law would add an appreciable dimension and depth to any positive
rule of law that is also consistent with the orientation of those questions.
Strictly speaking, though, it is not necessary to dwell on those questions
and their answers. For they are not in themselves dispositive of the debate
regarding the position of international law on the matter of criminal
responsibility of heads of state for international crimes in the proceedings
of international courts.

Regardless of any role that morality may have played in the formulation
of the current position of international law, it is enough that the present
state of international law, as a positive statement of command, does not
recognize immunity for heads of state.

In that regard, it is enough to consider that there is as yet no occasion when and where the positive lawmakers of international law have
recognized such immunity, when called upon to consider that question.
To the contrary, at every assembly of international lawmakers—beginning

with the adoption of the Versailles Treaty[14] at the Paris Peace Conference of 1919, through the adoption of the Charter of the International Military Tribunal at Nuremberg[15] at the London Conference of 1945 and the companion Control Council Law no. 10,[16] through the United Nations General Assembly's adoption of the Convention for the Prevention and Punishment of the Crime of Genocide,[17] the United Nations Security Council's adoption of the Statute of the International Criminal Tribunal for the former Yugoslavia,[18] and the Statute of the International Criminal Tribunal for Rwanda[19] or the Security Council's authorization of the Statute of the Special Court for Sierra Leone,[20] and culminating in the adoption of the ICC Statute[21] at the Rome Conference of 1998, not to talk of the Nuremberg Principles[22] and draft international criminal codes,[23] respectively adopted by the ILC in 1951, 1954, and 1996—the convening representatives of the international community have consistently stated the relevant norm in the terms that there is no immunity for heads of state when charged with an international crime.

EPILOGUE: THE FALLACIES OF THE "DELEGATION THEORY" OF JURISDICTION OF INTERNATIONAL COURTS

Apopular argument of legal scholars who have argued in favor of immunity of heads of state and heads of government before international criminal courts seeking to exercise jurisdiction over officials of states not party to the founding treaty of the court is the argument that international courts are merely surrogates "through" which their founding states exercise jurisdiction. A leading proponent of that argument cast it as follows:

> The immunities are conferred to *prevent foreign states from unduly interfering in the affairs of other states and from exercising judicial jurisdiction over another state* in circumstances where it has not consented. *It makes little difference whether the foreign states seek to exercise this judicial jurisdiction unilaterally or through some collective body that the state concerned has not consented to.* To suggest that immunity is nonexistent before an international tribunal that has not been consented to by the relevant state is to allow subversion of the policy underpinning international law immunities.[1]

Reiterating that argument in relation to the International Criminal Court (ICC), the same scholar wrote as follows: "Indeed since the ICC operates in effect *by 'delegation' from (or in the place of) its states parties*, the immunity of officials of nonparties applies not only in relation to states parties, but also in relation to the ICC itself. Thus, the Court itself is prevented by international law from taking steps that would amount to a violation of those immunities."[2]

For scholars struggling to make sense of all the ins and outs of jurisdiction of an international court, the foregoing explanation has an attractive logic to it, hence the popularity of the "delegation" theory of jurisdiction of international criminal courts.

෨

On close examination, however, the theory is beset with serious shortcomings. As a preliminary matter, we may look past the awkwardness that the nature of things presents to the argument that states party to a treaty-based international court cannot do "through" the international court what none of the founding states can do *alone*. For one thing, natural laws of biology allow no one to procreate *alone*. This is no mere caricature of a serious debate. Procreation may involve two parents, each of whom is limited in the ability to perform certain physical or intellectual activities. Would such a limitation in a parent or both parents necessarily limit the child as well?

Beyond the laws of progeneration, the laws of physics plainly undermine the thinking in question at the elementary level. Indeed, the primary reason for joint action is the impossibility or serious inconvenience of doing certain important things *alone*. Acting alone, no human being can lift a weight of five hundred kilograms: but 192 people can join hands and very easily do so.

Eleanor Roosevelt translated the relevant laws of natural sciences into a norm of international relations, in the following exhortation to her compatriots: "Our own land and our own flag cannot be replaced by any other land or any other flag. But you can join with other nations, under a joint flag, to *accomplish something good for the world that you cannot accomplish alone*."[3]

Quite apart from the foregoing, as a matter of legal reasoning, deeper hazards still snare the argument that international courts must respect head-of-state immunity that has, as a general rule, been accepted in state-to-state relations, lest it be seen that two or more states are exercising jurisdiction over another state "through" a court they created.

A careful reflection will see the misdirection that the argument entails. It is so for the confused crossing of wires between immunity and jurisdiction. An argument that seeks to demonstrate the existence of immunity does not, at the same time, demonstrate the existence of jurisdiction if that immunity were removed. To put it differently, to say that there is no immunity before a court that two or more states have created does not mean that the court in question has—without more—jurisdiction in the first place in a given case. There is a clear non sequitur in the argument that the *immunity* that has been established to guide state-to-state relations must also be respected at an international court or other treaty-based courts, to avoid an outcome in which two or more states would have exercised *jurisdiction* over a different state "through" a court they created.

There is yet a more fundamental difficulty with the suggestion that the several states that create a court would have been doing "through" the court what none of them can do alone. For one thing, the contention supposes the application of a well-known maxim in the law of agency: *qui facit per alium facit per se* (he who does something through another, does it himself).

But is it really the case that an international organization or institution is a mere agent "through" which the members do things in their notional units?

Many serious legal scholars have rejected the suggestion for various reasons. Professor Claus Kreß, for instance, contends that criminal responsibility for international crimes is an obligation owed to the whole world. The resulting ethos of accountability, and the criminal jurisdiction required to ensure that accountability, belong to no particular state to be "delegated" as such. Rather, the jurisdiction belongs to the international community as a whole, as a matter of their right to punish the violation of conducts that threaten the peace and security of the community of nations (an idea that some international lawyers describe as *ius puniendi*). But it so happens that the actions of states are needed to activate that *ius puniendi*, either on the national or the international plane. This would explain why it was acceptable to the international community that Charles Taylor, as the president of Liberia, was indicted to stand trial before the Special Court for Sierra Leone, though Liberia was no party to the agreement between Sierra Leone and the United Nations Secretary General that established the Special Court for Sierra Leone.[4]

In also rejecting the idea that international courts and tribunals exercise their jurisdiction as agents of states, Maurice Mendelson put the point well enough, though evidently addressing a more positive version of the unfortunate view. He did not "regard it as helpful to classify the decisions of *international courts and tribunals* as instances of State practice, even if their competence to act derives from States," he wrote. "In the first place," he continued, "the purpose of international courts and tribunals is to act *independently* of those appointing them. To treat them as State's agents is therefore misleading as well as—in a sense—demeaning. Furthermore, the real significance of the decisions of international courts and tribunals (apart from their role in settling a particular dispute) lies in their precedential value as determinations of the law."[5]

But "demeaning" may well be beside the point. It is one thing to say that the jurisdiction of an international court might be seen in theory as the "pooling" of jurisdictions of all the states that have ratified the court's founding treaty, if that reasoning is made only to counter the theory that the jurisdiction of the court represents the jurisdiction of any state. Such an argument still leaves intact the independence of the international court, which Professor Mendelson is keen to stress.

As a legal proposition, however, it is fatally flawed to say that an international court of law is an agent "through" which states parties to its founding treaty act.

Alert international lawyers should immediately see what is wrong with the argument. It begins with the judgment of the International Court of Justice in the *Reparation* case. There, the court held that the United Nations—an international organization—enjoys legal personality that is independent of its member states, notwithstanding that the UN Charter is silent on that very question.[6] Hence, the UN is not a mere agent of its member states "through" which they act.

While the UN Charter is notably silent on the matter of independent legal personality of the organization, article 4 of the Rome Statute of the International Criminal Court is quite explicit in that regard. "The Court," it says, "shall have international legal personality. It shall also have such legal capacity as may be necessary for the exercise of its functions and the fulfilment of its purposes."

But it may be considered that the understanding of the significance of "legal personality" requires no legal education at all. In some countries, even high school pupils are taught that a business entity with *legal personality* is not to be mistaken as an alter ego "through" which the shareholders do things. It goes without saying that first-year law students take that principle for granted.

Similarly, the fallacy of the agency argument is readily seen in the following example, among many. That no state may use force against the territorial integrity or political independence of another state is a cardinal principle of international law, recognized in article 2(4) of the UN Charter. But, down the line, article 42 of the UN Charter authorizes the Security Council to use force, when necessary, to maintain international peace and security, or to contain a threat to those ideals. When that happens, is it to be understood that member states would have done "through" the UN what they are forbidden to do individually? When the UN required Belgium to withdraw its troops from the Congo in 1960, would that action be seen as Belgium acting "through" the UN to require itself to withdraw from the Congo? Similarly, when the UN commissioned an inquiry into the situation in Darfur and consequently referred that situation to the ICC, was Sudan doing those things to itself "through" the UN?

Finally, the misadventures of the agency argument when lawyers make it in the context of the immunity debate are magnified in relation to courts of law. In other words, the argument ignores the matter of judicial independence. It is an essential attribute of a court of law. Lawyers know that, even if it is not spelled out as explicitly as it is in article 40(1) and 42(1) of the Rome Statute.

ACKNOWLEDGMENTS

The first push for me to get going on this book came from a purely academic source. In November 2021, I delivered a public lecture at Western University in Canada at the invitation of Professor Valerie Oosterveld, one of Canada's leading scholars in international criminal law. The discussion was on the nonavailability of head-of-state immunity before international courts. In light of materials engaged during the discussion, much of which were unfamiliar to the average legal scholar who studies the subject, Valerie urged me to write a book on it, for the benefit of law students, legal scholars, UN diplomats, and national policy decision makers who often grapple with that question. As I mulled the idea, Baroness Helena Kennedy, KC, gave the urge a moral propulsion, and so the book idea took off.

I'm especially grateful to Jake Bonar, my editor at Globe Pequot; his colleague, Nicole Carty Myers (senior production editor); and Nancy Syrett (copyeditor) for processing the manuscript and helping to keep it readable and interesting to the general audience. I also thank my agent, Peter Rubie, for helping to shepherd the process. It goes without saying that I remain entirely responsible for all errors and omissions in the book.

More important, I remain forever grateful to my wife, Shannon, and our three children (Ula, Chile, and Amara) for their understanding and tolerance of the constructive absences that the labors of writing this book occasioned.

NOTES

1. U.S. Department of State, *Report of Robert H. Jackson, United States Representative to the International Conference on Military Trials: London 1945*, International Organization and Conference Series 2, European and British Commonwealth 1 (Washington, DC: U.S. Department of State, 1947), 47.

2. David Lloyd George, *The Truth about the Peace Treaties* (London: Gollancz, 1938), 1:100.

Prologue

1. See, for instance, Ken Bredemeier, "Biden Warns Putin on Russian Troop Buildup Near Ukraine," Voice of America, 13 April 2021, accessed 17 December 2023, https://www.voanews.com/a/europe_biden-warns-putin-russian-troop -buildup-near-ukraine/6204541.html.

2. See "Kremlin Denies Plans to Invade Ukraine, Alleges NATO Threats," *Politico*, 12 November 2021, accessed 17 December 2023, https://www.politico .com/news/2021/11/12/russia-kremlin-ukraine-nato-threats-521031.

3. *Encyclopaedia Britannica*, s.v. "Sevastopol," accessed 17 December 2023, https://www.britannica.com/place/Sevastopol.

4. "Ukraine Crisis: Don't Create Panic, Zelensky Tells West," BBC, 28 January 2022, accessed 17 December 2023, https://www.bbc.com/news/world -europe-60174684.

5. "Ukraine Crisis."

6. See "Russian Forces Launch Full-Scale Invasion of Ukraine," Al Jazeera, 24 February 2022, accessed 17 December 2023, https://www.aljazeera.com/news/ 2022/2/24/putin-orders-military-operations-in-eastern-ukraine-as-un-meets.

7. See Krysztof Janowski, "Civilian Deaths in Ukraine War Top 10,000, UN Says," United Nations Press Release, 21 November 2023, accessed 17 December 2023, https://ukraine.un.org/en/253322-civilian-deaths-ukraine-war

-top-10000-un-says#:~:text=At%20least%2010%2C000%20civilians%2C%20 including,Ukraine%20(HRMMU)%20said%20today.

8. See "Lviv Commemorates 243 Dead Children in Ukraine War with School Buses Memorial," *Guardian*, 2 June 2022, accessed 15 June 2022, https://www .theguardian.com/world/2022/jun/02/lviv-commemorates-243-dead-children -in-ukraine-war-with-school-buses-memorial.

9. See "Ukraine: At Least Two Children Killed in War Every Day, Says UNICEF," *UN News*, 1 June 2022, accessed 15 June 2022, https://news.un.org/ en/story/2022/06/1119432.

10. See Woodrow Wilson, speech given at a dinner of the International Law Association, Paris, 9 May 1919, cited in *Commercial and Financial Chronicle* 108 (28 June 1919): 2598.

11. Paul Mantoux, *The Deliberations of the Council of Four (March 24–June 28, 1919): Notes of the Official Interpreter*, ed. and trans. Arthur S. Link, with the assistance of Manfred F. Boemeke (Princeton, NJ: Princeton University Press, 1992), 193.

12. David Lloyd George, *The Truth about the Peace Treaties* (London: Gollancz, 1938), 1:100.

13. Wilson, speech, Paris, 9 May 1919.

14. Wilson, speech, Paris, 9 May 1919.

15. Wilson, speech, Paris, 9 May 1919.

16. See Leo Strauss, *Natural Right and History* (Chicago: University of Chicago Press, 1953), 7.

17. See Roman A. Kolodkin, "Annex A: Immunity of State Officials from Foreign Criminal Jurisdiction," in "Report of the International Law Commission on the Work of Its Fifty-Eighth Session," by International Law Commission, in *Yearbook of the International Law Commission*, vol. 2, pt. 2 (New York: United Nations, 2006), 191.

18. See International Law Commission, "Report of the International Law Commission on the Work of Its Sixtieth Session," in *Yearbook of the International Law Commission*, vol. 2, pt. 2 (New York: United Nations, 2008), 136, para. 265.

19. The other dissenting judge was the judge from China.

20. See "Declaration of Vice-President Gevorgian," in "Case Concerning Allegations of Genocide under the Convention on the Prevention and Punishment of the Crime of Genocide (*Ukraine v. Russian Federation*) (Provisional Measures)," International Court of Justice, 16 March 2022, accessed 15 June 2022, https://www.icj-cij.org/public/files/case-related/182/182-20220316-ORD-01 -01-EN.pdf.

21. See "Case Concerning Allegations of Genocide under the Convention on the Prevention and Punishment of the Crime of Genocide (*Ukraine v. Russian Federation*) (Provisional Measures)," International Court of Justice, 16 March 2022, accessed 15 June 2022, https://www.icj-cij.org/public/files/case-related/182/182 -20220316-ORD-01-00-EN.pdf.

22. Kolodkin, "Annex A: Immunity of State Officials," vol. 2, pt. 2, 191, para. 1 (emphases added).

23. See Kolodkin, "Annex A: Immunity of State Officials," vol. 2, pt. 2, 193, para. 19 (emphasis added).

24. Sergio Beltrán-García, "Trump's Threat to Destroy Iranian Heritage Would Be a War Crime," *Guardian*, 6 January 2020, accessed 15 June 2022, https://amp.theguardian.com/artanddesign/2020/jan/06/trump-threat-destruction-iran-heritage-war-crime. See also "In Menacing Iran's Cultural Sites, Trump Threatens to Commit 'a War Crime,'" France 24, 6 January 2020, accessed 15 June 2022, https://amp.france24.com/en/20200106-in-menacing-iran-s-cultural-sites-trump-threatens-to-commit-a-war-crime.

25. According to the records, Pavel Šturma was the only "abstention." The following members voted "no": Huikang Huang, Roman A. Kolodkin, Ahmed Laraba, Sean D. Murphy, Georg Nolte, Ernest Petrič, Aniruddha Rajput, and Michael Wood. The following members voted "yes": Carlos J. Argüello Gomez, Yacouba Cissé, Concepción Escobar Hernández, Patrícia Galvão Teles, Juan Manuel Gómez-Robledo, Hussein A. Hassouna, Mahmoud D. Hmoud, Charles Chernor Jalloh, Marja Lehto, Shinya Murase, Hong Thao Nguyen, Nilüfer Oral, Hassan Ouazzani Chahdi, Ki Gab Park, Chris Maina Peter, August Reinisch, Juan José Ruda Santolaria, Gilberto Vergne Saboia, Dire D. Tladi, Eduardo Valencia-Ospina, and Marcelo Vázquez-Bermúdez. See UN General Assembly, *Report of the International Law Commission, Sixty-Ninth Session (1 May–2 June and 3 July–4 August 2017)* (New York: United Nations, 2017), doc. A/72/10, para. 74.

26. See "Symposium on the Present and Future of Foreign Official Immunity," *AJIL Unbound* 112 (2018).

27. See also the observations of Professor Adil Ahmad Haque who observed that another of the contributors to the *AJIL Unbound* symposium had erroneously created the impression that more states were against the draft article than was actually so. See Adil Ahmad Haque, "Immunity for International Crimes: Where Do States Really Stand?," *Just Security*, 17 April 2018, accessed 15 June 2022, www.justsecurity.org/54998/immunity-international-crimes-states-stand/.

28. UN International Law Commission, Sixty-Ninth Session (Second Part), Provisional Summary Record of the 3,378th meeting held at the Palais des Nations, Geneva, 20 July 2017, 10:00 a.m.; doc. A/CN.4/SR.3378 (13 August 2017), 10.

29. UN International Law Commission, Provisional Summary Record, 10 (emphasis added).

30. H. E. Ambassador Dr. Michael Koch, Legal Adviser, German Federal Foreign Office, statement on the occasion of the Seventy-Second Session of the UN General Assembly, Sixth Committee, New York, International Law Week, 2017.

31. Koch, statement, Seventy-Second Session of the UN General Assembly, 1.

32. Koch, statement, Seventy-Second Session of the UN General Assembly, 2.

33. For instance, in uncharacteristic nondiplomatic language, the statement charged that the special rapporteur's "report displays grave methodological flaws" (Koch, statement, Seventy-Second Session of the UN General Assembly, 1).

34. See, generally, Claus Kreß, Peter Frank, and Christoph Barthe, "Functional Immunity of Foreign State Officials before National Courts: A Legal Opinion by Germany's Federal Public Prosecutor," *Journal of International Criminal Justice* 19, no. 3 (2021): 697–716, https://doi.org/10.1093/jicj/mqab042.

35. Kreß, Frank, and Barthe, "Functional Immunity of Foreign State Officials," 706; see the main text preceding footnote 30.

36. Kreß, Frank, and Barthe, "Functional Immunity of Foreign State Officials," 734; see the main text following footnote 187.

Chapter 1

1. "American Society of International Law: Regulation on the Honors Committee," American Society of International Law, accessed 1 April 2024, https://www.asil.org/sites/default/files/ASILHonors.pdf?v=202101.

2. Uliana Pavlova, "Russian Officer Reveals Why He Risked It All to Quit Putin's War," CNN, 23 May 2022, https://www.cnn.com/2022/05/22/europe/ukraine-russian-officer-resigns/index.html.

3. See Oliver Wendell Holmes Jr., "The Soldier's Faith" (address delivered on Memorial Day, 30 May 1885, at a meeting called by the Graduating Class of Harvard University), in *The Essential Holmes*, ed. Richard A. Posner (Chicago: University of Chicago Press, 1992), 93.

4. See *Prosecution v. Kenyatta* (Decision on the Prosecution's motion for reconsideration of the decision excusing Mr. Kenyatta from continuous presence at trial), 26 November 2013, [ICC Trial Chamber], Dissenting Opinion of Judge Eboe-Osuji, Part V, para. 37 and following.

5. International Military Tribunal, Nuremberg, "Nuremberg Judgment," in *Trial of the Major War Criminals before the International Military Tribunal, 14 November 1945 to 1 October 1946* (Nuremberg: International Military Tribunal, 1947), 1:186.

6. See Gordon Brown, "How We Plan to Prosecute Putin at the International Criminal Court," Office of Gordon and Sarah Brown, 14 April 2022, https://gordonandsarahbrown.com/2022/04/gordon-brown-today-we-publish-the-text-of-a-criminal-indictment-against-president-putin.

7. See U.S. Department of State, *Report of Robert H. Jackson, United States Representative to the International Conference on Military Trials: London 1945*, International Organization and Conference Series 2, European and British Commonwealth 1 (Washington, DC: U.S. Department of State, 1947), vii–viii.

8. U.S. Department of State, *Report of Robert H. Jackson*, vii.

9. U.S. Department of State, *Report of Robert H. Jackson*, viii.

10. U.S. Department of State, *Report of Robert H. Jackson*, viii.

11. See Harold Hongju Koh and Todd F. Buchwald, "The Crime of Aggression: The United States Perspective," *American Journal of International Law* 109 (2015): 257–95.

12. The union of views among all five permanent members of the UN Security Council is adequately captured in the official records of the Review Conference held in Kampala, where the Rome Statute's substantive provisions were adopted. See Rome Statute Assembly of States Parties, *Review Conference of the Statute of the International Criminal Court*, Kampala, 31 May–1 June 2010, in *Official Records*, doc. RC/9/11 (2010), 122 (France); 124 (United Kingdom); 125 (China); 126 (Russia); 126 (United States).

13. Rome Statute Assembly of States Parties, *Review Conference of the Statute of the International Criminal Court*, 257.

14. Rome Statute Assembly of States Parties, *Review Conference of the Statute of the International Criminal Court*, 258.

15. Rome Statute Assembly of States Parties, *Review Conference of the Statute of the International Criminal Court*, 260. See also Vijay Padmanabhan, Council on Foreign Relations, "From Rome to Kampala: The U.S. Approach to the 2010 International Criminal Court Review Conference," *Special Report*, no. 55 (2010): 4.

16. Padmanabhan, "From Rome to Kampala," 4.

17. Robert H. Jackson, "The Rule of Law among Nations," *American Society of International Law Proceedings* 39 (1945): 17–18.

18. See Christian Tomuschat, "Uniting for Peace," United Nations Audiovisual Library of International Law, accessed 11 March 2024, https://legal.un.org/avl/pdf/ha/ufp/ufp_e.pdf.

19. See, for instance, Advisory Opinion No. 13 (Competence of the International Labour Organization to regulate, incidentally, the personal work of the employer) (1926) PCIJ (ser B) No. 13 [Permanent Court of International Justice].

20. *Prosecutor v. Al-Bashir* (Jordan Referral re-Al-Bashir), 6 May 2019. See especially Joint Concurring Opinion of Judges Eboe-Osuji, Morrison, Hofmanski, and Bossa.

21. See Dapo Akande, "A Criminal Tribunal for Aggression Tribunal in Ukraine," Chatham House Webinar, 4 March 2022, counter 38:57 et seq., https://www.chathamhouse.org/events/all/research-event/criminal-tribunal-aggression-ukraine.

22. Akande, "A Criminal Tribunal."

23. See Dapo Akande, "ICC Issues Detailed Decision on Bashir's Immunity (. . . At long Last . . .) but Gets the Law Wrong," *EJIL:Talk!*, 15 December 2011, https://www.ejiltalk.org/icc-issues-detailed-decision-on-bashir's-immunity-at-long-last-but-gets-the-law-wrong. See also Dapo Akande, "The Immunity of Heads of States of Nonparties in the Early Years of the ICC," *AJIL Unbound* 112 (2018): 174, https://doi.org/10.1017/aju.2018.56.

24. International Military Tribunal, Nuremberg, *Trial of the Major War Criminals before the International Military Tribunal, Nuremberg, 14 November 1945–1 October*

1946, vol. 2, *Proceedings of 14 November 1945 to 30 November 1945* (Nuremberg: International Military Tribunal, 1947), 99.

25. International Military Tribunal, *Trial of the Major War Criminals*, 2:101.

26. International Military Tribunal, *Trial of the Major War Criminals*, 2:101.

27. International Military Tribunal, *Trial of the Major War Criminals*, 2:102.

28. International Military Tribunal, *Trial of the Major War Criminals*, 2:102.

29. See Emer de Vattel, *The Law of Nations* (1758), ed. and with an introduction by Béla Kapossy and Richard Whatmore (Indianapolis, IN: Liberty Fund, 2008), 104–9, especially 105.

30. Vattel, *The Law of Nations*, 104.

Chapter 2

1. See, for instance, *Prosecutor v. Kayishema and Ruzindana* (Judgment), 1 June 2001 (ICTR Appeals Chamber), para. 367.

2. *Prosecutor v. Kayishema and Ruzindana.*

3. See Hugo Grotius, *De Jure Belli ac Pacis*, trans. Francis W. Kelsey (Oxford: Clarendon, 1925), bk. 2, chap. 22, §iii, para. 2. See also St. Augustine, *De Civitate Dei*, trans. John Healey (London: Eld, 1610), bk. 4, chap. 6. See also St. Augustine, *De Civitate Dei*, bk. 4, chap. 4.

4. Grotius, *De Jure Belli ac Pacis*, footnote 3. See also Grotius, *De Jure Belli ac Pacis*, bk. 2, chap. 1, §i. 3.

5. See "Study: 'False Pretences' Led US to War," CBS, 23 January 2008, https://www.cbsnews.com/news/study-false-pretences-led-us-to-war. See also Charles Lewis and Mark Reading-Smith, "False Pretences," Center for Integrity, 23 January 2003, https://publicintegrity.org/politics/false-pretenses.

6. See, for instance, Ewen MacAskill and Julian Borger, "Iraq War Was Illegal and Breached UN Charter, Says Annan," *Guardian*, 16 September 2004, https://www.theguardian.com/world/2004/sep/16/iraq.iraq. See also Tim Hume, "Chilcot Report Delivers Damning Verdict on British Role in Iraq War," CNN, 6 July 2016, https://www.cnn.com/2016/07/06/europe/uk-iraq-inquiry-chilcot-report/index.html. See also "The Report of the Iraq Inquiry," Iraq Inquiry and Cabinet Office, 6 July 2016, https://www.gov.uk/government/publications/the-report-of-the-iraq-inquiry.

7. See "Ukraine: UN General Assembly Demands Russia Reverse Course on 'Attempted Illegal Annexation,'" *UN News*, 12 October 2022, https://news.un.org/en/story/2022/10/1129492.

8. Thomas Hobbes, *Leviathan*, ed. J. C. A. Gaskin (Oxford: Oxford University Press, 1996), chap. 10, §49.

9. See "Declaration Respecting Maritime Law, Paris, 16 April 1856," International Humanitarian Law Databases, accessed 14 March 2024, https://ihl-databases.icrc.org/assets/treaties/105-IHL-1-EN.pdf.

10. See "Instructions for the Government of Armies of the United States in the Field (Lieber Code) 24 April 1863," International Humanitarian Law Databases, accessed 14 March 2024, https://ihl-databases.icrc.org/en/ihl-treaties/liebercode -1863.

11. See "Convention for the Amelioration of the Condition of the Wounded in Armies in the Field, Geneva, 22 August 1864," International Humanitarian Law Databases, accessed 14 March 2024, https://ihl-databases.icrc.org/en/ihl -treaties/gc-1864.

12. See "Declaration Renouncing the Use, in Time of War, of Explosive Projectiles under 400 Grammes Weight, Saint Petersburg, 29 November / 11 December 1868," International Humanitarian Law Databases, accessed 14 March 2024, https://ihl-databases.icrc.org/en/ihl-treaties/st-petersburg-decl-1868/ declaration?activeTab=default.

13. See "Project of an International Declaration Concerning the Laws and Customs of War, Brussels, 27 August 1874," International Humanitarian Law Databases, accessed 14 March 2024, https://ihl-databases.icrc.org/en/ihl-treaties/ brussels-decl-1874.

14. See "Final Act of the International Peace Conference, The Hague, 29 July 1899," International Humanitarian Law Databases, accessed 14 March 2024, https:// ihl-databases.icrc.org/en/ihl-treaties/hague-finact-1899?activeTab=historical.

15. See James Brown Scott, ed., *The Texts of the Peace Conferences: At The Hague, 1899 and 1907* (1908), foreword by Elihu Root (Whitefish, MT: Kessinger, 2008), iii. See also David D. Caron, "War and International Adjudication: Reflections on the 1899 Peace Conference," *American Journal of International Law* 94 (2000): 4.

16. See "Convention on Pacific Settlement of International Disputes," in Scott, *The Texts of the Peace Conferences*, 21.

17. "Convention with Respect to Laws and Customs of War on Land, and the Annexed Regulations," in Scott, *The Texts of the Peace Conferences*, 45.

18. "Convention for the Adaptation to Maritime Warfare of the Principles of the Geneva Convention of 22 August 1864," in Scott, *The Texts of the Peace Conferences*, 71.

19. "Declaration Concerning Launching of Projectiles and Explosives from Balloons," in Scott, *The Texts of the Peace Conferences*, 79.

20. "Declaration Concerning Asphyxiating Gases," in Scott, *The Texts of the Peace Conferences*, 81.

21. "Declaration Concerning Expanding Bullets," in Scott, *The Texts of the Peace Conferences*, 83.

22. "Convention on Pacific Settlement of International Disputes," in Scott, *The Texts of the Peace Conferences*, 155.

23. "Convention with Respect to Laws and Customs of War on Land, and the Annexed Regulations," in Scott, *The Texts of the Peace Conferences*, 203.

24. "Convention for the Adaptation to Naval Warfare of the Principles of the Geneva Convention of 22 August 1864," in Scott, *The Texts of the Peace Conferences*, 267.

25. "Declaration Concerning Launching of Projectiles and Explosives from Balloons," in Scott, *The Texts of the Peace Conferences*, 332.

26. "Convention Respecting the Limitation of the Employment of Force for the Recovery of Contract Debts," in Scott, *The Texts of the Peace Conferences*, 193.

27. "Convention Relative to the Opening of Hostilities," in Scott, *The Texts of the Peace Conferences*, 198.

28. "Convention Respecting the Rights and Duties of Neutral Powers and Persons in Case of War on Land," in Scott, *The Texts of the Peace Conferences*, 230.

29. "Convention Concerning the Rights and Duties of Neutral Powers in Naval War," in Scott, *The Texts of the Peace Conferences*, 317.

30. "Convention Relative to the Status of Enemy Merchant Ships at the Outbreak of Hostilities," in Scott, *The Texts of the Peace Conferences*, 240.

31. "Convention Relative to the Conversion of Merchant Ships into War Ships," in Scott, *The Texts of the Peace Conferences*, 246.

32. "Convention Relative to the Laying of Automatic Submarine Contact Mines," in Scott, *The Texts of the Peace Conferences*, 252.

33. "Convention Respecting Bombardment by Naval Forces in Times of War," in Scott, *The Texts of the Peace Conferences*, 259.

34. "Convention Relative to Certain Restrictions with Regard to the Exercise of the Right of Capture in Naval War," in Scott, *The Texts of the Peace Conferences*, 281.

35. "Convention Relative to the Creation of an International Prize Court," in Scott, *The Texts of the Peace Conferences*, 288.

36. See *Encyclopaedia Britannica*, s.v. "Battle of Waterloo," accessed 14 March 2024, https://www.britannica.com/event/Battle-of-Waterloo. See also Alan Forrest, *Waterloo* (Oxford: Oxford University Press, 2015), 52.

37. See André Tardieu, *The Truth about the Treaty* (Indianapolis, IN: Bobbs-Merrill, 1921), 431.

38. See David Lloyd George, *The Truth about the Peace Treaties* (London: Gollancz, 1938), 1:86–87.

39. Woodrow Wilson, "Address to the Peace Conference in Paris," in *Papers Relating to Foreign Relations of the United States: The Paris Peace Conference, 1919*, ed. Joseph V. Fuller (Washington, DC: Government Printing Office, 1943), 3:178. See also Woodrow Wilson, "Address to the Peace Conference in Paris, France," 25 January 1919, American Presidency Project, accessed 14 March 2024, https://www.presidency.ucsb.edu/node/317821.

40. "First Interim Report Presented to Sir Frederick E. Smith, KC, His Majesty's Attorney General," Committee of Enquiry into Breaches of the Laws of War, 13 January 1919, 6 (emphasis added).

41. "First Interim Report Presented to Sir Frederick E. Smith, KC, His Majesty's Attorney General."

42. See "First Interim Report Presented to Sir Frederick E. Smith, KC, His Majesty's Attorney General," 7.

43. "First Interim Report Presented to Sir Frederick E. Smith, KC, His Majesty's Attorney General," 6.

44. "First Interim Report Presented to Sir Frederick E. Smith, KC, His Majesty's Attorney General," 7.

45. "First Interim Report Presented to Sir Frederick E. Smith, KC, His Majesty's Attorney General," 7.

46. "First Interim Report Presented to Sir Frederick E. Smith, KC, His Majesty's Attorney General," 7.

47. "First Interim Report Presented to Sir Frederick E. Smith, KC, His Majesty's Attorney General," 7.

48. "First Interim Report Presented to Sir Frederick E. Smith, KC, His Majesty's Attorney General," 98.

49. "First Interim Report Presented to Sir Frederick E. Smith, KC, His Majesty's Attorney General," 97.

50. See Ferdinand Larnaude and Albert Geouffre de La Pradelle, *Examen de la responsabilité pénale de l'Empereur Guillaume II* (Paris: La Paix des Peuples, 1918), 18.

51. Paul Mantoux, *The Deliberations of the Council of Four (March 24–June 28, 1919): Notes of the Official Interpreter,* ed. and trans. Arthur S. Link, with the assistance of Manfred F. Boemeke (Princeton, NJ: Princeton University Press, 1992), 119.

52. James F. Willis, *Prologue to Nuremberg* (Westport, CT: Greenwood, 1982), 73, citing David Lloyd George Papers: Philip Kerr to David Lloyd George, 28 February 1919 (File 89/2/34); Kerr to Lloyd George, 1 March 1919 (File 89/2/36); and Kerr to Lloyd George, 3 March 1919 (File 89/2/38).

53. Commission on the Responsibility of the Authors of the War and on Enforcement of Penalties, "Report Presented to the Preliminary Peace Conference, 29 March 1919," *American Journal of International Law* 14, no. 1–2 (1920): 140.

54. Commission on the Responsibility of the Authors of the War and on Enforcement of Penalties, "Report Presented to the Preliminary Peace Conference, 29 March 1919," 127.

55. See Commission on the Responsibility of the Authors of the War and on Enforcement of Penalties, "Report Presented to the Preliminary Peace Conference, 29 March 1919," 128.

56. See Commission on the Responsibility of the Authors of the War and on Enforcement of Penalties, "Report Presented to the Preliminary Peace Conference, 29 March 1919," 139.

57. See article 227 of the Treaty of Versailles.

58. See "Declaration Respecting Maritime Law, Paris, 16 April 1856," International Humanitarian Law Databases, accessed 14 March 2024, https://ihl-databases.icrc.org/en/ihl-treaties/paris-decl-1856?activeTab=undefined.

59. Wilson, "Address to the Peace Conference in Paris, France."

60. See "United Nations Charter: Preamble," United Nations, accessed 14 March 2024, https://www.un.org/en/about-us/un-charter/preamble.

61. See Godfrey Hodgson, *The Colonel: Life and Wars of Henry Stimson, 1867–1950* (New York: Knopf, 1990), 29.

62. See Hodgson, *The Colonel*, 7.

63. Hodgson, *The Colonel*, 5.

64. *Encyclopaedia Britannica*, s.v. "Henry L. Stimson: United States Statesman," accessed 14 March 2024, https://www.britannica.com/biography/Henry-L-Stimson.

65. See Hodgson, *The Colonel*, 4.

66. Hodgson, *The Colonel*, 5.

67. Hodgson, *The Colonel*, 6.

68. Henry L. Stimson, "The Pact of Paris: The Three Years of Development," *Foreign Affairs* 11, no. 1 (1932): vi.

69. Stimson, "The Pact of Paris," i.

70. Stimson, "The Pact of Paris," ii.

71. Stimson, "The Pact of Paris," ii.

72. Stimson, "The Pact of Paris," ii.

73. Stimson, "The Pact of Paris," ii.

74. See Stimson, "The Pact of Paris."

75. See Stimson, "The Pact of Paris."

76. Stimson, "The Pact of Paris," iii.

77. Stimson, "The Pact of Paris," iii.

78. Stimson, "The Pact of Paris," iii.

79. Stimson, "The Pact of Paris," iii.

80. Stimson, "The Pact of Paris," iii.

81. Briand–Kellogg Pact, article 1 (emphasis added).

82. Briand–Kellogg Pact, article 2 (emphasis added).

83. Stimson, "The Pact of Paris," iv.

84. See Stimson, "The Pact of Paris," vii.

85. See Stimson, "The Pact of Paris," iii–iv.

86. U.S. Department of State, *Report of Robert H. Jackson, United States Representative to the International Conference on Military Trials: London 1945* (Washington, DC: U.S. Department of State, 1947), 3.

87. U.S. Department of State, *Report of Robert H. Jackson*, 6.

88. U.S. Department of State, *Report of Robert H. Jackson*, 22.

89. U.S. Department of State, *Report of Robert H. Jackson*, 24.

90. U.S. Department of State, *Report of Robert H. Jackson*, 31–32.

91. U.S. Department of State, *Report of Robert H. Jackson*, 40, 58, 65, 67, 84, 87, 98, 99, 100, 114, 121, 126, 130, 197, 205, 254, 259–60, 273, 274, 293–309, 312, 317, 327–32, 334–37, 351, 359, 361–64, 373–76, 379–80, 383–90, 392–95.

92. U.S. Department of State, *Report of Robert H. Jackson*, 423.

93. See "Agreement no. 251," in *United Nations Treaty Series* (Geneva: United Nations, 1951), 82:280.

94. U.S. Department of State, *Report of Robert H. Jackson*, 21.

95. U.S. Department of State, *Report of Robert H. Jackson*, 52 (emphasis added).

96. See U.S. Department of State, *Report of Robert H. Jackson*, 52–53.

97. See U.S. Department of State, *Report of Robert H. Jackson*, 53. Indeed, pursuant to a resolution sponsored by Poland, the Eighth Assembly of the League of Nations adopted a resolution on 24 September 1927, in the following terms:

> The Assembly,
> *Recognizing* the solidarity which unites the community of nations;
> *Being inspired* by a firm desire for the maintenance of general peace;
> *Being convinced* that a war of aggression can never serve as a means of settling international disputes and is, in consequence, *an international crime*;
> *Considering* that a solemn renunciation of all wars of aggression would tend to create an atmosphere of general confidence calculated to facilitate the progress of the work undertaken with a view to disarmament;
> Declares:
> (1) That all wars of aggression are, and shall always be, prohibited;
> (2) That every pacific means must be employed to settle disputes, of every description, which may arise between States.
> The Assembly declares that the States Members of the League are under an obligation to conform to these principles. [Emphasis added.]

See UN General Assembly, Seventh Session, "The Question of Defining Aggression," report of the Secretary General, doc. A/2211, 3 October 1952, para. 42.

98. U.S. Department of State, *Report of Robert H. Jackson*, 53. The text of the Havana resolution is as follows:

> Considering:
> That the American nations should always be inspired in solid co-operation for justice and the general good;
> That nothing is so opposed to this co-operation as the use of violence;
> That there is no international controversy, however serious it may be, which can not be peacefully arranged if the parties desire in reality to arrive at a pacific settlement;
> That war of aggression constitutes an international crime against the human species;
> Resolves:
> (1) All aggression is considered illicit and as such is declared prohibited;
> (2) The American States will employ all pacific means to settle conflicts which may arise between them.

See UN General Assembly, "The Question of Defining Aggression," para. 43.

99. International Military Tribunal, Nuremberg, *Trial of the Major War Criminals before the International Military Tribunal, Nuremberg, 14 November 1945–1 October 1946* (Nuremberg: International Military Tribunal, 1947), 1:29.

100. International Military Tribunal, Nuremberg, *Trial of the Major War Criminals before the International Military Tribunal, Nuremberg, 14 November 1945–1 October 1946*, vol. 2, *Proceedings of 14 November 1945 to 30 November 1945* (Nuremberg: International Military Tribunal, 1947), 98.

101. International Military Tribunal, Nuremberg, *Trial of the Major War Criminals*, 2:103.

102. International Military Tribunal, Nuremberg, *Trial of the Major War Criminals*, 2:99.

103. International Military Tribunal, Nuremberg, *Trial of the Major War Criminals*, 2:99.

104. International Military Tribunal, Nuremberg, *Trial of the Major War Criminals*, 2:99.

105. International Military Tribunal, Nuremberg, *Trial of the Major War Criminals*, 2:132–35 and following.

106. International Military Tribunal, Nuremberg, *Trial of the Major War Criminals*, 2:145.

107. International Military Tribunal, Nuremberg, *Trial of the Major War Criminals*, 2:145.

108. International Military Tribunal, Nuremberg, *Trial of the Major War Criminals*, 2:146.

109. International Military Tribunal, Nuremberg, *Trial of the Major War Criminals*, 2:147.

110. International Military Tribunal, Nuremberg, *Trial of the Major War Criminals*, 2:147.

111. See Harry S. Truman, "Address in New York City at the Opening Session of the United Nations General Assembly," 23 October 1946, American Presidency Project, accessed 14 March 2024, https://www.presidency.ucsb.edu/documents/address-new-york-city-the-opening-session-the-united-nations-general-assembly.

112. See UN General Assembly, "Affirmation of the Principles of International Law Recognized in the Charter of the Nürnberg Tribunal," resolution 95(I), 11 December 1946, World Legal Information Institute, accessed 14 March 2024, www.worldlii.org/int/other/UNGA/1946/70.pdf.

113. International Military Tribunal, Nuremberg, *Trial of the Major War Criminals*, 2:155.

114. International Military Tribunal, Nuremberg, *Trial of the Major War Criminals*, 1:42.

115. International Military Tribunal, Nuremberg, *Trial of the Major War Criminals before the International Military Tribunal, Nuremberg, 14 November 1945–1 October 1946* (Nuremberg: International Military Tribunal, 1947), 3:96.

116. International Military Tribunal, Nuremberg, *Trial of the Major War Criminals*, 3:96.

117. International Military Tribunal, Nuremberg, *Trial of the Major War Criminals*, 3:96.

118. International Military Tribunal, Nuremberg, *Trial of the Major War Criminals*, 3:96–99.

119. International Military Tribunal, Nuremberg, *Trial of the Major War Criminals*, 3:99–100.

120. International Military Tribunal, Nuremberg, *Trial of the Major War Criminals*, 3:104.

121. International Military Tribunal, Nuremberg, *Trial of the Major War Criminals*, 3:104.

122. International Military Tribunal, Nuremberg, *Trial of the Major War Criminals*, 3:105.

123. International Military Tribunal, Nuremberg, *Trial of the Major War Criminals*, 1:186.

124. See, for instance, Robert Cryer, Håkan Friman, Darryl Robinson, and Elizabeth Wilmshurst, *An Introduction to International Criminal Law and Procedure* (Cambridge: Cambridge University Press, 2007), 267; Guénaël Mettraux, ed., *Perspectives on the Nuremberg Trial* (Oxford: Oxford University Press, 2008), 141; Kirsten Sellers, *"Crimes against Peace" and International Law* (Cambridge: Cambridge University Press, 2013), 165.

125. International Military Tribunal, Nuremberg, *Trial of the Major War Criminals*, 1:186.

126. International Military Tribunal, Nuremberg, *Trial of the Major War Criminals*, 1:216.

127. International Military Tribunal, Nuremberg, *Trial of the Major War Criminals*, 1:222.

128. International Military Tribunal, Nuremberg, *Trial of the Major War Criminals*, 1:218.

129. International Military Tribunal, Nuremberg, *Trial of the Major War Criminals*, 1:218.

130. International Military Tribunal, Nuremberg, *Trial of the Major War Criminals*, 1:218.

131. See International Military Tribunal, Nuremberg, *Trial of the Major War Criminals*, 1:219–22.

132. International Military Tribunal, Nuremberg, *Trial of the Major War Criminals*, 1:223.

133. International Military Tribunal, Nuremberg, *Trial of the Major War Criminals*, 1:223.

134. International Military Tribunal, Nuremberg, *Trial of the Major War Criminals*, 1:223.

135. See UN General Assembly, "Affirmation of the Principles of International Law."

136. UN General Assembly, "Affirmation of the Principles of International Law."

137. See "Judgment of the International Military Tribunal for the Far East," November 1948, 7–9, Library of Congress, accessed 14 March 2024, https://tile.loc.gov/storage-services/service/ll/llmlp/Judgment-IMTFE-Vol-I-PartA/Judgment-IMTFE-Vol-I-PartA.pdf.

138. Article 5(a) of the Charter of the International Military Tribunal for the Far East provided as follows: "The Tribunal shall have the power to try and punish Far Eastern war criminals who as individuals or as members of organizations are charged with offenses which include Crimes against Peace. The following acts, or any of them, are crimes coming within the jurisdiction of the Tribunal for which there shall be individual responsibility: a. Crimes against Peace: Namely, the planning, preparation, initiation or waging of a declared or undeclared war of aggression, or a war in violation of international law, treaties, agreements or assurances, or participation in a common plan or conspiracy for the accomplishment of any of the foregoing." For its part, article 6(a) of the Charter of the International Military Tribunal (at Nuremberg) provides as follows: "The Tribunal established by the Agreement referred to in Article 1 hereof for the trial and punishment of the major war criminals of the European Axis countries shall have the power to try and punish persons who, acting in the interests of the European Axis countries, whether as individuals or as members of organisations, committed any of the following crimes. The following acts, or any of them, are crimes coming within the jurisdiction of the Tribunal for which there shall be individual responsibility: (a) Crimes against peace: namely, planning, preparation, initiation or waging of a war of aggression, or a war in violation of international treaties, agreements or assurances, or participation in a common plan or conspiracy for the accomplishment of any of the foregoing."

139. See "Judgment of the International Military Tribunal for the Far East," 23–24.

140. "Judgment of the International Military Tribunal for the Far East," 23.

141. "Judgment of the International Military Tribunal for the Far East," 23.

142. "Judgment of the International Military Tribunal for the Far East," 25.

143. "Judgment of the International Military Tribunal for the Far East," 26.

144. "Judgment of the International Military Tribunal for the Far East," 26.

145. See article 6(a) of the Charter of the Nuremberg Tribunal and article 5(a) of the Charter of the Tokyo Tribunal.

146. See article 7 of the Charter of the Nuremberg Tribunal and article 6 of the Charter of the Tokyo Tribunal.

147. See "Judgment of the International Military Tribunal, Nuremberg," in International Military Tribunal, Nuremberg, *Trial of the Major War Criminals*, vol. 1.

148. See "Judgment of the International Military Tribunal for the Far East."

149. See UN General Assembly, "Affirmation of the Principles of International Law Recognized by the Charter of the Nurnberg Tribunal," resolution 95(I) of 11 December 1946, UN Documents, accessed 14 March 2024, http://www.un-documents.net/a1r95.htm. See also the United Nations' Audiovisual Library, "Affirmation of the Principles of International Law Recognized by the Charter of the Nürnberg Tribunal," United Nations Office of Legal Affairs, accessed 14 March 2024, https://legal.un.org/avl/pdf/ha/ga_95-I/ga_95-I_ph_e.pdf.

150. Henry L. Stimson, "The Nuremberg Trial: Landmark in Law," *Foreign Affairs* 25 (1947): 179.

151. Stimson, "The Nuremberg Trial," 179.

152. Stimson, "The Nuremberg Trial," 179.

153. Stimson, "The Nuremberg Trial," 179. Notably, a faction of the U.S. administration led by Henry Morgenthau, the treasury secretary, had insisted that, upon capture and identification, the alleged war criminals "should be shot at once": see Henry L. Stimson, *On Active Service in Peace and War* (New York: Harper, 1947), 584. The British government was initially similarly in favor of an extrajudicial solution, rather than the judicial process: see U.S. Department of State, *Report of Robert H. Jackson*, 6.

154. Stimson, "The Nuremberg Trial," 179.

155. It has been suggested that such pressure had been experienced by the Imperial Cabinet of the United Kingdom, where some of its senior members (including Prime Minister Lloyd George and Attorney General F. E. Smith) had at some point expressed a desire to shoot the kaiser, while Lord Curzon wanted him exiled without trial. But an eventual resolve to prosecute him was able to divert energy away from the desire for extrajudicial solutions. See Alan Sharp, *The Versailles Settlement—Peacemaking in Paris, 1919* (New York: St. Martin's, 1991), 125–26.

156. Stimson, "The Nuremberg Trial," 180.

157. Stimson, "The Nuremberg Trial," 180.

158. Stimson, "The Nuremberg Trial," 181.

159. Stimson, "The Nuremberg Trial," 181.

160. Stimson, "The Nuremberg Trial," 181–82.

161. Stimson, "The Nuremberg Trial," 182.

162. Stimson, "The Nuremberg Trial," 182.

163. Stimson, "The Nuremberg Trial," 182.

164. See Tardieu, *The Truth about the Treaty*, 431; Lloyd George, *The Truth about the Peace Treaties*, 1:86–87.

165. Stimson, "The Nuremberg Trial," 182.

166. Stimson, "The Nuremberg Trial," 182.

167. Stimson, "The Nuremberg Trial," 182.
168. Stimson, "The Nuremberg Trial," 182.
169. Stimson, "The Nuremberg Trial," 182 (emphasis added).
170. Stimson, "The Nuremberg Trial," 182.
171. Stimson, "The Nuremberg Trial," 182–83.
172. Stimson, "The Nuremberg Trial," 183.
173. Stimson, "The Nuremberg Trial," 185.

Chapter 3

1. Carnegie Endowment for International Peace, *Proceedings of the Hague Conferences—Translation of Official Texts* (New York: Oxford University Press, 1920), 224.

2. See Carnegie Endowment for International Peace, *Proceedings of the Hague Conferences*, 9.

3. Carnegie Endowment for International Peace, *Proceedings of the Hague Conferences*, 222.

4. Carnegie Endowment for International Peace, *Proceedings of the Hague Conferences*, 12, 222, 225, 228, 306.

5. See the second *voeux* in the Final Act of the Hague Peace Conference of 1899: "The Conference expresses the wish that the questions of the rights and duties of neutrals may be inserted in the program of *a Conference in the near future*" (emphasis added). See also "Final Act of the International Peace Conference, The Hague, 29 July 1899," International Humanitarian Law Databases, accessed 14 March 2024, https://ihl-databases.icrc.org/en/ihl-treaties/hague-fin act-1899?activeTab=historical.

6. See James Brown Scott, "The Work of the Second Hague Peace Conference," *American Journal of International Law* 2, no. 1 (1908): 1–28.

7. James Brown Scott, "Prefatory Introduction," in Carnegie Endowment for International Peace, *Proceedings of the Hague Conferences*, v–vi: "The Peace Conferences held at The Hague were the first truly international assemblies meeting in time of peace for the purpose of preserving peace, not of concluding a war then in progress. They marked an epoch in the history of international relations. They showed on a large scale that international cooperation is possible, and they created institutions—imperfect it may be, as is the work of human hands—which, when improved in the light of experience, will both by themselves and by the force of their example promote the administration of justice and the betterment of mankind."

8. See "Final Act of the Second Peace Conference" (18 October 1907), International Humanitarian Law Databases, accessed 14 March 2024, https://ihl -databases.icrc.org/en/ihl-treaties/hague-finact-1907/final-act.

9. Margaret MacMillan, *Paris 1919* (New York: Random House, 2001), xxv.

10. MacMillan, *Paris 1919*, 26.

11. MacMillan, *Paris 1919*, 26.

12. MacMillan, *Paris 1919*, 26.

13. MacMillan, *Paris 1919*, 26.

14. MacMillan, *Paris 1919*, xxvii.

15. MacMillan, *Paris 1919*, xxviii.

16. MacMillan, *Paris 1919*, 3.

17. MacMillan, *Paris 1919*, xxviii.

18. MacMillan, *Paris 1919*, xxix.

19. See *Encyclopaedia Britannica*, s.v. "Congress of Vienna," accessed 14 March 2024, https://www.britannica.com/event/Congress-of-Vienna.

20. MacMillan, *Paris 1919*, xxix.

21. David Lloyd George, *The Truth about the Peace Treaties* (London: Gollancz, 1938), 1:565.

22. MacMillan, *Paris 1919*, xxv.

23. See "First Interim Report Presented to Sir Frederick E. Smith, KC, His Majesty's Attorney General," Committee of Enquiry into Breaches of the Laws of War, 13 January 1919, 7.

24. In a brief biography written in an Australian newspaper, when he went to teach as a professor of law at the University of Adelaide, it was reported that Lord Birkenhead had once described him as "one of the greatest living authorities on International Law" (*Jewish Herald*, 10 September 1920, 16).

25. Coleman Phillipson, *International Law and the Great War* (New York: Dutton, 1915), vi.

26. "First Interim Report Presented to Sir Frederick E. Smith, KC, His Majesty's Attorney General," 6–7.

27. See Frederick Edwin Smith Birkenhead, *The Speeches of Lord Birkenhead* (London: Cassell, 1929), 93.

28. See F. P. Copland Simmons, "Free Churches: England and Wales," *Christianity Today* 5, no. 22 (31 July 1961): 8.

29. David Lloyd George, "A Real League of Nations" (from an address delivered in the City Temple, London, to the National Council of Evangelical Free Churches), *New York Times Current History* 8, pt. 2 (April 1918–September 1918): 351.

30. Lloyd George, "A Real League of Nations," 351 (emphases added).

31. See Paul Mantoux, *The Deliberations of the Council of Four (March 24–June 28, 1919): Notes of the Official Interpreter*, ed. and trans. Arthur S. Link, with the assistance of Manfred F. Boemeke (Princeton, NJ: Princeton University Press, 1992), 191.

32. Lloyd George, *The Truth about the Peace Treaties*, 1:140 (emphasis added). "M. CLEMENCEAU said that he thought it would show an immense progress if we could punish the man who was guilty of a great historic crime like the declaration of war in August, 1914. All the Governments represented here to-day were proud of the principle of responsibility. As a rule, it only meant responsibility in

newspaper articles and books, which the great criminals of the world could afford to laugh at. He was not one of those who was sure we could immediately set up a League of Nations. A great step, however, would have been taken towards internal understanding if the peoples of the world could feel that the greatest criminals, such as the ex-Kaiser, would be brought to trial. He therefore supported energetically the proposition of Mr. Lloyd George that the ex-Kaiser and his accomplices should be brought before an international tribunal" (Lloyd George, *The Truth about the Peace Treaties*, 1:139, emphasis added).

33. Lloyd George, *The Truth about the Peace Treaties*, 1:144.

34. Lloyd George, *The Truth about the Peace Treaties*, 1:145.

35. "Reply of the Allied and Associated Powers to the Observations of the German Delegation on the Conditions of Peace" (16 June 1919), 30.

36. "Reply of the Allied and Associated Powers."

37. "Reply of the Allied and Associated Powers."

38. See Margaret MacMillan, "The Lessons from History? The Paris Peace Conference 1919" (O. D. Skelton Memorial Lecture), Global Affairs Canada, 2003, accessed 14 March 2024, https://www.international.gc.ca/gac-amc/pro grams-programmes/od_skelton/margaret_olwen_macmillan_lecture-conference .aspx?lang=eng.

Chapter 4

1. Malcolm M. Shaw, *International Law*, 6th ed. (Cambridge: Cambridge University Press, 2008), 79.

2. David Lloyd George, "A Real League of Nations" (from an address delivered in the City Temple, London, to the National Council of Evangelical Free Churches), *New York Times Current History* 8, pt. 2 (April 1918–September 1918): 351.

3. Lloyd George, "A Real League of Nations," 351.

4. David Lloyd George, *The Truth about the Peace Treaties* (London: Gollancz, 1938), 1:100.

5. See, for instance, Alan Sharp, *The Versailles Settlement—Peacemaking in Paris, 1919* (New York: St. Martin's, 1991), 19.

6. Sharp, *The Versailles Settlement*, 22.

7. Paul Mantoux, *The Deliberations of the Council of Four (March 24–June 28, 1919): Notes of the Official Interpreter*, ed. and trans. Arthur S. Link, with the assistance of Manfred F. Boemeke (Princeton, NJ: Princeton University Press, 1992), 191.

8. Mantoux, *The Deliberations of the Council of Four*, 191.

9. Mantoux, *The Deliberations of the Council of Four*, 191.

10. Mantoux, *The Deliberations of the Council of Four*, 191–92.

11. Mantoux, *The Deliberations of the Council of Four*, 192.

12. Mantoux, *The Deliberations of the Council of Four*, 192.

13. Mantoux, *The Deliberations of the Council of Four*, 193.

14. Jean Martet, *Georges Clemenceau* (London: Longmans, Green, 1930), x, xi, 246, 287.

15. Mantoux, *The Deliberations of the Council of Four*, 193.

16. Mantoux, *The Deliberations of the Council of Four*, 193.

17. See Lloyd George, "A Real League of Nations," 351.

18. See "First Interim Report Presented to Sir Frederick E. Smith, KC, His Majesty's Attorney General," Committee of Enquiry into Breaches of the Laws of War, 13 January 1919, 6–7.

19. Mantoux, *The Deliberations of the Council of Four*, 193.

20. Mantoux, *The Deliberations of the Council of Four*, 193.

21. Mantoux, *The Deliberations of the Council of Four*, 193.

22. Mantoux, *The Deliberations of the Council of Four*, 193.

23. Mantoux, *The Deliberations of the Council of Four*, 193–94.

24. Mantoux, *The Deliberations of the Council of Four*, 194.

25. Mantoux, *The Deliberations of the Council of Four*, 195.

Chapter 5

1. See James F. Willis, *Prologue to Nuremberg* (Westport, CT: Greenwood, 1982), xi. See also Arthur Walworth, *Wilson and His Peacemakers—American Diplomacy at the Paris Peace Conference* (New York: Norton, 1986), 216.

2. See David Lloyd George, *The Truth about the Peace Treaties* (London: Gollancz, 1938), 1:86–87.

3. See *Encyclopaedia Britannica*, s.v. "Friedrich Karl von Savigny," accessed 15 March 2024, https://www.britannica.com/biography/Friedrich-Karl-von-Savigny.

4. Willis, *Prologue to Nuremberg*, 51.

5. Willis, *Prologue to Nuremberg*, 50.

6. Willis, *Prologue to Nuremberg*, 56 (emphasis added).

7. Willis, *Prologue to Nuremberg*, 50.

8. Willis, *Prologue to Nuremberg*, 51.

9. Willis, *Prologue to Nuremberg*, 51.

10. Willis, *Prologue to Nuremberg*, 51.

11. Willis, *Prologue to Nuremberg*, 51.

12. Willis, *Prologue to Nuremberg*, 51–52.

13. Willis, *Prologue to Nuremberg*, 52.

14. Willis, *Prologue to Nuremberg*, 52.

15. Willis, *Prologue to Nuremberg*, 52.

16. Willis, *Prologue to Nuremberg*, 52.

17. Willis, *Prologue to Nuremberg*, 55.

18. Willis, *Prologue to Nuremberg*, 55.

19. Willis, *Prologue to Nuremberg*, 55.

20. Willis, *Prologue to Nuremberg*, 55.

21. Willis, *Prologue to Nuremberg*, 55.

22. Willis, *Prologue to Nuremberg*, 55.

23. Willis, *Prologue to Nuremberg*, 53.

24. Willis, *Prologue to Nuremberg*, 56–57.

25. See Alan Sharp, *The Versailles Settlement—Peacemaking in Paris, 1919* (New York: St. Martin's, 1991), 125–26.

26. See Willis, *Prologue to Nuremberg*, 49.

27. Willis, *Prologue to Nuremberg*, 52–54.

28. See Bruce Weber, "Umaru Dikko, Ex-Nigerian Official Who Was Almost Kidnapped, Dies," *New York Times*, 8 July 2014, https://www.nytimes.com/2014/07/08/world/africa/umaru-dikko-ex-nigerian-official-who-was-almost-kidnapped-dies.html.

29. See William Schabas, *The Trial of the Kaiser* (Oxford: Oxford University Press, 2018), chap. 7.

30. See Robert Hunt, "Luke Lea, the Legionnaires, and the Legacy of Two Wars: The Politics of Memory in the Mind of a Nashville Progressive, 1915–1945," *Journal of Southern History* 83, no. 3 (2017): 619.

31. See Luke Lea and William T. Alderson, "The Attempt to Capture the Kaiser," *Tennessee Historical Quarterly* 20, no. 3 (1961): 224. See also Mary Louise Lea Tidwell, *Luke Lea of Tennessee* (Bowling Green, KY: Bowling Green State University Popular Press, 1993), 105.

32. See Tidwell, *Luke Lea of Tennessee*, 109.

33. Tidwell, *Luke Lea of Tennessee*, 109.

34. See Mitchell Yockleson, "The Bizarre Tale of a Kidnapping Attempt, the German Kaiser and a Beloved Ashtray," *Washington Post*, 14 August 2018, https://www.washingtonpost.com/news/retropolis/wp/2018/08/05/the-bizarre-tale-of-a-kidnapping-attempt-the-german-kaiser-and-a-beloved-ashtray.

35. See William Schabas, *The Trial of the Kaiser* (Oxford: Oxford University Press, 2018), 92.

36. Schabas, *Trial of the Kaiser*, 93.

37. Schabas, *Trial of the Kaiser*, 85.

38. Schabas, *Trial of the Kaiser*, 97.

39. Schabas, *Trial of the Kaiser*, 97 (emphasis added).

40. Schabas, *Trial of the Kaiser*, 81.

41. See Tidwell, *Luke Lea of Tennessee*, 105–6.

42. See Lea and Alderson, "The Attempt to Capture the Kaiser," 233.

43. See "Law Officers of the Crown," Crown Law, accessed 15 March 2024, https://www.crownlaw.govt.nz/about-us/law-officers.

44. Lloyd George, *The Truth about the Peace Treaties*, 1:100–101.

45. The committee members were: Sir John Macdonell, KC (chairman); Professor J. H. Morgan (vice-chairman); Sir E. B. D. Acland, KC; Captain V. Brandon (Royal Navy); Sir John Butcher, KC; Brigadier-General G. K. Cockerill;

Mr. C. P. Gill, KC; Admiral Sir W. Reginald Hall, KC; Mr. A. Pearce Higgins, LLD; Sir Alfred Hopkinson, KC; Mr. C. J. B. Hurst, KC; Mr. T. W. H. Inskip; Mr. H. P. Manisty, KC; the Honorable Mr. Justice Peterson; Sir E. M. Pollock; KC; the Right Honorable Sir F. Pollock; Mr. C. A. Russell, KC; Mr. Walter A. Stewart; Mr. J. F. More; Major V. R. M. Gattie; Colonel E. H. Davidson; Sir Ellis Hume Williams, KC; Mr. Maurice L. Gwyer; Major M. Beachcropt; Sir Archibald H. Bodkin; and Mr. C. R Brigstocke. The committee secretaries were Mr. Hugh H. L. Bellot, DCL, and Mr. J. E. G. de Montmorency, LLB. See "First Interim Report Presented to Sir Frederick E. Smith, KC, His Majesty's Attorney General," Committee of Enquiry into Breaches of the Laws of War, 13 January 1919, 3, 4.

46. See Pearce Higgins, CBE, KC, LLD, *Studies in International Law and Relations* (Cambridge: Cambridge University Press, 1928).

47. Lloyd George, *The Truth about the Peace Treaties*, 1:101.

48. Lloyd George, *The Truth about the Peace Treaties*, 1:112.

49. See F. E. Smith, Second Earl of Birkenhead, *Frederick Edwin, Earl of Birkenhead: The Last Phase* (London: Thornton Butterworth, 1935), 115.

50. Lloyd George, *The Truth about the Peace Treaties*, 1:101–2, 113–14.

51. "First Interim Report Presented to Sir Frederick E. Smith, KC, His Majesty's Attorney General," 6 (emphasis added).

52. "First Interim Report Presented to Sir Frederick E. Smith, KC, His Majesty's Attorney General, 6.

53. "First Interim Report Presented to Sir Frederick E. Smith, KC, His Majesty's Attorney General, 7.

54. See A. J. P. Taylor, *The First World War, an Illustrated History* (London: Hamilton, 1963), 158.

55. See *Encyclopaedia Britannica*, s.v. "World War I: Major Developments," accessed 15 March 2024, https://www.britannica.com/event/World-War-I/Major-developments-in-1916.

56. "The point of essential difference between Municipal Law and International Law has long been a commonplace with those who have written or thought upon such subjects. *In our Municipal Laws punishment waits upon the wrong doer, and the presence of punishment—immediate, inevitable—is one of the primary and essential marks of a civilised community*. All of us have been familiar, all those, who have contributed immeasurable industry and great learning to the gradual evolution of the doctrine of International Law, have been well aware of *the weakness of International Law upon this point*. But they have been content to believe, since the day when the genius and the humanity of Grotius first created the foundations upon which the great doctrines of International Law were to be built, that there would never be such a retrogression into savagery that any great community would challenge these doctrines with the result of *flinging the whole world back from civilisation into a welter of savagery*. Gentlemen, that challenge was made. As I have said, happily and providentially, with how *narrow a margin of success*—few even of those who are

here know completely, only those can know completely who have partaken of the immediate secrets of the Government in the last four and a half years—it has failed and it has definitively failed, and *the question has now arisen, what steps ought to be taken*, not for the purpose of wreaking any spirit of idle vindictiveness, but *for the purpose of re-establishing the authority of International Law*. I hope, gentlemen, and I believe that when we say, as we say to-day, that *we are determined to take any steps that are necessary to reassert, and to reassert under circumstances of the utmost possible notoriety*, the authority of those doctrines, that we say so not in the spirit of men who are greatly concerned to exercise or take pleasure in exercising punitive functions (I do not think that is in the minds of any of us) but *looking as far as we can with cool and passion less eyes into the future of the World, we are determined that our children and our grandchildren, and those even who come after them, shall be spared what this generation has gone through.*" "First Interim Report Presented to Sir Frederick E. Smith, KC, His Majesty's Attorney General," 7 (emphasis added).

57. "First Interim Report Presented to Sir Frederick E. Smith, KC, His Majesty's Attorney General," 7 .

58. "First Interim Report Presented to Sir Frederick E. Smith, KC, His Majesty's Attorney General," 7 (emphasis added).

59. "First Interim Report Presented to Sir Frederick E. Smith, KC, His Majesty's Attorney General," 7.

60. "First Interim Report Presented to Sir Frederick E. Smith, KC, His Majesty's Attorney General," 7 (emphasis added).

61. See Frederick Edwin Smith Birkenhead, *The Speeches of Lord Birkenhead* (London: Cassell, 1929), 109.

62. "First Interim Report Presented to Sir Frederick E. Smith, KC, His Majesty's Attorney General," 8.

63. "First Interim Report Presented to Sir Frederick E. Smith, KC, His Majesty's Attorney General," 12.

64. "First Interim Report Presented to Sir Frederick E. Smith, KC, His Majesty's Attorney General," 14.

65. "First Interim Report Presented to Sir Frederick E. Smith, KC, His Majesty's Attorney General," 14.

66. "First Interim Report Presented to Sir Frederick E. Smith, KC, His Majesty's Attorney General," 19 (emphasis added).

67. "First Interim Report Presented to Sir Frederick E. Smith, KC, His Majesty's Attorney General," 96 (emphases added).

68. "First Interim Report Presented to Sir Frederick E. Smith, KC, His Majesty's Attorney General," 13–15.

69. "First Interim Report Presented to Sir Frederick E. Smith, KC, His Majesty's Attorney General," 15, 27, 99.

70. "First Interim Report Presented to Sir Frederick E. Smith, KC, His Majesty's Attorney General," 15. Now a staple in international humanitarian law instruments, the full text of the Martens Clause appearing in the preamble of the

Hague Regulations appears as follows: "Until a more complete code of the laws of war has been issued, the High Contracting Parties deem it expedient to declare that, in cases not included in the Regulations adopted by them, the inhabitants and the belligerents remain under the protection and the rule of the law of nations, as they result from the usages established among civilized peoples, from the laws of humanity and the dictates of public conscience."

71. "First Interim Report Presented to Sir Frederick E. Smith, KC, His Majesty's Attorney General," 53.

72. "First Interim Report Presented to Sir Frederick E. Smith, KC, His Majesty's Attorney General," 53.

73. "First Interim Report Presented to Sir Frederick E. Smith, KC, His Majesty's Attorney General," 53 (emphasis added).

74. "First Interim Report Presented to Sir Frederick E. Smith, KC, His Majesty's Attorney General," 53.

75. "First Interim Report Presented to Sir Frederick E. Smith, KC, His Majesty's Attorney General," 31 (emphasis added).

76. "First Interim Report Presented to Sir Frederick E. Smith, KC, His Majesty's Attorney General," 31 (emphasis added).

77. "First Interim Report Presented to Sir Frederick E. Smith, KC, His Majesty's Attorney General," 32 (emphasis added).

78. "First Interim Report Presented to Sir Frederick E. Smith, KC, His Majesty's Attorney General," 33.

79. See Herbert Rowen, "'L'état, c'est moi': Louis XIV and the State," *French Historical Studies* 2 (1961): 83–98.

80. "First Interim Report Presented to Sir Frederick E. Smith, KC, His Majesty's Attorney General," 33.

81. "First Interim Report Presented to Sir Frederick E. Smith, KC, His Majesty's Attorney General," 33.

82. "First Interim Report Presented to Sir Frederick E. Smith, KC, His Majesty's Attorney General," 33.

83. "First Interim Report Presented to Sir Frederick E. Smith, KC, His Majesty's Attorney General," 33. However, Macdonell was careful to point out that Richard Zouche had also written as follows: "Et si cum in territorio principis in quem conjurarunt deprehensi sunt, præsenti vindicta uti melius videbitur; juri gentium convenit pro hostibus declarare, unde, non expectato judicio, cuivis eos interficere impune liceat." Google Translate suggests the following translation: "And if when they were discovered in the territory of the prince in whom they had conspired, it will seem better to use the present vengeance; it belongs to the law of the nations to declare it as an enemy." Assuming the general correctness of that translation, the suggestion appears to be that international law, according to Zouche, permits one sovereign to take extrajudicial action against the second sovereign caught in the act of hostility against the first sovereign. That understanding of Google Translate appears correct, because Zouche had, according to

J. L. Brierly's translation of his work, suggested that there is no immunity where a foreign sovereign impliedly submitted to the forum jurisdiction by making a contract, or by committing a wrong within the jurisdiction. Richard Zouche, *An Exposition of Fecial Law and Procedure, or of Law between Nations, and Questions concerning the Same* (1650), trans. J. L. Brierly (Washington, DC: Carnegie Institute of Washington, 1911), 2:65.

84. "First Interim Report Presented to Sir Frederick E. Smith, KC, His Majesty's Attorney General," 33.

85. *Prosecutor v. Al-Bashir* (Jordan Referral re-Al-Bashir), dated 6 May 2019. Joint Concurring Opinion of Judges Eboe-Osuji, Morrison, Hofmanski, and Bossa, para. 46.

86. "First Interim Report Presented to Sir Frederick E. Smith, KC, His Majesty's Attorney General," 33.

87. "First Interim Report Presented to Sir Frederick E. Smith, KC, His Majesty's Attorney General," 33.

88. "First Interim Report Presented to Sir Frederick E. Smith, KC, His Majesty's Attorney General," 33. As Vattel put that qualifier: "Mais ce n'est point une loi de guerre d'épargner en toute recontre la personne du roi ennemi; et on n'y obligé que quand on a la facilité de le faire prisonnier (But it is not one of the laws of war that we should on every occasion spare the person of the hostile king; we are not bound to observe that moderation except where we have a fair opportunity of making him prisoner)." See Emer de Vattel, *The Law of Nations* (1758), ed. and with an introduction by Béla Kapossy and Richard Whatmore (Indianapolis, IN: Liberty Fund, 2008), 566, §159.

89. See Ferdinand Larnaude and Albert Geouffre de La Pradelle, "Inquiry into the Penal Liabilities of Emperor William II" (memorandum), Annex to Minutes of the First Meeting, 3 February 1919, 3:00 p.m., Paris Peace Conference 1919, Commission on the Responsibility of the Authors of the War and on Enforcement of Penalties, U.S. National Archives, File Unit 181.1201/16, microcopy M 820, roll 142, 13. See also *Prosecutor v. Al-Bashir* (Jordan Referral re-Al-Bashir), para. 93.

90. See "First Interim Report Presented to Sir Frederick E. Smith, KC, His Majesty's Attorney General," 34–35 (emphasis added).

91. See "First Interim Report Presented to Sir Frederick E. Smith, KC, His Majesty's Attorney General," 34 (emphasis added).

92. "First Interim Report Presented to Sir Frederick E. Smith, KC, His Majesty's Attorney General," 35.

93. "First Interim Report Presented to Sir Frederick E. Smith, KC, His Majesty's Attorney General," 35.

94. "First Interim Report Presented to Sir Frederick E. Smith, KC, His Majesty's Attorney General," 51.

95. "First Interim Report Presented to Sir Frederick E. Smith, KC, His Majesty's Attorney General," 12.

96. "First Interim Report Presented to Sir Frederick E. Smith, KC, His Majesty's Attorney General," 95.

97. Lloyd George, *The Truth about the Peace Treaties*, 1:131.

98. Lloyd George, *The Truth about the Peace Treaties*, 1:101.

99. Lloyd George, *The Truth about the Peace Treaties*, 1:102.

100. See Lloyd George, *The Truth about the Peace Treaties*, 1:109.

101. Lloyd George, *The Truth about the Peace Treaties*, 1:105.

102. Lloyd George, *The Truth about the Peace Treaties*, 1:107.

103. Lloyd George, *The Truth about the Peace Treaties*, 1:107.

104. Lloyd George, *The Truth about the Peace Treaties*, 1:112–13.

105. Lloyd George, *The Truth about the Peace Treaties*, 1:113.

106. Juvenal, *Satire II*, 63.

107. Lloyd George, *The Truth about the Peace Treaties*, 1:105.

108. Lloyd George, *The Truth about the Peace Treaties*, 1:114.

109. Lloyd George, *The Truth about the Peace Treaties*, 1:114.

110. Lloyd George, *The Truth about the Peace Treaties*, 1:112.

111. Lloyd George, *The Truth about the Peace Treaties*, 1:112.

112. Lloyd George, *The Truth about the Peace Treaties*, 1:139.

113. Lloyd George, *The Truth about the Peace Treaties*, 1:139.

114. Lloyd George, *The Truth about the Peace Treaties*, 1:139.

115. Lloyd George, *The Truth about the Peace Treaties*, 1:139.

116. Lloyd George, *The Truth about the Peace Treaties*, 1:140 (emphasis added).

117. Lloyd George, *The Truth about the Peace Treaties*, 1:140.

118. Lloyd George, *The Truth about the Peace Treaties*, 1:140.

119. Lloyd George, *The Truth about the Peace Treaties*, 1:144.

120. "First Interim Report Presented to Sir Frederick E. Smith, KC, His Majesty's Attorney-General," 29.

121. "First Interim Report Presented to Sir Frederick E. Smith, KC, His Majesty's Attorney-General," 30.

122. "First Interim Report Presented to Sir Frederick E. Smith, KC, His Majesty's Attorney-General," 30.

123. See Ferdinand Larnaude and Albert Geouffre de La Pradelle, *Examen de la responsabilité pénale de l'Empereur Guillaume II* (Paris: La Paix des Peuples, 1918), fn1.

124. Larnaude and La Pradelle, "Inquiry into the Penal Liabilities of Emperor William II," 8, 12, 13.

125. See Larnaude and La Pradelle, "Inquiry into the Penal Liabilities of Emperor William II," 6–9.

126. Larnaude and La Pradelle, *Examen de la responsabilité pénale de l'Empereur Guillaume II*, 11 (emphasis added). "*A tribunal must be found* which by its composition, the position it occupies, and the authority with which it is clothed, is able to deliver the most solemn judgment the world has ever heard." See Larnaude and La Pradelle, "Inquiry into the Penal Liabilities of Emperor William II," 8, 12, 13.

127. "First Interim Report Presented to Sir Frederick E. Smith, KC, His Majesty's Attorney General," 96.

128. Larnaude and La Pradelle, *Examen de la responsabilité pénale de l'Empereur Guillaume II*, 11 (emphasis added).

129. Larnaude and La Pradelle, *Examen de la responsabilité pénale de l'Empereur Guillaume II*, 11.

130. Larnaude and La Pradelle, *Examen de la responsabilité pénale de l'Empereur Guillaume II*, 12.

131. For instance, in the memorandum by Larnaude and La Pradelle, "Inquiry into the Penal Liabilities of Emperor William II," they contended that the individual criminal responsibility of William II must be dealt with as a matter of priority as a necessary consequence of "the new law born of the war" (12–13). They also contended that the merit of their solution was "in harmony with this new principle of free and honourable peoples who are desirous that every right should be accompanied by a duty" (13). They thought it required repeating that "the League of Nations is developing continuously and daily under our very eyes. A new international law is arising and forming under the pressure of circumstances" (14); and they remarked that the "new international law to which circumstances give birth and which leaps fully armed from the universal conscience, awakened so energetically by President Wilson's messages, demands that it should be the Allied and Associated nations who should create this high tribunal" (15).

132. Larnaude and de La Pradelle, *Examen de la responsabilité pénale de l'Empereur Guillaume II*, 17.

133. Larnaude and La Pradelle, *Examen de la responsabilité pénale de l'Empereur Guillaume II*, 17: "La solution que nous adoptons a d'ailleurs le mérite d'être en harmonie avec ce principe nouveau des peuples libres et honnêtes qui veut que tout droit s'accompagne d'un devoir. Le droit moderne ne connaît plus d'autorités irresponsables, même au sommet des hiérarchies. Il fait descendre d'Etat de son piédestal en le soumettant à la règle du juge. Il ne peut dès lors être question de soustraire au juge celui qui est au sommet de la hiérarchie, soit dans l'application du droit interne, soit dans l'application du droit international. Chef d'Etat, l'Empereur allemand avait droit à toutes les prérogatives du droit international: immunité juridictionnelle, honneurs, préséances. Au regard du droit international, il doit avoir aussi la charge des responsabilités internationales. *Ubi emolumentum, ibi onus esse debet.* Qu'on réfléchisse enfin, et ce sera notre conclusion, à l'irrémédiable atteinte que porterait au droit international nouveau l'impunité de l'Empereur allemand." ("The solution which we adopt has moreover the merit of being in harmony with this new principle of free and honourable peoples who are desirous that every right should be accompanied by a duty. Modern law does not know irresponsible authorities, even at the apex of hierarchies. The State must be taken down from its highest pedestal and subjected to the decisions of the judge. Therefore, there can be no debate about exempting from judgment the man who is at the summit of the hierarchy, in the application of either municipal or international

law. As Chief of a State, the German Emperor was entitled to all the privileges national accorded—immunity from suit, honours and precedence. Before international law, he must also assume international responsibilities. *Ubi emolumentum, ibi onus esse debet.* Let us therefore consider—and it will be our conclusion—the irremediable blow which would be struck against the new international law if the German Emperor were granted immunity" [See the "Annex to Minutes of the First Meeting of the Commission," Commission on the Responsibility of the Authors of the War and on the Enforcement of Penalties, Paris Peace Conference doc. no. 181.1201/16, U.S. National Archives Microfilm Publications, microcopy no. 820, roll 142, doc. 0327, 13].)

134. Larnaude and La Pradelle, *Examen de la responsabilité pénale de l'Empereur Guillaume II*, 158.

135. See "Minutes of the Meetings of the Commission," Commission on the Responsibility of the Authors of the War and on the Enforcement of Penalties, Paris Peace Conference doc. no. 181.1201/16, U.S. National Archives Microfilm Publications, microcopy no. 820, roll 142, doc. 0318, 1–2.

136. "Minutes of the Meetings of the Commission," doc. 0318, 2–4.

137. *Encyclopaedia Britannica*, s.v. "James Brown Scott," accessed 15 March 2024, https://www.britannica.com/biography/James-Brown-Scott.

138. See "The Death of William Massey," New Zealand History, accessed 15 March 2024, https://nzhistory.govt.nz/page/death-william-massey. See also Bruce Farland, *Farmer Bill: William Ferguson Massey & the Reform Party* (Wellington, NZ: Farland, 2009).

139. Sydney Edward Mezes, "Preparations for Peace," in *What Really Happened at Paris*, ed. Edward Mandell House and Charles Seymour (London: Hodder & Stoughton, 1921), 1, 2.

140. See John Royde-Smith and Dennis Showalter, "World War I," in *Encyclopaedia Britannica*, accessed 15 March 2024, https://www.britannica.com/event/World-War-I.

141. Royde-Smith and Showalter, "World War I," 3.

142. Royde-Smith and Showalter, "World War I," 10. See also Robert Lansing, *The Peace Negotiations* (Boston, MA: Houghton Mifflin, 1921), 14, 21, 36, 42, 54, 73, 79, 117, 122, 136, 146, 154, 160, 186, 214, 216.

143. Edward M. House, foreword to House and Seymour, *What Really Happened at Paris*, ix.

144. James Brown Scott, "The Trial of the Kaiser," in House and Seymour, *What Really Happened at Paris*, 239–40.

145. Scott, "The Trial of the Kaiser," in House and Seymour, *What Really Happened at Paris*, 239–40.

146. See Lord Hanworth, *Lord Chief Baron Pollock* (London: Murray, 1929), v, vi.

147. Scott, "The Trial of the Kaiser," in House and Seymour, *What Really Happened at Paris*, 240.

148. See U.S. Department of State, *Papers Relating to the Foreign Relations of the United States: The Paris Peace Conference, 1919*, ed. Joseph V. Fuller (Washington, DC: U.S. Government Printing Office, 1946), 6:678.

149. André Tardieu, *The Truth about the Treaty* (Indianapolis, IN: Bobbs-Merrill, 1921), 431.

150. Tardieu, *The Truth about the Treaty*, 431.

151. Lloyd George, *The Truth about the Peace Treaties*, 1:87.

152. Lloyd George, *The Truth about the Peace Treaties*, 1:87.

153. Lloyd George, *The Truth about the Peace Treaties*, 1:86–87.

154. Lloyd George, *The Truth about the Peace Treaties*, 1:87.

155. Lloyd George, *The Truth about the Peace Treaties*, 1:87.

156. See Mezes, "Preparations for Peace," 8. See also Tardieu, *The Truth about the Treaty*, 2.

157. "Proceedings of a Meeting of Sub-commission no. 3 of the Commission on the Responsibilities for the War, etc.," 25 February 1919, 11:00 a.m., U.S. National Archives Microfilm Publications, General Records of the American Commission to Negotiate Peace 1918–1931, microcopy no. 820, roll 144, vol. 118, 2–3.

158. "Proceedings of a Meeting of Sub-commission no. 3 of the Commission on the Responsibilities for the War, etc.," 25 February 1919, 11:00 a.m., 2–3.

159. "First Interim Report Presented to Sir Frederick E. Smith, KC, His Majesty's Attorney-General, 96.

160. "Proceedings of a Meeting of Sub-commission no. 3 of the Commission on the Responsibilities for the War, etc.," 25 February 1919, 11:00 a.m., 2–3.

161. "Proceedings of a Meeting of Sub-commission no. 3 of the Commission on the Responsibilities for the War, etc.," 25 February 1919, 11:00 a.m., 2–3 (emphasis added).

162. "Proceedings of a Meeting of Sub-commission no. 3 of the Commission on the Responsibilities for the War, etc.," 25 February 1919, 11:00 a.m., 4.

163. "Proceedings of a Meeting of Sub-commission no. 3 of the Commission on the Responsibilities for the War, etc.," 25 February 1919, at 11:00 a.m., 4.

164. "Proceedings of a Meeting of Sub-commission no. 3 of the Commission on the Responsibilities for the War, etc.," 25 February 1919, 11:00 a.m., 4.

165. "Proceedings of a Meeting of Sub-commission no. 3 of the Commission on the Responsibilities for the War, etc.," 25 February 1919, 11:00 a.m., 4.

166. "Proceedings of a Meeting of Sub-commission no. 3 of the Commission on the Responsibilities for the War, etc.," 25 February 1919, 11:00 a.m., 5.

167. "Proceedings of a Meeting of Sub-commission no. 3 of the Commission on the Responsibilities for the War, etc.," 25 February 1919, 11:00 a.m., 6.

168. "Proceedings of a Meeting of Sub-commission no. 3 of the Commission on the Responsibilities for the War, etc.," 25 February 1919, 11:00 a.m., 6.

169. "Proceedings of a Meeting of Sub-commission no. 3 of the Commission on the Responsibilities for the War, etc.," 25 February 1919, 11:00 a.m., 11.

170. "Proceedings of a Meeting of Sub-commission no. 3 of the Commission on the Responsibilities for the War, etc.," 25 February 1919, 11:00 a.m., 13–14.

171. "Proceedings of a Meeting of Sub-commission no. 3 of the Commission on the Responsibilities for the War, etc.," 25 February 1919, 11:00 a.m., 14.

172. "Proceedings of a Meeting of Sub-commission no. 3 of the Commission on the Responsibilities for the War, etc.," 25 February 1919, 11:00 a.m., 14.

173. "Proceedings of a Meeting of Sub-commission no. 3 of the Commission on the Responsibilities for the War, etc.," 25 February 1919, 11:00 a.m., 15.

174. "Proceedings of a Meeting of Sub-commission no. 3 of the Commission on the Responsibilities for the War, etc.," 25 February 1919, 11:00 a.m., 15.

175. "Proceedings of a Meeting of Sub-commission no. 3 of the Commission on the Responsibilities for the War, etc.," 25 February 1919, 11:00 a.m., 16.

176. "Proceedings of a Meeting of Sub-commission no. 3 of the Commission on the Responsibilities for the War, etc.," 25 February 1919, 11:00 a.m., 16.

177. "Proceedings of a Meeting of Sub-commission no. 3 of the Commission on the Responsibilities for the War, etc.," 25 February 1919, 11:00 a.m., 17.

178. "Proceedings of a Meeting of Sub-commission no. 3 of the Commission on the Responsibilities for the War, etc.," 25 February 1919, 11:00 a.m., 17.

179. "Proceedings of a Meeting of Sub-commission no. 3 of the Commission on the Responsibilities for the War, etc.," 25 February 1919, 11:00 a.m., 17.

180. "Proceedings of a Meeting of Sub-commission no. 3 of the Commission on the Responsibilities for the War, etc.," 25 February 1919, 11:00 a.m., 17.

181. "Proceedings of a Meeting of Sub-commission no. 3 of the Commission on the Responsibilities for the War, etc.," 25 February 1919, 11:00 a.m., 18.

182. "Proceedings of a Meeting of Sub-commission no. 3 of the Commission on the Responsibilities for the War, etc.," 25 February 1919, 11:00 a.m., 18.

183. "Proceedings of a Meeting of Sub-commission no. 3 of the Commission on the Responsibilities for the War, etc.," 25 February 1919, 11:00 a.m., 18.

184. "Proceedings of a Meeting of Sub-commission no. 3 of the Commission on the Responsibilities for the War, etc.," 25 February 1919, 11:00 a.m., 18.

185. "First Interim Report Presented to Sir Frederick E. Smith, KC, His Majesty's Attorney General," 26.

186. Larnaude and La Pradelle, *Examen de la responsabilité pénale de l'Empereur Guillaume II*, 11.

187. "Proceedings of a Meeting of Sub-commission no. 3 of the Commission on the Responsibilities for the War, etc.," 25 February 1919, 11:00 a.m., 18.

188. "Proceedings of a Meeting of Sub-commission no. 3 of the Commission on Responsibilities for the War, etc.," 25 February 1919, 11:00 a.m., 19.

189. "Proceedings of a Meeting of Sub-commission no. 3 of the Commission on the Responsibilities for the War, etc.," 4 March 1919, 11:00 a.m., U.S. National Archives Microfilm Publications, General Records of the American Commission to Negotiate Peace 1918–1931, microcopy no. 820, roll 144, vol. 118, 1.

190. "Proceedings of a Meeting of Sub-commission no. 3 of the Commission on the Responsibilities for the War, etc.," 4 March 1919, 11:00 a.m., 2.

191. "Proceedings of a Meeting of Sub-commission no. 3 of the Commission on the Responsibilities for the War, etc.," 4 March 1919, 11:00 a.m., 2–3.

192. "Proceedings of a Meeting of Sub-commission no. 3 of the Commission on the Responsibilities for the War, etc.," 4 March 1919, 11:00 a.m., 3.

193. "Proceedings of a Meeting of Sub-commission no. 3 of the Commission on the Responsibilities for the War, etc.," 4 March 1919, 11:00 a.m., 3.

194. "Proceedings of a Meeting of Sub-commission no. 3 of the Commission on the Responsibilities for the War, etc.," 4 March 1919, 11:00 a.m., 4.

195. "Proceedings of a Meeting of Sub-commission no. 3 of the Commission on the Responsibilities for the War, etc.," 4 March 1919, 11:00 a.m., 4.

196. "First Interim Report Presented to Sir Frederick E. Smith, KC, His Majesty's Attorney General," 96.

197. See Larnaude and La Pradelle, *Examen de la responsabilité pénale de l'Empereur Guillaume II*, 11. See also Larnaude and La Pradelle, "Inquiry into the Penal Liabilities of Emperor William II," 8, 12, 13.

198. "Proceedings of a Meeting of Sub-commission no. 3 of the Commission on the Responsibilities for the War, etc.," 4 March 1919, 11:00 a.m., 4.

199. "Proceedings of a Meeting of Sub-commission no. 3 of the Commission on the Responsibilities for the War, etc.," 4 March 1919, 11:00 a.m., 4.

200. "Proceedings of a Meeting of Sub-commission no. 3 of the Commission on the Responsibilities for the War, etc.," 4 March 1919, 11:00 a.m., 4.

201. "Proceedings of a Meeting of Sub-commission no. 3 of the Commission on the Responsibilities for the War, etc.," 4 March 1919, 11:00 a.m., 5.

202. "Proceedings of a Meeting of Sub-commission no. 3 of the Commission on the Responsibilities for the War, etc.," 4 March 1919, 11:00 a.m., 5 et seq.

203. "Proceedings of a Meeting of Sub-commission no. 3 of the Commission on the Responsibilities for the War, etc.," 4 March 1919, 11:00 a.m., 11.

204. "Proceedings of a Meeting of Sub-commission no. 3 of the Commission on the Responsibilities for the War, etc.," 4 March 1919, 11:00 a.m., 12.

205. See *Encyclopaedia Britannica*, s.v. "Nikolaos Sokrates Politis," accessed 15 March 2024, https://www.britannica.com/biography/Nikolaos-Sokrates-Politis. See also Percy Thomas Fenn Jr., review of *La justice international*, by N. Politis, *American Journal of International Law* 19 (1925): 662.

206. "Proceedings of a Meeting of Sub-commission no. 3 of the Commission on the Responsibilities for the War, etc.," 4 March 1919, 11:00 a.m., 12.

207. "Proceedings of a Meeting of Sub-commission no. 3 of the Commission on the Responsibilities for the War, etc.," 4 March 1919, 11:00 a.m., 12.

208. "Proceedings of a Meeting of Sub-commission no. 3 of the Commission on the Responsibilities for the War, etc.," 4 March 1919, 11:00 a.m., 12.

209. "Proceedings of a Meeting of Sub-commission no. 3 of the Commission on the Responsibilities for the War, etc.," 4 March 1919, 11:00 a.m., 13.

210. "Proceedings of a Meeting of Sub-commission no. 3 of the Commission on the Responsibilities for the War, etc.," 4 March 1919, 11:00 a.m., 14.

211. Lansing, *The Peace Negotiations*, 127.

212. "Proceedings of a Meeting of Sub-commission no. 3 of the Commission on the Responsibilities for the War, etc.," 4 March 1919, 11:00 a.m., 3.

213. "Proceedings of a Meeting of Sub-commission no. 3 of the Commission on the Responsibilities for the War, etc.," 4 March 1919, 11:00 a.m., 14.

214. "Proceedings of a Meeting of Sub-commission no. 3 of the Commission on the Responsibilities for the War, etc.," 4 March 1919, 11:00 a.m., 15.

215. "Proceedings of a Meeting of Sub-commission no. 3 of the Commission on the Responsibilities for the War, etc.," 4 March 1919, 11:00 a.m., 15–16.

216. "Proceedings of a Meeting of Sub-commission no. 3 of the Commission on the Responsibilities for the War, etc.," 4 March 1919, 11:00 a.m., 16.

217. "Proceedings of a Meeting of Sub-commission no. 3 of the Commission on the Responsibilities for the War, etc.," 4 March 1919, 11:00 a.m., 16.

218. "Proceedings of a Meeting of Sub-commission no. 3 of the Commission on the Responsibilities for the War, etc.," 4 March 1919, 11:00 a.m., 17.

219. "Proceedings of a Meeting of Sub-commission no. 3 of the Commission on the Responsibilities for the War, etc.," 4 March 1919, 11:00 a.m., 17.

220. "Proceedings of a Meeting of Sub-commission no. 3 of the Commission on the Responsibilities for the War, etc.," 4 March 1919, 11:00 a.m., 18.

221. "Proceedings of a Meeting of Sub-commission no. 3 of the Commission on the Responsibilities for the War, etc.," 4 March 1919, 11:00 a.m., 18.

222. "Proceedings of a Meeting of Sub-commission no. 3 of the Commission on the Responsibilities for the War, etc.," 4 March 1919, 11:00 a.m., 18.

223. "Proceedings of a Meeting of Sub-commission no. 3 of the Commission on the Responsibilities for the War, etc.," 4 March 1919, 11:00 a.m., 18.

224. "Proceedings of a Meeting of Sub-commission no. 3 of the Commission on the Responsibilities for the War, etc.," 4 March 1919, 11:00 a.m., 18.

225. "Proceedings of a Meeting of Sub-commission no. 3 of the Commission on the Responsibilities for the War, etc.," 4 March 1919, 11:00 a.m., 18.

226. "Proceedings of a Meeting of Sub-commission no. 3 of the Commission on the Responsibilities for the War, etc.," 4 March 1919, 11:00 a.m., 18.

227. "Proceedings of a Meeting of Sub-commission no. 3 of the Commission on the Responsibilities for the War, etc.," 4 March 1919, 11:00 a.m., 18.

228. "Proceedings of a Meeting of Sub-commission no. 3 of the Commission on the Responsibilities for the War, etc.," 4 March 1919, 11:00 a.m., 18.

229. "Proceedings of a Meeting of Sub-commission no. 3 of the Commission on the Responsibilities for the War, etc.," 4 March 1919, 11:00 a.m., 19.

230. See U.S. Department of State, "Minutes of the Meetings of the American Commissioners Plenipotentiary," in *Papers Relating to the Foreign Relations of the United States: The Paris Peace Conference, 1919*, ed. Joseph V. Fuller (Washington, DC: U.S. Government Printing Office, 1946), 11:93–94. The text of the

minutes is as follows: "Mr. Lansing explained the great difficulties which he had encountered on his sub-committee to determine the responsibility for the war. At the request of the American Delegation a drafting committee had submitted to this Commission a report proposing that military commissions be established to try cases for violations of the laws of war. At first the British Delegates did not approve of such a scheme but had finally given in at the insistence of the American delegates. The British had desired that a tribunal be established on which all the different nations concerned should be represented, which should try individuals, including the ex-Kaiser of Germany. This proposal Mr. Lansing had been unable to agree to particularly as it had involved the trial of individuals for acts committed before the United States entered the war. He had therefore stated that the United States could not entertain such a project. The British Delegate had evidently been displeased by the American point of view as expressed by Mr. Lansing and therefore withdrew his consent to the establishing of military commissions as suggested by Mr. Lansing. Owing to this impasse Mr. Lansing stated that he would withdraw the American member of the Drafting Committee because the American wishes in this matter seemed to be completely overlooked. Immediately after this statement the French and Italian Delegates as well as the Delegates from Greece and Rumania attempted to smooth matters over and suggested a compromise between the British and the American points of view. This was the first time that a wedge had been driven between the French and British, who had so far stood solidly together on this whole question. It was Mr. Lansing's opinion that the British Delegates were not very sincere in their desire to try the Kaiser etc., but merely felt that they had to urge this measure because of a political pledge. The situation was much the same as it had been on the Reparations Committee where both the French and British were trying to accomplish the impossible, knowing that it was impossible, but wishing to place the blame for the failure upon the United States."

231. U.S. Department of State, "Minutes of the Meetings of the American Commissioners Plenipotentiary," in Fuller, *Papers Relating to the Foreign Relations of the United States: The Paris Peace Conference, 1919*, 11:93–94.

232. The entire surviving membership of Germany's World War II government, including Grand Admiral Dönitz (Hitler's successor as the German head of state), were tried for international crimes.

233. The entire surviving membership of Japan's World War II imperial cabinet were put on trial for international crimes. The emperor was spared prosecution, not for reasons of legal inadmissibility of prosecuting him.

234. Slobodan Mladić was indicted for trial at the International Criminal Tribunal for the former Yugoslavia while he was the president of Serbia, and later prosecuted at the tribunal.

235. "Draft Report of Sub-commission III (Prepared by the Drafting Committee and Submitted to the Sub-Commission, 4 March 1919)," U.S. National Archives Microfilm Publications, General Records of the American Commission

to Negotiate Peace 1918–1931, microcopy no. 820, roll 144, vol. 118, 7 (emphasis added).

236. See "Report of Sub-commission III on the Violation of the Laws of War (as adopted by the Sub-commission, 8 March 1919, etc.)," U.S. National Archives Microfilm Publications, General Records of the American Commission to Negotiate Peace 1918–1931, microcopy no. 820, roll 144, vol. 118, 3 (emphasis added).

237. See "Proceedings of a Meeting of Sub-commission no. 3 of the Commission on the Responsibilities for the War, etc.," 8 March 1919, 11:00 a.m., U.S. National Archives Microfilm Publications, General Records of the American Commission to Negotiate Peace 1918–1931, microcopy no. 820, roll 144, vol. 118, doc. 0140, 2.

238. "Proceedings of a Meeting of Sub-commission no. 3 of the Commission on the Responsibilities for the War, etc.," 8 March 1919, 11:00 a.m., 2.

239. "Proceedings of a Meeting of Sub-commission no. 3 of the Commission on the Responsibilities for the War, etc.," 8 March 1919, 11:00 a.m., 2.

240. "Proceedings of a Meeting of Sub-commission no. 3 of the Commission on the Responsibilities for the War, etc.," 8 March 1919, 11:00 a.m., 2–3.

241. "Proceedings of a Meeting of Sub-commission no. 3 of the Commission on the Responsibilities for the War, etc.," 8 March 1919, 11:00 a.m., 3.

242. "Proceedings of a Meeting of Sub-commission no. 3 of the Commission on the Responsibilities for the War, etc.," 8 March 1919, 11:00 a.m., 3.

243. "Proceedings of a Meeting of Sub-commission no. 3 of the Commission on the Responsibilities for the War, etc.," 8 March 1919, 11:00 a.m., 3–4.

244. "Proceedings of a Meeting of Sub-commission no. 3 of the Commission on the Responsibilities for the War, etc.," 8 March 1919, 11:00 a.m., 4.

245. "Proceedings of a Meeting of Sub-commission no. 3 of the Commission on the Responsibilities for the War, etc.," 8 March 1919, 11:00 a.m., 4.

246. "Proceedings of a Meeting of Sub-commission no. 3 of the Commission on the Responsibilities for the War, etc.," 8 March 1919, 11:00 a.m., 4–5.

247. "Proceedings of a Meeting of Sub-commission no. 3 of the Commission on the Responsibilities for the War, etc.," 8 March 1919, 11:00 a.m., 5.

248. "Proceedings of a Meeting of Sub-commission no. 3 of the Commission on the Responsibilities for the War, etc.," 8 March 1919, 11:00 a.m., 5.

249. "Proceedings of a Meeting of Sub-commission no. 3 of the Commission on the Responsibilities for the War, etc.," 8 March 1919, 11:00 a.m., 6.

250. See Adam Hochschild, "Leopold II," in *Encyclopaedia Britannica*, accessed 16 March 2024, https://www.britannica.com/biography/Leopold-II-king-of-Belgium. For a detailed account of King Leopold's brutality, see Adam Hochschild, *King Leopold's Ghost* (Boston, MA: Houghton Mifflin, 1998).

251. See "Proceedings of a Meeting of Sub-commission no. 3 of the Commission on the Responsibilities for the War, etc.," 8 March 1919, 11:00 a.m., 6–7.

252. "Proceedings of a Meeting of Sub-commission no. 3 of the Commission on the Responsibilities for the War, etc.," 8 March 1919, 11:00 a.m., 7.

253. "Proceedings of a Meeting of Sub-commission no. 3 of the Commission on the Responsibilities for the War, etc.," 8 March 1919, 11:00 a.m., 8.

254. "Proceedings of a Meeting of Sub-commission no. 3 of the Commission on the Responsibilities for the War, etc.," 8 March 1919, 11:00 a.m., 8.

255. "Proceedings of a Meeting of Sub-commission no. 3 of the Commission on the Responsibilities for the War, etc.," 8 March 1919, 11:00 a.m., 8.

256. "Proceedings of a Meeting of Sub-commission no. 3 of the Commission on the Responsibilities for the War, etc.," 8 March 1919, 11:00 a.m., 8.

257. "Proceedings of a Meeting of Sub-commission no. 3 of the Commission on the Responsibilities for the War, etc.," 8 March 1919, 11:00 a.m., 8.

258. "Proceedings of a Meeting of Sub-commission no. 3 of the Commission on the Responsibilities for the War, etc.," 8 March 1919, 11:00 a.m., 9.

259. "Proceedings of a Meeting of Sub-commission no. 3 of the Commission on the Responsibilities for the War, etc.," 8 March 1919, 11:00 a.m., 9.

260. "Proceedings of a Meeting of Sub-commission no. 3 of the Commission on the Responsibilities for the War, etc.," 8 March 1919, 11:00 a.m., 11.

261. See "UK Notes," U.S. National Archives Microfilm Publications, General Records of the American Commission to Negotiate Peace 1918–1931, microcopy no. 820, roll 144, vol. 118, doc. 189.

262. See "Proceedings of a Meeting of Sub-commission no. 3 of the Commission on the Responsibilities for the War, etc.," 8 March 1919, 11:00 a.m., 11.

263. "Proceedings of a Meeting of Sub-commission no. 3 of the Commission on the Responsibilities for the War, etc.," 8 March 1919, 11:00 a.m., 11.

264. "Proceedings of a Meeting of Sub-commission no. 3 of the Commission on the Responsibilities for the War, etc.," 8 March 1919, 11:00 a.m., 11–12.

265. "Minutes of the Meetings of the Commission," Commission on the Responsibility of the Authors of the War and on the Enforcement of Penalties, Paris Peace Conference doc. no. 181.1201/3, U.S. National Archives Microfilm Publications, microcopy no. 820, roll 141, vol. 115, doc. 5.

266. "Minutes of the Meetings of the Commission," doc. 5, 5.

267. "Minutes of the Meetings of the Commission," doc. 5, 8.

268. "Minutes of the Meetings of the Commission," doc. 5, 8.

269. "Minutes of the Meetings of the Commission," doc. 5, 8.

270. "Minutes of the Meetings of the Commission," doc. 5, 8.

271. "Minutes of the Meetings of the Commission," doc. 5, 9.

272. "Minutes of the Meetings of the Commission," doc. 5, 9.

273. "Minutes of the Meetings of the Commission," doc. 5, 9–10.

274. "Minutes of the Meetings of the Commission," doc. 5, 10–14.

275. "Minutes of the Meetings of the Commission," doc. 5, 14–16.

276. "Minutes of the Meetings of the Commission," doc. 5, 16.

277. "Minutes of the Meetings of the Commission," doc. 5, 17.

278. Lloyd George, *The Truth about the Peace Treaties*, 1:139.

279. "Minutes of the Meetings of the Commission," doc. 5, 17.

280. "Minutes of the Meetings of the Commission," doc. 5, 14.

281. "Minutes of the Meetings of the Commission," doc. 5, 14.

282. "Minutes of the Meetings of the Commission," doc. 5, 18.

283. "Minutes of the Meeting of the Commission, 13 March 1919, 10:30 a.m.," Commission on the Responsibility of the Authors of the War and on the Enforcement of Penalties, Paris Peace Conference doc. no. 181.1201/4, U.S. National Archives Microfilm Publications, microcopy no. 820, roll 141, vol. 115, doc. 156, 7.

284. "Minutes of the Meeting of the Commission, 13 March 1919, 10:30 a.m.," 7.

285. "Minutes of the Meeting of the Commission, 13 March 1919, 10:30 a.m.," 7.

286. "Minutes of the Meeting of the Commission, 13 March 1919, 10:30 a.m.," 7.

287. "Minutes of the Meeting of the Commission, 13 March 1919, 10:30 a.m.," 7.

288. "Minutes of the Meeting of the Commission, 13 March 1919, 10:30 a.m.," 7.

289. "Minutes of the Meeting of the Commission, 13 March 1919, 10:30 a.m.," 10.

290. "Minutes of the Meeting of the Commission, 13 March 1919, 10:30 a.m.," 10.

291. "Minutes of the Meeting of the Commission, 13 March 1919, 10:30 a.m.," 12.

292. "Minutes of the Meeting of the Commission, 13 March 1919, 10:30 a.m.," 19–20.

293. "Minutes of the Meeting of the Commission, 14 March 1919, 11:00 a.m.," Commission on the Responsibility of the Authors of the War and on the Enforcement of Penalties, Paris Peace Conference doc. no. 181.1201/5, U.S. National Archives Microfilm Publications, microcopy no. 820, roll 141, vol. 115, doc. 264, 7.

294. "Minutes of the Meeting of the Commission, 14 March 1919, 11:00 a.m.," 7.

295. "Minutes of the Meeting of the Commission, 14 March 1919, 11:00 a.m.," 8.

296. "Minutes of the Meeting of the Commission, 14 March 1919, 11:00 a.m.," 10.

297. "Minutes of the Meeting of the Commission, 14 March 1919, 11:00 a.m.," 11.

298. "Minutes of the Meeting of the Commission, 14 March 1919, 11:00 a.m.," 13.

299. "Minutes of the Meeting of the Commission, 14 March 1919, 11:00 a.m.," 13.

300. "Minutes of the Meeting of the Commission, 14 March 1919, 11:00 a.m.," 14.

301. "Minutes of the Meeting of the Commission, 14 March 1919, 11:00 a.m.," 12.

302. "Minutes of the Meeting of the Commission, 14 March 1919, 11:00 a.m.," 16.

303. "Minutes of the Meeting of the Commission, 17 March 1919, 11:30 a.m.," Commission on the Responsibility of the Authors of the War and on the Enforcement of Penalties, Paris Peace Conference doc. no. 181.1201/7, U.S. National Archives Microfilm Publications, microcopy no. 820, roll 141, vol. 115, doc. 403, 1.

304. "Minutes of the Meeting of the Commission, 17 March 1919, 11:30 a.m.," Commission on the Responsibility of the Authors of the War and on the Enforcement of Penalties, Paris Peace Conference doc. no. 181.1201/7, U.S. National Archives Microfilm Publications, microcopy no. 820, roll 141, vol. 115, doc. 264, 1.

305. "Minutes of the Meeting of the Commission, 17 March 1919, 11:30 a.m.," doc. 403, 2.

306. "Minutes of the Meeting of the Commission, 17 March 1919, 11:30 a.m.," doc. 403, 2.

307. "Minutes of the Meeting of the Commission, 17 March 1919, 11:30 a.m.," doc. 403, 3.

308. "Minutes of the Meeting of the Commission, 17 March 1919, 11:30 a.m.," doc. 403, 3.

309. "Minutes of the Meeting of the Commission, 17 March 1919, 11:30 a.m.," doc. 403, 4.

310. "Minutes of the Meeting of the Commission, 17 March 1919, 11:30 a.m.," doc. 403, 4.

311. "Minutes of the Meeting of the Commission, 17 March 1919, 11:30 a.m.," doc. 403, 11–12.

312. "Minutes of the Meeting of the Commission, 17 March 1919, 11:30 a.m.," doc. 403, 12.

313. "Minutes of the Meeting of the Commission, 17 March 1919, 11:30 a.m.," doc. 403, 14.

314. "Minutes of the Meeting of the Commission, 17 March 1919, 11:30 a.m.," Commission on the Responsibility of the Authors of the War and on the Enforcement of Penalties, Paris Peace Conference doc. no. 181.1201/7, U.S. National Archives Microfilm Publications, microcopy no. 820, roll 141, vol. 115, doc. 435.

315. As of this intervention, the commissioners were sitting under the configuration of the plenary Commission on Responsibilities, no longer as Subcommission III.

316. See "Minutes of the Meeting of the Commission, 17 March 1919, 11:30 a.m.," doc. 403, 16.

317. "Minutes of the Meeting of the Commission, 17 March 1919, 11:30 a.m.," doc. 403, 17.

318. "Minutes of the Meetings of the Commission," Commission on the Responsibility of the Authors of the War and on the Enforcement of Penalties, Paris Peace Conference doc. no. 181.1201/16, U.S. National Archives Microfilm Publications, microcopy no. 820, roll 142, doc. 0318, 115–19. See also Commission on the Responsibility of the Authors of the War and on Enforcement of Penalties, "Report Presented to the Preliminary Peace Conference, 29 March 1919," *American Journal of International Law* 14, no. 1–2 (1920): 98–112.

319. "Minutes of the Meetings of the Commission," doc. 0318, 121–23. See also Commission on the Responsibility of the Authors of the War and on Enforcement of Penalties, "Report Presented to the Preliminary Peace Conference, 29 March 1919," 112–15.

320. "Minutes of the Meetings of the Commission," doc. 0318, 123 (emphasis added). See also Commission on the Responsibility of the Authors of the War and on Enforcement of Penalties, "Report Presented to the Preliminary Peace Conference, 29 March 1919," 116.

321. "Minutes of the Meetings of the Commission," doc. 0318, 123. See also Commission on the Responsibility of the Authors of the War and on Enforcement of Penalties, "Report Presented to the Preliminary Peace Conference, 29 March 1919," 116.

322. "Minutes of the Meetings of the Commission," doc. 0318, 123. See also Commission on the Responsibility of the Authors of the War and on Enforcement of Penalties, "Report Presented to the Preliminary Peace Conference, 29 March 1919," 116.

323. "Minutes of the Meetings of the Commission," doc. 0318, 124. See also Commission on the Responsibility of the Authors of the War and on Enforcement of Penalties, "Report Presented to the Preliminary Peace Conference, 29 March 1919," 117.

324. "Minutes of the Meetings of the Commission," doc. 0318, 124. See also Commission on the Responsibility of the Authors of the War and on Enforcement of Penalties, "Report Presented to the Preliminary Peace Conference, 29 March 1919," 117.

325. "Minutes of the Meetings of the Commission," doc. 0318, 125. See also Commission on the Responsibility of the Authors of the War and on Enforcement of Penalties, "Report Presented to the Preliminary Peace Conference, 29 March 1919," 120.

326. "Minutes of the Meetings of the Commission," doc. 0318, 125–26. See also Commission on the Responsibility of the Authors of the War and on Enforcement of Penalties, "Report Presented to the Preliminary Peace Conference, 29 March 1919," 121.

327. "Minutes of the Meetings of the Commission," doc. 0318, 126 (emphasis added). See also Commission on the Responsibility of the Authors of the War

and on Enforcement of Penalties, "Report Presented to the Preliminary Peace Conference, 29 March 1919," 122.

328. See Commission on the Responsibility of the Authors of the War and on Enforcement of Penalties, "Report Presented to the Preliminary Peace Conference, 29 March 1919," 128.

329. Commission on the Responsibility of the Authors of the War and on Enforcement of Penalties, "Report Presented to the Preliminary Peace Conference, 29 March 1919," 128.

330. Commission on the Responsibility of the Authors of the War and on Enforcement of Penalties, "Report Presented to the Preliminary Peace Conference, 29 March 1919," 133–34, 135, 137, 144.

331. Commission on the Responsibility of the Authors of the War and on Enforcement of Penalties, "Report Presented to the Preliminary Peace Conference, 29 March 1919," 135.

332. Commission on the Responsibility of the Authors of the War and on Enforcement of Penalties, "Report Presented to the Preliminary Peace Conference, 29 March 1919," 136.

333. Commission on the Responsibility of the Authors of the War and on Enforcement of Penalties, "Report Presented to the Preliminary Peace Conference, 29 March 1919," 140–41, 145, 146.

334. Commission on the Responsibility of the Authors of the War and on Enforcement of Penalties, "Report Presented to the Preliminary Peace Conference, 29 March 1919," 141. See also Commission on Responsibilities of the Authors of the War and on Enforcement of Penalties, "Report Presented to the Preliminary Peace Conference, 29 March 1919," 142.

335. Commission on the Responsibility of the Authors of the War and on Enforcement of Penalties, "Report Presented to the Preliminary Peace Conference, 29 March 1919," 142.

336. Commission on the Responsibility of the Authors of the War and on Enforcement of Penalties, "Report Presented to the Preliminary Peace Conference, 29 March 1919," 145.

337. *U.S. v. Hudson* (1812) 7 Cranch 32.

338. Commission on the Responsibility of the Authors of the War and on Enforcement of Penalties, "Report Presented to the Preliminary Peace Conference, 29 March 1919," 146.

339. *U.S. v. Hudson*, 33.

340. *U.S. v. Hudson*, 33.

341. *U.S. v. Hudson*, 34.

342. *U.S. v. Hudson*, 34.

343. See "Minutes of the Meeting of the Commission, 17 March 1919, 11:30 a.m.," doc. 403, 6.

344. See Sheldon Glueck, *The Nuremberg Trial and Aggressive War* (New York: Knopf, 1946), 60–64, citing *Republica v. De Longchamps*, 1 U.S. 111 (1784) (Dall.).

345. *Republica v. De Longchamps*, cited in Glueck, *The Nuremberg Trial and Aggressive War*, 116.

346. See Rome Statute of the International Criminal Court, article 28; Statute of the International Criminal Tribunal for Rwanda, article 6(3); Statute of the International Criminal Tribunal for the former Yugoslavia, article 7(3); Statute of the Special Court for Sierra Leone, article 6(3).

347. Commission on the Responsibility of the Authors of the War and on Enforcement of Penalties, "Report Presented to the Preliminary Peace Conference, 29 March 1919," 143.

348. Commission on the Responsibility of the Authors of the War and on Enforcement of Penalties, "Report Presented to the Preliminary Peace Conference, 29 March 1919," 151–52.

349. See "Report Presented to the Preliminary Peace Conference by the Commission on the Responsibility of the Authors of the War and on the Enforcement of Penalties, 29 March 1919," Paris Peace Conference doc. no. 181.1202/7, U.S. National Archives Microfilm Publications, microcopy no. 820, roll 142, vol. 115, doc. 435.

350. See "Note from Secretary of State Robert Lansing to President Wilson," 4 April 1919, Paris Peace Conference doc. no. 181.1202/7, U.S. National Archives Microfilm Publications, microcopy no. 820, roll 142, vol. 115, doc. 0539.

351. See Paul Mantoux, *The Deliberations of the Council of Four (March 24–June 28, 1919): Notes of the Official Interpreter*, ed. and trans. Arthur S. Link, with the assistance of Manfred F. Boemeke (Princeton, NJ: Princeton University Press, 1992), 110.

352. Mantoux, *The Deliberations of the Council of Four*, 111.

353. Mantoux, *The Deliberations of the Council of Four*, 118.

354. Mantoux, *The Deliberations of the Council of Four*, 119.

355. Mantoux, *The Deliberations of the Council of Four*, 119.

356. Mantoux, *The Deliberations of the Council of Four*, 119.

357. See "First Interim Report Presented to Sir Frederick E. Smith, KC, His Majesty's Attorney General," 97.

358. See Larnaude and La Pradelle, *Examen de la responsabilité pénale de l'Empereur Guillaume II*, 18.

359. "Note from Secretary of State Robert Lansing to President Wilson."

360. See U.S. Department of State, "Minutes of the Meetings of the American Commissioners Plenipotentiary," in Fuller, *Papers Relating to the Foreign Relations of the United States: The Paris Peace Conference, 1919*, 11:94.

Chapter 6

1. Claus Kreß, "Peacemaking Process after the Great War and the Origins of International Criminal Law *Stricto Sensu,*" *German Yearbook of International Law* 62 (2019): 185–86.

2. William Schabas, *The Trial of the Kaiser* (Oxford: Oxford University Press, 2018), 119.

3. See Commission on the Responsibility of the Authors of the War and on Enforcement of Penalties, "Report Presented to the Preliminary Peace Conference, 29 March 1919," *American Journal of International Law* 14, no. 1–2 (1920): 135.

4. See Commission on the Responsibility of the Authors of the War and on Enforcement of Penalties, "Report Presented to the Preliminary Peace Conference, 29 March 1919," 136.

5. The view that the United States dissented to article 227 of the Versailles Treaty is not expressed by Professor Schabas alone. Other commentators have also registered that impression: see Matthew Lipmann, "The Convention on the Prevention and Punishment of the Crime of Genocide: Fifty Years Later," *Arizona Journal of International and Comparative Law* 15 (1998): 418.

6. See Kreß, "Peacemaking Process," 185–86. See Commission on the Responsibility of the Authors of the War and on Enforcement of Penalties, "Report Presented to the Preliminary Peace Conference, 29 March 1919," 135, 142, 144.

7. See Commission on the Responsibility of the Authors of the War and on Enforcement of Penalties, "Report Presented to the Preliminary Peace Conference, 29 March 1919," 143.

8. Kreß, "Peacemaking Process after the Great War," 185–86. See also Commission on the Responsibility of the Authors of the War and on Enforcement of Penalties, "Report Presented to the Preliminary Peace Conference, 29 March 1919," 129, 142.

9. Kreß, "Peacemaking Process after the Great War," 185–86.

10. In the *majority* were the British Empire (Ernest Pollock and William F. Massey), France (André Tardieu and Ferdinand Larnaude), Italy (V. Scialoja and Mariano D'Amelio), Belgium (Edouard Rolin-Jaequemyns), Greece (Nikolaos Politis), Poland (L. Lubienski), Romania (S. Rosental), and Serbia (Slobodan Yovanovitch). And in the *minority* were the United States (Robert Lansing and James Brown Scott) and Japan (Mineichirō Adachi and S. Tachi). See also Commission on the Responsibility of the Authors of the War and on Enforcement of Penalties, "Report Presented to the Preliminary Peace Conference, 29 March 1919," 125–26.

11. See E. J. Dillon, *The Inside Story of the Peace Conference* (New York: Harper, 1920), 493.

12. According to article 21 of the Covenant, "Nothing in this Covenant shall be deemed to affect the validity of international engagements, such as treaties of

arbitration or regional understandings like the Monroe doctrine, for securing the maintenance of peace."

13. Patrick Gallagher, *America's Aims and Asia's Aspirations* (New York: Century, 1920), 331.

14. See, generally, Paul Gordon Lauren, "Human Rights in History: Diplomacy and Racial Equality at the Paris Peace Conference," *Diplomatic History* 2, no. 3 (1978): 257–78, especially 269.

15. Lauren, "Human Rights in History," 263, 266–67, 270.

16. See Dillon, *The Inside Story of the Peace Conference*, 493.

17. Lauren, "Human Rights in History," 264.

18. See Becky Little, "How Woodrow Wilson Tried to Reverse Black American Progress," History, 14 July 2020, https://www.history.com/news/woodrow -wilson-racial-segregation-jim-crow-ku-klux-klan.

19. Little, "How Woodrow Wilson Tried to Reverse Black American Progress," 272.

20. See Margaret MacMillan, *Paris 1919* (New York: Random House, 2001), 320.

21. See Schabas, *Trial of the Kaiser*, 193.

22. Paul Mantoux, *Deliberations of the Council of Four (March 24–June 28, 1919): Notes of the Official Interpreter*, ed. and trans. Arthur S. Link, with the assistance of Manfred F. Boemeke (Princeton, NJ: Princeton University Press, 1992), 120.

23. Mantoux, *Deliberations of the Council of Four*, 119.

24. Mantoux, *Deliberations of the Council of Four*, 120.

25. Mantoux, *Deliberations of the Council of Four*, 120.

26. Mantoux, *Deliberations of the Council of Four*, 119.

27. James F. Willis, *Prologue to Nuremberg* (Westport, CT: Greenwood, 1982), 77.

28. Mantoux, *Deliberations of the Council of Four*, 119.

29. See Robert Lansing, *The Peace Negotiations: A Personal Narrative* (London: Constable, 1921), 6.

30. See Schabas, *Trial of the Kaiser*, 180–81.

31. See Schabas, *Trial of the Kaiser*, 188.

32. Mantoux, *Deliberations of the Council of Four*, 118.

33. Mantoux, *Deliberations of the Council of Four*, 118fn2.

34. Commission on the Responsibility of the Authors of the War and on Enforcement of Penalties, "Report Presented to the Preliminary Peace Conference, 29 March 1919," 120, also 137–38.

35. Commission on the Responsibility of the Authors of the War and on Enforcement of Penalties, "Report Presented to the Preliminary Peace Conference, 29 March 1919," 120, also 137–38.

36. Commission on the Responsibility of the Authors of the War and on Enforcement of Penalties, "Report Presented to the Preliminary Peace Conference, 29 March 1919," 121–24.

37. Commission on the Responsibility of the Authors of the War and on Enforcement of Penalties, "Report Presented to the Preliminary Peace Conference, 29 March 1919," 125–26.

38. Schabas, *Trial of the Kaiser*, 119.

39. Commission on the Responsibility of the Authors of the War and on Enforcement of Penalties, "Report Presented to the Preliminary Peace Conference, 29 March 1919," 116, 117, 121.

40. Commission on the Responsibility of the Authors of the War and on Enforcement of Penalties, "Report Presented to the Preliminary Peace Conference, 29 March 1919," 146.

41. Commission on the Responsibility of the Authors of the War and on Enforcement of Penalties, "Report Presented to the Preliminary Peace Conference, 29 March 1919," 145–46.

42. See Commission on the Responsibility of the Authors of the War and on Enforcement of Penalties, "Report Presented to the Preliminary Peace Conference, 29 March 1919," 140–42, 145, 146. Among many instances during the proceedings of the Commission on Responsibilities, Lansing had pressed his objection to creating an international tribunal against his own observations such as this: "[T]he position of the United States is that there have been direct violations of the laws of war; that those laws have been embodied in the various codes of the nations; that to their violation there is attached a measure of penalty; that so far as such violations are concerned, persons are liable to trial and punishment; that so far as the other class of offences are concerned, which are to me much greater, the moral wrongs that have been committed against the world. I believe that only moral sanctions apply. Beyond that, I do not see how we can go." "Minutes of Meeting of 17 March 1919," Commission on the Responsibility of the Authors of the War and on the Enforcement of Penalties, Paris Peace Conference doc. no. 181.1201/7, U.S. National Archives Microfilm Publications, microcopy 820, roll 141, vol. 115, doc. 403, 5.

43. See article 38(3) of the Statute of the Permanent Court of International Justice (1920).

44. See Schabas, *Trial of the Kaiser*, 186.

45. See Schabas, *Trial of the Kaiser*, 183, 192–93.

46. See Schabas, *Trial of the Kaiser*, 183, 192–93.

47. "Minutes of the Meetings of the Commission," 12 March 1919, Commission on the Responsibility of the Authors of the War and on the Enforcement of Penalties, Paris Peace Conference doc. no. 181.1201/3, U.S. National Archives Microfilm Publications, microcopy no. 820, roll 141, vol. 115, doc. 5, 5–9.

48. See also Commission on the Responsibility of the Authors of the War and on Enforcement of Penalties, "Report Presented to the Preliminary Peace Conference, 29 March 1919," 128.

49. See U.S. Department of State, *Papers Relating to the Foreign Relations of the United States: The Paris Peace Conference, 1919*, ed. Joseph V. Fuller (Washington, DC: U.S. Government Printing Office, 1946), 5:401–2.

50. U.S. Department of State, *Papers Relating to the Foreign Relations of the United States: The Paris Peace Conference, 1919*, 5:389.

51. See Schabas, *Trial of the Kaiser*, 199.

52. See, for instance, Schabas, *Trial of the Kaiser*, 199. See also M. Cherif Bassiouni, "World War I: The War to End All Wars and the Birth of a Handicapped International Criminal Justice System," *Denver Journal of International Law and Policy* 30, no. 3 (2002): 271; Kirsten Sellars, "The First World War, Wilhelm II and Article 227: The Origin of the Idea of 'Aggression' in International Criminal Law," in *Crime of Aggression: A Commentary*, ed. Claus Kreß and Stephan Barrigar (Cambridge: Cambridge University Press, 2017), 35–36.

53. See Schabas, *Trial of the Kaiser*, 194 (emphasis added).

54. See "Convention (IV) Respecting the Laws and Customs of War on Land and Its Annex: Regulations Concerning the Laws and Customs of War on Land, The Hague, 18 October 1907," International Humanitarian Law Databases, accessed 17 March 2024, https://ihl-databases.icrc.org/applic/ihl/ihl.nsf/States .xsp?xp_viewStates=XPages_NORMStatesParties&xp_treatySelected=195.

55. See, generally, C. P. Sanger and H. T. J. Norton, *England's Guarantee to Belgium and Luxembourg* (London: Allen & Unwin, 1915).

56. Germany signed the convention upon its adoption on 18 October 1907 and ratified it on 27 November 1909. See "Convention (V) Respecting the Rights and Duties of Neutral Powers and Persons in Case of War on Land, The Hague, 18 October 1907," International Humanitarian Law Databases, accessed 17 March 2024, https://ihl-databases.icrc.org/applic/ihl/ihl.nsf/States .xsp?xp_viewStates=XPages_NORMStatesParties&xp_treatySelected=200.

57. Lansing, *The Peace Negotiations*, generally, especially pages 3–4.

58. Schabas reports of an occasion when Lansing's wife interceded with Wilson's social secretary Edith Benham, with the observation that Lansing "knows nothing of anything that is going on, that he is left out of everything and the French and British just leave him alone because they know this." Schabas, *Trial of the Kaiser*, 182.

59. Robert Lansing, *The Big Four and Others of the Peace Conference* (New York: Houghton Mifflin, 1922), 44–47.

60. Commission on the Responsibility of the Authors of the War and on Enforcement of Penalties, "Report Presented to the Preliminary Peace Conference, 29 March 1919," 133–34, 137, 144, 145.

61. L. Oppenheim, ed., *Collected Papers of John Westlake on Public International Law* (Cambridge: Cambridge University Press, 1914), 16.

62. In the relevant part, the Declaration provides as follows:

On the proposition of the Imperial Cabinet of Russia, an International Military Commission having assembled at St. Petersburg in order to examine the expediency of forbidding the use of certain projectiles in time of war between civilized nations, and that Commission having by common agreement fixed the technical limits at which the necessities of war ought to yield to *the requirements of humanity*, the Undersigned are authorized by the orders of their Governments to declare as follows:

Considering:

That the progress of civilization should have the effect of alleviating as much as possible the calamities of war;

That the only legitimate object which States should endeavour to accomplish during war is to weaken the military forces of the enemy;

That for this purpose it is sufficient to disable the greatest possible number of men;

That this object would be exceeded by the employment of arms which uselessly aggravate the sufferings of disabled men, or render their death inevitable;

That the employment of such arms would, therefore, be *contrary to the laws of humanity* (emphasis added).

63. See, generally, Lansing's memoirs of both the peace conference and his relationship with President Wilson, respectively, in Lansing, *The Peace Negotiations*, and Lansing, *The Big Four*, especially 16–17, 19–20, 21–22, 24, 40–41, 44–45. Marcus Payk conveys that impression charitably as follows: "The U.S. secretary of state, delegate to the Paris Peace Conference of 1919 and *one of its most notorious critics*, found the formal arrangements of the finished Treaty of Versailles much better than expected. *Lansing had been critical of the disorganization of the proceedings in general, and of the high-minded attitude of US President Woodrow Wilson in particular, and had therefore been left out of much of the decision-making process.* But the systematic composition and rationality of the treaty structure nonetheless met with his approval as a professional lawyer." Marcus M. Payk, "The Draughtsmen: International Lawyers and the Crafting of the Paris Peace Treaties, 1919–1920," in *Crafting the International Order: Practitioners and Practices of International Law since c. 1800*, ed. Marcus M. Payk and Kim Christian Priemel (Oxford: Oxford University Press, 2021), 142 (emphasis added).

64. The wife of President Wilson, Mrs. Edith Wilson, who accompanied her husband and the American entourage to Paris, recalled the painstaking and constant drills they were put through during their voyage, just on account of that danger. See Edith Bolling Wilson, *My Memoir* (Indianapolis, IN: Bobbs-Merrill, 1939), 174.

65. Lansing, *The Peace Negotiations*, 21. See also Lansing, *The Big Four*, 38–39.

66. Lansing, *The Peace Negotiations*, 21 (emphasis added).

67. Lansing, *The Big Four*, 39.

68. As Lansing put it, "it would have been futile to have attempted to dissuade him [Wilson] from this purpose." Lansing, *The Peace Negotiations*, 23.

69. Lansing, *The Big Four*, 3–4: "It is manifestly difficult to treat the subject impersonally and to avoid the petty influences which ought not to, but so often do, warp individual opinion and a just appraisement of public men. Yet it cannot be denied that traits of character are as frequently shown by trivial incidents

as by those of greater moment, though it is on latter that popular reputations are founded."

70. Lansing, *The Peace Negotiations*, 22–23 (emphasis added).

71. Lansing, *The Peace Negotiations*, 23–24.

72. Lansing, *The Peace Negotiations*, 5.

73. Lansing, *The Peace Negotiations*, 5–6.

74. Lansing, *The Peace Negotiations*, 3.

75. Lansing, *The Peace Negotiations*, 3.

76. See President Woodrow Wilson, speech at a dinner of the International Law Association, Paris, 9 May 1919, cited in *Commercial & Financial Chronicle* 108 (28 June 1919): 2598.

77. Lansing, *The Peace Negotiations*, 107. See also Lansing, *The Big Four*, 41.

78. Lansing, *The Peace Negotiations*, 107.

79. Robert Tucker, *Woodrow Wilson and the Great War: Reconsidering America's Neutrality 1914–1917* (Charlottesville: University of Virginia Press, 2007), 193.

80. Tucker, *Woodrow Wilson and the Great War*, 193.

81. Tucker, *Woodrow Wilson and the Great War*, 193. See also MacMillan, *Paris 1919*, 5.

82. David Lloyd George, *The Truth about the Peace Treaties* (London: Gollancz, 1938), 1:243. "Lansing Wilson had always treated more as a negligible clerk than as a responsible Foreign Secretary" (David Lloyd George, *The Truth about the Peace Treaties* [London: Gollancz, 1938], 2:1266).

83. Lansing, *The Big Four*, 42.

84. Schabas, *Trial of the Kaiser*, 184.

85. As Lloyd George subtly hinted, "I would go so far as to say that it would not be worth the trouble to make peace if one believed that all these crimes would go unpunished." Mantoux, *Deliberations of the Council of Four*, 122.

86. Lloyd George, *The Truth about the Peace Treaties*, 1:88, 1:92. Clemenceau quoted in André Tardieu, *The Truth about the Treaty* (Indianapolis, IN: Bobbs-Merrill, 1921), 353.

Chapter 7

1. See "Nigeria to Give Up Charles Taylor to Face Charges," *Irish Times*, 25 March 2006, https://www.irishtimes.com/news/nigeria-to-give-up-charles -taylor-to-face-charges-1.776822. See also *Prosecutor v. Taylor* (Judgment), 18 May 2012, 2484 [Trial Chamber, SCSL].

2. See James F. Willis, *Prologue to Nuremberg* (Westport, CT: Greenwood, 1982), chap. 6, 7. See also William Schabas, *The Trial of the Kaiser* (Oxford: Oxford University Press, 2018), chap. 17.

3. See Sally Marks, "'My Name Is Ozymandias': The Kaiser in Exile," *Central European History* 16, no. 2 (1983): 122–70. See also Willis, *Prologue to Nuremberg*, 66; Schabas, *Trial of the Kaiser*, chap. 3.

4. U.S. Department of State, *Papers Relating to the Foreign Relations of the United States: The Paris Peace Conference, 1919*, ed. Joseph V. Fuller (Washington, DC: U.S. Government Printing Office, 1946), 2:76.

5. See Schabas, *Trial of the Kaiser*, 88. The Dutch government had posted Carlos Bentinck to Amerongen to help his father manage affairs concerning the kaiser. Carlos was the son of Count Godard Bentinck, the owner of the castle where the kaiser was residing at the time in Amerongen, before the kaiser bought his own estate in Doorn.

6. U.S. Department of State, *Papers Relating to the Foreign Relations of the United States: The Paris Peace Conference, 1919*, 2:77.

7. U.S. Department of State, *Papers Relating to the Foreign Relations of the United States: The Paris Peace Conference, 1919*, 2:79.

8. See Schabas, *Trial of the Kaiser*, 267.

9. See David Lloyd George, *The Truth about the Peace Treaties* (London: Gollancz, 1938), 1:141.

10. U.S. Department of State, *Papers Relating to the Foreign Relations of the United States: The Paris Peace Conference, 1919*, 2:653–54.

11. U.S. Department of State, *Papers Relating to the Foreign Relations of the United States: The Paris Peace Conference, 1919*, 2:653–54, doc. no. 67.

12. See Willis, *Prologue to Nuremberg*, chap. 6, 7.

13. See Schabas, *Trial of the Kaiser*, 81.

14. U.S. Department of State, *Papers Relating to the Foreign Relations of the United States: The Paris Peace Conference, 1919*, ed. Joseph V. Fuller (Washington, DC: U.S. Government Printing Office, 1946), 6:670.

15. U.S. Department of State, *Papers Relating to the Foreign Relations of the United States: The Paris Peace Conference, 1919*, 6:671.

16. U.S. Department of State, *Papers Relating to the Foreign Relations of the United States: The Paris Peace Conference, 1919*, 6:678.

17. U.S. Department of State, *Papers Relating to the Foreign Relations of the United States: The Paris Peace Conference, 1919*, 6:699–700.

18. U.S. Department of State, *Papers Relating to the Foreign Relations of the United States: The Paris Peace Conference, 1919*, 6:710.

19. U.S. Department of State, *Papers Relating to the Foreign Relations of the United States: The Paris Peace Conference, 1919*, 6:721.

20. U.S. Department of State, *Papers Relating to the Foreign Relations of the United States: The Paris Peace Conference, 1919*, 6:740–41.

21. U.S. Department of State, *Papers Relating to the Foreign Relations of the United States: The Paris Peace Conference, 1919*, 6:751.

22. U.S. Department of State, *Papers Relating to the Foreign Relations of the United States: The Paris Peace Conference, 1919*, 6:757.

23. U.S. Department of State, *Papers Relating to the Foreign Relations of the United States: The Paris Peace Conference, 1919*, 6:757.

24. U.S. Department of State, *Papers Relating to the Foreign Relations of the United States: The Paris Peace Conference, 1919*, 6:752.

25. U.S. Department of State, *Papers Relating to the Foreign Relations of the United States: The Paris Peace Conference, 1919*, 6:752.

26. U.S. Department of State, *Papers Relating to the Foreign Relations of the United States: The Paris Peace Conference, 1919*, 2:654–55.

27. U.S. Department of State, *Papers Relating to the Foreign Relations of the United States: The Paris Peace Conference, 1919*, 2:655–56.

28. U.S. Department of State, *Papers Relating to the Foreign Relations of the United States: The Paris Peace Conference, 1919*, 2:656.

29. U.S. Department of State, *Papers Relating to the Foreign Relations of the United States: The Paris Peace Conference, 1919*, 2:656.

30. U.S. Department of State, *Papers Relating to the Foreign Relations of the United States: The Paris Peace Conference, 1919*, 2:657.

31. U.S. Department of State, *Papers Relating to the Foreign Relations of the United States: The Paris Peace Conference, 1919*, 2:657.

32. Telegram from the Secretary of State [Lansing] to the Chargé in the Netherlands [Gunther], 13 December 1919, 2 p.m., in U.S. Department of State, *Papers Relating to the Foreign Relations of the United States: The Paris Peace Conference, 1919*, 2:657.

33. Telegram from the Secretary of State [Lansing] to the Chargé in the Netherlands [Gunther], 13 December 1919, 2 p.m., in U.S. Department of State, *Papers Relating to the Foreign Relations of the United States: The Paris Peace Conference, 1919*, 2:657.

34. Telegram from the Secretary of State [Lansing] to the Chargé in the Netherlands [Gunther], 13 December 1919, 2 p.m., in U.S. Department of State, *Papers Relating to the Foreign Relations of the United States: The Paris Peace Conference, 1919*, 2:657.

35. Telegram from the Secretary of State [Lansing] to the Chargé in the Netherlands [Gunther], 13 December 1919, 2 p.m., in U.S. Department of State, *Papers Relating to the Foreign Relations of the United States: The Paris Peace Conference, 1919*, 2:657.

36. Telegram from the Secretary of State [Lansing] to the Chargé in the Netherlands [Gunther], 13 December 1919, 2 p.m., U.S. Department of State, *Papers Relating to the Foreign Relations of the United States: The Paris Peace Conference, 1919*, 2:657 (emphasis added).

37. See Daniel M. Smith, "Robert Lansing and the Wilson Interregnum, 1919–1920," *Historian* 21 (1959): 135–61.

38. Smith, "Robert Lansing and the Wilson Interregnum," 144.

39. See Smith, "Robert Lansing and the Wilson Interregnum," generally. See also Dimitri D. Lazo, "A Question of Loyalty: Robert Lansing and the Treaty of Versailles," *Diplomatic History* 9, no. 1 (1985): 35–53, generally. See also Robert Lansing, *The Peace Negotiations: A Personal Narrative* (London: Constable, 1921).

40. See Stockton Axson, *Brother Woodrow: A Memoir of Woodrow Wilson by Stockton Axson*, ed. Stockton Axson and Arthur S. Link (Princeton, NJ: Princeton University Press, 1993), 211–12.

41. See Edith Bolling Wilson, *My Memoir* (Indianapolis, IN: Bobbs-Merrill, 1939), 233–34, 236–37.

42. Bolling Wilson, *My Memoir*, 300.

43. Bolling Wilson, *My Memoir*, 298.

44. Bolling Wilson, *My Memoir*, 300.

45. Bolling Wilson, *My Memoir*, 300.

46. Bolling Wilson, *My Memoir*, 301.

47. See Willis, *Prologue to Nuremberg*, 91. See also Willis, *Prologue to Nuremberg*, 104–5.

48. U.S. Department of State, *Papers Relating to the Foreign Relations of the United States: The Paris Peace Conference, 1919*, ed. Joseph V. Fuller (Washington, DC: U.S. Government Printing Office, 1946), 9:886–87.

49. U.S. Department of State, *Papers Relating to the Foreign Relations of the United States: The Paris Peace Conference, 1919*, 9:888–889 (emphases added).

50. See The Hague (website), https://www.denhaag.nl/en/municipality-of -the-hague/international-the-hague/history-of-the-city-of-peace-and-justice .htm.

51. See "Advisory Opinion on the Extraterritorial Application of *Non-Refoulement* Obligations under the 1951 Convention Relating to the Status of Refugees and Its 1967 Protocol," United Nations High Commissioner for Refugees, accessed 18 March 2024, https://www.unhcr.org/4d9486929.pdf.

52. See Convention Relating to the Status of Refugees (1951), article 33:

1. No Contracting State shall expel or return ("*refouler*") a refugee in any manner whatsoever to the frontiers of territories where his life or freedom would be threatened on account of his race, religion, nationality, member-ship of a particular social group or political opinion.

2. The benefit of the present provision may not, however, be claimed by a refugee whom there are reasonable grounds for regarding as a danger to the security of the country in which he is, or who, having been convicted by a final judgment of a particularly serious crime, constitutes a danger to the community of that country.

53. See the Asylum Case (Colombia/Peru) (1950) ICJ Reports 266, 276.

54. Willis, *Prologue to Nuremberg*, 68.

55. Tom Geoghegan, "What Happens to Deposed Leaders?," *BBC News Magazine*, 14 April 2011, https://www.bbc.com/news/magazine-13052996.

56. See F. E. Adcock, "The Exiles of Peisistratus," *Classical Quarterly* 18, no. 3 (1924): 174–81.

57. See Mrs. [Margaret] Oliphant, *The Makers of Venice: Doges, Conquerors, Painters and Men of Letters* (London: Macmillan, 1887), 20–23.

58. See John V. A. Fine Jr., *The Late Mediaeval Balkans* (Ann Arbor: University of Michigan Press, 1987), 226.

59. See *Encyclopaedia Britannica*, s.v. "Muḥammad XII," accessed 18 March 2024, https://www.britannica.com/biography/Muhammad-XII.

60. See *Encyclopaedia Britannica*, s.v. "Piero di Cosimo de' Medici," accessed 18 March 2024, https://www.britannica.com/biography/Piero-di-Cosimo-de-Medici.

61. See *Encyclopaedia Britannica*, s.v. "António, prior of Crato," accessed 18 March 2024, https://www.britannica.com/biography/Antonio-prior-of-Crato.

62. See Henry Godfrey Roseveare, "Charles II," in *Encyclopedia Britannica*, accessed 18 March 2024, https://www.britannica.com/biography/Charles-II-king-of-Great-Britain-and-Ireland.

63. John Kenyon, "James II," in *Encyclopedia Britannica*, accessed 18 March 2024, https://www.britannica.com/biography/James-II-king-of-England-Scotland-and-Ireland.

64. See *Encyclopaedia Britannica*, s.v. "Agustín de Iturbide," accessed 18 March 2024, https://www.britannica.com/biography/Agustin-de-Iturbide.

65. See *Encyclopaedia Britannica*, s.v. "Charles X," accessed 18 March 2024, https://www.britannica.com/biography/Charles-X.

66. See *Encyclopaedia Britannica*, s.v. "Antonio López de Santa Anna," accessed 18 March 2024, https://www.britannica.com/biography/Antonio-Lopez-de-Santa-Anna.

67. See *Encyclopaedia Britannica*, s.v. "Constantine I," accessed 18 March 2024, https://www.britannica.com/biography/Constantine-I-king-of-Greece.

68. See *Encyclopaedia Britannica*, s.v. "Ferdinand," accessed 18 March 2024, https://www.britannica.com/biography/Ferdinand-king-of-Bulgaria.

69. See *Encyclopaedia Britannica*, s.v. "Odumegwu Ojukwu," accessed 18 March 2024, https://www.britannica.com/biography/Odumegwu-Ojukwu.

70. See *Encyclopaedia Britannica*, s.v. "Idi Amin," accessed 18 March 2024, https://www.britannica.com/biography/Idi-Amin.

71. See *Encyclopaedia Britannica*, s.v. "Mohammad Reza Shah Pahlavi," accessed 18 March 2024, https://www.britannica.com/biography/Mohammad-Reza-Shah-Pahlavi.

72. See Tim Cocks and Lamin Jahateh, "Gambia's Former Leader Jammeh Flies into Exile in Equatorial Guinea," Reuters, 20 January 2017, https://www.reuters.com/article/idUSKBN15505N.

73. See *Encyclopaedia Britannica*, s.v. "Samuel K. Doe," accessed 18 March 2024, https://www.britannica.com/biography/Samuel-K-Doe.

74. See *Encyclopaedia Britannica*, s.v. "Muammar al-Qaddafi," accessed 18 March 2024, https://www.britannica.com/biography/Muammar-al-Qaddafi.

Chapter 8

1. See Commission on the Responsibility of the Authors of the War and on Enforcement of Penalties, "Report Presented to the Preliminary Peace

Conference, 29 March 1919," *American Journal of International Law* 14, no. 1–2 (1920): 148 (emphasis added).

2. James W. Garner, "Limitations on National Sovereignty in International Relations," *American Political Science Review* 19, no. 1 (1925): 1.

3. Garner, "Limitations on National Sovereignty," 20.

4. Garner, "Limitations on National Sovereignty," 20–21.

5. Garner, "Limitations on National Sovereignty," 21.

6. Commission on the Responsibility of the Authors of the War and on Enforcement of Penalties, "Report Presented to the Preliminary Peace Conference, 29 March 1919," 140–41.

7. See "Provisional Summary Record of the 3378th Meeting," Palais des Nations, Geneva, 20 July 2017, 10:00 a.m., UN International Law Commission, Sixty-Ninth Session (Second Part), doc. no. A/CN.4/SR.3378, dated 13 August 2017, 10. See also "Report of the International Law Commission, Sixty-Ninth Session (1 May–2 June and 3 July–4 August 2017)," UN General Assembly, doc. no. A/72/10, para. 74. See also "Symposium on the Present and Future of Foreign Official Immunity," *AJIL Unbound* 112 (2018). See also Adil Ahmad Haque, "Immunity for International Crimes: Where Do States Really Stand?," *Just Security*, 17 April 2018, https://ww.justsecurity.org/54998/immunity-international -crimes-states-stand.

8. International Military Tribunal, Nuremberg, *Trial of the Major War Criminals before the International Military Tribunal, Nuremberg, 14 November 1945–1 October 1946*, vol. 2, *Proceedings of 14 November 1945 to 30 November 1945* (Nuremberg: International Military Tribunal, 1947), 101.

9. See, generally, Chatham House, "The Treatment of War Crimes and Crimes Incident to the War," *Bulletin of International News* 22 (1945).

10. Chatham House, "The Treatment of War Crimes and Crimes Incident to the War."

11. See *Encyclopædia Britannica*, s.v. "Paul von Hindenburg," accessed 18 March 2024, https://www.britannica.com/biography/Paul-von-Hindenburg.

12. See Chatham House, "The Treatment of War Crimes and Crimes Incident to the War."

13. Chatham House, "The Treatment of War Crimes and Crimes Incident to the War."

14. Chatham House, "The Treatment of War Crimes and Crimes Incident to the War," 102.

15. Dapo Akande, "International Law Immunities and the International Criminal Court," *American Journal of International Law* 98 (2004): 407.

Chapter 9

1. International Military Tribunal, Nuremberg, *Trial of the Major War Criminals before the International Military Tribunal, Nuremberg, 14 November 1945–1 October*

1946, vol. 2, *Proceedings of 14 November 1945 to 30 November 1945* (Nuremberg: International Military Tribunal, 1947), 101.

2. U.S. Department of State, "Punishment of War Criminals" (statement by Acting Secretary Grew, released to the press 1 February 1945), *Bulletin* 12, no. 293 (4 February 1945): 154.

3. U.S. Department of State, "Punishment of War Criminals," 154. See also Franklin D. Roosevelt, "Statement Warning Neutral Nations against Asylum for War Criminals," 30 July 1943, American Presidency Project, accessed 19 March 2024, https://www.presidency.ucsb.edu/documents/statement-warning-neutral -nations-against-asylum-for-war-criminals.

4. Franklin D. Roosevelt, "Fireside Chat no. 23: Report on the Home Front," radio broadcast, 12 October 1942. See Franklin D. Roosevelt, *The War Messages of Franklin D. Roosevelt—December 8, 1941 to October 12, 1942* (Washington, DC: Office of War Information, 1942), 71.

5. U.S. Department of State, *Report of Robert H. Jackson, United States Representative to the International Conference on Military Trials: London 1945*, International Organization and Conference Series 2, European and British Commonwealth 1 (Washington, DC: U.S. Department of State, 1947), 16–17 (emphasis added).

6. U.S. Department of State, *Report of Robert H. Jackson*, 17.

7. See Roosevelt, "Statement Warning Neutral Nations."

8. Roosevelt, "Statement Warning Neutral Nations."

9. See U.S. Department of State, *Report of Robert H. Jackson*, 13.

10. U.S. Department of State, *Report of Robert H. Jackson*, 13.

11. See "Moscow Conference, October 1943: Joint Four-Nation Declaration," Avalon Project at Yale Law School, accessed 19 March 2024, https://avalon .law.yale.edu/wwii/moscow.asp.

12. See U.S. Department of State, *Report of Robert H. Jackson*, 3.

13. *Encyclopaedia Britannica*, s.v. "Adolf Hitler," accessed 19 March 2024, https://www.britannica.com/biography/Adolf-Hitler.

14. See U.S. Department of State, *Report of Robert H. Jackson*, 3.

15. U.S. Department of State, *Report of Robert H. Jackson*, 4.

16. U.S. Department of State, *Report of Robert H. Jackson*, 5.

17. See U.S. Department of State, *Report of Robert H. Jackson*, 5.

18. See U.S. Department of State, *Report of Robert H. Jackson*, 6 (emphasis added).

19. U.S. Department of State, *Report of Robert H. Jackson*, 6.

20. U.S. Department of State, *Report of Robert H. Jackson*, 18 (emphasis added).

21. U.S. Department of State, *Report of Robert H. Jackson*, 18 (emphasis added).

22. U.S. Department of State, *Report of Robert H. Jackson*, 18.

23. U.S. Department of State, *Report of Robert H. Jackson*, 18.

24. U.S. Department of State, *Report of Robert H. Jackson*, 18–19.

25. U.S. Department of State, *Report of Robert H. Jackson*, 19.

26. See *Encyclopaedia Britannica*, s.v. "Franklin D. Roosevelt: Declining Health and Death," accessed 19 March 2024, https://www.britannica.com/biography/Franklin-D-Roosevelt/Relations-with-the-Allies.

27. *Encyclopaedia Britannica*, s.v. "Franklin D. Roosevelt: Declining Health and Death."

28. See U.S. Department of State, *Report of Robert H. Jackson*, 22.

29. U.S. Department of State, *Report of Robert H. Jackson*, 22.

30. U.S. Department of State, *Report of Robert H. Jackson*, 24.

31. U.S. Department of State, *Report of Robert H. Jackson*, 30.

32. U.S. Department of State, *Report of Robert H. Jackson*, 34.

33. U.S. Department of State, *Report of Robert H. Jackson*, 31.

34. U.S. Department of State, *Report of Robert H. Jackson*, 35.

35. U.S. Department of State, *Report of Robert H. Jackson*, 36.

36. U.S. Department of State, *Report of Robert H. Jackson*, 33.

37. U.S. Department of State, *Report of Robert H. Jackson*, 34 (emphasis added).

38. U.S. Department of State, *Report of Robert H. Jackson*, 35 (emphasis added).

39. U.S. Department of State, *Report of Robert H. Jackson*, 22.

40. U.S. Department of State, *Report of Robert H. Jackson*, 21.

41. U.S. Department of State, *Report of Robert H. Jackson*, 39.

42. U.S. Department of State, *Report of Robert H. Jackson*, 39.

43. See U.S. Department of State, *Report of Robert H. Jackson*, 41.

44. U.S. Department of State, *Report of Robert H. Jackson*, 46.

45. U.S. Department of State, *Report of Robert H. Jackson*, 46–47.

46. U.S. Department of State, *Report of Robert H. Jackson*, 47.

47. U.S. Department of State, *Report of Robert H. Jackson*, 47.

48. U.S. Department of State, *Report of Robert H. Jackson*, 47.

49. U.S. Department of State, *Report of Robert H. Jackson*, 47.

50. U.S. Department of State, *Report of Robert H. Jackson*, 51.

51. U.S. Department of State, *Report of Robert H. Jackson*, 51.

52. U.S. Department of State, *Report of Robert H. Jackson*, 51.

53. U.S. Department of State, *Report of Robert H. Jackson*, 51.

54. U.S. Department of State, *Report of Robert H. Jackson*, 51. Grotius indeed wrote that "[r]ight reason . . . and the nature of society . . . do not prohibit all use of force, but only that use of force which is in conflict with society, that is which attempts to fake away the rights of another" (Hugo Grotius, *De Jure Belli ac Pacis*, trans. Francis W. Kelsey, vol. 2 [Oxford: Clarendon, 1925], bk. 2, chap. 2, 53). In other words, "the use of force which does not violate the rights of others is not unjust" (Grotius, *De Jure Belli ac Pacis*, bk. 2, chap. 2, 54).

55. U.S. Department of State, *Report of Robert H. Jackson*, 51.

56. U.S. Department of State, *Report of Robert H. Jackson*, 51.

57. U.S. Department of State, *Report of Robert H. Jackson*, 51.

58. U.S. Department of State, *Report of Robert H. Jackson*, 52.

59. U.S. Department of State, *Report of Robert H. Jackson*, 52.

60. U.S. Department of State, *Report of Robert H. Jackson*, 52.

61. U.S. Department of State, *Report of Robert H. Jackson*, 51.

62. U.S. Department of State, *Report of Robert H. Jackson*, 52.

63. U.S. Department of State, *Report of Robert H. Jackson*, 52.

64. U.S. Department of State, *Report of Robert H. Jackson*, 52.

65. U.S. Department of State, *Report of Robert H. Jackson*, 42.

Chapter 10

1. See John Dower, *Embracing Defeat: Japan in the Wake of World War II* (New York: Norton, 1999), 278.

2. See Wilhelm II, *The Kaiser's Memoirs: Wilhelm II, Emperor of Germany, 1888–1918* (New York: Harper, 1922), 292–96.

3. See Douglas MacArthur, *Reminiscences* (Westport, CT: Heinemann, 1964), 288.

4. As one of General MacArthur's aides recalled: "The pressure from Washington to 'hang Hirohito' was great at the time." Faubion Bowers, "The Day the General Blinked," *New York Times*, 30 September 1988. See also Herbert P. Bix, "The Showa Emperor's 'Monologue' and the Problem of War Responsibility," *Journal of Japanese Studies* 18, no. 2 (1992): 329.

5. Dower, *Embracing Defeat*, 278. See also Hal Brands, "Who Saved the Emperor? The MacArthur Myth and US Policy toward Hirohito and the Japanese Imperial Institution, 1942–1946," *Pacific Historical Review* 75, no. 2 (2006): 271–306.

6. See MacArthur, *Reminiscences*, 288. See also Brands, "Who Saved the Emperor?"; Dale Hellegers, *We, the Japanese People: World War II and the Origins of the Japanese Constitution* (Stanford, CA: Stanford University Press, 2001), 1:227, 1:230; Dower, *Embracing Defeat*, 282–86; Haruo Iguchi, "Bonner Fellers and US-Japan Relations, June 1945–June 1946," *Journal of American and Canadian Studies* 20 (2002): 74.

7. Iguchi, "Bonner Fellers and US-Japan Relations," 67.

8. Iguchi, "Bonner Fellers and US-Japan Relations," 68, 74.

9. Indeed, the Soviets had attempted a claim to the occupation of Hokkaido, which would have split Japan into an American zone and a Soviet zone. But MacArthur bluntly rebuffed the approach. See MacArthur, *Reminiscences*, 285, 292–93.

10. See Arnold C. Brackman, *The Other Nuremberg: The Untold Story of the Tokyo War Crimes Trials* (New York: Morrow, 1987), 40–42.

11. See Bix, "The Showa Emperor's 'Monologue.'"

12. See, for instance, Hellegers, *We, the Japanese People*, 223. See also Richard B. Frank, "The Fate of Emperor Hirohito," National WWII Museum, 26 August 2020, https://www.nationalww2museum.org/war/articles/what-happened-to-emperor-hirohito; Ryan Fan, "Japan Surrendered—but Hirohito Stayed

Emperor for 44 Years. Why?," Medium, 2 January 2022, https://medium.com/
frame-of-reference/japan-surrendered-but-hirohito-stayed-emperor-for-44-years
-why-9472e33e163b.

13. See Dower, *Embracing Defeat*, 281.

14. See Paul Mantoux, *Deliberations of the Council of Four (March 24–June 28, 1919): Notes of the Official Interpreter*, ed. and trans. Arthur S. Link, with the assistance of Manfred F. Boemeke (Princeton, NJ: Princeton University Press, 1992), 120.

15. See "His Majesty's Government: The Cabinet," UK Parliament, accessed 19 March 2024, https://members.parliament.uk/Government/Cabinet.

16. See Official Website of the British Monarchy (website), https://web.archive.org/web/20100414023100/http://www.royal.gov.uk/MonarchUK/QueenandGovernment/QueenandPrimeMinister.aspx.

17. See Official Website of the British Monarchy.

18. See Official Website of the British Monarchy.

19. See Official Website of the British Monarchy.

20. See Official Website of the British Monarchy.

21. See Official Website of the British Monarchy.

22. See Ben Johnson, "King's Speech," Historic UK, accessed 19 March 2024, https://www.historic-uk.com/HistoryUK/HistoryofBritain/The-Kings-Speech. See also "King George VI Speech—Declaration of War against Germany 1939," Brit Politics, accessed 19 March 2024, https://www.britpolitics.co.uk/speeches -george-vi-declaration-of-war.

23. See Hellegers, *We, the Japanese People*, 230.

24. See Dower, *Embracing Defeat*, 282–83, 286. See also Bix, "The Showa Emperor's 'Monologue,'" 349.

25. See, for instance, Hellegers, *We, the Japanese People*, 173.

26. See Brackman, *The Other Nuremberg*, 37, 39, 133, 272.

27. See Harry S. Truman Library, "President Truman Announces the Bombing of Hiroshima," YouTube, accessed 19 March 2024, https://www.youtube .com/watch?v=n_A8LPtuX5c.

Chapter 11

1. See International Military Tribunal, Nuremberg, *Trial of the Major War Criminals before the International Military Tribunal, 14 November 1945–1 October 1946* (Nuremberg: International Military Tribunal, 1947), 1:365–67.

2. International Military Tribunal, Nuremberg, *Trial of the Major War Criminals*, 1:342–56.

3. See *Encyclopaedia Britannica*, "Nürnberg Trials," accessed 16 November 2023, https://www.britannica.com/event/Nurnberg-trials.

4. See Antonio Cassese, "Affirmation of the Principles of International Law Recognized by the Charter of the Nürnberg Tribunal," United Nations, 2009,

https://legal.un.org/avl/pdf/ha/ga_95-I/ga_95-I_e.pdf. See also "Affirmation of the Principles of International Law Recognized by the Charter of the Nürnberg Tribunal," United Nations, 2008, https://legal.un.org/avl/pdf/ha/ga_95-I/ga_95 -I_ph_e.pdf.

5. See V. V. Pella, "Towards an International Criminal Court," *American Journal of International Law* 44 (1950): 41fn11.

6. Harry S. Truman, "Letter to Francis Biddle in Response to His Report on the Nurnberg Tribunal," 12 November 1946, in United States Office of the Federal Register, National Archives and Records Service, General Services Administration, *Public Papers of the Presidents of the United States: Harry S. Truman—Containing the Public Messages, Speeches and Statements of the President—January 1 to December 31, 1946* (Washington, DC: U.S. Government Printing Office, 1962), 480–81 (emphasis added); see also Harry S. Truman, "Letter to Francis Biddle in Response to His Report on the Nurnberg Tribunal," 12 November 1946, American Presidency Project, accessed 19 March 2024, https://www.presidency.ucsb.edu/docu ments/letter-francis-biddle-response-his-report-the-nurnberg-tribunal.

7. Truman, "Letter to Francis Biddle," 12 November 1946, 480–81.

8. Truman, "Letter to Francis Biddle," 12 November 1946, 480–81.

9. Truman, "Letter to Francis Biddle," 12 November 1946, 480–81.

10. Truman, "Letter to Francis Biddle," 12 November 1946, 480–81.

11. Truman, "Letter to Francis Biddle," 12 November 1946, 480–81.

12. See Francis Biddle, "Report to President Truman, 9 November 1946," *U.S. Department of State Bulletin* 15, no. 386 (24 November 1946): 954.

13. Biddle, "Report to President Truman, 9 November 1946," 956.

14. Biddle, "Report to President Truman, 9 November 1946," 956.

15. Biddle, "Report to President Truman, 9 November 1946," 956.

16. Biddle, "Report to President Truman, 9 November 1946," 956.

17. Biddle, "Report to President Truman, 9 November 1946," 956.

18. Biddle, "Report to President Truman, 9 November 1946," 956.

19. Biddle, "Report to President Truman, 9 November 1946," 956.

20. Biddle, "Report to President Truman, 9 November 1946," 956.

21. Biddle, "Report to President Truman, 9 November 1946," 956.

22. Biddle, "Report to President Truman, 9 November 1946," 956–57.

23. See Harry S. Truman, "Address in New York City at the Opening Session of the United Nations General Assembly," 23 October 1946, American Presidency Project, accessed 19 March 2024, https://www.presidency.ucsb.edu/documents/ address-new-york-city-the-opening-session-the-united-nations-general-assembly.

24. Truman, "Address in New York City."

25. Truman, "Address in New York City."

26. See Harry S. Truman, "Letter to Judge Biddle dated 12 November 1946," *U.S. Department of State Bulletin* 15, no. 386 (24 November 1946): 954.

27. United Nations Secretary General, "Supplementary Report on the Work of the Organization," 24 October 1946, United Nations doc. no. A/65/Add.1, 10–11 (emphasis added).

28. United Nations Secretary General, "Supplementary Report on the Work of the Organization," 10–11.

29. United Nations Secretary General, "Supplementary Report on the Work of the Organization," 10–11.

30. United Nations Secretary General, "Supplementary Report on the Work of the Organization," 10–11.

31. United Nations Secretary General, "Supplementary Report on the Work of the Organization," 10–11.

32. United Nations Secretary General, "Supplementary Report on the Work of the Organization," 10–11 (emphasis added).

33. See M. H. Mendelson, "The Formation of Customary International Law," in *Collected Courses of the Hague Academy of International Law*, 272:200–201, Brill Online, accessed 19 March 2024, https://referenceworks.brillonline.com/entries/the-hague-academy-collected-courses/*A9789041112378_02.

34. Mendelson, "The Formation of Customary International Law," 201.

35. Mendelson, "The Formation of Customary International Law," 201.

36. Mendelson, "The Formation of Customary International Law," 201.

37. See "Affirmation of the Principles of International Law Recognized by the Charter of the Nürnberg Tribunal," United Nations Audiovisual Library of International Law, accessed 19 March 2024, https://legal.un.org/avl/pdf/ha/ga_95-I/ga_95-I_ph_e.pdf.

38. International Military Tribunal, Nuremberg, *Trial of the Major War Criminals*, 1:218.

39. International Military Tribunal, Nuremberg, *Trial of the Major War Criminals*, 1:223.

40. International Military Tribunal, Nuremberg, *Trial of the Major War Criminals*, 1:223.

41. International Military Tribunal, Nuremberg, *Trial of the Major War Criminals*, 1:223.

42. See "Formation of the Principles Recognized in the Charter of the Nürnberg Tribunal and in the Judgment of the Tribunal," in *Yearbook of the International Law Commission 1949* (Geneva: United Nations, 1949), 130, para. 9.

43. "Formation of the Principles Recognized in the Charter of the Nürnberg Tribunal," 131, para. 16.

44. "Report of the International Law Commission on Its Second Session, 5 June to 29 July 1950," Official Records of the General Assembly, Fifth Session, Supplement no. 12 (A/1316), in *Yearbook of the International Law Commission 1950* (Geneva: United Nations, 1950), 2:374, para. 96.

45. "Report of the International Law Commission on Its Second Session," 374–78.

46. "Report of the International Law Commission on Its Second Session," 376, para. 110.

47. "Report of the International Law Commission on Its Second Session," 376, para. 111.

48. "Report of the International Law Commission on Its Second Session," 378, para. 127.

49. See Commission on the Responsibility of the Authors of the War and on Enforcement of Penalties, "Report Presented to the Preliminary Peace Conference, 29 March 1919," *American Journal of International Law* 14, no. 1–2 (1920): 122.

50. See, generally, "Draft Code of Offences against Peace and Security of Mankind—Report of the Secretary General," UN General Assembly, 22 September 1981, doc. No A/36/416, 3. See also *Yearbook of the International Law Commission* (1982), vol. 2, pt. 1, 274 et seq.

51. See "Report of the International Law Commission on the Work of Its Forty-Third Session," in *Yearbook of the International Law Commission* (1991), vol. 2, pt. 2, 93 (para. 173) and 94 (paras. 174, 175).

52. See *Yearbook of the International Law Commission* (1993), vol. 2, pt. 1, 59 et seq.

53. *Yearbook of the International Law Commission* (1993), vol. 2, pt. 1, 100, para. 17.

54. *Yearbook of the International Law Commission* (1994), vol. 2, pt. 1, 108, para. 132.

55. Commission on the Responsibility of the Authors of the War and on Enforcement of Penalties, "Report Presented to the Preliminary Peace Conference, 29 March 1919," 116.

56. See *Yearbook of the International Law Commission* (1993), vol. 2, pt. 1, 95, para. 37.

57. See *Yearbook of the International Law Commission* (1996), vol. 2, pt. 2, 27, para. 6.

Chapter 12

1. See "Agreement between the United Nations and the Government of Sierra Leone on the Establishment of a Special Court for Sierra Leone," Human Rights Library, University of Minnesota, accessed 20 March 2024, http://hrlibrary.umn.edu/instree/SCSL/SierraLeoneUNAgreement.pdf.

2. See article 7(2) of the ICTY Statute; article 6(2) of the ICTR Statute; and article 6(2) of the SCSL Statute.

3. See indictment against Slobodan Milošević: "The Prosecutor of the Tribunal against Slobodan Milosevic et al. (Indictment)," International Criminal Tribunal for the Former Yugoslavia, 22 May 1999, https://www.icty.org/x/cases/slobodan_milosevic/ind/en/mil-ii990524e.htm.

4. See Judge Kevin Parker, "Report to the President: Death of Slobodan Milošević," International Criminal Tribunal for the Former Yugoslavia, 30 May 2006, https://www.icty.org/x/cases/slobodan_milosevic/custom2/en/parkerrep ort.pdf.

5. See "Prosecutor v. Bagosora and Nsengiyumva (Judgment)," International Criminal Tribunal for Rwanda [ICTR Appeals Chamber], 14 December 2011, https://www.cdiph.ulaval.ca/sites/cdiph.ulaval.ca/files/bagosora_arret_en.pdf.

6. See "Prosecutor v. Kambanda (Judgment and Sentence)," International Criminal Tribunal for Rwanda [ICTR Trial Chamber], 4 September 1998, https://ucr.irmct.org/LegalRef/CMSDocStore/Public/English/Judgement/ NotIndexable/ICTR-97-23/MSC14050R0000529818.PDF.

7. See "Prosecutor v. Taylor (Judgment)," Residual Special Court of Sierra Leone [SCSL Appeals Chamber], 26 September 2013, https://www.rscsl.org/ Documents/Decisions/Taylor/Appeal/1389/SCSL-03-01-A-1389.pdf.

8. See "Prosecutor v. Taylor (Judgment)," 26 September 2013, para. 4. See also "Prosecutor v. Taylor (Decision on Immunity from Jurisdiction)," Residual Special Court of Sierra Leone [SCSL Appeals Chamber], 31 May 2004, para, 1, https://www.rscsl.org/Documents/Decisions/Taylor/Appeal/059/SCSL-03-01 -I-059.pdf.

9. "Prosecutor v. Taylor (Decision on Immunity from Jurisdiction)," 6.

10. "Prosecutor v. Taylor (Decision on Immunity from Jurisdiction)," para. 7.

11. "Prosecutor v. Taylor (Decision on Immunity from Jurisdiction)," para. 52.

12. "Prosecutor v. Taylor (Decision on Immunity from Jurisdiction)," para. 2.

13. See "Prosecutor v. Taylor (Decision on Immunity from Jurisdiction)," 3 (recitals).

14. "Prosecutor v. Taylor (Decision on Immunity from Jurisdiction)," para. 17.

15. "Prosecutor v. Taylor (Decision on Immunity from Jurisdiction)," para. 17.

16. *Arrest Warrant of 11 April 2000* (Democratic Republic of the Congo v. Belgium), [2002] ICJ Reports, 3, §58 (emphasis added).

17. Antonio Cassese, "When May Senior State Officials Be Tried for International Crimes? Some Comments on the Congo v. Belgium Case," *European Journal of International Law* 13 (2002): 870 et seq.

18. Some of the data in that regard include but are not limited to: Lieber Code (1863) IV and V; for instance, article 71 provides: "Whoever intentionally inflicts additional wounds on an enemy already wholly disabled, or kills such an enemy, or who orders or encourages soldiers to do so, shall suffer death, if duly convicted, whether he belongs to the Army of the United States, or is an enemy captured after having committed his misdeed." See also the *Oxford Manual on the Laws of War on Land* (Oxford: Institute of International Law, 1880), article 84: "If any of the foregoing rules be violated, the offending parties should be punished, after a judicial hearing, by the belligerent in whose hands they are. Therefore . . . Offenders against the laws of war are liable to the punishments specified in the penal law." See also L. Oppenheim, *International Law*, vol. 2, *War and Neutrality*,

2nd ed. (New York: Longmans, Green, 1912), §251. See also *United States v. Bopp* 237 F 283 (1916) [ND Cal]. See also Versailles Treaty 1919, article 228. See also Commission on the Responsibility of the Authors of the War and on Enforcement of Penalties, "Report Presented to the Preliminary Peace Conference, 29 March 1919," *American Journal of International Law* 14, no. 1–2 (1920): 121. See also William Hall, *A Treatise on International Law*, ed. Pearce Higgins, 8th ed. (Cambridge: Cambridge University Press, 1924), §135. See also Ex Parte Quirin, 317 U.S. 1 (1942) [U.S. Supreme Court], 30–31, 35–36. See Hartley Shawcross, "Opening Statement of Sir Hartley Shawcross, Attorney-General of UK," in *Trial of the Major War Criminals before the International Military Tribunal, Nuremberg, 14 November 1945–1 October 1946* (Nuremberg: International Military Tribunal, 1947), 3:92. See also Telford Taylor, "Final Report to the Secretary of the Army on the Nuernberg War Crimes Trials under Control Council Law no. 10," 15 August 1949, 4, Crime of Aggression, accessed 1 April 2024, https://crimeofaggression .info/documents//6/1945_Control_Council_Law_No10.pdf. See also Geneva Convention for the Amelioration of the Conditions of the Wounded and Sick in Armed Forces in the Field (First Geneva Convention), 12 August 1949, article 49; Geneva Convention for the Amelioration of the Condition of Wounded, Sick and Shipwrecked Members of Armed Forces at Sea (Second Geneva Convention), 12 August 1949, article 50; Geneva Convention Relative to the Treatment of Prisoners of War (Third Geneva Convention), 12 August 1949, article 129; and Geneva Convention Relative to the Protection of Civilian Persons in Time of War (Fourth Geneva Convention), 12 August 1949, article 146.

19. "Prosecutor v. Taylor (Decision on Immunity from Jurisdiction)," para. 18.

20. "Prosecutor v. Taylor (Decision on Immunity from Jurisdiction)," para. 18.

21. "Prosecutor v. Taylor (Decision on Immunity from Jurisdiction)," para. 19.

22. See *Prosecutor v. Al-Bashir* (Jordan Referral re Al-Bashir Appeal Judgment), 6 May 2019, Joint Concurring Opinion of Judges Eboe-Osuji, Morrison, Hofmański and Bossa, para. 344–69.

23. See article 5 of the Rome Statute.

24. See *Yearbook of the International Law Commission* (1993), vol. 2, pt. 1, 95, para. 37.

25. See *Yearbook of the International Law Commission* (1993), vol. 2, pt. 1, 100, para. 17.

26. See "Regulation 2000/15," sec. 1.3, and sec. 4, 5, 6, 7, United Nations Transitional Administration of East Timor, 6 June 2000, https://www.legal-tools .org/doc/c082f8/pdf/.

27. See "Regulation 2000/15," sec. 8, 9.

28. See "Background," Kosovo Specialist Chamber and Specialist Office of the Prosecutor, accessed 20 March 2024, https://www.scp-ks.org/en/background.

29. See "Council of Europe Parliamentary Assembly Report on 'Inhuman Treatment of People and Illicit Trafficking in Human Organs in Kosovo,'" Kosovo Specialist Chambers and Specialist Prosecutor's Office, 7 January 2011,

https://www.scp-ks.org/en/documents/council-europe-parliamentary-assembly
-report-inhuman-treatment-people-and-illicit.

Chapter 13

1. Joanne Suter, *Fearon's World History* (Belmont, CA: Fearon Education, 1990), 3.

2. See Suetonius, *Lives of the Twelve Caesars*, trans. H. M. Bird (Ware, Hertfordshire: Wordsworth Editions, 1997), for instance, "Caius Caesar Caligula," chap. 29.

3. Woodrow Wilson, speech given at a dinner of the International Law Association, Paris, 9 May 1919, cited in *Commercial & Financial Chronicle* 108 (28 June 1919): 2598.

4. See U.S. Department of State, *Report of Robert H. Jackson, United States Representative to the International Conference on Military Trials: London 1945*, International Organization and Conference Series 2, European and British Commonwealth 1 (Washington, DC: U.S. Department of State, 1947), 46–47.

5. Notably, the Japanese delegation had displayed no keenness for a rule of immunity that would prosecute a head of state.

6. Paul Mantoux, *Deliberations of the Council of Four (March 24–June 28, 1919): Notes of the Official Interpreter*, ed. and trans. Arthur S. Link, with the assistance of Manfred F. Boemeke (Princeton, NJ: Princeton University Press, 1992), 120.

7. Mantoux, *Deliberations of the Council of Four*, 120.

8. Mantoux, *Deliberations of the Council of Four*, 120.

9. Notably, the records of The Hague Peace Conference of 1899 contain the following "Nomenclature of the Sovereigns and Rulers of States Represented at the Peace Conference": "His Majesty the Emperor of Germany, King of Prussia; His Majesty the Emperor of Austria, King of Bohemia, etc., and Apostolic King of Hungary; His Majesty the King of the Belgians; His Majesty the Emperor of China; His Majesty the King of Denmark; His Majesty the King of Spain and in His Name Her Majesty the Queen Regent of the Kingdom; the President of the United States of America; the President of the United States of Mexico; the President of the French Republic; Her Majesty the Queen of the United Kingdom of Great Britain and Ireland, Empress of India; His Majesty the King of the Hellenes; His Majesty the King of Italy; His Majesty the Emperor of Japan; His Royal Highness the Grand Duke of Luxemburg, Duke of Nassau; His Highness the Prince of Montenegro; Her Majesty the Queen of the Netherlands; His Imperial Majesty the Shah of Persia; His Majesty the King of Portugal and of the Algarves, etc.; His Majesty the King of Roumania; His Majesty the Emperor of All the Russias; His Majesty the King of Siam; His Majesty the King of Sweden and Norway: the Swiss Federal Council; His Majesty the Emperor of the Ottomans, and His Royal Highness the Prince of Bulgaria." See Carnegie Endowment for International

Peace, *Proceedings of The Hague Peace Conferences: Translation of the Official Texts* (New York: Oxford University Press, 1920), 219.

10. Seneca, *De Clementia* (1532 CE), bk. 1, chap. 1, v. 1, in *Calvin's Commentary on Seneca's* De Clementia (55 CE), by John Calvin, ed. and trans. F. L. Battles and A. M. Hugo (Leiden: Brill, 1969), 19 (emphasis added).

11. See Suetonius, *Lives of the Twelve Caesars*, for instance, "Caius Caesar Caligula," chap. 23–36.

12. Suetonius, *Lives of the Twelve Caesars*, 1.

13. Suetonius, *Lives of the Twelve Caesars*, "Caius Caesar Caligula," chap. 29.

14. Suetonius, *Lives of the Twelve Caesars*, chap. 22.

15. Suetonius, *Lives of the Twelve Caesars*, chap. 56–59.

16. See R. W. Carlyle and A. J. Carlyle, *History of Mediaeval Political Theory in the West* (Edinburgh: Blackwood, 1903), 1:147.

17. See Carlyle and Carlyle, *History of Mediaeval Political Theory in the West*, 1:150, 1:152.

18. See 1 Samuel 17–23 (New International Version).

19. See 1 Samuel 24 (NIV).

20. See Romans 13:1–5 (NIV).

21. 1 Peter 2:13–20 (NIV).

22. See Carlyle and Carlyle, *History of Mediaeval Political Theory in the West*, 1:149.

23. Carlyle and Carlyle, *History of Mediaeval Political Theory in the West*, 1:147.

24. Carlyle and Carlyle, *History of Mediaeval Political Theory in the West*, 1:148.

25. Carlyle and Carlyle, *History of Mediaeval Political Theory in the West*, 1:151.

26. R. W. Carlyle and A. J. Carlyle, *History of Mediaeval Political Theory in the West* (Edinburgh: Blackwood, 1915), 3:122.

27. Carlyle and Carlyle, *History of Mediaeval Political Theory in the West*, 3:116.

28. Carlyle and Carlyle, *History of Mediaeval Political Theory in the West*, 3:116.

29. See R. W. Carlyle and A. J. Carlyle, *History of Mediaeval Political Theory in the West* (Edinburgh: Blackwood, 1915), 6:272.

30. Carlyle and Carlyle, *History of Mediaeval Political Theory in the West*, 6:272–73.

31. Carlyle and Carlyle, *History of Mediaeval Political Theory in the West*, 6:275.

32. See Carlyle and Carlyle, *History of Mediaeval Political Theory in the West*, 6:273.

33. See Carlyle and Carlyle, *History of Mediaeval Political Theory in the West*, 6:274.

34. See Carlyle and Carlyle, *History of Mediaeval Political Theory in the West*, 6:278–79.

35. See Carlyle and Carlyle, *History of Mediaeval Political Theory in the West*, 6:288.

36. See Carlyle and Carlyle, *History of Mediaeval Political Theory in the West*, 6:288.

37. See Carlyle and Carlyle, *History of Mediaeval Political Theory in the West*, 6:288 ("Hereby seest thou that the kyng is in this worlde without law, and may at his lust do right or wrong, and shall give accomptes but to God only").

38. See Carlyle and Carlyle, *History of Mediaeval Political Theory in the West*, 6:291.

39. See Carlyle and Carlyle, *History of Mediaeval Political Theory in the West*, 6:291.

40. See John Locke, *Two Treatises of Government: With a Supplement, Patriarcha, by Robert Filmer*, ed. Thomas I. Cook (New York: Hafner, 1947), 251.

41. See Locke, *Two Treatises of Government*, 251.

42. See Locke, *Two Treatises of Government*, 252.

43. See Locke, *Two Treatises of Government*, x.

44. See Locke, *Two Treatises of Government*, x–xi.

45. William Blackstone, *Commentaries on the Laws of England in Four Books* (1753), ed. George Sharswood (Philadelphia, PA: Lippincott, 1868), vol. 1, bk. 1, §244.

46. Blackstone, *Commentaries on the Laws of England*, vol. 1, bk. 1, §246 (emphasis in original).

47. Blackstone, *Commentaries on the Laws of England in Four Books*, vol. 1, bk. 1, §246.

48. Frederick Pollock and William Maitland, *The History of English Law before the Time of Edward I* (Cambridge: Cambridge University Press, 1895), 1:496.

49. Blackstone, *Commentaries on the Laws of England in Four Books*, vol. 1, bk. 1, §246.

50. Blackstone, *Commentaries on the Laws of England in Four Books*, vol. 1, bk. 1, §246.

51. A. V. Dicey, *Introduction to the Study of Law of the Constitution*, 9th ed. (London: Macmillan, 1952), 8–9.

52. Blackstone, *Commentaries on the Laws of England in Four Books*, vol. 1, bk. 1, §241.

53. Blackstone, *Commentaries on the Laws of England in Four Books*, vol. 1, bk. 1, §242.

54. William Holdsworth, *A History of English Law* (London: Methuen, 1938), 10:345–46.

55. Pollock and Maitland, *The History of English Law before the Time of Edward I*, 1:517, para. 502.

56. Pollock and Maitland, *The History of English Law before the Time of Edward I*, 1:517, para. 502.

57. Pollock and Maitland, *The History of English Law before the Time of Edward I*, 1:517, para. 502.

58. David Lloyd George, *Truth about the Peace Treaties* (London: Gollancz, 1938), 1:105.

Chapter 14

1. George Stuart Robertson, *Law and the Practice of Civil Proceedings by and against the Crown and Departments of the Government: With Numerous Forms and Precedents* (London: Stevens, 1908), 2.

2. William Blackstone, *Commentaries on the Laws of England in Four Books* (1753), ed. George Sharswood (Philadelphia, PA: Lippincott, 1868), vol. 1, bk. 1, §242.

3. Blackstone, *Commentaries on the Laws of England*, vol. 1, bk. 1, §242.

4. William Holdsworth, *A History of English Law* (London: Methuen, 1938), 10:346.

5. See *Matthews v. Minister of Defence* [2003] UK House of Lords 4, para. 4–8 (Lord Bingham) and para. 54–57 (Lord Hope).

6. *The Schooner Exchange v. McFaddon*, 11 US 116 (1812).

7. The Case of the SS *Lotus* (1927) PCIJ Judgments, series A, no. 10.

8. The Case of the SS *Lotus*, 18.

9. The Case of the SS *Lotus*, 21 (emphasis added).

10. Frederick Pollock and William Maitland, *The History of English Law before the Time of Edward I* (Cambridge: Cambridge University Press, 1895), 1:499.

11. See *Oxford Reference*, s.v. "Royal Titles Act 1876," accessed 21 March 2024, https://www.oxfordreference.com/view/10.1093/oi/authority.20110803100 431780.

12. Blackstone, *Commentaries on the Laws of England*, vol. 1, bk. 1, §242 (emphasis in original).

13. Blackstone, *Commentaries on the Laws of England*, vol. 1, bk. 1, §242 (emphasis in original).

14. Blackstone, *Commentaries on the Laws of England*, vol. 1, bk. 1, §242.

15. Blackstone, *Commentaries on the Laws of England*, vol. 1, bk. 1, §242.

16. Blackstone, *Commentaries on the Laws of England*, vol. 1, bk. 1, §242.

17. In 2008, a sitting president of Israel was forced to resign from office when he was indicted for rape. He was convicted in his eventual trial. See "Israel ex-President Moshe Katsav Found Guilty of Rape," BBC, 30 December 2010, https://www.bbc.com/news/world-middle-east-12091982. Such insistence on accountability makes a state stronger. It does not destroy the constitution.

18. See, generally, John Morrill and Geoffrey Elton, "Henry VIII," in *Encyclopedia Britannica*, last updated 14 March 2022, accessed 5 June 2022, https://www .britannica.com/biography/Henry-VIII-king-of-England.

19. *Encyclopaedia Britannica*, s.v. "Thirty Years' War," last updated 6 May 2021, accessed 5 June 2022, https://www.britannica.com/event/Thirty-Years-War.

20. See *Encyclopaedia Britannica*, s.v. "Thirty Years' War."

21. *Encyclopaedia Britannica*, s.v. "Peace of Westphalia," *Encyclopedia Britannica*, last updated 23 January 2022, accessed 5 June 2022, https://www.britannica.com/event/Peace-of-Westphalia.

22. See the Peace of Münster, 24 October 1648, article 64. Article 65 also gave each state party the right to conduct its own foreign relations and enter into foreign military pacts as long as those were not aimed at the emperor or the empire or against public peace.

23. See the Peace of Münster, articles 28 and 29. See also articles 15–24 of the Peace of Augsburg, 25 September 1555.

24. See *Encyclopaedia Britannica*, s.v. "End of the Holy Roman Empire," accessed 21 March 2024, https://www.britannica.com/place/Germany/End-of -the-Holy-Roman-Empire.

25. The contrast with the horizontal axis is the vertical axis that involves relations that include international organizations and institutions.

26. Edward Andrew, "Jean Bodin on Sovereignty," *Republics of Letters: A Journal for the Study of Knowledge, Politics, and the Arts* 2, no. 2 (2011): 75, accessed 21 March 2024, https://arcade.stanford.edu/sites/default/files/article_pdfs/roflv 02i02_Andrew_060111_0.pdf.

27. See Andrew, "Jean Bodin on Sovereignty," generally, but especially page 77.

28. See Andrew, "Jean Bodin on Sovereignty," 78. See also Jean Bodin, *Six Books of the Commonwealth*, abr. and trans. M. J. Tooley (Oxford: Basil Blackwell, 1955), 38–39, https://www.yorku.ca/comninel/courses/3020pdf/six_books.pdf.

29. Mario Turchetti, "Jean Bodin," in *Stanford Encyclopedia of Philosophy*, ed. Edward N. Zalta (Stanford, CA: Stanford University, 2018), sec. 3; article published 25 March 2005, last updated 30 July 2018, https://plato.stanford.edu/ archives/fall2018/entries/bodin.

30. See Bodin, *Six Books of the Commonwealth*, 28–31. See also Julian H. Franklin, ed., *Jean Bodin* (New York: Routledge, 2006), 107–9.

31. Andrew, "Jean Bodin on Sovereignty," 78.

32. According to Grotius, justifiable causes of war include defense, the obtaining of that which belongs to us or is our due, and the inflicting of punishment. Hugo Grotius, *De Jure Belli ac Pacis*, trans. Francis Kelsey (Oxford: Clarendon, 1925), bk. II, chap. 1, §II.

33. See Mary Ellen O'Connell and Lenore Vanderzee, "The History of International Adjudication," in *The Oxford Handbook of International Adjudication*, ed. Cesare Romano, Karen Alter, and Yuval Shany (Oxford: Oxford University Press, 2013), 47 et seq.

Chapter 15

1. Coleman Phillipson, *International Law and the Great War* (London: Fisher Unwin, 1915), vi (emphasis added).

Conclusion

1. James Brown Scott, "The Trial of the Kaiser," in *What Really Happened at Paris*, ed. Edward Mandell House and Charles Seymour (London: Hodder & Stoughton, 1921), 239–40.

2. "One of the proposals in the [Henry] Morgenthau memorandum of September 6 was that a list should be made of German archcriminals—men whose obvious guilt was generally recognized by the United Nations—and that upon capture and identification these men should be shot at once": see Henry L. Stimson, *On Active Service in Peace and War* (New York: Harper, 1947), 584.

3. Stimson, *On Active Service in Peace and War*, 584–87.

4. International Military Tribunal, Nuremberg, *Trial of the Major War Criminals before the International Military Tribunal, Nuremberg, 14 November 1945–1 October 1946*, vol. 2, *Proceedings of 14 November 1945 to 30 November 1945* (Nuremberg: International Military Tribunal, 1947), 101–2.

5. "ICTR in Brief," International Criminal Tribunal for Rwanda, accessed 28 June 2022, https://unictr.irmct.org/en/tribunal.

6. See "Key Figures of the Cases," International Criminal Tribunal for the Former Yugoslavia, accessed 28 June 2022, https://www.icty.org/en/cases/key-figures-cases.

7. Matti Koskenniemi, "What Is International Law For?," in *International Law*, ed. Malcolm D. Evans (Oxford: Oxford University Press, 2003), 89, 110–11.

8. Chile Eboe-Osuji, "The High Commissioner for Human Rights: On the Legal Obligation of Corporations to Respect International Human Rights Norms," in *For the Sake of Present and Future Generations*, ed. Suzannah Linton et al. (Leiden: Brill, 2015), 198.

9. See H. L. A. Hart, *The Concept of Law* (Oxford: Oxford University Press, 1961).

10. See Ronald Dworkin, *Law's Empire* (Cambridge, MA: Harvard University Press, 1986).

11. See Joseph Raz, *The Concept of a Legal System* (New York: Oxford University Press, 1970).

12. See John Finnis, *Natural Law and Natural Rights* (Oxford: Clarendon, 1980).

13. See Alf Ross, *On Law and Justice* (Berkeley and Los Angeles: University of California Press, 1959).

14. See the Versailles Treaty, article 227.

15. See article 7.

16. See article II(4)(a).

17. See article IV.

18. See article 7(2).

19. See article 6(2).

20. See article 6(2).

21. See article 27.

22. See Principle III.

23. See the draft Code of Offences against the Peace and Security of Mankind (1954), article 3; and the draft Code of Crimes against the Peace and Security of Mankind (1996), article 7.

Epilogue

1. Dapo Akande, "International Law Immunities and the International Criminal Court," *American Journal of International Law* 98, no. 3 (2004): 409 (emphases added).

2. Akande, "International Law Immunities and the International Criminal Court," 421 (emphasis added).

3. Eleanor Roosevelt, "My Day: October 30, 1950," Eleanor Roosevelt Papers Project, accessed 21 March 2024, https://erpapers.columbian.gwu.edu/browse -my-day-columns (emphasis added).

4. See Claus Kreß, "Article 98—Cooperation with Respect to Waiver of Immunity and Consent to Surrender," in *Rome Statute of the International Criminal Court: Article-by-Article Commentary*, 4th ed., ed. Kai Ambos (Munich: Beck, Hart, Nomos, 2021), para. 126–30.

5. M. H. Mendelson, "The Formation of Customary International Law," in *Collected Courses of the Hague Academy of International Law*, 272:202, accessed 21 March 2024, http://dx.doi.org/10.1163/1875-8096_pplrdc_A9789041112378_02 (emphasis in original).

6. Reparation for Injuries Suffered in the Service of the United Nations, Advisory Opinion [1949] ICJ Reports 174, 182–84.

INDEX

absentia, prosecution in, 8
absolute authority, 265–66
absolute perfection, 250–51
absolute submission, to monarchy, 249
absolute theory, of sovereignty, 185–86
accountability. *See specific topics*
actus reus, *mens rea* compared to, 5
Adachi, Mineichirō, 120
ad hominem, 119; for crime of aggression, 12
advocacy, objections and, 161
Afghanistan, xxvi
African Bar Association, 236
African Union, 16
agency, 286–87
aggression. *See* crime of aggression; wars of aggression
Agrast, Mark, 1
AJIL. *See American Journal of International Law*
AJIL Unbound symposium, xxv
Alexander II (Czar), 30
Alfaro, Ricardo, 223
Allied and Associated Powers, 64–65; article 227 and, 67, 158–59; Bethmann Hollweg relation to, 172–73; Netherlands relation to, 102–3, 167, 170, 174; Paris Peace Conference and, 66; precedent and, 157; Treaty of Versailles and, 34; U.S. relation to, 110

Ambrose (Saint), 247
Ambrosiaster, 246–47
American Civil War, 29, 270
American Journal of International Law (AJIL), xxv, 14
American Society of International Law (ASIL), 1
apartheid, 228
Appeals Chamber: of ICC, xxiv, xxv, 19, 88; of SCSL, 234–35
armed robbery, war compared to, 26
arms limitation, 29–30
Arrest Warrant case, xxii, 235–36
Arthur (Prince), 78
article 2(4), of UN Charter, 286
article 7, of IMTN Charter, 226, 229, 231
article 13(b), of Rome Statute, 17
article 15bis(5), of Rome Statute, 17, 273
article 227, of Treaty of Versailles, 67–73, 75, 81, 167, 183, 199–200; article 7, of IMTN Charter relation to, 226; Council of Four relation to, 156–57, 159; ICC relation to, 149; Lloyd George and, 231; Netherlands relation to, 180; Nuremberg Charter compared to, 206; Schabas on, 154–55; U.S. relation to, 152–53, 330n5; Wilson, W., and, 144, 152–53, 158–59, 165
article 228, of Treaty of Versailles, 150, 187–88

ASIL. *See* American Society of
    International Law
asylum: non-refoulment and, 180–81; of
    Wilhelm II, 167–68
atomic bombing, 37, 211
Auchincloss, Gordon, 162n†
Augustine (Saint), 26, 28n†, 247
Australia, 181; racism and, 151

Bacon, Francis, 254
Bagosora, Theonéste, xv, 2, 115n★, 233; at
    ICTR, xvi
Balfour, Arthur, 151; Netherlands relation
    to, 172
Balkan Wars, 272
balloons, 30
Barnes, Robert, 248, 249
Al-Bashir, Omar, xxiv
Battle of Solferino, 270–71
Battle of Waterloo, 31
Belgium, 33, 286–87; Democratic
    Republic of Congo and, 235; Lloyd
    George relation to, 156n★; Ndombasi
    and, xxii; in World War I, 59
Bentinck (Count), 79, 167
Berlin Wall, 237
Bethmann Hollweg, Theobald von,
    172–73
Bidault, Georges, 197
Biddle, Francis, 194, 201; IMTN and, 213;
    International Criminal Code and, 217–
    18; resolution 95(I) relation to, 214–15;
    Truman relation to, 216, 218–19
Biden, Joe, xiii–xiv, 200; Putin relation to,
    2–3, 12
*The Big Four and Others of the Peace
    Conference* (Lansing), 163
biology, natural law of, 284
Birkenhead (Lord Chancellor), 63, 82, 84,
    99, 255; Crown Liability Act relation
    to, 258; Macdonell Committee and,
    104. *See also* Smith, Frederick E., KC
Birkett (Justice), 213
Blackstone, William, 250–53, 257–58, 262;
    on emperors, 260–61
blood feud, 54
Bodin, Jean, 265, 266, 267

Bohlen und Halbach, Gustab Krupp von,
    213
Bonaparte, Napoleon, 20, 101, 102, 142,
    277–78; exile of, 181; *Schooner Exchange*
    case relation to, 258; U.S. relation to,
    139
Bormann, Martin, 8; conviction of,
    213–14
Briand, Aristide, 38
Briand-Kellogg Pact, 36–40, 42, 44, 47;
    IMTN relation to, 49; Nazis relation
    to, 48; Tokyo Tribunal relation to, 51;
    wars of aggression relation to, 55
Brierly, J. L., 313n83
British Empire, 125; *haut tribunal* and, 109–
    11; Pollock, E., relation to, 116–17,
    129; racism and, 151; stature of, 152.
    See also United Kingdom
British House of Lords, 8; Pinochet and,
    xxii
Brown, Gordon, 12, 19
Brussels Declaration (1874), 29n★, 30
Bynkershoek, Cornelius, 88, 89–90

Cadogan, Alexander, 195, 201
Caligula, 102, 241; divine right of kings
    and, 244
Cambodia, Khmer Rouge in, xv
Cardinals, 262
Cardogan, Alexander, 278
Carlyle, A. J., 249
Carlyle, R. W., 249
Cassese, Antonio, 235
Castlereagh (Lord), 61
Chad, 16
Charlemagne, 262
Charles I, 70, 142, 261n★
charter: of IMTFE, 304n138; of IMTN,
    45–46, 48–49, 50, 56, 121, 205–7, 218,
    220–23, 226, 229, 231, 242, 271; of
    Tokyo Tribunal, 50–52; of UN, 286
China, 40
Christian (Queen), 86
Churchill, Winston, 201; Declaration
    of Atrocities relation to, 193; Hitler
    relation to, 3; Yalta Memorandum and,
    40

Church of England, 263
civilization, war relation to, 270
"civilized nations," 43, 85
civil liability: for crime of aggression, 274; sovereignty and, 261
Clause 10, of Yalta Memorandum, 198
Clausewitz, Carl von, 28n★
Clemenceau, Georges, xvii, 64, 66, 147, 172; Council of Four relation to, 97; Curzon and, 84; Germany relation to, 171; at Inter-Allied meeting, 65, 93–95; judicial process and, 278; Lloyd George and, 68–69, 72–73, 307n32; moral condemnation and, 124; Netherlands relation to, 173–74; at Paris Peace Conference, 69–72, 98; prosecution relation to, 170; on Supreme Council, 178; Wilhelm II relation to, 3; Wilson, W., relation to, 155, 169
Clement VII (Pope), 263
coercive orders, 7
Cold War, 15–16, 200, 236–37
The Colonel (Hodgson), 37–38
Commentaries on the Laws of England (Blackstone), 250–51
commerce, 57
commercial interests, in wars of aggression, 276
Commission on the Responsibility of the Authors of the War and the Enforcement of Penalties, of Paris Peace Conference, 33, 69, 98–99, 105, 131–36; Council of Four and, 141–44; international tribunal and, 108; Lansing and, 99, 121–23, 146, 332n42; Pollock, E., relation to, 230; prosecution and, 155. See also Sub-commission III, of Paris Peace Conference
Committee of Enquiry into Breaches of the Laws and Customs of War. See Macdonell Committee
common law crimes, 139–40
common sense, 280
condemnation, morality and, 122, 124, 158
Congress of Vienna (1815), 60–61
constitutional monarchies, 52n★
contract debts, 30

Control Council Law no. 10, 206–7
Convention on the Punishment and Prevention of the Crime of Genocide, 271
convictions, of IMTN, 213–14
corruption, 255
Council of Europe, 16; Parliamentary Assembly Report of, 239
Council of Four, 34, 35, 64, 69–72; article 227 relation to, 156–57, 159; Clemenceau relation to, 97; Commission on the Responsibility of the Authors of the War and the Enforcement of Penalties, of Paris Peace Conference and, 141–44; jus ad bellum and, 155–56; Orlando relation to, 156n†
Council on Foreign Relations, 14; Stimson at, 38–39
covenant, of League of Nations, 151, 330n12
Crimea, Sevastopol, xiii
Crimean Conference, 40
Crimean War, 29, 270
crime of aggression, 19–20, 44–45, 202–3; accountability and, 12–13; debate of, 25–26; global superpowers and, 14–15; ICC relation to, 27; in IMTFE trial, 207; jus ad bellum and, 99; prosecution of, 273, 274; Rome Statute relation to, 4–6, 272–73; self-interest and, 16–17; soldiers and, 4–10, 273; Tokyo Tribunal relation to, 51–53; UN Security Council and, 11–12, 13–14; of Wilhelm II, 33–34, 69–70
crimes against humanity, 3, 65, 161; culpability and, 9; of Hitler, 193; IMTN and, 215; individual criminal responsibility for, 223; in Nuremberg Principles, 227; prosecution of, 206; punishment for, 95; in Sierra Leone, 119; of Wilhelm II, 69–70
crimes against peace, 41, 42, 50, 223, 304n138; wars of aggression relation to, 225
criminal omission, 150
criticism, of article 227, 159

Crown Liability Act (1947), 258
Cuban Missile Crisis, 37
cuius regio, eius religio, 264
culpability, 5–9
Currant (newspaper), 139
Curzon (Lord), 68–69, 95, 278, 305n155;
   Clemenceau and, 84
customary international law, 59, 240;
   debate of, xx–xxi

Daily Mail (newspaper), 76
D'Amelio, Mariano, 113, 132
Darfur, 287
David, in Old Testament, 244–45, 248
death penalty, 261, 261n★
debate: of crime of aggression, 25–26; of
   customary international law, xx–xxi
debts, contract, 30
Declaration of Atrocities, in Moscow
   Declaration, 193, 333n62
Declaration of St. Petersburg (1868), 161
De Clementia (Seneca), 243–44, 246
Decree of Infallibility, 164
De Jure Belli ac Pacis (Grotius), 26
delegation theory, 283–84
democracy, 249
Democratic Republic of Congo, 235,
   286–87
Demons (Lieutenant), 259
derivative jurisdiction, 21–22
Dicey, A. V., 251–52
Dikko, Umaru, 77–78
Disraeli, Benjamin, 260
divine being, 253
divine right of kings, 201–2, 266, 267;
   Caligula and, 244; immunity and,
   242–43, 254, 260; in New Testament,
   245–46; in Old Testament, 244–45,
   248; patriarchy and, 249–50; Protestant
   Reformation and, 248–49; punishment
   relation to, 247; royal dignity and,
   252–53
Dönitz, Karl, xvi; prosecution of, 231
Doyle, Arthur Conan, 77
draft article 7, of ILC, xxv–xxvii, 135,
   187, xxvinn★–†, xxvn★

Draft Code of Crimes against the Peace
   and Security of Mankind, 227, 228–30,
   238
Draft Code of Offences against the Peace
   and Security of Mankind, 227
drafting committee, 108–9, 113, 121;
   Politis and, 114
due process, 278–79
Dunant, Henry, 29, 270–71
duty, 316n133
Dworkin, Ronald, 280

Eastern Galicia, 142
East Timor, 238–39
Eden, Anthony, 197
effective control, 116
Eighth Army, of Germany, 188
Eighth Assembly, of League of Nations, 42
Eighty Years' War, 270
ejusdem generis rule, 130
emperors, 260–61; of Holy Roman
   Empire, 262–63. *See also* Hirohito
   (Emperor)
equality, of sovereigns, 20, 266
Escobar Hernández, Concepción, xxii, xxv
ethnic cleansing, in Yugoslavia, 236–37
European Court of Human Rights, 8
European Union, 239
ex abundanti cautela, 238
*Examen de la responsabilité pénale de
   l'Empereur Guillaume II*, 96
exile, 181–83, 288
extrajudicial banishment, 20

Falco, R., 213
federal courts, 140
Ferdinand II, 263, 264
fiction, 250, 254–55; "Vicar of God," 257
Filmer, Robert, 249–50
Finlay (Lord), 77
Finnis, John, 280
Fireside Chat no. 23 (Roosevelt, F.), 192
First Hague Peace Conference (1899), 30,
   36, 58, 58nn★–†
first limitation, to Rome Statute, 10
force, use of, 342n54

Foreign Affairs (magazine), 53
France, 68, 76, 125; *haut tribunal* and, 109; *Lotus* case and, 259; Ministry of War of, 96; public opinion in, 105; stature of, 152; War of Religion in, 265; in World War I, 75, 103, 124
Francis II, 264
freedom, 249
frozen assets, 275

G7, international criminal tribunal of, 16
G77, 16
Garçon, Emile Auguste, 96
Garner, James W., 185–86
Garrett, John W., 168
Gembloux, 247
Geneva, 151
Geneva Convention, 29, 30, 85, 270–71
Geneva Protocol for the Pacific Settlement of International Disputes (1924), 42
genocide, 2, 3, 6, 25, 228, 271; accountability for, 22; culpability and, 9; in Nuremberg Principles, 227; in Rwanda, 236–37; wars of aggression and, 10
Gentilis, Alberico, 87, 88
Geoghegan, Tom, 182
geopolitical power, scholarship relation to, 22
George V, 255
George VI, 210
Germany, 76, 173; draft article 7 and, xxvi–xxvii, xxvin†; Lloyd George relation to, 170–71; Macdonell Committee relation to, 82–83; Mexico relation to, 100; Poland and, xiv–xv; Reichsgericht of, 187–88; treaties relation to, 160; wars of aggression of, 132, 243; Wilhelm II relation to, 70–71; in World War I, 32, 59
gerrymandering, in immunity reasoning, 22
Gestapo, 194–95
Gevorgian, Kirill, xxi
Ghana, 234
Gigantia (fictional), 6
glasnost, 237

global superpowers, crime of aggression and, 14–15
Goler T. Butcher Medal, 1
Gorbachev, Mikhail, 200
Göring, Hermann, xvi; conviction of, 213–14
Gough, Alfred, 77
GPPN. *See* Group of Prosperous and Progressive Nations
Great Britain, 46
Great Peasants' Revolt, 248
Greetham, William, 258
Gregorian school, 247
Gregory (Saint), 244, 246, 248
Grey, Jane, 261n★
Grotius, Hugo, 26, 28n★, 44, 88, 203, 266; on force, 342n54; on war, 354n32
Group of Prosperous and Progressive Nations (GPPN), 6
Gunther, Franklin Mott, 174–76
Guterres, Antonio, 269
Guttery, Arthur, 77

Habré, Hissène, 16
Habyarimana, Juvénal, xv, 233
The Hague, Netherlands, 180
Hague Conventions, 29n★, 85, 132, 350n9; international relations and, 306n7; Respecting the Laws and Customs of War on Land, 62, 161–62, 161n★; Respecting the Rights and Duties of Neutral Powers and Persons in Case of War on Land, 160, 171–72
Hague Peace conferences, 85, 271
Hague Regulations, 312n70
Hampshire, HMS, 83
Hankey, Maurice, 83
Hariri, Rafik, 238
Harrison, Frederic, 77
Hart, H. L. A., 280
The Hashemite Kingdom of Jordan, xxiv
Hatton, Christopher, 87
haut tribunal (high tribunal), 109–11
Havana Resolution, 301n98
heads of state. *See* sovereigns
Henry VIII, 248, 263
Hess, Rudolf, xvi, 213–14

Hewart, Gordon, KC, 92, 99
Higgins, Pearce, 81
high tribunal (*haut tribunal*), 109–11
Hindenburg, Paul von, 188
Hirohito (Emperor), 50, 52n★, 211; HMG compared to, 210; prosecution of, 208–9; punishment of, 343n4; Wilhelm II compared to, 207–8
Hiroshima, 37, 38, 211
His Britannic Majesty's Government (HMG), 195–97, 201, 209–10
historical documents, xx
Hitler, Adolf, xiii, xv, xvi, 2, 3, 53; crimes against humanity of, 193; Hindenburg relation to, 188; immunity and, 22; prosecution of, 191–92, 196–97; punishment of, 194, 195–96, 198–99
HMG. *See* His Britannic Majesty's Government
Hobbes, Thomas, 27–28
Hodgson, Godfrey, 37–38
Holdsworth, William, 253–54, 258
Holmes, Oliver Wendell, Jr., 7
Holocaust, 25
Holy Roman Empire, 262, 265; Peace of Westphalia relation to, 263–64
honors-based international humanitarian law system, 63
Hoover (President), 37
House, Edward Mandell, 95, 162n†, 169; on Lansing, 164; at Paris Peace Conference, 101
Hughes, Billy, 151; article 227 and, 159
Huguenots, 265
humanity, laws of, 85, 162n★
Human Rights Committee, UN, 8
Hussein, Saddam, 27

ICC. *See* International Criminal Court
ICJ. *See* International Court of Justice
ICTR. *See* International Criminal Tribunal for Rwanda
ICTY. *See* International Criminal Tribunal for the former Yugoslavia
Igbo parable, 18
ILC. *See* UN International Law Commission

Immunities of State Officials from Foreign Criminal Jurisdictions, of ILC, xxii, 135
immunity. *See specific topics*
immunity *ratione materiae*, 149–50–150, 235
immunity *ratione personae*, 150
immunity reasoning, gerrymandering in, 22
immunity-tolerant scholarship, 20, 21, 22, 121
impartiality, in international tribunal, 138
Imperial Cabinet, of United Kingdom, 305n155
imperialism, 44
Imperial War Cabinet, 92–93
IMTFE. *See* International Military Tribunal for the Far East
IMTN. *See* International Military Tribunal in Nuremberg
individual criminal responsibility, 223, 285; official position relation to, 230; punishment and, 225–26; of Wilhelm II, 316n131
Industrial Revolution, 39
insurgency, xix
Inter-Allied meeting (1918), 65, 91–95
Inter-Allied Parliamentary Committee, 77
International Commission on the Inquiry, 123
International Court of Justice (ICJ), xxii; *Arrest Warrant* case in, 235–36; *Reparation* case in, 286
international courts: derivative jurisdiction in, 21–22; national courts relation to, xxiii
International Criminal Code, 214, 217–18
International Criminal Court (ICC), 236–37, 272; absentia prosecution in, 8; Appeals Chamber of, xxiv, xxv, 19, 88; article 227 relation to, 149; crime of aggression relation to, 27; jurisdiction of, 283; Rome Statute and, 4, 10–11; Trump relation to, 200; UN General Assembly relation to, 17–18, 273; U.S. relation to, 14–15. *See also* Rome Statute
International Criminal Tribunal for Rwanda (ICTR), xvi, 279; Nuremberg Principles and, 233

International Criminal Tribunal for the former Yugoslavia (ICTY), 233, 279; Mladić and, 322n234
international law. *See specific topics*
International Law Association, 241–42
International Military Tribunal for the Far East (IMTFE), 207–8, 271; charter of, 304n138
International Military Tribunal in Nuremberg (IMTN), xvi, xxiii, 41, 47, 53–54; charter of, 45–46, 48–49, 50, 56, 121, 205–7, 218, 220–23, 226, 229, 231, 242, 271; convictions of, 213–14; ILC relation to, 224–25; Jackson relation to, 42–43, 191; new international order and, 215–16; Paris Peace Conference compared to, 200; precedent and, 203; Tokyo Tribunal relation to, 51–52; UN relation to, 216, 218, 219–21; wars of aggression relation to, 10, 42–43
international morality, 34–35, 67
international relations, 354n25; Hague Conventions and, 306n7; natural sciences compared to, 284; sovereignty relation to, 264–65
international tribunal, 84–85, 115, 219, 307n32; Commission on the Responsibility of the Authors of the War and the Enforcement of Penalties, of Paris Peace Conference and, 108; judicial process in, 277–78; jurisdiction of, 147–48, 283–86; Lansing and, 105–7, 123, 164–65, 321n230; Larnaude-La Pradelle study and, 110–11, 146; Politis and, 125–26; precedent for, 137–39, 164–65; for prosecution, 91, 94, 95, 146n★, 160, 205–6; punishment by, 137; for sovereigns, 117–20, 127; Sub-commission III, of Paris Peace Conference and, 104–8, 160; U.S. and, 109–10, 112–13, 321n230, 332n42
interpretation, of treaties, 159
"Invasion of Belgium and Luxemburg in Breach of Treaties," 33
Iraq, U.S. and, 12, 27
Irenaeus (Saint), 247

Iron Curtain, 237
Isidore (Saint), 247
isolation, of U.S., 100–101
Israel, 78, 353n17
Italy, 104
ius puniendi, 285

Jackson, Robert H., 16–17, 20–21, 41, 187, 197, 203–4; on crime of aggression, 44–45; divine right of kings and, 242, 243, 253; on due process, 278–79; IMTN relation to, 42–43, 191; on international law, 45–46; London Conference relation to, 194; Truman relation to, 199, 200, 201–2, 206
Japan, 40, 153; IMTFE and, 208; MacArthur relation to, 210n★; memoranda of reservations of, 136, 141; at Paris Peace Conference, 151; surrender of, 210–11; in World War II, 322n233
Johnson, Boris, 2
Jordan Referral re Al-Bashir (2019), xxiv, xxv, 19, 183
judicial accountability, monarchy and, 257–58
judicial process, in international tribunal, 277–78
Judiciary Act (1789), 139
jurisdiction: derivative, 21–22; of international tribunal, 147–48, 283–86; of national courts, 135; nationality principle of, 109–10, 112; sovereigns and, 89–90; of state courts, 140; in U.S., 139
jurisprudence, of international law, 25
jus ad bellum, 92, 99, 132, 134–35; Council of Four and, 155–56. *See also* wars of aggression
jus in bello, 92, 132–35; laws and customs relation to, 99; prosecution of, 137. *See also* war crimes
jus puniendi, 56, 62, 66, 83, 243; Lloyd George and, 68
justice, 122, 279–80; international law relation to, 69; neutrality in, 112; punishment relation to, 198;

sovereignty relation to, 189; summary execution relation to, 199; Yalta Memorandum relation to, 195
Juvenal, 92

Kambanda, Jean, 115n★, 233
Kampala, Review Conference in, 295n12
Kampala Conference, 14
Karnebeek, Harman van, 174
Katsav, Moshe, 353n17
Kellogg, Frank B., 38
Kennedy (President), 37
Kerr, Philip, 34
Khmer Rouge, xv
kidnapping, of Dikko, 77–78
Kipling, Rudyard, 46
Kitchener (Lord), 83
Kolodkin, Roman, xxi–xxiii
Koskenniemi, Matti, 279–80
Kosovo, 239–40
Kreß, Claus, 149–50, 285
Ku Klux Klan, 151

laissez-faire, martial, 35–36
Lansing, Robert, 34–35, 69, 72, 103; Commission on the Responsibility of the Authors of the War and the Enforcement of Penalties and, 99, 121–23, 146, 332n42; on condemnation, 158; *haut tribunal* and, 109–11; immunity *ratione materiae* and, 149–50; international tribunal and, 105–7, 123, 164–65, 321n230; Larnaude relation to, 113–14, 124–25; memoranda of reservations and, 136–38, 141; nationality principle and, 112; Netherlands relation to, 170, 174–76, 199–200; Pollock, E., relation to, 113–14, 116–18, 122, 126–27, 128, 140, 152n★; sovereignty relation to, 185, 186–87; on Sub-commission III, 104, 107–8, 115–16, 120, 130–32, 145, 146n★, 164; *U.S. v. Hudson* and, 139, 140; Wilson, W., relation to, 112, 127, 138, 141–42, 144–46, 147, 152–55, 154nn★–†, 157, 160–64, 162n†, 169, 176–77, 334n63

La Poittevin, Alfred, 96
La Pradelle, Albert Geouffre de, 33, 34, 88–89, 95–97, 96n★; Larnaude and, 146–47; at Paris Peace Conference, 98; on Sub-commission III, 100
Larnaude, Ferdinand, 33, 34, 88–89, 95–97, 96n★; *haut tribunal* and, 111; Lansing relation to, 113–14, 124–25; La Pradelle and, 146–47; Massey relation to, 128; at Paris Peace Conference, 98; Pollock, E., and, 105, 106, 119–20, 121, 131–32; on Sub-commission III, 100
Larnaude–La Pradelle study, 96, 97, 108, 125, 144, 316n131; international tribunal and, 110–11, 146
Law Officers of the Crown, 80
law of nations, 57; in *Respublica v. De Longchamps*, 141
law of neutrality, 171–72
Lawrence (Lord Justice), 213
laws and customs: *jus in bello* relation to, 99; of war, 137, 139, 143, 155, 187–88
laws of humanity, 85, 162n★
Lea, Luke, 78–80, 208
League of Nations, 39, 63–64, 301n97, 307n32; Clemenceau relation to, 94; covenant of, 151, 330n12; Eighth Assembly of, 42; Netherlands in, 179–80; Paris Peace Conference relation to, 59, 271; U.S. relation to, 40; Wilson, W., and, 36, 76, 316n131
Lebanon, 238
legal fictions, 68
legal personality, 286
legal philosophy, 280
legal responsibility, 70–71
legislative fact, 4
Leipzig proceedings, 187–89
Leopold II, 118–19
Lerner (Baron), 188, 189
Ley, Robert, 213
Liberia, 234, 285; Sierra Leone and, 20
Lie, Trygve, 219
Lieber Code, 29, 29n★, 270, 348n18
Lincoln, Abraham, 29, 62
Lloyd George, David, xvii, 3, 33–34, 61–62, 66, 103; Belgium relation to,

156n★; Clemenceau and, 68–69, 72–73, 307n32; on Council of Four, 142–43; on criminal law, 159; divine right of kings and, 242–43; Germany relation to, 170–71; Hankey and, 83; at Inter-Allied meeting, 65, 91, 93–95; on Italy, 104; judicial process and, 278; Lansing relation to, 164, 165; on League of Nations, 63; on Macdonell Committee, 82; at Paris Peace Conference, 69–70, 98, 231; on peace, 335n85; prosecution relation to, 77, 182–83; on punishment, 76; on Supreme Council, 178; on treaties, 64; on Treaty of Versailles, 165–66; Wilson, W., relation to, 65, 155, 169, 181, 209

London Agreement (1945), 41
London Conference (1945), 12–13, 193, 201, 205, 237; Jackson relation to, 194
Lotus case, 259
Louis XIV, 87; divine right of kings and, 243, 244
Louis XVI, 70, 261n★
Ludendorff, Erich, 188
Lusitania, 100
Luther, Martin, 247–48

MacArthur, Douglas, 50, 207, 208; Japan relation to, 210n★
Macdonell, John, KC, 81, 86–87, 313n83; on Grotius, 88; on Phillimore, 90
Macdonell Committee, 32–34, 63, 81, 98, 125, 134n★; Birkenhead and, 104; Germany relation to, 82–83; immunity and, 86; international tribunal and, 110–11, 146; Larnaude–La Pradelle study compared to, 96, 97; precedent and, 85; on prosecution, 144; Special Sub-committee on Law of, 91, 93
MacMillan, Margaret, 57, 60, 61
Macron, Emmanuel, 2
Maitland, William, 251, 254, 260
Makino (Baron), 170, 172
Mandela, Nelson, 237
Mantoux, Paul, 155, 172–73
Marie Antoinette, 261n★
maritime warfare, 30

Marshall, John, 259
Martens, Fyodor Fyodorovich, 85
Martens Clause, 85, 161–62, 162n★, 312n70
martial laissez-faire, 35–36
Mary, Queen of Scots, 86–87, 88, 142
Massey, William, 77, 121, 124, 126–27; Larnaude relation to, 128; on Sub-commission III, 99–100
Matsui, 178
McFaddon, John, 258
memoranda, of reservations, 136–38, 141, 144–45
Mendelson, M. H., 220, 285–86
mens rea, actus reus compared to, 5
Mexico, 100
Midleton (Lord), 77
military expenditure, 58, 58n★
Millerand, Alexandre, 189
Milošević, Slobodan, 233
Ministry of War, of France, 96
Minoria (fictional), 6
Mladić, Slobodan, 322n234
Molotov, Vyacheslav, 192, 197
monarchy, 52n★, 209–10, 243, 265; absolute perfection and, 250–51; absolute submission to, 249; judicial accountability and, 257–58
Monroe Doctrine, 151, 330n12
moral choice, crime of aggression and, 7, 9
moral condemnation, 122, 124, 158
morality, 280; condemnation and, 122, 124, 158; international, 34–35, 67
moral sanctions, 136, 332n42
Morgan (Professor), 90–91
Morgenthau, Henry, 278, 354n2
Morris (Lord), 77
Moscow Declaration, 196; Declaration of Atrocities in, 193
multilateral clearinghouse arrangement, 264–65
municipal law, 63; international law compared to, 311n56
Mussolini, 192–93; punishment of, 195–96

Nagasaki, 37, 38, 211
Napoleonic Wars, 60–61

narrative synthesis, xvii
National Council of Evangelical Free
    Churches, 63, 66, 68, 76
national courts: international courts
    relation to, xxiii; jurisdiction of, 135
national criminal code, 239
nationality principle, of jurisdiction, 109–
    10, 112
natural law, 280; of biology, 284
natural sciences, 284
Nazis, xiv–xv, 42, 45, 46; accountability
    of, 53–54; treaties relation to, 48; Yalta
    Memorandum relation to, 194–95. *See
    also* International Military Tribunal in
    Nuremberg
Ndombasi, Yerodia, xxii
Nero, 243–44, 246
Netherlands, 199–200; Allied and
    Associated Powers relation to, 102–3,
    167, 170, 174; Balfour relation to,
    172; Clemenceau relation to, 173–74;
    neutrality of, 180–81; Supreme Council
    relation to, 178–80; U.S. relation to,
    174–76; Wilhelm II in, 78–80, 101,
    102–3, 167–68
neutrality, 180n★; in justice, 112; law of,
    171–72; of Netherlands, 180–81
new international order, IMTN and,
    215–16
New Testament, 245–46
New York State Bar Association, 63, 76, 84
New York Times (newspaper), 77
Nicholas II (Czar), 30, 58, 255
Nigeria, 77–78, 167
Nikitchenko, I. T., 213, 214
Nolte, Georg, xxviii★
"Nomenclature of the Sovereigns and
    Rulers of States Represented at the
    Peace Conference," 243, 350n9
non-refoulment, 180–81
Noriega, Manuel, xxii
North Korea, wars of aggression of, 18
nullum crimen sine lege, 139, 140, 157
Nuremberg Principles, 224–28, 231, 233;
    Kosovo relation to, 239–40; Rome
    Statute relation to, 236, 237–38

Nuremberg Tribunal. *See* International
    Military Tribunal in Nuremberg

The Obedience of Christian Men (Tyndale),
    248–49
objections, advocacy and, 161
Die Obriegkeit, 248
official position, individual criminal
    responsibility relation to, 230
Old Testament, divine right of kings in,
    244–45, 248
opinio juris, xx
Orentlicher, Diane, 234; *Arrest Warrant*
    case and, 235–36
Orlando, Vittorio, 65; Council of Four
    relation to, 156n†; at Inter-Allied
    meeting, 93–95; at Paris Peace
    Conference, 69–71, 72
Oxford Manual, 180n★

Palais de Nation, xxvi
Papen, Franz von, 188
parable, Igbo, 18
Paris Declaration (1856), 29, 270
Paris Peace Conference (1919), xvii,
    31, 66, 71, 98; Congress of Vienna
    compared to, 60–61; IMTN
    compared to, 200; Japan at, 151;
    League of Nations relation to, 59,
    271; Lloyd George at, 69–70, 98,
    231; wars of aggression relation to,
    34–35, 55; Wilson, W., at, 60, 69,
    72, 101, 165, 199, 241–42. *See also*
    Commission on the Responsibility
    of the Authors of the War and the
    Enforcement of Penalties, of Paris
    Peace Conference
Parker, John J., 213
Parliamentary Assembly Report, of
    Council of Europe (2011), 239
Patriacha (Filmer), 249–50
patriarchy, divine right of kings and,
    249–50
Paul (Saint), 245–46, 248
PCIJ. *See* Permanent Court of
    International Justice

peace, 218, 285; crimes against, 41, 42, 50, 223, 225, 304n138; punishment and, 335n85; right to, 274–76
The Peace Negotiations (Lansing), 163
Peace of Augsburg, 264
Peace of Westphalia, 57–58, 262, 263–65, 266, 270
Peisistratus, 182
penal regulation, 62
peremptory capability, 6
perestroika, 237
Permanent Court of International Justice (PCIJ), 259
personal responsibility, of sovereigns, 133
Peter (Saint), 245–46
Phillimore (Lord), 89–90
Phillips, William, 169
Phillipson, Coleman, 63, 274
Philo, of Alexandria, 26
physics, 284
Pichon, Stephen, 76
Pinochet, Augusto, xxii
Pinochet cases, 234–35
Poland, xiii, 231, 301n97; Draft Code of Crimes against the Peace and Security of Mankind and, 238; Germany and, xiv–xv; Ukraine and, 142
political expediency, Rome Statute and, 16–17
politics, 68
Politis, Nikolaos, 111–12, 113, 118, 119, 128–29; drafting committee and, 114; international tribunal and, 125–26; Pollock, E., relation to, 133
Pollock, Charles, 102
Pollock, Ernest, KC, 34, 98, 102; British Empire relation to, 116–17, 129; Commission on the Responsibility of the Authors of the War and the Enforcement of Penalties, of Paris Peace Conference relation to, 230; on drafting committee, 109; on *ejusdem generis* rule, 130; *haut tribunal* and, 110–11; Lansing relation to, 113–14, 116–18, 122, 126–27, 128, 140, 152n★; Larnaude and, 105, 106, 119–20, 121, 131–32; Politis relation to, 133;

Scott relation to, 107, 152n★; on Subcommission III, 99, 104, 107–8
Pollock, Frederick, KC, 81, 251, 254, 260; on precedent, 85
the pope, 246, 248, 261, 262, 266; divine right of kings and, 244; Peace of Westphalia relation to, 263–64
positive law, 23
Pot, Pol, xv, xvi, 2, 22
Potsdam Declaration, 193
precedent, 68–73, 75; Allied and Associated Powers and, 157; in article 227, 159; IMTN and, 203; for international tribunal, 137–39, 164–65; Lansing relation to, 153; Macdonell Committee and, 85; sovereignty and, 186
princep legibus solutus, 90, 97, 243, 260
principal perpetrators, in crime of aggression, 9
prisoners, of war, 88
private duels, 27–28, 28n★
procreation, 284
pro-immunity advocates, xxi
prosecution, 134; in absentia, 8; Commission on the Responsibility of the Authors of the War and the Enforcement of Penalties, of Paris Peace Conference and, 155; of crime of aggression, 273, 274; of crimes against humanity, 206; of Dönitz, 231; of Hirohito, 208–9; of Hitler, 191–92, 196–97; international tribunal for, 91, 94, 95, 146n★, 160, 205; of *jus in bello*, 137; Lloyd George relation to, 77, 182–83; Netherlands relation to, 170; of sovereigns, 125, 137, 144, 183; by UN, 193; of war crimes, 76–77, 144, 197, 206, 214; of wars of aggression, 136, 144; Wilhelm II and, 80, 84, 86, 91–95, 100, 104–5, 124, 153, 160, 169, 174–75, 180, 240; Wilson, W., relation to, 157, 170
Prosecutor v. Charles Taylor, 183
Protestant Reformation, 248–49
public opinion, 11, 100, 110, 111, 123, 279; in France, 105; retribution and,

122; of war crimes, 21, 76–77; of
   Wilhelm II, 80
publish-or-perish culture, xix
Pufendorf, Samuel von, 88
Punch cartoon, 177, *177*, 178
punishment, 64, 65–66, 285; for crimes
   against humanity, 95; divine right
   of kings relation to, 247; exile as,
   181–83, 288; of Hirohito, 343n4;
   of Hitler, 194, 195–96, 198–99;
   individual criminal responsibility and,
   225–26; by international tribunal,
   137; justice relation to, 198; in Lieber
   Code, 348n18; peace and, 335n85; of
   summary execution, 195–96; for war,
   68, 76–77, 354n32; of Wilhelm II, 75,
   92, 142, 305n155
Putin, Vladimir, 4, 16, 23, 200, 243; Biden
   relation to, 2–3, 12; crime of aggression
   and, 10, 19–20; Ukraine and, xiii–xiv,
   xv, xvi, xxiv

qui facit per alium facit per se, 285

R2P. *See* Responsibility to Protect
racial equality clause, in League of Nations
   Covenant, 151
racism, 151
rage, 272
rationalization, in crime of aggression,
   14–15
Raz, Joseph, 280
Red Cross Society, 270
Reformation movement, 248, 263
Refugee Convention (1950), 181
Reichsgericht, of Germany, 187–88
reparation, 275
Reparation case, 286
reservations, memoranda of, 136–38, 141,
   144–45
resignation, of soldiers, 4–5
resolution 36/106, of UN General
   Assembly, 228
resolution 95(I), of UN General Assembly,
   50; IMTN Charter relation to, 220–21;
   Truman relation to, 214–15

resolution 177(II), of UN General
   Assembly, 220, 227; ILC relation to,
   221–24
Respecting the Laws and Customs of
   War on Land, Hague Convention, 62,
   161–62, 161n*
Respecting the Rights and Duties of
   Neutral Powers and Persons in Case of
   War on Land, Hague Convention, 160,
   171–72
Responsibility to Protect (R2P), 272
Respublica v. De Longchamps, 141
retribution, public opinion and, 122
retroactivity, 150
retrospective law, 138–39
Review Conference, in Kampala, 295n12
rex non potest preccare, 243, 260
right to peace, 274–76
right to reparation, 275
Robertson, George Stuart, 257, 258
Rolin-Jaequemyns, Edouard, 118–19,
   131–32
Rome Statute, 10, 215, 277, 287;
   article 15bis(5) of, 17, 273; crime of
   aggression relation to, 4–6, 272–73;
   legal personality in, 286; Nuremberg
   Principles relation to, 236, 237–38;
   political expediency and, 16–17;
   Review Conference relation to,
   295n12; Russia and, 11–12; UN
   General Assembly relation to, 236;
   UN Security Council relation to, 18;
   U.S. relation to, 14. *See also* crime of
   aggression
Roosevelt, Eleanor, 284
Roosevelt, Franklin D., 37, 197;
   Declaration of Atrocities relation
   to, 193; Hitler relation to, 3;
   on prosecution, 191–92; Yalta
   Memorandum and, 40
Roosevelt, Teddy, 162n†
Root, Elihu, 37
Rosenman, Samuel, 195, 197
Rosental, S., 109, 113
Ross, Alf, 280
royal dignity, 252–53

royal prerogatives, 254
Royal Titles Act (1876), 260
Ruijs de Beerenbrouck, Charles, 167
rules-based order, international law as, 185
Russia, 23; crime of aggression and, 17, 26; Rome Statute and, 11–12; Ukraine and, xiii–xiv, xv, xxi–xxii, 2, 10, 13, 103, 269–70; UN relation to, 27; UN Security Council relation to, 15
"Russian Officer Reveals Why He Risked It All to Quit Putin's War," 4
Rwanda, xv, 272; genocide in, 236–37
Rwandan Civil War, 272

SA. *See* Sturmabteilung
sanctions, 32, 63, 274; moral, 136, 332n42
Sands, Philippe, 234–35
Sandström, Emile, 223
San Francisco Conference for the United Nations Organization, 40, 197
San Francisco Memorandum, 198–99
Satires (Juvenal), 92
Saul (King), 245, 248
Savigny, Friedrich Karl von, 75
Schabas, William, 78, 149, 152, 330n5; on article 227, 154–55; on Treaty of Versailles, 168
scholarship, immunity-tolerant, 20, 21, 22, 121
Schooner Exchange case, 127, 150, 243, 258–60
Schutzstaffel (SS), 194–95
Scott, James Brown, 34–35, 101–3, 127–28; on Bonaparte, 277–78; drafting committee and, 109, 113–14; immunity *ratione materiae* and, 149–50; international tribunal and, 123; memoranda of reservations and, 136–38, 141; Netherlands relation to, 174–75; Pollock, E., relation to, 107, 152n★; sovereignty relation to, 185, 186–87; on Sub-commission III, 99, 104; *U.S. v. Hudson* and, 139, 140; Wilson, W., relation to, 152
SCSL. *See* Special Court for Sierra Leone
Second Hague Peace Conference (1907), 30–31, 36; Respecting Laws and Customs of War on Land of, 62, 161–62, 161n★; treaties at, 58–59
Second Italian War of Independence, 29, 270–71
sedition charges, 139–40
self-defense, 276; war of, 20, 36–37
self-interest, crime of aggression and, 16–17
Seneca, 243–44, 246
Sevastopol, Crimea, xiii
Shaw, Malcolm, 68
Shawcross, Hartley, KC, 46–47
Sierra Leone, xvi; crimes against humanity in, 119; Liberia and, 20. *See also* Special Court for Sierra Leone
Sigebert, 247
Simon (Viscount), 200–201
Les six livres de la république (Bodin), 265
Sixth Pan-American Conference (1928), 42
slavery, 241
Smith, Frederick E., KC, 32–33, 63, 70, 76, 91–93; as Birkenhead (Lord Chancellor), 99, 255, 258; Macdonell Committee and, 82–83
soldiers, crime of aggression and, 4–10, 273
Sonnino, Sidney, 94, 170, 172
sovereign equality, of states, 125, 234, 266–67
sovereigns, 143; *ejusdem generis* relation to, 130; equality of, 20, 266; immunity of, 86–90, 96n★, 97, 121, 134, 149, 201–2; international tribunal for, 117–20, 127; jurisdiction and, 89–90; personal responsibility of, 133; prosecution of, 125, 137, 144, 183
sovereignty, 35–36, 54–55, 70, 187, 250; absolute authority and, 265–66; absolute theory of, 185–86; civil liability and, 261; international relations relation to, 264–65; justice relation to, 189; Peace of Westphalia relation to, 263–64; prosecution relation to, 137; R2P relation to, 272; wars of aggression relation to, 49
Soviet Union, 192, 237; Japan relation to, 208

Special Court for Sierra Leone (SCSL), xvi–xvii, 20, 115n†, 167, 183, 285; Appeals Chamber of, 234–35; Nuremberg Principles and, 233

Special Sub-committee on Law, of Macdonell Committee, 91, 93

Special Tribunal for Lebanon, 238

"the spirit of the people" (volksgeist), 75, 80

SS. See Schutzstaffel

Stalin, Joseph: Declaration of Atrocities relation to, 193; Hitler relation to, 3; Yalta Memorandum and, 40

Stanford Law School, 5

state courts, jurisdiction of, 140

stature, 152

St. Bartholomew's Day massacre, 265

Stettinius, Edward, Jr., 194; war crime prosecution and, 214

Stimson, Henry Lewis, 28n★, 37, 59, 201, 278; on Briand-Kellogg Pact, 40, 55; at Council on Foreign Relations, 38–39; on IMTN, 53, 54; war crime prosecution and, 214; on wars of aggression, 55–56; Yalta Memorandum and, 194

Stimson Doctrine, 40

St. Petersburg Declaration (1868), 29–30, 271

Strauss, Leo, xxi

Stuart, Mary. See Mary, Queen of Scots

Sturmabteilung (SA), 194–95

Sub-commission III, of Commission on the Responsibility, 64, 99–100, 113–14, 121, 128–29; immunity and, 150; international tribunal and, 104–8, 160; Lansing on, 104, 107–8, 115–17, 120, 130–32, 145, 146n★, 164; Politis relation to, 111–12

sublunary beings, 253

Sudan, 287

summary execution, 53–54, 195–96; justice relation to, 199

superior courts, common law crimes in, 140

Supreme Council, 170, 172; Netherlands relation to, 178–80

surrender, of Japan, 210–11

Taft (President), 37

Tardieu, André, 103

Taylor, Charles, xvi, xvi–xvii, 20, 115n†, 233, 285; African Bar Association and, 236; in Nigeria, 167; Prosecutor v., 183

Le Temps (newspaper), 76

territoriality principle, of jurisdiction, 109–10

Thatcher administration, 77–78

theft, 28n†

Thiam, Doudou, 228

Third Reich, xiv, xvi; Yalta Memorandum relation to, 194–95

Thirty Years' War, 262, 263, 266, 270

Times (newspaper), 76

Tojo, Hideki, 192–93, 209; at IMTN trial, 207

Tokyo Tribunal, 50; crime of aggression relation to, 51–53

tort lawsuits, 262

trade, 57

transactional scholarship, 22

treaties, xx, 64, 274; Germany relation to, 160; interpretation of, 159; Nazis relation to, 48; Peace of Westphalia, 57–58, 262, 263–65, 266, 270; at Second Hague Peace Conference, 58–59

Treaties of London, 160

Treaty of Versailles, 34, 48, 64, 65, 165–66, 271; article 228 of, 150, 187–88; Germany relation to, 171; Lansing relation to, 334n63; precedent and, 157; U.S. Senate and, 169, 175–76; Wilson, W., relation to, 164. See also article 227, of Treaty of Versailles; Paris Peace Conference

The Trial of the Kaiser (Schabas), 78, 149

Trudeau, Justin, 2

Truman, Harry S., 37, 41–42, 197, 204, 242; Biddle relation to, 216, 218–19; Jackson relation to, 199, 200, 201–2, 206; resolution 95(I) relation to, 214–15

Trump, Donald, xxiv, 200

Turkey, 259

Tutsi people, xv

Tyndale, William, 248–49
tyrants, 102, 244; divine right of kings relation to, 247

ubi jus ibi remedium, 275
Ukraine, 63; Poland and, 142; Rome Statute and, 11–12; Russia and, xiii–xiv, xv, xxi–xxii, 2, 10, 13, 103, 269–70; war of self-defense of, 20
UN. *See* United Nations
UN General Assembly, 19; ICC relation to, 17–18, 273; resolution 36/106 of, 228; resolution 95(I) of, 50, 214–15, 220–21; resolution 177(II) of, 220–24, 227; Rome Statute relation to, 236
UN International Law Commission (ILC), xxi, xxiii, 220, 277; draft article 7 of, xxv–xxvii, 187, xxvinn★–†, xxvn★; Immunities of State Officials from Foreign Criminal Jurisdictions of, xxii, 135; IMTN relation to, 224–25; Nuremberg Principles and, 224, 226, 227, 228, 231; resolution 177(II) relation to, 221–24; UNTAET Regulation 2000/15 and, 239
United Kingdom, 27, 68; Draft Code of Crimes against the Peace and Security of Mankind and, 229–30; Imperial Cabinet of, 305n155; in World War I, 75, 104
United Nations (UN), 36, 271; Human Rights Committee of, 8; IMTN relation to, 216, 218, 219–21; legal personality of, 286; prosecution by, 193; Russia relation to, 27; Truman at, 218; on Ukraine, xiv. *See also* International Law Commission
United Nations Commission for the Investigation of War Crimes, 191–92
United States (U.S.), 130–31; article 227 relation to, 152–53, 330n5; Bonaparte relation to, 139; crime of aggression and, 17; ICC relation to, 14–15; international tribunal and, 109–10, 112–13, 321n230, 332n42; Iraq and, 12, 27; isolation of, 100–101; League

of Nations relation to, 40; Lieber Code and, 348n18; memoranda of reservations of, 136–38, 144–45; Netherlands relation to, 174–76; stature of, 152; war crime prosecution and, 214; in World War I, 103, 123
"Uniting for Peace" procedure, 17–18, 273
Universal Declaration of Human Rights, 271
UN Security Council, 272, 295n12; crime of aggression and, 11–12, 13–14; ICC relation to, 15; Special Tribunal for Lebanon and, 238; veto power of, 17–18, 236, 273, 274
UNTAET. *See* UN Transitional Administration in East Timor
UNTAET Regulation 2000/15, 239
UN Transitional Administration in East Timor (UNTAET), 238–39
U.S. *See* United States
U.S. Army 114th Field Artillery, 78
U.S. Congress, 140
U.S. Department of Defense, 36–37
U.S. Federal Court for the District of Pennsylvania, 259
U.S. Senate, Treaty of Versailles and, 169, 175–76
U.S. Supreme Court, 200; *Respublica v. De Longchamps* in, 141; *Schooner Exchange* case in, 127, 150, 243, 258–60; *U.S. v. Hudson* in, 139, 140
U.S. v. Hudson, 139, 140

Vae victis!, 20, 28, 75, 87–88, 255; summary execution and, 54
Varbres, Donnedieu de, 213
Vattel, Emer de, 22, 88–89, 314n88
veto power, of UN Security Council, 17–18, 236, 273, 274
"Vicar of God," 244, 246–47, 253, 257
Victoria (Queen), 255, 260
Volchkov, A. F., 213
volksgeist ("the spirit of the people"), 75, 80

"Waging an Aggressive and Unjust War," 33

Wallace, Hugh, 178

war, 44, 83, 202–4, 269; armed robbery compared to, 26; civilization relation to, 270; Industrial Revolution relation to, 39; laws and customs of, 137, 139, 143, 155, 187–88; prisoners of, 88; punishment for, 68, 76–77, 354n32; of self-defense, 20, 36–37

War (MacMillan), 57

war crimes, 3, 6, 99, 132–33; culpability and, 9; draft article 7 and, 187; individual criminal responsibility for, 223; of Japan, 210; national courts and, 135; in Nuremberg Principles, 227; prosecution of, 76–77, 144, 197, 206, 214; public opinion of, 21, 76–77; in wars of aggression, 8; of Wilhelm II, 69–70, 92

War of Religion, 265

wars of aggression, 36–38, 46–48, 50, 155, 215–18, 304n138; accountability for, 54–56; commercial interests in, 276; crimes against peace relation to, 225; genocide and, 10; of Germany, 132, 243; Havana Resolution and, 301n98; immunity and, 222–23; IMTN relation to, 10, 42–43; Jackson on, 203–4; *jus ad bellum* and, 99; League of Nations relation to, 301n97; of North Korea, 18; Paris Peace Conference relation to, 34–35, 55; private duels compared to, 27–28, 28n★; prosecution of, 136, 144; sovereignty relation to, 49; Tokyo Tribunal and, 51; Ukraine and, 269–70; war crimes in, 8; of Western nations, 26–27; of Wilhelm II, 33–35; Yalta Memorandum and, 40–41. *See also* crime of aggression; jus ad bellum

Weimar Republic, 188

Western nations, wars of aggression of, 26–27

Westlake, John, 161

White, Henry, 162n†

White, Thomas, 77

Whitlock (Ambassador), 79–80

Wilhelm II (Kaiser), 2, 3, 135n★, 260, 316n133; crime of aggression of, 33–34, 69–70; Germany relation to, 70–71; Hirohito compared to, 207–8; individual criminal responsibility of, 316n131; in Netherlands, 78–80, 101, 102–3, 167–68; prosecution and, 80, 84, 86, 91–95, 100, 104–5, 124, 153, 159–60, 169, 174–75, 180, 240; punishment of, 75, 92, 142, 305n155; wars of aggression of, 33–35

Wilhelmina (Queen), 58

William II. *See* Wilhelm II (Kaiser)

Willis, James, 76; on Lloyd George, 181

Wilson, Edith, 176–77, 334n64

Wilson, Woodrow, xvii–xviii, 34, 44n★, 95; article 227 and, 144, 152–53, 158–59, 165; on Council of Four, 143–44, 159; divine right of kings and, 242, 243; Germany relation to, 100, 171, 173; on imperialism, 44; Lansing relation to, 112, 127, 138, 141–42, 144–46, 147, 152–55, 154nn★–†, 157, 160–64, 162n†, 169, 176–77, 334n63; League of Nations and, 36, 76, 316n131; Lloyd George relation to, 65, 155, 169, 181, 209; Netherlands relation to, 103, 175; at Paris Peace Conference, 60, 69, 72, 101, 165, 199, 241–42; prosecution relation to, 157, 170; racism and, 151; Wilhelm II relation to, 3; on World War I, 31

World War I, xvii, 31, 38–39, 54–55, 271, 277; France in, 75, 103, 124; Germany in, 32, 59; laws and customs of war in, 139; Netherlands relation to, 180; Reichsgericht and, 187; United Kingdom in, 75, 104; U.S. in, 103, 123

World War II, 56, 271, 277; Japan in, 322n233; prosecution and, 191–92

Wrenbury (Lord), 77

Yalta Conference (1945), 197

Yalta Memorandum, 40–41, 194–95, 197; Clause 10 of, 198

Yerodia case, 234–35

Yugoslavia, 272; ethnic cleansing in, 236–37. *See also* International Criminal Tribunal for the former Yugoslavia

Zelensky, Volodymyr, xiii–xiv

Zimmerman Telegram, 100

Zouche, Richard, 88, 313n83

ABOUT THE AUTHOR

Chile Eboe-Osuji is former president of the International Criminal Court. He earlier served as the legal advisor to the United Nations High Commissioner for Human Rights in Geneva. Since completing his term at the ICC, Eboe-Osuji has continued to serve the international community through scholarship, including as the Herman Phlegar Visiting Professor of Law at Stanford Law School, senior fellow of the Carr Center at the Harvard Kennedy School, Distinguished International Jurist in the Lincoln Alexander School of Law at Toronto Metropolitan University, Paul Martin Senior Professor of Political Science in international relations and law at the University of Windsor, visiting professor in the UCLA School of Law, and Distinguished Visitor at the University of Toronto Faculty of Law. He was the 2022 recipient of the Goler T. Butcher Medal of the American Society of International Law for outstanding global contribution to human rights. Eboe-Osuji holds doctorate degrees (academic and honorary) from universities in the Netherlands, England, and Canada.